Christianity
AND THE
Constitution

Christianity
AND THE
Constitution

48 5701

The Faith of
Our Founding Fathers

John Eidsmoe

261.7
Ei29

A Mott Media Book

BAKER BOOK HOUSE
Grand Rapids, Michigan 49506

Copyright 1987 by
Baker Book House Company

ISBN: 0-8010-3444-2

Third Printing, August 1988

Library of Congress
Catalog Card Number: 87-70789

Printed in the United States of America

This book is dedicated, in the words of the Mayflower Compact of 1620, to "the glorie of God and advancemente of ye Christian faith";

That Americans may better understand, in the words of the Declaration of Independence, the "Laws of Nature and of Nature's God," which are the only sure foundation for the God-given rights of life, liberty, and the pursuit of happiness;

So that with a "firm reliance on the protection of Divine Providence," we may, in the words of the Preamble to our Constitution, "secure the Blessings of Liberty to ourselves and our Posterity";

In the hope that my own children, David Christopher Eidsmoe and Kirsten Heather Eidsmoe, may not only enjoy the blessings of life in a free society, but also possess the godly moral character that alone makes freedom possible;

For, "Righteousness exalteth a nation: but sin is a reproach to any people" (Prov. 14:34);

And, "where the Spirit of the Lord is, there is liberty." (2 Cor. 3:17 KJV).

Contents

Part Three
The Constitution: *Then and Now*

Foreword

The question of church and state is an issue which truly perplexes our national life today. Battles are continually waged over this issue—in the schools, in the courts, and on the campaign trails. Many people, including Christians, are confused on what the relationship between church and state should be. Many have fallen prey to the propaganda that, by its antiestablishment clause, the Constitution has meant there should be no relationship between God or Christianity and the government. No assertion could be further from the historical facts.

John Eidsmoe has documented many of these facts in his latest book, *Christianity and the Constitution: The Faith of Our Founding Fathers*. I believe that through this book, he has made an outstanding contribution to the church-state debate.

Dr. Eidsmoe shows clearly how most of our founding fathers were not secular men, as we often hear today. He explains how the influence of Calvinism gave rise to our republican form of government. He also documents how our founding fathers embodied several biblical principles in the Constitution.

I recommend this book to anyone who wants to learn about our nation's truly Christian heritage, which has been virtually expunged by the secular revisionists. I pray God will use it to educate a new generation of informed, Christian Americans.

D. James Kennedy
Senior Pastor, Coral Ridge Presbyterian Church
Fort Lauderdale, Florida

Introduction

The Dawn of the Great Convention
"An Assembly of Demigods"

I t is really an assembly of demigods," Thomas Jefferson wrote to John Adams.[1] Later Jefferson added, "A more able assembly never sat in America."[2] Nor, we may add, has a more able assembly ever sat since.

Most of America's great minds assembled as the Great Convention in Independence Hall in Philadelphia on May 14, 1787, to propose changes in America's plan of government. The men were hopeful; they intended to pool their learning and wisdom, draw from the best of past governments and thinkers, and perhaps try a few new ideas. They had experienced tyranny under Great Britain with a government that was too powerful. They had fought a major war to be freed from that oppression. They had experienced anarchy under the Articles of Confederation which created a government that was too weak and the nation had nearly collapsed as a result. So they hoped to formulate a system of government powerful enough to prevent anarchy but appropriately restricted to prevent tyranny.

Right from the beginning the convention was beset with problems. First, the convention was without funds. The delegates who came, did so at their own expense. Second, the convention began

1. Thomas Jefferson to John Adams, August 30, 1787, reprinted in *The Works of Thomas Jefferson*, ed. H. A. Washington (New York: Townsend, 1884), 2:260.
2. Thomas Jefferson to M. Dumas, September 10, 1787, ibid., 2:264.

11

with only seven of the thirteen states represented, some by a partial delegation. Eventually more delegations arrived, although some also left. Finally twelve of the thirteen states were represented. Rhode Island chose not to participate. How could a new nation be formed with so little cooperation and enthusiasm?

It soon became apparent that those present were by no means of one accord. Alexander Hamilton, the distinguished and brilliant New Yorker, distrusted the masses and wanted a strong central government. In contrast, Roger Sherman of Connecticut and others, strong defenders of states' rights, didn't trust a central government. Delegates from the large states, like James Madison of Virginia, wanted proportional representation in Congress. Men like William Patterson of New Jersey, felt smaller states would be abused by the larger states unless each state had an equal voice in Congress.

There was also the underlying issue of slavery. Some northern delegates totally opposed slavery and wanted it abolished. Other delegates morally opposed slavery but were slaveholders themselves. Some delegates defended slavery as an institution and declared that the South would not ratify the Constitution if it contained antislavery provisions.

Debating this point and that, the convention dragged listlessly on. It passed some measures, defeated others, referred some matters to committees and then seemingly lost sight of them. The state delegations were unwilling to compromise; each wanted its own way. A discouraged George Washington, the convention chairman, wrote a friend saying that he doubted the convention would ever agree on a new plan of government.

On June 28, 81-year-old Benjamin Franklin, the oldest delegate at the convention, delivered what was probably the most famous speech of the entire meeting. He noted that

> "the small progress we have made after 4 or 5 weeks [was] melancholy proof of the imperfection of the Human Understanding." Rather than mere human understanding, the delegates needed something more: "the Father of lights to illuminate our understandings"! He reminded the delegates that during the War for Independence they had prayed regularly to God in that very Hall: "Our prayers, Sir, were heard, and they were graciously answered." All of them could remember God's intervention on their behalf, and to that intervention they owed their victory over Great Britain. "And have we forgotten that powerful friend? or do we imagine that we no longer need his assistance? I have lived, Sir, a long time, and the longer I live, the more convincing proofs I see of this truth—*that God*

governs in the affairs of men. And if a sparrow cannot fall to the ground without his notice, is it probable that an empire can rise without his aid? We have been assured, Sir, in the sacred writings, that 'except the Lord build the House they labour in vain that build it.' I firmly believe this; and I also believe that without his concurring aid we shall succeed in this political building, no better than the builders of Babel.'' Franklin then suggested daily prayers, led by one or more Philadelphia clergymen.[3]

How was Franklin's suggestion received? Did the delegates become conscious of their need for God's help? Did they turn to God and implore his assistance? Was God present at the Great Convention in Philadelphia? Did he intervene and forge unity out of discord? Does the U.S. Constitution bear God's imprint, reflect his wisdom and his precepts?

Before we answer those questions, let us fade from Independence Hall and reflect on the forces that influenced these men. We will investigate their background, education, what they read, whom they respected. And then we will examine in detail the religious beliefs of a representative dozen of the delegates. All of these factors have a bearing on the document they forged: the United States Constitution.

---

3. Benjamin Franklin, quoted by James Madison in *Notes on Debates in the Federal Convention of 1787* (Athens: Ohio University Press, 1966, 1985), p. 209. As we shall see in chapter 12 on Benjamin Franklin, he probably never became a Christian in the orthodox sense of the word, but as his autobiography reveals, he had come a long way from the deism of his teenage years. He clearly believed in a prayer-answering God.

PART **1**

The Background

1 Calvinism

olonists came from many lands and arrived at many different times to build a new nation. Some landed at Jamestown in 1607; others landed at Plymouth Rock in 1620, having crossed the Atlantic on the *Mayflower*. In 1630 the *Arabella* arrived at Salem with a group of settlers. Throughout the 1600s shiploads of eager settlers arrived at various ports to begin a new life.

Some colonists were wealthy; some were slaves or indentured servants. Other colonists owned nothing but the clothes on their backs.

Although many colonists came empty-handed, they did not come empty-minded. They brought with them the heritage, culture, and ideas from the lands of their birth.

In forming a new nation and developing its Constitution the following century, the delegates at the 1787 Convention did not intend to put into practice new and untried ideas. The framers of the American Constitution based their political concepts on the tried and tested ideas of the past. These men were intelligent, well-educated, and widely read. They combined the best ideas they read about to establish a government for the United States.

Therefore, it is appropriate to ask: What influenced the founders of this nation? Which books did they read? Which thinkers did they respect? To which theological, philosophical, and political systems did they subscribe?

17

Their ideas came from a variety of sources but one source stands out above all others. Dr. E. W. Smith says it well:

> If the average American citizen were asked, who was the founder of America, the true author of our great Republic, he might be puzzled to answer. We can imagine his amazement at hearing the answer given to this question by the famous German historian, Ranke, one of the profoundest scholars of modern times. Says Ranke, 'John Calvin was the virtual founder of America.'

Dr. Smith continues:

> These revolutionary principles of republican liberty and self-government, taught and embodied in the system of Calvin, were brought to America, and in this new land where they have borne so mighty a harvest were planted, by whose hands?—the hands of the Calvinists. The vital relation of Calvin and Calvinism to the founding of the free institutions of America, however strange in some ears the statement of Ranke may have sounded, is recognized and affirmed by historians of all lands and creeds.[1]

Dr. Smith is not alone in his assessment. Bancroft, probably the leading American historian of the nineteenth century, simply called Calvin the "father of America." Bancroft, far from being a Calvinist himself, added, "He who will not honor the memory and respect the influence of Calvin knows but little of the origin of American liberty."[2]

D'Aubigne, a leading Reformation scholar, echoed a similar theme:

> Calvin was the founder of the greatest of republics. The Pilgrims who left their country in the reign of James I, and landing on the barren soil of New England, founded populous and mighty colonies, were his sons, his direct and legitimate sons; and that American nation which we have seen growing so rapidly boasts as its father the humble Reformer on the shore of Lake Leman.[3]

The Roman Catholic scholar Emilio Castelar, Professor of Philosophy at the University of Madrid and later President of the Republic of Spain in 1873, acknowledged,

---

1. E. W. Smith, quoted by Loraine Boettner, *The Reformed Doctrine of Predestination* (Philadelphia: Presbyterian and Reformed, 1972), p. 389.

2. George Bancroft; ibid., pp. 389–90.

3. D'Aubigne; ibid., p. 389.

It was necessary for the republican movement that there should come a morality more austere than Luther's, the morality of Calvin, and a Church more democratic than the German, the Church of Geneva. The Anglo-Saxon democracy has for its lineage a book of a primitive society--the Bible. It is the product of a severe theology learned by the few Christian fugitives in the gloomy cities of Holland and Switzerland, where the morose shade of Calvin still wanders. . . . And it remains serenely in its grandeur, forming the most dignified, most moral and most enlightening portion of the human race.[4]

Many, if not the vast majority of colonial Americans came from Calvinistic backgrounds.

The colonists lived in the shadow of the Reformation. Luther nailed his ninety-five theses on the door of Wittenberg Castle October 31, 1517; the Mayflower sailed just over a century later. John Calvin died in 1564, fifty-six years before the Mayflower sailed. Events like the Thirty Years' War between Catholics and Protestants (1618-1648) were current events to the Pilgrims and Puritans.[5]

As Dr. Loraine Boettner has noted,

It is estimated that of the 3,000,000 Americans at the time of the American Revolution, 900,000 were of Scotch or Scotch-Irish origin, 600,000 were Puritan English, and 400,000 were German or Dutch Reformed. In addition to this the Episcopalians had a Calvinistic confession in their Thirty-nine Articles; and many French Huguenots also had come to this western world. Thus we see that about two-thirds of the colonial population had been trained in the school of Calvin.[6]

What does Calvinism, a theological system, have to do with constitutions and forms of government?

The answer is: A great deal. For Calvinism, like any theological system, encompasses both a world view and a view of human nature. The way one views the world and human nature will determine one's choice for effective government. As James Madison asked in *Federalist No. 51*, "What is government itself but the greatest of all reflections on human nature?"

---

4. Emilio Castelar; ibid., p. 384.
5. At this point I wish to emphasize, lest I be accused of a Calvinistic bias, that I am an ordained minister of the Church of the Lutheran Brethren. While I respect Calvinism, I cannot consider myself a Calvinist. But any objective reading of American history will clearly demonstrate that it was Calvinism, not Lutheranism or any other theological system, that made the most profound, widespread and significant impact on the thinking of early Americans.
6. Boettner, *Reformed Doctrine of Predestination*, p. 382.

For example, suppose a person believes that human beings are basically good, or that human nature is improving and perfectable, as many eighteenth-century French philosophes believed. That person would see little need to impose strict criminal penalties if he believed people are altruistic and have the best interest of others at heart. He would probably favor a system of socialism or communism whereby work and wealth are apportioned "from each acccording to his ability, to each according to his needs." In addition, he would trust the good intentions of the nation's rulers and would see little need to impose constitutional restraints on their power. He would also trust the good intentions of other nations and see little need for national defense.

On the other hand, suppose a person believes men to be basically evil and self-interested. He also believes human nature to be basically constant, unchanging, and unchangeable (apart from the saving grace of Jesus Christ). Holding this view of human nature, this person would favor a form of government with strict laws and strict punishments for criminal behavior. He would also be skeptical of efforts to reform and rehabilitate criminals. Believing with Lord Acton that "power corrupts; absolute power corrupts absolutely," he would distrust the intentions of government officials and seek to, in Jefferson's words, "bind them down with the chains of the Constitution."[7] He would be suspicious of foreign powers and favor a strong military presence to deter attacks and preserve the nation's liberty and security.

Total Depravity (Inability) of Human Nature

One's view of human nature does then profoundly affect one's view of government. Calvinists (along with Lutherans and others) stress the total depravity of human nature—that man is by nature sinful and unable to please God.

Calvinists, and other Christians to greater or lesser degrees, believe God created man in an ideal state—but man fell into sin. Man possesses a sinful nature and is totally unable to please God by his own efforts. As Paul says, "In my flesh dwelleth no good thing" (Rom. 7:18). Man is powerless to save himself from eternal damnation, nor can he earn or purchase redemption in any way. His only hope for salvation lies in Jesus Christ, the second person of the

---

7. Thomas Jefferson, quoted by Attorney General Edwin Meese, "The Law of the Constitution," a bicentennial lecture, Tulane University, New Orleans, Louisiana, October 21, 1986.

Trinity, who died on a cross to pay the penalty for man's sins. Those who are the elect and predestined of God are saved through faith in Jesus Christ.

The fact man has a sinful nature does not mean he is incapable of doing good. God bestowed his common grace on all mankind, and it is manifested through human reason and human conscience. The law of God written upon men's hearts (Rom. 2:14-15) gives even the heathen man a basic knowledge of right and wrong, enabling him to be a good citizen, a good employee and a good husband and father. But since this civil righteousness proceeds out of mixed motives, it is flawed. Therefore it cannot be pleasing to God. As Isaiah says, "All our righteousnesses are as filthy rags" (Isa. 64:6).

The founders of this nation held this view of human nature and were not interested in the utopian schemes of the French freethinkers of that time. They knew that human beings are not capable of functioning, most of the time, with unselfish motives such as the good of society. Rather, the best that can be expected of most men most of the time is that they pursue an enlightened self-interest—working at productive jobs in order to earn money for themselves and their families, obeying laws because they don't want to go to jail, etc. They designed a government with this view of human nature in mind.

First, they recognized that the government must be powerful enough to restrain the evil impulses of the masses. A system of government that is too weak to restrain the masses will eventually degenerate into anarchy and chaos. The designers of the Constitution saw this happen under the Articles of Confederation.

But they also recognized that rulers possess sinful natures. Therefore rulers cannot be trusted with absolute power. Rulers will use power to enhance themselves and oppress the masses. As a result they will become tyrants.

So most of the problems the founders of the U.S. Constitution were faced with when they gathered at the Great Convention in 1787 had to do with setting up checks and balances relating to sin and power. Given the sinful nature of mankind, how should the government's power be allocated to give the government sufficient power to serve and restrain the masses effectively without giving it so much power that it becomes tyrannical and oppressive?

Their solutions to this problem showed a Calvinistic background.

Priesthood of All Believers

A second Calvinist concept that indirectly influenced the U.S. system of government was the priesthood of all believers. Because of the sacrifice of Jesus Christ on the cross, Calvinists and other Protestants believe that Christians need not go through intermediaries such as priests and bishops, but may come before the throne of grace themselves in prayer without an intermediary (Heb. 4:16). In Luther's words, every plowboy should be able to read and interpret the Scripture for himself rather than be bound to follow the interpretation given to him by his priest, for he himself is responsible to God for his own soul.

This concept promoted the belief that every plowboy must learn to read. As a result, Protestant societies strongly encouraged universal education.

Colonial Americans then provided widespread and high-quality education for their children. Nowhere was this more true than in the most Calvinistic part of early America, New England. The high caliber of learning at that time is evident from the entrance requirements for colonial colleges. In the 1700s an undergraduate freshman at William and Mary College had to be able to read, write, converse, and debate in Greek.[8] When John Jay applied for admission to King's College in New York at the age of fourteen, one of the entrance requirements he had to fulfill was to translate the first ten chapters of the Gospel of John from Greek into Latin.[9] John Adams wrote to Thomas Jefferson that he had carefully studied Plato using two Latin translations, one French, one English, and the original Greek.[10] As early as 1765, John Adams observed that "a native American, especially in New England, who cannot read and write is as rare a Phenomenon as a Comet."[11]

Around 1800 Pierre Samuel Dupont de Nemours, founder of the famous Dupont lineage in America, conducted a study on education in America on behalf of Thomas Jefferson. He concluded: "Most young Americans . . . can read, write and cipher. Not more than four in a thousand are unable to write legibly—even neatly." He compared the low rate of literacy throughout the world to the relatively high literacy rate in the United States, England, Holland,

8. John Adams to Thomas Jefferson, *Jefferson's Works*, Vol. 15, p. 156; quoted by W. Cleon Skousen, *"Miracle of America" Study Guide* (Salt Lake City: Freemen Institute, 1981), pp. 37–38.

9. Frank Monaghan, *John Jay: Defender of Liberty* (Indianapolis: Bobbs-Merrill, 1935, 1972), p. 26.

10. Sheldon Emry, *God's Law on Property and Inheritance*, cassette lecture, March 15, 1981 (*America's Promise*, Box 5334, Phoenix, Arizona 85010).

11. John Adams, *Diary and Autobiography of John Adams*, ed. L. Butterfield (Cambridge: Harvard University Press, 1961); quoted by John W. Whitehead and Wendell R. Bird, *Home Education and Constitutional Liberties* (Westchester, Illinois: Crossway Books, 1984, 1986), p. 24.

and the Protestant Cantons of Switzerland. He attributed the difference to the fact that "in those countries the Bible is read; it is considered a duty to read it to the children; and in that form of religion the sermons and liturgies in the language of the people tend to increase and formulate ideas of responsibility." He went on to say that for the most part, education in America was accomplished in the home through reading Bibles and newspapers.[12]

Daniel Webster, speaking in Plymouth, Massachusetts in 1820, made the same observation: In New England every child possessed the means of learning to read and write, and "A youth of fifteen, of either sex, who cannot read and write, is very seldom to be found."[13] The Frenchman Alexis de Tocqueville also observed the high quality of American education when he traveled throughout the United States in the 1830s.[14]

The widespread high quality of American education during the formative years of the nation made it possible for most Americans to understand and participate in their system of government.

Emphasis on Biblical Law

The relevance of biblical law to contemporary institutions also found its way into American political thinking.

Calvinists believe that God's law, as revealed in his Word, the Bible, contains absolute and unchanging principles that are (for the most part) relevant to modern society. (Certain ceremonial laws had been fulfilled in Christ and therefore no longer apply.) Calvin stressed that both moral and judicial laws of Scripture needed to be applied as principles, not as hard-and-fast rules. The laws reflected the eternal and unchanging character and will of God and could not be ignored.

Ahlstrom notes that "the intense concern of Reformed theology for God's revealed Law" flows from the Calvinistic doctrines of

12. Pierre Samuel DuPont de Nemours, *National Education in the United States of America* (Newark: University of Delaware Press, 1923), pp. 3–5; quoted in R. J. Rushdoony, *The Messianic Character of American Education* (Nutley, N.J.: Prague Press, 1963), pp. 329–30.

13. Daniel Webster, Discourse on Education, December 22, 1820, in *The Works of Daniel Webster*, 2 vols. (Boston: 1851); quoted by Verna M. Hall, *The Christian History of the American Revolution: Consider and Ponder* (San Francisco: Foundation for American Christian Education, 1976), p. 222.

14. Alexis de Tocqueville, *Democracy in America*, 1:315–16; see also George W. Pierson, *Tocqueville in America* (Garden City: Anchor Books, 1959), pp. 293–94. For full quotations from de Tocqueville on the subject of education, see John Eidsmoe, *The Christian Legal Advisor* (Grand Rapids: Baker, 1984, 1987), pp. 289–90.

divine sovereignty and human depravity: ". . . . the first use of the
Law was to proclaim God as the Creator of the universe; in this
context the law in all its forms, but especially as enforced by
governments, keeps the sinful proclivities of men in check."[15]

In a later chapter it will be pointed out that this application of
God's revealed law to civil government was especially prominent in
Puritan New England.

Covenant Theology

Calvinists generally hold covenant theology. The central theme of
covenant theology is that God's covenant with man is two-fold: a
covenant of law and a covenant of grace. The covenant of law
consists of God's revelation of the Old Testament law, the Ten
Commandments, and man's promise to obey it; the covenant of
grace is God's promise of redemption through man's faith in the
finished work of Jesus Christ on the cross.

Many Calvinists applied the covenant concept to civil government.

The practical implications of covenant theory were developed by
the Rev. Samuel Rutherford (1600-1661) in his classic work, *Lex,
Rex,* or *The Law and the Prince.* Rutherford stressed that rulers
derive authority from God, as declared in Romans 13:1-4 and other
passages of Scripture. But God gives this authority to rulers through
the people. The people establish a form of government and choose
a particular man to be their ruler. The ruler then acts under the
direction of God. Rutherford cited biblical passages to prove his
point:

> II Samuel 16:18, "Hushai said to Absalom, Nay, but whom the
> Lord and the people, and all the men of Israel choose, his will I be,
> and with him will I abide"; Judges 8:22, "The men of Israel said to
> Gideon, Rule thou over us"; Judges 9:6, "The men of Shechem made
> Abimelech king"; II Kings 14:21, "The people made Azariah king";
> I Samuel 12:1; II Chronicles 23:3.[16]

The covenant view of government also found secular expression
in John Locke's social contract theory—the belief that men in a
state of nature formed a government by mutual consent and gave it

15. Sydney E. Ahlstrom, *A Religious History of the American People* (Garden City:
Doubleday, 1972, 1975), 1:119.

16. Samuel Rutherford, *Lex, Rex, or The Law and the Prince,* 1644 (reprinted
Harrisonburg, Virginia: Sprinkle Publications, 1982), pp. 1, 6–7.

certain limited authority to act in order to protect their basic rights of life, liberty, and property. Locke, a Puritan by background, based his political theories on Rutherford's *Lex, Rex*.

For Americans the covenant concept finds its ultimate expression in the Preamble to the Constitution: "We the People of the United States, in order to form a more perfect Union, . . . do ordain and establish this Constitution for the United States of America."

Limited Government

Calvinists not only believe civil government is ordained and established by God, they also believe that God has given civil government only limited authority. The same power that grants authority to government, also limits that authority.

The concept of limited government is a fundamental principle of U.S. constitutional theory—ours is a government of limited, delegated powers. The framers of the Constitution envisioned our federal government with only the powers delegated to it by the people through the Constitution.

Rutherford in particular emphasized limited government. The people, acting under the will of God, had given the civil government only limited authority, and they had given it conditionally—they reserved the right to terminate their covenant with the ruler if the ruler violated the covenant terms. Consequently the ruler is acting without legitimate authority if he violates the laws of God and nature by suppressing the basic liberties of the people. In such instances he is not to be obeyed. In fact, he is to be resisted. It is the Christian's *duty* to resist—by force if necessary.[17]

Limited government also formed the basis for resistance to British oppression in the War of Independence. The colonists' slogan, "Rebellion against tyrants is obedience to God!" grew from roots firmly planted in Calvinist soil.

The Declaration of Independence appears to have been adapted, at least in part, from a Calvinistic predecessor, the Mecklenburg Declaration. On May 20, 1775—more than a year before the Declaration of Independence—a group of Scotch-Irish Presbyterians gathered in Charlotte, North Carolina, out of concern over the conflict with Britain. They declared the colonies to be free and independent and used such phrases as "We do hereby dissolve the political bands which have connected us with the mother-country, and hereby absolve ourselves from all allegiance to the British

---

17. Ibid., pp. 118–19.

crown." And, "We hereby declare ourselves a free and independent people; are, and of right ought to be, a sovereign and self-governing association, under control of no power other than that of our God and the general government of Congress; to the maintenance of which we solemnly pledge to each other our mutual cooperation and our lives, our fortunes and our most sacred honor." The document, prepared by Presbyterian elder Ephraim Brevard, was sent by special messenger to the Continental Congress. That fact, coupled with the almost identical language used, makes it likely that Jefferson and his committee drew from the Mecklenburg Declaration when they drafted the Declaration of Independence.[18]

Local Church Government

Calvinists generally practiced presbyterian or congregational church government. In contrast, Catholics and Anglicans (Episcopalian) practiced hierarchical forms of church government—that is, government by bishops and high church officials with centralized authority.

Presbyterian church government consisted of local elders governing each church. Churches organized into various local synods. Congregational church government was even more democratic in form. Each local church was autonomous, owning its own property, calling its own pastor, choosing its own officials.

The practice of presbyterian and congregational church government gave colonial Americans practical experience in local self-government. It helped form a basis for representative and decentralized government, both of which are cornerstones of the American constitutional system. This was particularly true in New England where the meetings of the Congregational churches developed into the town meetings that are a hallmark of New England politics even today.

18. Boettner, *Reformed Doctrine of Predestination*, pp. 387-88.

2 Puritanism

Pilgrims and Puritans occupy a special place in American history. Being among America's earliest European settlers, the Pilgrims are remembered for America's first Thanksgiving. As for the Puritans, their zeal, industriousness, morals, and dedication to God are remembered with profound respect. Yet, their stocks, whipping posts, ducking stools, and Salem witch trials are regarded as one of the worst chapters of American history.

Before considering the lasting effect Puritanism had on American society, a distinction needs to be made between Pilgrims and Puritans. The Pilgrims who landed at Plymouth Rock in 1620 were separatists. They believed the Church of England was so worldly and corrupt that they had to separate from it and establish their own church, one which was true to biblical principles. They were not allowed to form their own church in England so they first went to Holland and then came to America.

The Puritans agreed with the Pilgrims that the Church of England was worldly and corrupt; it was too lenient with regard to vice and heresy. However, they believed they should stay in the church to "purify" it. The title *Puritan* defined their cause. In contrast to the Pilgrims, Puritans didn't object to the concept of a state church. They came to America to establish a state church and run it strictly according to the commands of God. Many Puritans believed that after gaining strength during their sojourn in the New World's wilderness, they would return to England, take control of the Church, and set things aright.[1]

The Pilgrims arrived before the Puritans, but were quickly outnumbered by them. By 1700 the Pilgrims had been completely absorbed into Puritan society, and there was no distinction between the two groups thereafter.

Both Pilgrims and Puritans were staunch Calvinists. Not all Calvinists were Puritans, but all Puritans were Calvinistic. The things said about Calvinists in chapter 1 are true about Puritans. Puritans stressed the total depravity of human nature, and strongly believed that the state, like the church, was an instrument God used to combat sin.

They also believed in the priesthood of all believers and wanted everyone to know how to read the Word of God. Consequently, there has seldom, if ever, been a society in which education was as high in quality and as widespread as in colonial New England. As early as 1640, Massachusetts passed a law requiring parents to make sure their children knew how to read and write. In 1647 Massachusetts enacted the famous "Old Deluder Satan Law" which established common schools to teach reading because it was "one chief project of the old deluder, Satan, to keep men from the knowledge of the Scriptures."[2] Using the *New England Primer*, a widely-circulated text written from a distinctively Calvinistic standpoint, colonial children learned a world view that clearly taught sin and salvation, law and gospel.

Puritans, like other Calvinists, believed in covenant theology and therefore held a covenant view of government, in which the government possessed only limited powers. In colonial New England, congregational church government was common. Township meetings usually took place in the church, and only members of the church were allowed to vote and hold civil office.

The Holy Commonwealth

The Puritans made unique contributions to American political thinking. Following Calvinism, they believed God established the state for the purpose of restraining sin. And to control sin God entered into covenants with men—covenants to establish churches as well as covenants to establish civil governments.

1. J. Steven O'Malley, lectures, "Theology of Jonathan Edwards," Oral Roberts University, Autumn 1982.

2. *The Laws and Liberties of Massachusetts*, 1648 (reprinted Cambridge: 1929), cited in *McCollum v. Board of Education*, 68 S.Ct. 461, 333 U.S. 203 (1948).

In contrast to other Calvinists, the Puritans wanted to establish a "Holy Commonwealth" in which only believers in the Lord Jesus Christ were fully part of the community.

Before going ashore at Plymouth, the Pilgrims signed a covenant for civil government which created a Holy Commonwealth. It was called the "Mayflower Compact," and it reads in part:

> In ye name of God, Amen. We whose names are underwritten, the loyall subjects of our dread soveraigne Lord, King James, by ye grace of God, of Great Britaine, Franc, & Ireland king, defender of ye faith, &c., haveing undertaken, for ye glorie of God, and advancemente of ye Christian faith, and honour of our king & countrie, a voyage to plant ye first colonie in ye Northerne parts of Virginia, doe by these presents solemnly & mutually in ye presence of God, and one of another, covenant & combine our selves togeather into a civill body politick, for our better ordering & preservation & furtherance of ye ends aforesaid; and by ye vertue hearof to enacte, constitute, and frame such just & equall lawes, ordinances, acts, constitutions, & offices, from time to time, as shall be thought most meete & convenient for ye generall good of ye Colonie, unto which we promise all due submission and obedience. In witnes wherof we have hereunder subscribed our names at Cap-Codd ye 11. of November, in ye year of ye raigne of our soveraigne lord, King James, of England, France, & Ireland ye eighteenth, and of Scotland ye fiftie fourth. Ano: Dom. 1620.

In 1630 Governor John Winthrop laid out a similar exclusive covenant for the Holy Commonwealth of Massachusetts, as the *Arabella* approached Salem.

> It is of the nature and essence of every society to be knit together by some covenant, either expressed or implied. . . .
>
> For the work we have in hand, it is by mutual consent, through a special over-ruling providence and a more than ordinary approbation of the churches of Christ, to seek out a place of cohabitation and consortship, under a due form of government both civil and ecclesiastical. . . .
>
> Therefore we must not content ourselves with usual ordinary means. Whatsoever we did or ought to have done when we lived in England, the same we must do, and more also where we go. . . .
>
> Neither must we think that the Lord will bear such failings at our hands as He doth from those among whom we have lived. . . .
>
> Thus stands the cause between God and us: we are entered into a

covenant with Him for this work; we have taken out a commission, the Lord hath given us leave to draw our own articles. . . .

We shall find that the God of Israel is among us, when ten of us shall be able to resist a thousand of our enemies, when He shall make us a praise and glory, that men of succeeding plantations shall say, "The Lord make it like that of New England." For we must consider that we shall be as a city upon a hill, the eyes of all people are upon us; so that if we shall deal falsely with our God in this work we have undertaken and so cause him to withdraw his present help from us, we shall be made a story and a by-word through the world, we shall open the mouths of enemies to speak evil of the ways of God and all professors for God's sake; we shall shame the faces of many of God's worthy servants, and cause their prayers to be turned into curses upon us till we be consumed out of the good land whether we are going. . . .[3]

It was by blending the covenants of church and government, and allowing only church members the privilege of voting and holding public office, that the Holy Commonwealth was established and maintained. Nonmembers derived benefits such as security for the basic rights of life, liberty, and property from living in Puritan society. They were obligated to obey the rules of society but they were not fully a part of either covenant.

The Holy Commonwealth, created and then controlled through the dictatorship of the holy and regenerate, lasted for over a century. It broke down in the 1700s as the Puritan zeal began to fade.

Postmillennialism

In dealing with eschatology most Puritans adopted a postmillennial interpretation of Scripture. They believed the thousand-year reign of the kingdom of God, or the golden age, on earth was about to begin. God was working through the saints, the church, and the state to bring about conditions conducive to Christ's return. Many Puritans believed God was using New England to lead the revival which would bring about the millennium.

In contrast, Calvin and the early Calvinists were amillennial in their view of the last days. They believed there would be no literal thousand-year golden age. The Scripture references to the millennium must be interpreted other than literally. Amillennialists under-

3. John Winthrop, "A Model of Christian Charity," 1630 (language updated), quoted by Perry Miller and Thomas H. Johnson in *The Puritans: A Sourcebook of Their Writings*, Vol. 1 (New York: Harper & Row, 1938, 1963), pp. 195–99.

stood the passages to refer to heaven, or interpreted them as meaning the church age.

Rev. Jonathan Edwards, an intellectual and well-known Puritan, described the Puritan viewpoint on postmillennialism and New England's role in his sermon, "The Latter-Day Glory Is Probably to Begin in America." In it he suggests that God had created two continents, the Old World and the New; and since the Old had been given the honor of being the place of Christ's first coming, the New would probably be given the honor of hosting his second coming. He noted that the "sun of righteousness" had been traveling from east to west, and therefore

> when the time comes of the church's deliverance from her enemies, so often typified by the Assyrians, the light will rise in the west, till it shines through the world like the sun in its meridian brightness.
> . . . And if we may suppose that this glorious work of God shall begin in any part of America, I think, if we consider the circumstances of the settlement of New England, it must needs appear the most likely, of all American colonies, to be the place whence this work shall principally take its rise. . . .[4]

Postmillennial eschatology[5] helped determine Puritan political thinking in several ways. First, it assumed an upward direction of history—God was using believers to prepare the world for the return of Christ.

Second, it placed special responsibility on New England's most devout religious leaders to do God's work well. God was using them to prepare the way for the culmination of human history and the return of his son Jesus Christ. Therefore, the covenant and the Holy Commonwealth assumed even greater roles.

Third, it placed more emphasis on biblical law.[6] The postmillennial Puritans saw the church as the successor to Israel's promises

4. Jonathan Edwards, "The Latter-Day Glory Is Probably to Begin in America"; reprinted in Conrad Cherry, *God's New Israel: Religious Interpretations of American Destiny* (Englewood Cliffs, N.J.: Prentice-Hall, 1971), pp. 55–59.

5. The postmillennial views of Puritanism are well summarized by Iain Murray in *The Puritan Hope* (Carlisle: Banner of Truth, 1971, 1975).

6. As a dispensational premillennialist, I reject the view of some of my dispensational colleagues that the Mosaic law is irrelevant today. While the ceremonial portions of God's law are fulfilled in Christ and are valuable today only for teaching purposes, the moral law remains. It is, as Paul says, "holy, just, and good," and therefore reflects the character and will of God. While it was given specially to Israel and is binding as a covenant obligation solely on Israel, its principles are universal, unchanging, and applicable to all societies including ours. It is of course not a way of salvation, but it was never intended that way—not even for Israel.

and obligations. They held no reservations about applying biblical law since the covenant of the church and the covenant of civil government were interdependent.

Without actually identifying themselves as the new Israel, the Puritans thought of themselves as a people specially chosen of God. They freely drew comparisons between themselves and the Israelites and assumed that God would either bless or punish them for their faith and actions just as he had Israel.

Postmillennialism was the predominant eschatology of the 1600s, 1700s, and early 1800s. It almost died out in the middle 1900s. Within the past decade it has undergone a revival among some Calvinists and charismatics.

It is possible that postmillennial theology has also affected secular thought in America throughout the centuries. It finds expression in "Manifest Destiny," the notion that God planned for America to expand its boundaries to the Pacific Ocean; in the Monroe Doctrine, which gave the United States special authority to protect the western hemisphere from outside interference; in the idea of America as the "arsenal of democracy" engaged in a war to "make the world safe for democracy"; and in America as that "bright, shining city on a hill" as described by President Reagan. These and other forms of the "American Dream" which suggest that America has a special place in the plan of God, probably had their roots in Puritan postmillennialism.

The Application of Biblical Law

The concept of the Holy Commonwealth, coupled with postmillennialism, led to the strict enforcement of biblical law in New England society.

In 1636 the General Court of Massachusetts resolved to make code of laws "agreeable to the word of God."[7] About the same tin the Rev. John Cotton drafted a code of laws which made referenc to "the Law of Nature, delivered by God," and which closed with a reference to Isaiah 33:22:

The Lord is our Judge.
The Lord is our Law-giver.
The Lord is our King, He will save us.[8]

7. *Massachusetts Colonial Records*, 1:174; quoted by Benjamin Fletcher Wright, Jr., *American Interpretations of Natural Law* (New York: Russell & Russell, 1962), p. 33.
  8. Wright, *American Interpretations*, pp. 17–18.

The legal code adopted in 1641 as the Massachusetts Body of Liberties, reads as follows:

The free fruition of such liberties, Immunities and Priveledges as humanitie, Civilitie, and Christianitie call for as due to every man in his place and proportion without impeachment and Infrigement hath ever bene and ever will be the tranquillitie and Stabilitie of Churches and Commonwealths. And the deniall or deprivall thereof, the disturbance if not the ruine of both.

58. Civill Authoritie hath power and libertie to see the peace, ordinances and rules of Christ observed in every church according to his word. So it be done in a civill and not in an Ecclesiastical way.

59. Civill Authoritie hath power and libertie to deale with any Church member in a way of Civill Justice, notwithstanding any Church relation, office or interest.

60. No church censure shall degrad or depose any man from any Civill dignitie, office, or Authoritie he shall have in commonwealth.

94.

    1. If any man after legall conviction shall have or worship any other god, but the lord god, he shall be put to death.

    2. If any men or women be a witch, (that is hath or consulteth with a familiar spirit), They shall be put to death.

    3. If any man shall Blaspheme the name of god, the father, Sonne or Holie ghost, with direct, expresse, presumptous or high handed blasphemie, or shall curse god in the like manner he shall be put to death.

95.

    1. All the people of god within this Jurisdiction who are not in the church way, and the orthodox Judgment, and not scandalous in life, shall have full libertie to gather themselves into a Church Estaite. Provided they doe it in a Christian way, with due observation of the rules of Christ revealed in his word . . .

    10. Wee allow private meetings for edification in religion amongst Christians of all Sortes of people. So be it without just offence for number, time, place, and other cercumstances.

Almost twenty years later, John Eliot, the Puritan missionary to the Indians, wrote a treatise entitled *The Christian Commonwealth: or, The Civil Policy of the Rising Kingdom of Jesus Christ* (1659). The treatise formulated a plan of government for the Natick Indian community. He declared,

That which the Lord now calleth England to attend is not to search humane Polities and Platformes of Government, contrived by the wisdom of man; but as the Lord hath carried on their works for them, so they ought to go unto the Lord, and enquire at the Word of

his mouth, what Platforme of Government he hath therein commanded; and humble themselves to embrace that as the best, how
mean soever it may seem to Humane Wisdom.

There is undoubtedly a forme of Civil Government instituted by
God himself in the holy Scriptures; whereby any Nation may enjoy all
the ends and effects of Government in the best manner, were they but
perswaded to make trial of it. We should derogate from the suffi-
ciency and perfection of the Scriptures, if we should deny it. The
scripture is able thoroughly to furnish the man of God (whether
Magistrate in the Commonwealth, or elder in the Church, or any
other) unto every good work. . . .

(The) written Word of God is the perfect System or Frame of
Laws, to guide all the Moral actions of man, either towards God or
man.[9]

The application and enforcement of biblical law had its basis in
the Puritan belief that the Scriptures contained the general principles of government. God left it up to men to work out the details of
applying those principles to concrete situations.

The Work Ethic

Both Calvinists and Puritans believed in the sacredness of all
vocations and stressed the virtue of hard and honest work. These
teachings provided a basis for American prosperity and the free-
enterprise system, which were extolled by others who did not share
Puritan theology. Benjamin Franklin, who was raised in Puritan
New England, is sometimes called a "secular Puritan" because his
Poor Richard's Almanac positively depicts the Puritan work ethic.

The Fear of Power

Puritans refused to give anyone too much power because of their
belief in human depravity. Power had a corrupting influence and
could be used to oppress others. For that reason, the authority of
their rulers was carefully monitored. The Rev. John Cotton put it
well:

Let all the world learn to give mortall men no greater power than
they are content they shall use, for use it they will: and unless they be
better taught of God, they will use it ever and anon . . . . . . for what

9. John Eliot, *Massachusetts Historical Collections*, 3d ser., 9:133–134, 163; quoted by
Wright, *American Interpretations*, pp. 19–21.

ever transcendent power is given, will certainly over-run those that give it, and those that receive it: there is a straine in a mans heart that will sometime or other runne out to excesse, unlesse the Lord restraine it, but it is not good to venture it: It is necessary therefore, that all power that is on earth be limited, Church-power or other . . . It is counted a matter of danger to the State to limit Prerogatives; but it is a further danger, not to have them limited: They will be like a Tempest, if they be not limited: A Prince himselfe cannot tell where hee will confine himselfe, nor can the people tell. . . . It is therefore fit for every man to be studious of the bounds which the Lord hath set: and for the People, in whom fundamentally all power lyes, to give as much power as God in his word gives to men: And it is meet that Magistrates in the commonwealth, and so Officers in Churches should desire to know the utmost bounds of their own power, and it is safe for both: All intrenchment upon the bounds which God hath not given, they are not enlargments, but burdens and snares: They will certainly lead the spirit of a man out of his way sooner or later. It is wholesome and safe to be dealt withall as God deales with the vast Sea; Hitherto shalt thou come, but there shalt thou stay thy proud waves: and therefore if they be but banks of simple sand, they will be good enough to check the vast roaring Sea.[10]

The fear of power led Puritans to distrust majority rule. Unbridled majorities were likely to err because they were not necessarily possessed with divine wisdom. Furthermore, as Rev. Cotton wrote,

Democracy, I do not conceyve that ever God did ordeyne as a fit government eyther for church or commonwealth. If the people be governors, who shall be governed? As for monarchy, and aristocracy, they are both of them clearly approoved, and directed in scripture, yet so as referreth the soveraigntie to himselfe, and setteth up Theocracy in both, as the best forme of government in the common-wealth, as well as in the church.[11]

It was by limiting voting privileges to freeholders and church members that the Puritans held elections. As Rev. Thomas Hooker emphasized, "the choice of public magistrates belongs unto the people, by God's allowance. . . . (T)he privilege of election, which belongs to the people, therefore must not be exercised according to their humours, but according to the blessed will and law of God."[12]

10. John Cotton, quoted by Miller and Johnson, *The Puritans*, pp. 212–14.

11. John Cotton, 1636; ibid., pp. 209–12.

12. Thomas Hooker, 1638, *Collections of the Connecticut Historical Society*, 1:20; quoted by Wright, *American Interpretations*, p. 23.

Protection of Individual Rights

Individual rights were valued and defended in colonial New England. Those rights were part of the basic law, and the slightest infraction of the law was a threat to the order of society:

> Puritans were not content to let abject submission totally define their relationship to authority. Even more than persons living in a permissive atmosphere, they felt the need to raise defenses against the fathers who constantly threatened judgment and rebuke. This inward impulse was expressed in Puritan political philosophy as the doctrine of rights and the rule of law. Even conservatives asserted that "God has not Subjected the Lives and Liberty's of the Ruled, to the Arbitrary Will and Pleasure of Rulers." He gave "Laws to their Authority," so that they were not "at Liberty to Pursue and Accomplish their own Desires." The law defined the line beyond which rulers became tyrants and resistance became a duty.
>
> The spirited opposition to English and colonial authority when subjects thought their rights violated was a defense of the self. Property rights, for example, represented more than physical comfort or social prestige, for property was an extension of the person. Hence the legal safeguards against government invasion of these rights protected the individual as well. When action in England threatened their titles, Connecticut men complained that if "we may not secure the liberty of the law for the security of our freeholds . . . we shall then be the most miserable of any Christian people." The Stonington men who objected to a tax imposed by the Assembly, out of fear that their "estates, liberties and persons [would be] subject unto servitude" were not being melodramatic when they blew up one dubious tax into a threat against their lives. Without the bulwark of law they would be in their own minds defenseless against the crushing force of authority. They were "very tender" of their lawful liberties which protected the self against total domination by the fathers of society.[13]

Professor Bushman explains that lawsuits over trivial matters were common in colonial Connecticut, because men were very concerned about their rights:

> In the seventeenth century the occasions for justifiable resistance to colonial authority in Connecticut were few, but the sensitive concern for lawful liberties showed up every day in the courts. *Connecticut men were extraordinarily quick to drag their neighbors*

---

13. Richard L. Bushman, *From Puritan to Yankee: Character and the Social Order in Connecticut, 1690–1765* (Cambridge: Harvard University Press, 1967, 1980), pp. 20–21.

*to law at the least offense and to battle ferociously for justice. A
trespass by a fellow subject was resented because the neighbor
seemed to be exercising authority falsely. Angered by the slightest
hint of oppression, Puritans jealously defended their rights against
attacks from any source.*

Thus his awe of the rulers did not reduce the Puritan to slavish
servitude, for the general respect for power led to stress on the limits
of government. The law both restrained and strengthened the
individual in his testy relations with authority.[14]

Religious Liberty

Puritans became precursors of religious liberty although at first
they were the opposite. Initially, dissenters were banished from
New England. This explains well the Puritan viewpoint:

> To allow no dissent from the truth was exactly the reason they had
> come to America. They maintained here precisely what they had
> maintained in England, and if they exiled, fined, jailed, whipped or
> hanged those who disagreed with them in New England, they would
> have done the same thing in England could they have secured the
> power. It is almost pathetic to trace the puzzlement of New England
> leaders at the end of the seventeenth century, when the idea of
> toleration was becoming more and more respectable in European
> thought. They could hardly understand what was happening in the
> world, and they could not for a long time be persuaded that they had
> any reason to be ashamed of their record of so many Quakers
> whipped, blasphemers punished by amputation of ears, Antinomians
> exiled, Anabaptists fined, or witches executed. By all the lights which
> had prevailed in Europe at the time the Puritans had left, these were
> achievements to which any government could point with pride.[15]

Things changed, however. In the 1680s Rev. Increase Mather
was a staunch foe of religious toleration. But forty years later he and
his son the Rev. Cotton Mather participated in the ordination of a
Baptist minister in Boston, and Increase then preached a sermon
about the need for harmony between differing denominations.[16]

The establishing of Rhode Island by Roger Williams in 1636 was
one factor that led to the development of religious liberty. Williams,
an advocate of religious liberty, had been banished from Massachusetts for his religious views. He argued that of the "Two Tables" on

14. Ibid., p. 21 (emphasis added).
15. Miller and Johnson, *The Puritans*, p. 185.
16. Ibid., p. 186.

which the law of God had been given to man, only the second (Thou shalt not kill, steal, etc.) was within the jurisdiction of civil government, because those laws dealt with man's relationship with his fellow man. The first table (Thou shalt have no other gods before me, etc.) dealt with man's relationship with God and therefore was outside the jurisdiction of civil government.

Another factor which contributed to the development of religious liberty was the controversy over the "halfway covenant." The Puritan zeal began to wane in the 1700s. Church officials wondered what to do with the growing number of respectable citizens who were raised in the covenant yet showed no signs of regeneration. These people wanted to belong to the church because of the civic privileges church membership conferred. Many churches opted for a "halfway covenant" which would allow the people whose salvation was uncertain to attend church, vote on church matters, and receive the sacraments. That way they could vote, hold public office, etc.

Jonathan Edwards challenged the halfway covenant. He argued that there could be no such thing as a halfway covenant with God. The unregenerate should not be lulled into a false sense of security, and they should not have a voice in church affairs. But he was willing to give them their rights as citizens.

Jonathan Edwards was a conservative, calling his fellow New Englanders back to the stern Puritanism of earlier days. Edwards was willing to allow the unregenerate the rights of citizenship while refusing them church membership. He separated church membership from civic privileges. Edwards conceded that the Puritan ideal of a Holy Commonwealth was not feasible. He saw the choices as (1) a church-run society in which the church was little more than a social club; or (2) a society not run by the church, but with a strong and faithful church within it. Edwards chose the latter, and in effect opted for separation of church and state.[17]

The decline of Puritanism in the early 1700s was not the end of its influence. The ideas incorporated in the Holy Commonwealth and postmillennialism as well as the emphasis on biblical law, the work ethic, the fear of power, and the need for individual rights and religious liberty formed the foundation for American history and thinking. The first Great Awakening, the religious revival which shook the nation around 1742, called Americans back to the religious zeal of Puritan days.

Puritanism was never the same as in the 1600s, but it was never allowed to die.

17. J. Steven O'Malley, lectures, "Theology of Jonathan Edwards," Oral Roberts University, Autumn 1982.

3 Deism, Freemasonry, and Science

In 1985 I was a guest on "Point of View," a nationwide radio talk show originating out of Dallas. When I spoke of the Christian faith of the founding fathers, my host expressed surprise. His daughter had returned from school recently and said she had learned in class that the founders of this nation were, without exception, deists rather than Christians. That comment spurred me to do more research and resulted in my writing this book.

Beyond defining Calvinism and its influence on the founding fathers, it is necessary to study the non-Christian or thought-to-be non-Christian ideologies of the late 1700s. In this chapter we examine deism, freemasonry, and science.

Deism

Deism[1] "contradicts orthodox Christianity by denying any direct intervention in the natural order by God." "It would reduce God's function in creation to that of first cause only. According to the classical comparison of God with a clockmaker, which is found as

---

1. Some people confuse deism with theism. Literally, theism means a belief in the existence of God. Granted, there is a difference in beliefs held by theists. However, the perception of God as Creator and Sustainer of the universe, infinite in attributes, and the only God is the one usually accepted by Christians. An orthodox Christian must be a theist but could never be a deist.

early as Nicolaus of Oresmes (d. 1382), God wound up the clock of the world once and for all at the beginning, so that it now proceeds as world history without the need for further involvement."[2]

The *Encyclopedia Britannica* expands on this definition:

> The Deists argued that after God's initial work of creation, He withdrew into detached transcendence, leaving the world to operate according to rational natural rules. Borrowing upon the general prestige of Newton's vision of the universe as a mechanism obeying stable rational laws, they propounded variations on the classic argument for design wherein the existence of a creator is inferred from the evidence of the rational ordering of the world.[3]

Deism arose in Europe in the late 1600s, and was somewhat popular throughout the 1700s into the 1800s. The deist sees little reason for prayer, since God does not intervene to answer prayer. The deist does not believe in miracles performed by God. He does not believe that God sent Jesus Christ to atone for sin, or that God reveals himself through the Bible. The deist believes man learns about God through human reason and perhaps empirical evidence.

Deists did not agree among themselves on every detail. The deists in colonial America tended to be more moderate than those in Europe.

Deism and Law

Deism and Christianity are incompatible on many fundamental points of theology. But they are similar in the way they look at law and government. They both agree on the existence of natural laws and natural rights.

Deists believe God had infused the universe with certain physical laws.

In addition, before God left the universe, he established natural laws to govern human affairs and implanted these in the human mind and conscience. These natural laws, like the physical laws which govern the universe, are fixed, absolute, and unchanging. Natural law requires the observance of these natural rights.

2. M. H. Macdonald, "Deism" in *Evangelical Dictionary of Theology*, ed. Walter A. Elwell (Grand Rapids: Baker, 1984), p. 305.

3. *Encyclopedia Britannica*, 1986, s.v. "Deism." The *Macropaedia* adds, "Indeed, in the eighteenth century, there was a tendency to convert Newton into a matter-of-fact Deist—a transmutation that was contrary to the spirit of both his philosophical and his theological writings" (s.v. "Religious and Spiritual Belief, Systems of").

Christians also believe in some form of higher law or natural law. Paul wrote in Romans 2:15 of the conscience, the "work of the law written on their hearts." The early Christian theologians Augustine and Aquinas spoke of the law of nature, drawing from the Bible and classical Greek tradition. Calvin spoke of the law of nature as part of the "common grace" which God bestowed upon all men; Lutherans called it "gratia natura," or natural grace. Many Christians believe that God reveals his law through the Bible. On this point they part company with the deists. Some Christians also have less faith than deists in man's ability to understand natural law through human reason alone.

When Jefferson penned the Declaration of Independence, he wrote of the "Laws of Nature and of Nature's God." He declared that "All men are created equal, that they are endowed by their Creator with certain unalienable Rights, that among these are Life, Liberty and the pursuit of Happiness." He used terminology and expressed concepts to which both Christians and deists could subscribe.

Deism in America

The colonists were familiar with deist thinking. But deism never gained a strong foothold in America. The first Great Awakening, the religious revival of the 1740s, was partially responsible for cutting short the spread of deism.

In many states at the time of the Constitutional Convention, confessed deists were not allowed to hold public office.[4] Deism was generally held in low esteem, as such laws indicate.

Dr. M. E. Bradford of the University of Dallas has written a series of biographical sketches on the fifty-five delegates to the Constitutional Convention. He has included the following table[5] listing the church membership of the delegates.

New Hampshire
    John Langdon, *Congregationalist*
    Nicholas Gilman, *Congregationalist*

Massachusetts
    Elbridge Gerry, *Episcopalian*
    Rufus King, *Episcopalian*

---

4. Catherine Drinker Bowen, *Miracle at Philadelphia: The Story of the Constitutional Convention May to September 1787* (Boston: Little, Brown & Co., 1966), p. 215.

5. M. E. Bradford, *A Worthy Company: Brief Lives of the Framers of the United States Constitution* (Marlborough, N.H.: Plymouth Rock Foundation, 1982), pp. iv–v.

Caleb Strong, *Congregationalist*
Nathaniel Gorham, *Congregationalist*

Connecticut
Roger Sherman, *Congregationalist*
William Samuel Johnson, *Episcopalian*
Oliver Ellsworth, *Congregationalist*

New York
Alexander Hamilton, *Episcopalian*
John Lansing, *Dutch Reformed (?)*
Robert Yates, *Dutch Reformed*

New Jersey
William Patterson, *Presbyterian*
William Livingston, *Presbyterian*
Jonathan Dayton, *Episcopalian*
David Brearly, *Episcopalian*
William Churchill Houston, *Presbyterian*

Pennsylvania
Benjamin Franklin, *Deist*
Robert Morris, *Episcopalian*
James Wilson, *Episcopalian/Deist*
Gouverneur Morris, *Episcopalian*
Thomas Mifflin, *Quaker/Lutheran*
George Clymer, *Quaker/Episcopalian*
Thomas FitzSimmons, *Roman Catholic*
Jared Ingersoll, *Presbyterian*

Delaware
John Dickinson, *Quaker/Episcopalian*
George Read, *Episcopalian*
Richard Bassett, *Methodist*
Gunning Bedford, *Presbyterian*
Jacob Broom, *Lutheran*

Maryland
Luther Martin, *Episcopalian*
Daniel Carroll, *Roman Catholic*
John Francis Mercer, *Episcopalian*
James McHenry, *Presbyterian*
Daniel of St Thomas Jennifer, *Episcopalian*

Virginia
George Washington, *Episcopalian*
James Madison, *Episcopalian*
George Mason, *Episcopalian*
Edmund Jennings Randolph, *Episcopalian*
James Blair, Jr., *Episcopalian*

James McClung,
George Wythe, *Episcopalian*

North Carolina
William Richardson Davie, *Presbyterian*
Hugh Williamson, *Presbyterian/Deist (?)*
William Blount, *Presbyterian*
Alexander Martin, *Presbyterian/Episcopalian*
Richard Dobbs Spaight, Jr., *Episcopalian*

South Carolina
John Rutledge, *Episcopalian*
Charles Cotesworth Pinckney, *Episcopalian*
Pierce Butler, *Episcopalian*
Charles Pinckney, III, *Episcopalian*

Georgia
Abraham Baldwin, *Congregationalist*
William Leigh Pierce, *Episcopalian*
William Houstoun, *Episcopalian*
William Few, *Methodist*

Two religions are listed for several of the delegates. These delegates changed their religion at some time during their lives. Using only the last religion listed for each delegate, Bradford's list includes 28 Episcopalians, 8 Presbyterians, 7 Congregationalists, 2 Lutherans, 2 Dutch Reformed, 2 Methodists, 2 Roman Catholics, and 3 deists. One religious preference is unknown to historians. The chart indicates that deism was not the religion of most of our founding fathers. At most it was the religion of 3 out of 55, or 5½ percent.

It is possible some of the delegates belonged to other churches and might have held deist convictions. But as a condition for church membership, most colonial churches required sworn adherence to strict doctrinal creeds, which included belief in the Bible as God's revelation and trust in Jesus Christ as the Son of God. If the founding fathers held deist ideas while belonging to Christian churches it means they swore falsely in the presence of God.

The three delegates Bradford identifies as deists—Hugh Williamson of North Carolina, James Wilson of Pennsylvania, and Benjamin Franklin of Pennsylvania—were raised in staunch Calvinist homes. All three originally studied for the ministry. Hugh Williamson, licensed to preach by the Presbyterian Church, conducted church services. (Bradford places a question mark after Williamson's identification as a deist.) It seems that Williamson was influenced by Calvinist Christianity even if he did not accept all of its doctrines.

Whether Benjamin Franklin was actually a deist can also be questioned. At the Great Convention it was Franklin who called for prayer, declaring that "God governs in the affairs of men." According to deism, God does *not* so intervene.

Franklin was a deist as a young man, but he became disenchanted with deism. While Franklin probably never became a Christian in the orthodox sense, he came a long way from deism in his eighty-four years.

That leaves James Wilson. Wilson was raised by strict Calvinist parents in the shire of Fife in the Scottish lowlands, the heart of covenanter country. After college he entered seminary to prepare for the ministry. His studies were interrupted by his father's death, and perhaps by his own disinclination for a theological career. He came to America in 1765, studied law, and embarked on a career as a lawyer, land speculator, and politician. He maintained some association with the Episcopal church, having his children baptized there. He was buried in an Episcopal churchyard, but it is not clear whether or not he ever became a member.

Wilson frequently spoke at the Convention. But his legal philosophy gives the most insight into his religious beliefs. This is best described in his law lectures at the College of Philadelphia in 1789, in which he declared over and over that all law comes from God. He divided God's law into four categories: the "law eternal" which applies only to God himself and which only he can know; the "law celestial" which is "made for angels and the spirits of the just made perfect"; the "laws of nature" by which "the irrational and inanimate parts of the creation are governed." Finally, there is

> That law, which God has made for man in his present state; that law, which is communicated to us by reason and conscience, the divine monitors within us, and by the sacred oracles, the divine monitors without us. . . .
>
> As promulgated by reason and the moral sense it has been called natural; as promulgated by the holy scriptures, it has been called revealed law.
>
> As addressed to men, it has been denominated the law of nature; as addressed to political societies, it has been denominated the law of nations.
>
> But it should always be remembered, that this law, natural or revealed, made for men or for nations, flows from the same divine source; it is the law of God. . . .

> Human law must rest its authority, ultimately, upon the authority
> of that law, which is divine.[6]

Most of Wilson's ideas reflect the views of either a Christian or a deist, except for his recognition of revealed law as found in the "holy scriptures." In another passage he refers to the "will of God" as the "efficient cause of moral obligation—of the eminent distinction between right and wrong," and therefore, the "supreme law." But why should one obey the will of God?—"I can only say, I *feel* that such is my duty. Here investigation must stop; reasoning can go no further. The science of morals, as well as other sciences is founded on truths, that cannot be discovered or proved by reasoning."[7] And how do we discover the will of God?—"by our conscience, by our reason, and by the Holy Scriptures."[8]

These quotes do not prove Wilson was a Christian, but they do indicate that he was willing to give less place to human reason, and more credit to divine revelation, than the deists.

Deism, while it existed in America and was even accepted by a few leading Americans (Thomas Paine, Ethan Allen, and possibly James Wilson), was (1) less influential than Christianity and (2) fundamentally compatible with Christianity in its view of law and government.

Freemasonry

> Freemasonry is an old fraternal organization, the aim of which is to
> promote brotherhood and foster morality among its members. It is
> nondenominational, urging its members to worship one God as the
> "Great Architect of the Universe," and it brings together men of
> various beliefs, opinions, and denominations.[9]

Masons claim that their organization is not a religious denomination. Members are required to believe in God and in life after death, but beyond that their religious creeds are their own.

Many church bodies are critical of masonry, particularly the Catholic Church, some Lutheran synods, and many evangelical churches. They argue that masonry involves secrecy, promotes the

6. James DeWitt Andres, *Works of Wilson* (Chicago, 1896), 1:91–93; quoted by Charles Page Smith, *James Wilson: Founding Father* (Chapel Hill: University of North Carolina Press, 1956), p. 329.

7. Andrews, 1:93–95, 102–5; quoted by Smith, *James Wilson*, p. 331.

8. Smith, *James Wilson*, p. 331.

9. *World Book Encyclopedia*, 1985, s.v. "Masonry."

idea of salvation by works, accepts all religions whether true or false, and is corrupted by Eastern mysticism and occultism. Other Christians defend masonry because it encourages men to be faithful to their respective churches, promotes prayer, and engages in good works. This is not the occasion to take a position on whether or not Christians should be involved with freemasonry. The important point to note is that, then as now, Christians frequently were masons.

The influence of freemasonry on the founding fathers of this nation has been the subject of much discussion and concern. It is true that some of the founding fathers were masons. Benjamin Franklin was a master mason. George Washington was also a mason, although he wrote to a friend in 1797 that he had not attended lodge meetings more than once or twice in the preceding thirty years.

The fact that some of the founding fathers were masons in no way suggests that they were not Christians. There is evidence that even Rev. John Witherspoon, the orthodox Presbyterian minister who signed the Declaration of Independence and influenced many of the founding fathers, may have been a mason. Bradford refers to Daniel Carroll, delegate to the Convention from Maryland and brother of the Archbishop of Baltimore, as "a Mason; and a generous supporter of his church" (Roman Catholic)[10]

Part of the reason for concern over masonry is the fact that in some parts of the world, France in particular, the lodge was a hotbed of radical thinking. This does not appear to have been true in America. Carl Van Doren notes in his biography of Franklin that, "Freemasonry in America had been social and local, with little influence in politics. In France, it was freethinking and opposed to absolutism."[11]

An eighteenth-century American might join a masonic lodge for a variety of reasons: to find friends, to engage in social activities, to make business or political contacts, or to help promote the good works and lofty ideals supported by freemasonry. Lodge membership then says very little about a person's Christian faith, except that it confirms he does believe in God and in life after death.

Science

The advancement of the scientific age and scientific attitudes in America during the late 1700s is often suspected of drawing men,

10. Bradford, *A Worthy Company*, p. 122.
11. Carl Van Doren, *Benjamin Franklin* (New York: Viking Press, 1938, 1961), p. 656.

our founding fathers in particular, away from Christian beliefs and into science.

It is true that the founding fathers studied science. Most of them were well versed in various fields of science. Franklin and Jefferson gained recognition for their scientific discoveries. Charles Cotesworth Pinckney was known for his experiments in botany and chemistry. James McClurg was a medical doctor, Professor of Anatomy and Medicine at William and Mary College, and President of the Virginia Medical Society. Most other delegates were interested in science, directly or indirectly, if for no other reason than their prosperity depended on the science of agriculture. Physical sciences were part of the required curriculum at most colonial colleges. The well-educated man was expected to be familiar with various fields of science.

It is important to realize that the founding fathers lived before the theory of evolution became popular. The *Encyclopedia of Philoso phy* says that during colonial time, ". . . science was more generally used as a bulwark for Christianity than the reverse."[12]

Generally speaking, the Christian view of science has been that reason and evidence may supplement revelation, but may never supplant revelation. And faith may transcend reason, but faith is not inconsistent with reason. Science and Christianity should be accused of opposing each other only when scientific reasoning is antithetical to Christianity.

The interest in science and scientific discoveries during colonial days helped increase man's understanding of the world and the universe. The following four scientists of that period added new dimensions to human thinking—ideas that didn't necessarily go against Christian teachings.

Nicolas Copernicus (1473-1543) was the author of the heliocentric view of the universe which held that the earth revolves around the sun rather than the other way around, and that the stars appear to move only because the earth moves. As a young man Copernicus earned his doctorate in canon law and was appointed canon of the Cathedral at Frauenburg in 1497 though he did not actually assume that position until 1512. A church man himself, he in no way considered his conclusions contrary to Christianity. He believed he had developed a cosmology that was a true picture of the divinely ordered cosmos, and he considered the geocentric

---

12. *Encyclopedia of Philosophy*, s.v. "Deism."

(earth-centered) view to be contrary to experience, common sense, and Scripture.[13]

Galileo (1564-1642) was known for his invention of the telescope. He also developed the idea that the universe operates according to mathematical certainties. Galileo did not see himself as an enemy of Christianity. He had been educated in a monastery and was a strong believer in the inerrancy of the Bible. He declared, "As to the (physical) propositions which are stated but not rigorously demonstrated, anything contrary to the Bible involved in them must be considered undoubtedly false and should be proved so by every possible means."[14]

Like Copernicus a century earlier, Galileo's dispute was not with Scripture but with methods of interpreting Scripture. He argued that when the Bible comes into conflict with scientific truth, the Bible should be interpreted allegorically.

He further argued that it would be "a terrible detriment for the souls if people found themselves convinced by proof of something that it was made then a sin to believe."[15]

Sir Francis Bacon (1561-1626) was an attorney, statesman, and Lord Keeper of the Great Seal under James I. Bacon, along with Locke and Newton, was revered by Thomas Jefferson as part of his trinity of great men. Bacon is noted for his development of science as a systematic body of knowledge.

Bacon in no way meant to attack Christianity by systematizing science. He saw scientific knowledge as "a rich storehouse for the glory of the Creator and the relief of man's estate," referring to the ways in which scientific knowledge could improve the human condition. He stressed that knowledge was only partly natural or developed from our own endeavors; it was also partly supernatural, derived from God himself.[16]

Sir Isaac Newton (1642-1727) was perhaps the most significant scientist in the eyes of the founding fathers. Newton is remembered for his laws of gravity. He made many other discoveries, including his three laws of motion: (1) that every body continues in motion in a constant direction and speed unless opposed by force; (2) that the change of motion will be in exact proportion to the degree of resistance; and (3) to every action there is an equal reaction.

Newton also defended Christianity. According to the *Encyclope-*

13. Ibid., s.v. "Copernicus, Nicolas."
14. *New Catholic Encyclopedia*, s.v. "Galileo, Galilei."
15. *Encyclopedia Britannica: Macropaedia: Knowledge in Depth*, 1986, s.v. "Galileo."
16. *Encyclopedia of Philosophy*, s.v. "Bacon, Francis."

dia of Philosophy, "Newton himself was a student of Old Testament prophecies and believed in the Scriptures as inerrant guides."[17]

The main contribution of these scientists to the founding fathers' knowledge was the concept of a universe, created and sustained by God himself, which operates according to fixed, unchanging natural laws.

17. Ibid., s.v. "Deism."

4 Law and Government

Imagine yourself as a reporter for a twentieth-century publication in a time machine with the dial set for A.D. 1787, the days of the Constitutional Convention. Or perhaps you will represent yourself as a spokesman for the U.S. Bicentennial Commission of 1987, asking the founding fathers what they meant when they wrote the Constitution. Note pad in hand, your mind brimming with questions, you prepare to interview Washington, Hamilton, Madison, and the others for the news "scoop" of the year.

Obviously that is not possible. So how can we determine what the founders really thought? Whom did they read, whose ideas caught their imagination, whom did they respect? Where did they get their ideas? One way is to read what they wrote, and check the sources they cited.

Two professors, Donald S. Lutz and Charles S. Hyneman, have reviewed an estimated 15,000 items, and closely read 2,200 books, pamphlets, newspaper articles, and monographs with explicitly political content printed between 1760 and 1805. They reduced this to 916 items, about one-third of all public political writings longer than 2,000 words.

From these items, Lutz and Hyneman identified 3,154 references to other sources. The source most often cited by the founding fathers was the Bible, which accounted for 34 percent of all citations. The fifth book of the Bible, Deuteronomy, because of its

51

heavy emphasis on biblical law, was referred to frequently. Table 1
shows the breakdown of sources cited during that period.

Table 1.   Distribution of Citations by Decade (Percentage)[1]

	1760s	1770s	1780s	1790s	1800-05	Percent of Total Number
Bible	24	44	34	29	38	34
Enlightenment	32	18	24	21	18	22*
Whig	10	20	19	17	15	18
Common Law	12	4	9	14	20	11
Classical	8	11	10	11	2	9
Peers	6	2	3	6	5	4
Others	8	1	1	2	2	2
	100%	100%	100%	100%	100%	100%
N	216	544	1306	674	414	3154

*If we break Bailyn's Enlightenment category into the three sub-categories described by Lundberg and May, the results are not significantly altered. The "First Enlightenment," dominated by Montesquieu, Locke, and Pufendorf, comprises 16% of all citations. The more radical writers of the "Second Enlightenment," men like Voltaire, Diderot, and Helvetius, garner 2% of the citations. The "Third Enlightenment," typified by Beccaria, Rousseau, Mably, and Raynal, receives 4% of the citations, to bring the total back to the 22% listed here.

The most cited thinkers (see Table 2) were not deists and
philosophes, but conservative legal and political thinkers who often
were also Christians.

Table 2.   Ordering of Most Cited Thinkers, 1760-1805

	Percent		Percent
1. Montesquieu	8.3	19. Shakespeare	.8
2. Blackstone	7.9	20. Livy	.8
3. Locke	2.9	21. Pope	.7
4. Hume	2.7	22. Milton	.7
5. Plutarch	1.5	23. Tacitus	.6
6. Beccaria	1.5	24. Coxe	.6
7. Trenchard & Gordon	1.4	25. Plato	.5
8. Delolme	1.4	26. Abbé Raynal	.5
9. Pufendorf	1.3	27. Mably	.5
10. Coke	1.3	28. Machiavelli	.5
11. Cicero	1.2	29. Vattel	.5
12. Hobbes	1.0	30. Petyt	.5
13. Robertson	.9	31. Voltaire	.5
14. Grotius	.9	32. Robison	.5
15. Rousseau	.9	33. Sidney	.5
16. Bolingbroke	.9	34. Somers	.5
17. Bacon	.8	35. Harrington	.5
18. Price	.8	36. Rapin	.5

*Includes all thinkers cited at least sixteen times (.5% out of the total number of 3,154 citations). These 36 names account for 47.8% of all citations.

1. Donald S. Lutz, "The Relative Influence of European Writers on Late Eighteenth-Century American Political Thought," *American Political Science Review* 189 (1984): 189–97. My thanks to Dr. H. Wayne House of Dallas Theological Seminary for bringing this study by Lutz to my attention.

Baron Charles Montesquieu leads this list with 8.3 percent of all citations, followed closely by Sir William Blackstone with 7.9 percent and John Locke with 2.9 percent.

Table 3 shows the breakdown by decade for the twelve most often cited thinkers. Locke led in the 1760s and 1770s when America's foremost concern was independence and the rights of man; Montesquieu and Blackstone led in the 1780s and 1790s when attention was focused on the practical problems of forming a government to secure those rights.

Table 3. Most Cited Thinkers by Decade

	1760s	1770s	1780s	1790s	1800-05	Percent of Total Number
Montesquieu	8	7	14	4	1	8.3
Blackstone	1	3	7	11	15	7.9
Locke	11	7	1	1	1	2.9
Hume	1	1	1	6	5	2.7
Plutarch	1	3	1	2	0	1.5
Beccaria	0	1	3	0	0	1.5
Trenchard & Gordon	1	1	3	0	0	1.4
Delolme	0	0	3	1	0	1.4
Pufendorf	4	0	1	0	5	1.3
Coke	5	0	1	2	4	1.3
Cicero	1	1	1	2	1	1.2
Hobbes	0	1	1	0	0	1.0
	33	25	37	29	32	32.4
Others	67	75	63	71	68	67.6
	100%	100%	100%	100%	100%	100.0%
N	216	544	1306	674	414	3154

*This table is limited to those who were cited at least 32 times, which is 1% of the total of 3,154 citations. The extra decimal point in the last column is to allow more precise recovery of the number of citations over the era, whereas all other percentages are rounded off to the nearest whole number to ease the viewing of the table. The use of 0% indicates fewer than .5% of the citations for a given decade.

One weakness in the approach followed in these figures is that it fails to measure the value given to each citation. Major and minor as well as negative and positive references receive equal recognition. However, Lutz notes that negative references show familiarity with the work and use of the cited author's categories of thought.

By combining the research available in the figures with additional investigations into which books the founding fathers had in their libraries, which books they studied in school, and which sources they recommended to others, a group of notable thinkers emerges. These men were important sources of the founding fathers' political perspectives. These thinkers and their contributions will be examined in the remainder of this chapter.

Montesquieu

Charles Louis Joseph de Secondat, the Baron Montesquieu of France (1689-1755), was cited by the founders of this nation more frequently than any other source except the Bible. His best-known work, *The Spirit of Laws*, distinguished four forms of government: monarchy in which the guiding principle is honor, aristocracy in which the guiding principle is moderation, republican democracy in which the guiding principle is virtue, and despotism in which the guiding principle is fear. His main contribution to the thinking of the founders of this nation was the concept of separation of powers between legislative, executive, and judicial branches of government. This concept is so vital to the American constitutional system.

Because he lived in France and taught in French universities during the time of the philosophes, Montesquieu is sometimes identified as a deist. But he was born a Catholic, and remained a Catholic to his death. He did have some private questions concerning Catholic dogma. Stark suggests that Montesquieu moved closer and closer to Christian orthodoxy as he grew older, noting Montesquieu's comment that the establishment of Christianity among the Romans would be an absurdity if it were merely a natural historical event.[2] In any event, he received Communion shortly before he died, and he emphatically declared his belief that the elements were the true Body and Blood of Jesus Christ.[3]

Montesquieu believed all law has its source in God. As he says in the opening of *The Spirit of Laws*: "God is related to the universe, as Creator and Preserver; the laws by which He created all things are those by which He preserves them."[4] These laws apply to the physical world and human beings. Men make their own laws, but these laws must conform to the eternal laws of God.

> Particular intelligent beings may have laws of their own making, but they likewise have some which they never made. . . . Before laws were made, there were relations of possible justice. To say that there is nothing just or unjust but what is commanded or forbidden by positive laws, is the same as saying that before the describing of a circle all the radii were not equal.[5]

2. Werner Stark, *Montesquieu, Pioneer of the Sociology of Knowledge* (Toronto: University of Toronto Press, 1961), pp. 14–16.

3. Robert Shackleton, *Montesquieu: A Critical Biography* (Oxford: Oxford University Press, 1961), pp. 395–96.

4. Montesquieu, *The Spirit of Laws* (New York: Hafner, 1949, 1962), 1:1.

5. Ibid., 1:2.

Montesquieu believed man was basically evil and self-centered. His pessimism was due to the fact that he felt intelligent beings do not choose to follow God's laws:

> But the intelligent world is far from being so well governed as the physical. For though the former has also its laws, which of their own nature are invariable, it does not conform to them so exactly as the physical world. This is because, on the one hand, particular intelligent beings are of a finite nature, and consequently liable to error; and on the other, their nature requires them to be free agents. Hence they do not steadily conform to their primitive laws; and even those of their own instituting they frequently infringe. . . .
>
> Man, as a physical being, is like other bodies governed by invariable laws. As an intelligent being, he incessantly transgresses the laws established by God, and changes those of his own instituting. He is left to his private direction, though a limited being, and subject, like all finite intelligences, to ignorance and error: even his imperfect knowledge he loses; and as a sensible creature, he is hurried away by a thousand impetuous passions. Such a being might every instant forget his Creator; God has therefore reminded him of his duty by the laws of religion. Such a being is liable every moment to forget himself; philosophy has provided against this by the laws of morality. Formed to live in society, he might forget his fellow-creatures; legislators have, therefore, by political and civil laws, confined him to his duty.[6]

He compared Christianity to Islam and declared Christianity superior partly because of the better government it promotes, "a moderate Government is most agreeable to the Christian Religion, and a despotic Government to the Mahommedan":

> The Christian religion, which ordains that men should love each other, would, without doubt, have every nation blest with the best civil, the best political laws; because these, next to this religion, are the greatest good that men can give and receive. . . .
>
> The Christian religion is a stranger to mere despotic power. The mildness so frequently recommended in the gospel is incompatible with the despotic rage with which a prince punishes his subjects, and exercises himself in cruelty. . . .
>
> While the Mahommedan princes incessantly give or receive death, the religion of the Christians renders their princes less timid, and consequently less cruel. The prince confides in his subjects, and the subjects in the prince. How admirable the religion which, while it

---

6. Ibid., 1:2–3.

only seems to have in view the felicity of the other life, continues the happiness of this![7]

In addition he explained that "the Catholic Religion is most agreeable to a Monarchy, and the Protestant to a Republic," because "the people of the north have, and will forever have, a spirit of liberty and independence, which the people of the south have not; and, therefore, a religion which has no visible head is more agreeable to the independence of the climate than that which has one. . . ." This was more true of Calvinist societies than Lutheran societies.[8]

In his writings, Montesquieu explained the role of religion in fostering values which find expression in civil laws. He pointed out that this is also true in non-Christian societies. He expressed the orthodox conviction that Christianity is a religion revealed by God himself. "In a country so unfortunate as to have a religion that God has not revealed, it is necessary for it to be agreeable to morality; because even a false religion is the best security we can have of the probity of men."[9] Thus, even a false religion can positively affect society if it fosters values which find expression in good laws.

While Montesquieu's countrymen followed the way of the radical philosophes which ultimately led to destruction, the American founding fathers were receptive to his views. He recognized the value of religion, Christianity in particular, in fostering good laws and good government. Knowing the sinful nature of man, he advocated separation of powers by which power checks power. That was Montesquieu's main contribution to the thinking of the founders of this nation: the separation of powers between the legislative, executive, and judicial branches of government.

Blackstone

Noted for literary quality and readability as well as for legal and historical scholarship, Sir William Blackstone's famous *Commentaries on the Laws of England* are rated as the most famous treatise on common law.

Blackstone (1723-1780) was an English barrister whose talents and inclinations were more suited to teaching law than to practicing law. Harvard Law Professor Duncan Kennedy describes Black-

7. Ibid., 24:27–29.
8. Ibid., 26:30–31.
9. Ibid., 24:32.

stone's *Commentaries* as "an important 18th-century treatise that all legal scholars have heard of but practically no one knows anything about."[10] One reason may be that Blackstone's God-centered view of law is out of fashion in today's legal community.

Throughout the latter half of the 1700s and the first half of the 1800s Blackstone's popularity in America was uneclipsed. It is said that more copies of Blackstone's *Commentaries* were sold in America than in England, that his *Commentaries* were in the offices of every lawyer in the land, that candidates for the bar were routinely examined on Blackstone, that he was cited authoritatively in the courts, and that a quotation from Blackstone settled many a legal argument.[11]

The founders of the nation read Blackstone with great interest. At least one delegate to the Constitutional Convention, Charles Cotesworth Pinckney of South Carolina, had been Blackstone's student at Oxford and was Blackstone's firm disciple. James Madison wrote in 1821, "I very cheerfully express my approbation of the proposed edition of Blackstone's *Commentaries*. . . ."[12]

The founding fathers drew three major points from Blackstone. The first was his conviction that all law has its source in God. Blackstone wrote about various categories of law, one of which is the law of nature:

> Law of Nature. This will of his Maker is called the law of nature. For as God, when He created matter, and endued it with a principle of mobility, established certain rules for the perpetual direction of that motion; so, when He created man, and endued him with free will to conduct himself in all parts of life, He laid down certain immutable laws of human nature, whereby that free will is in some degree regulated and restrained, and gave him also the faculty of reason to discover the purport of those laws.
>
> Considering the Creator only a Being of infinite power, He was able unquestionably to have prescribed whatever laws He pleased to His creature, man, however unjust or severe. But as he is also a Being of infinite wisdom, He has laid down only such laws as were founded in those relations of justice, that existed in the nature of things antecedent to any positive precept. These are the eternal, immutable laws of good and evil, to which the Creator Himself in all his

10. Duncan Kennedy, "The Structure of Blackstone's Commentaries," *Buffalo Law Review* (1979), 28:203–375, 209.

11. Lutz, "Relative Influence of European Writers," pp. 195–96.

12. Madison, quoted by Verna M. Hall, *The Christian History of the Constitution of the United States of America: Christian Self-Government with Union* (San Francisco: Foundation for American Christian Education, 1962, 1979), p. 130A.

Dispensations conforms; and which He has enabled human reason to discover, so far as they are necessary for the conduct of human actions. Such, among others, are these principles: that we should live honestly, should hurt nobody, and should render to everyone his due; to which three general precepts Justinian has reduced the whole doctrine of law. . . .

This law of nature, being coeval with mankind and dictated by God Himself, is of course superior in obligation to any other. It is binding over all the globe in all countries, and at all times: no human laws are of any validity, if contrary to this. . . .

Blackstone then described revealed law, the law of God as found in the Bible.

Revealed Law. This has given manifold occasion for the interposition of divine providence; which in compassion to the frailty, the imperfection, and the blindness of human reason, hath been pleased, at sundry times and in divers manners, to discover and enforce its laws by an immediate and direct revelation. The doctrines thus delivered we call the revealed or divine law, and they are to be found only in the Holy Scriptures. These precepts, when revealed, are found upon comparison to be really a part of the original law of nature as they tend in all their consequences to man's felicity. But we are not from thence to conclude that the knowledge of these truths was attainable by reason, in its present corrupted state; since we find that, until they were revealed, they were hid from the wisdom of the ages. As then the moral precepts of this law are indeed of the same original with those of the law of nature, so their intrinsic obligation is of equal strength and perpetuity. Yet undoubtedly the revealed law is of infinitely more authenticity than that moral system, which is framed by ethical writers, and denominated the natural law. Because one is the law of nature, expressly declared so to be by God Himself; the other is only what, by the assistance of human reason, we imagine to be that law. If we could be as certain of the latter as we are of the former, both would have an equal authority; but, till then, they can never be put in any competition together.

Upon these two foundations, the law of nature and the law of revelation, depend all human laws; that is to say, no human law should be suffered to contradict these.[13]

For the founding fathers, a second significant point in Blackstone's writings was the role of judges. In Blackstone's view, judges discover and apply law; they do not "make" law. This closely

13. Sir William Blackstone, *Commentaries on the Laws of England*, quoted by Hall, *Christian History of the Constitution*, pp. 140–46.

follows from Blackstone's underlying view of law as part of the revealed law of God or the law of nature. Judges were not a source of law. There are only three sources of law—general custom, the court precedents which present-day judges are not free to alter; special custom, rights of private parties that had ripened into rights by prescription; and statute law, that which was passed by Parliament. In respect to the latter, the role of the judge is to interpret the will of the legislature, not to substitute his own ideas in their place.[14] Blackstone, like Montesquieu, saw three branches of government, but envisioned the legislative as superior to the judiciary.

A third significant point in Blackstone's *Commentaries* was his expert systematizing of the common law of England. While this systematizing was needed in England, it was even more necessary in America because America was a new nation that did not have England's long traditions.

The common law of England is generally founded on biblical principles. The Anglo-Saxon Alfred the Great, for example, started his legal code with a recitation of the Ten Commandments and excerpts from the Mosaic law. There were additions to the Anglo-Saxon law. In the eleventh century Henricus Bracton systematized the common law according to Roman law as revised by the Justinian Code. The result was a Christianized version of the Roman law.

The Jewish interpretation of the Old Testament influenced the commercial law of England and the rest of Europe. Throughout much of the Middle Ages the church prohibited money-lending at interest, based on the interpretation of certain passages of Scripture. The Jews interpreted these Scriptures differently and were willing to lend money at interest. Often the only place one could borrow money was in the Jewish community. Jewish scholars such as Rabbi Moses Ben Maimon (Maimondes) codified the Jewish law and it formed the basis for much of English commercial law.

The canon law of the church and the emphasis on individual rights found in the Viking law from portions of England controlled by Norwegians and Danes also influenced English common law.[15] The noblemen who forced King John to sign the Magna Carta in A.D. 1215 came mostly from areas which had been under Viking

14. Kennedy, "Structure of Blackstone's Commentaries," p. 250.
15. Thamar E. Dufwa, *The Viking Laws and the Magna Carta: A Study of the Northmen's Cultural Influence on England and France* (New York: Exposition Press, 1963), pp. 32–92. For a general discussion and detailed documentation of the Christian and Jewish influence on the development of English common law, see John Eidsmoe, *The Christian Legal Advisor* (Grand Rapids: Baker, 1984, 1987), pp. 26–29.

control. While the Vikings were not Christians until about A.D. 1000, their emphasis on individual rights was consistent with biblical principles.

Although for a time it was popular to belittle Blackstone and his beliefs,[16] his views are becoming increasingly valued by legal scholars. One of Blackstone's former students, Jeremy Bentham, charged that Blackstone was an arch-conservative and an "enemy of reformation." But, fortunately, Bentham never gained the following in America that he had in England.

The 1986 edition of *Encyclopedia Britannica* puts it well: "Blackstone's description of the law as it existed was accurate and comprehensive, and was of great use to those who wished to reform it."[17] The author adds that it is "amusing" (the 1911 edition changes this word to "curious") that even today Blackstone's *Commentaries* "probably express the most profound political convictions of the majority of the English people."

The common law of England is part of the Christian heritage of America. That so much of it survived the migration to America is due in large part to Sir William Blackstone.

Locke

John Locke (1632-1704) was the British philosopher and political theorist who inspired a generation of Americans to thoughts of independence and the rights of man. His best-known works are his "Essay Concerning Human Understanding" and his two treatises "On Civil Government."

John Locke was born into a Puritan family, the son of a rural Calvinist lawyer who fought on the side of the Puritans in the English civil war. He was educated at Calvinist institutions and emerged with a Calvinistic world view although he was a bit more moderate than some Calvinists.

Locke, sometimes identified as a deist and freethinker, was actually a staunch and fervent Christian. He placed a higher value

16. "[Blackstone] had only the vaguest possible grasp on the elementary conceptions of law. He evidently regards the law of gravitation, the law of nations, and the law of England, as different examples of the same principle—as rules of action or conduct imposed by a superior power on its subjects. He propounds in terms a fallacy which is perhaps not quite yet expelled from courts of law, viz., that municipal or positive laws derive their validity from their conformity to the so-called law of nature or law of God. 'No human laws,' he says, 'are of any validity or contrary to this'" (*Encyclopedia Britannica*, 1896, s.v. "Blackstone, Sir William"; cf. 1911 ed.).

17. *Encyclopedia Britannica: Micropedia*, 1986, s.v. "Blackstone, Sir William."

on human reason than most orthodox Christians; but he used his powers of reason to arrive at Christian truths. According to his understanding of original sin, children are born neither good nor bad, but rather with a "tabula rosa" or "blank slate" upon which good or bad can be written during life. He wrote a treatise titled "The Reasonableness of Christianity," in which he attempted to prove the truth of Christianity. Locke believed that if he showed people how logical and reasonable Christianity was, everyone would accept it. He did not realize that most objections to Christianity come from the heart and not the mind.

He was a pious man,[18] and always held a high view of Scripture. Locke studied the Bible extensively and wrote paraphrases of St. Paul's Epistles to the Romans, Corinthians, Galatians, and Ephesians, as well as "An Essay for the Understanding of St. Paul's Epistles, by consulting St. Paul himself." These were published after his death. He derived his view of Scripture largely from Richard Hooker's "On the Laws of Ecclesiastical Polity." Hooker, an Anglican theologian, took a middle-ground position between the Catholics who placed church tradition on a par with Scripture, and the Puritans who stood for Scripture alone. Hooker argued that where the Scripture is clear, Scripture alone must govern. Where Scripture is unclear, church tradition may be employed to help interpret it; and where both Scripture and church tradition are unclear, or where new circumstances arise, reason may also be employed to apprehend God's truth.[19]

Locke frequently cited the Bible in his political writings. In his first treatise on government he cited the Bible eighty times. Forty-two of these citations are from Genesis, mostly chapters 1 and 3. Twenty-two biblical citations appear in his second treatise in which he argued that parents have authority over their children based upon the creation of Adam and Eve and their offspring. He also argued that man has the right to possess property since God gave the earth to Adam and later to Noah. He based the social compact which government is established upon "that Paction which God made with Noah after the Deluge."(4)[20] His basic doctrines of parental authority, private property, and social compact were based on the historical existence of Adam and Noah.

John Locke made two major contributions to the thinking of America's founding fathers. The first was his doctrine of natural law

18. *Encyclopedia Britannica: Macropaedia: Knowledge in Depth*, 1986, s.v. "Locke."
19. *Encyclopedia Britannica: Micropedia*, 1986, s.v. "Hooker, Richard."
20. John Locke, *Of Civil Government, Book Two*, II:11, III:56; V:25, 55; XVIII:200.

and natural rights which the founding fathers were acquainted with from other sources but found most clearly expressed in Locke's writings. He based both of these concepts on Scripture:

> Human Laws are measures in respect of Men whose Actions they must direct, albeit such measures they are as have also their higher Rules to be measured by, which Rules are two, the Law of God, and the Law of Nature; so that Laws Human must be made according to the general Laws of Nature, and without contradiction to any positive Law of Scripture, otherwise they are ill made.[21]

Locke identified the basic natural rights of man as "life, liberty, and property." This phrase is part of the Fifth and Fourteenth Amendments to the Constitution as well as the Declaration of Independence, where Jefferson expanded "property" to "pursuit of happiness."

Second, Locke contributed the theory of social compact: the idea that men in a state of nature realize their rights are insecure, and compact together to establish a government and cede to that government certain power so that government may use that power to secure the rest of their rights. The social compact theory is similar to the Calvinist idea of covenant. The social compact theory, like the covenant, allows the government only the power God and/or people delegate. This is the cornerstone of limited government. It finds expression in the Tenth Amendment to the Constitution and in the Declaration of Independence which states that governments exist to secure human rights and "derive their just powers from the consent of the governed."

Grotius

Hugo Grotius (1583-1645), the famous Dutch lawyer, theologian, statesman and poet, was called "the father of the modern code of nations" by James Madison.[22]

A child prodigy and the son of the curator of the University of Leyden, Grotius rose to prominence rapidly. He entered the University at age 12, published his first scholarly work at 15, began the practice of law at 16 or 17, and at age 24 was appointed Advocate-General for the provinces of Holland and Zealand. In 1613, at the

---

21. Locke, ibid., XI:136n.
22. James Madison, "Examination of the British Doctrine" 1806; quoted by Hall, *Christian History of the Constitution*, p. 250.

age of 30, he became Chief Magistrate of Rotterdam. But in 1619, having taken the losing side in a political battle in Holland surrounding the meaning of Calvinism he was convicted of having raised an insurrection and sentenced to life imprisonment. After two years in prison, he escaped, with his wife's help, hidden in a linen chest. He fled to Paris, where he was well received. He later accepted an appointment as Sweden's ambassador to France, and eventually returned to the Netherlands after the political climate had changed.

His two great works are *The Rights of War and Peace* (1625) and *The Truth of the Christian Religion.* The second book is divided into three parts. In the first part, Grotius demonstrates the existence, attributes, and providence of God. In part two, he argues the divine origin of the Christian religion.

> The design of the second book (after having put up our petitions to Christ the King of heaven, that he would afford us such assistances of His holy spirit, as may render us sufficient for so great a business) is . . . to show that the Christian religion is most true and certain.[23]

The third part of the book is a defense of the authenticity of the books of the New Testament, followed by a refutation of paganism, Judaism, and Islam. He defends the authenticity and special divine purpose of the miracles of Jesus Christ.[24]

In his writings on law and government Grotius attempted to apply Christian principles to politics. He emphasized, perhaps more clearly than any other writer, that "What God has shown to be his will that is law."[25]

Grotius believed that God's laws are superior to human laws:

> Among all good men one principle at any rate is established beyond controversy, that if the authorities issue any order that is contrary to the law of nature or to the commandments of God, the order should not be carried out. For when the Apostles said that obedience should be rendered to God rather than men, they appealed to an infallible rule of action, which is written in the hearts of all men.[26]

---

23. Grotius, *The Truth of the Christian Religion*; quoted by William Vasilio Sotirovich, *Grotius' Universe: Divine Law and a Quest for Harmony* (New York: Vantage Press, 1978), p. 27.

24. Grotius, ibid.; quoted by Sotirovich, *Grotius' Universe*, pp. 28–30.

25. Grotius, *Commentary on the Law of Prize and Booty*, (Oxford: Clarendon Press, 1950), p. 8; quoted by Sotirovich, *Grotius' Universe*, p. 46.

26. Grotius, *The Rights of War and Peace*, (Amsterdam, 1933), I:4.1.3.; quoted by Sotirovich, *Grotius' Universe*, p. 51.

His beliefs formed the basis of his principles of international law. God's law transcends the laws of individual states and nations. It provides a basis by which both men and nations are to be judged. Grotius believed in just wars and capital punishment:

> If it were not permitted to punish certain Criminals with Death, nor to defend the Subject by Arms against Highwaymen and Pyrates, there would of Necessity follow a terrible Inundation of Crimes, and a Deluge of Evils, since even now that Tribunals are erected, it is very difficult to restrain the Boldness of profligate Persons. Wherefore if it had been the Design of CHRIST to have introduced a new Kind of Regulation, as was never heard of before, he would certainly have declared in most distinct and plain Words, that none should pronounce Sentence of Death against a Malefactor, or carry Arms in Defence of one's Country.[27]

He condoned just warfare but also believed rulers have a duty to settle disputes without war, if possible, using "Holy Writ" as a basis. The Christian ruler has both an advantage and a greater responsibility:

> Especially, however, Christian kings and states are bound to pursue this method of avoiding wars. . . . Both for this and for other reasons it would be advantageous to hold certain conferences of Christian powers, where those who have no interest at stake may settle the disputes of others, and where, in fact, steps may be taken to compel parties to accept peace on fair terms.[28]

Alliances, leagues, and confederations of Christian states were the best means of creating peace; occasionally alliances may be made with non-Christian states.[29]

Grotius saw his ideal as the "Christian prince" who would apply the will of God as found both in nature and the Old and New Testaments. He went beyond Luther, who would have magistrates apply God's law but not God's gospel in their civic duties, and moved in the direction of Calvin. He closes *The Rights of War and Peace* with a powerful prayer:

> May God, who alone hath the power, inscribe these teachings on the hearts of those who hold sway over the Christian world. May He

---

27. Grotius, *The Rights of War and Peace*, quoted by Hall, *Christian History of the Constitution*, p. 251.

28. Grotius, *The Rights of War and Peace*, II:23:3.4.; quoted by Sotirovich, *Grotius' Universe*, p. 58.

29. Sotirovich, *Grotius' Universe*, pp. 58–59.

grant to them a mind possessing knowledge of divine and human law, and having ever before it the reflection that it hath been chosen as a servant for the rule of man, the living thing most dear to God.[30]

Grotius was highly respected by the founders of this nation, although he was not quoted as often. His writings were standard studies in American colonial colleges, and the founding fathers recommended his books to others. Hamilton wrote, "Apply yourself, without delay, to the study of the law of nature. I would recommend to your perusal Grotius, Pufendorf, Locke. . . ."[31]

Pufendorf

Samuel de Pufendorf (1632-1694) is best remembered for his masterpiece, *The Law of Nature and Nations*. The son of a Lutheran minister, Pufendorf studied theology at the University of Leipzig but later turned to law. He held numerous diplomatic posts in Germany and Sweden but exercised his greatest influence as Professor of the Law of Nature, first at the University of Heidelberg (1661-1668) and then at the University of Lund in Sweden. He became the royal historian for Sweden and later for the Elector Frederick II of Brandenburg, Germany, and died in 1694. After his death his final treatise was published, entitled "Law of Diplomacy, Agreement and Disagreement of Protestants," in which he pleaded for union among Protestants, particularly those of Lutheran and Calvinist persuasion.

Pufendorf, influenced by Grotius, helped to establish the law of nature as the basis for international law.

First, Pufendorf emphasized that God is the creator of all and

exercises a Sovereignty not only over the whole World, or over mankind in general, but over every Individual Human Person: Whose Knowledge nothing can escape: Who, by Virtue of his Imperial Right, hath enjoin'd Men such certain Duties by Natural Law, the Observance of which will meet with his Approbation, the Breach or the Neglect, with his Displeasure: And that he will for his Purpose require an exact Account from every Man, of his Proceedings, without Corruption and without Partiality.[32]

30. Grotius, *The Rights of War and Peace*, III:25.8; quoted by Sotirovich, *Grotius' Universe*, pp. 7–8.

31. Alexander Hamilton, "The Farmer Refuted," 1775; quoted by Hall, *Christian History of the Constitution*, p. 250.

32. Samuel de Pufendorf, *The Law of Nature and Nations*; quoted by Hall, *Christian History of the Constitution*, p. 270.

Second, Pufendorf acknowledged, in keeping with Lutheran theology, that God gives a certain natural grace to the unsaved so that they can understand and obey the law of nature. He noted that

> God is not so far pleas'd with every Kind of Worship which Men pay him, as to embrace them with pecular Favour, and to give them a Title to Eternal Life which good Effects do follow only that Institution and Way of Service which he hath reveal'd in a singular Manner to the World.

Those who are not Christians but hold "a serious Perswasion concerning the Divine Existence and Providence" are thereby made more observant of their duty under the law of nature. Men who hold to paganism and Mahammedanism, "which we must own to be destructive to Salvation," because of their fear of God show "no inconsiderable Care and concern for Honesty and Justice; so as not to be outdone by many Christians, at least as to External Performances." He added that many professing Christians are sadly lacking in this regard, but suggests that the reason may be that Christianity has been forced upon them and "resides rather in their Mouth than in their Heart."[33] Pufendorf was an advocate of religious toleration.

Pufendorf said that some belief-systems fail to encourage men to be faithful in their duties; among these are atheism, Epicureanism, and Stoicism or determinism. The first denies faith in God and the latter deny human responsibility.[34] They undermine the concept of duty that is essential to observance of the law of nature: "Atheists are not, strictly speaking, God's Enemies . . . but his Rebellious Subjects, and consequently guilty of Treason against the Divine Majesty . . . It is no such obscure matter, therefore to assign the particular Species of Sin, to which Atheism belongs. . . ."[35]

Pufendorf expanded the concept of international law as expressed by Grotius, to include God-fearing non-Christians as well as Christians. Pufendorf did this by showing that the fear of God produces a sense of duty even in non-Christians. This is in keeping with Paul's words about "the law of God written on their hearts" (Rom. 2:14-15).

Alexander Hamilton, Benjamin Franklin, James Wilson, Samuel Adams and other founding fathers paid tribute to Pufendorf,

33. Pufendorf; ibid., p. 271.
34. Pufendorf; ibid., p. 271.
35. Pufendorf; ibid., p. 279.

acknowledged his influence on their thinking, and recommended his writings to others.

Vattel

Emmerich de Vattel (1714-1767) was the son of a German Protestant minister. As a German diplomat he spent most of his life on assignments to Bern, Switzerland. It was there he did most of his writing. His most famous work, *The Law of Nations,* was published in 1758 and was a popularization of the 1749 work of the same title by the German philosopher Christian Wolff.

Vattel stressed that men must live "agreeably to their nature, and in conformity to the views of their common Creator; a law that our own safety, our happiness, our most precious advantages, ought to render sacred to every one of us."[36]

This led to the "general law of society," which is "that each should do for others whatever their necessities require, and they are capable of doing, without neglecting what they owe to themselves."[37] The same is true of nations: each nation should lend its assistance to other nations so long as it can do so without injuring itself; but the primary obligation of each nation is to its own citizens.[38]

He stated that each nation has the liberty to govern itself as it pleases, even if that is offensive to others, so long as it hurts no other nation. He promoted the idea that all nations are on an equal footing in terms of sovereignty, regardless of size, just as all persons are equal whether they are giants or dwarfs.[39] Finally, he insisted that nations have a right to defend themselves and their citizens against foreign attack.[40] Vattel's emphasis on the liberty and equality of individuals and nations was of special interest to the founding fathers. Samuel Adams, James Wilson, Alexander Hamilton, James Madison, and others give evidence of Vattel's influence in their thinking.

Adam Smith

Adam Smith (1723-1790), a Scotsman, was not quoted much in the political writings of the founding fathers because his interest was

---

36. Emmerich de Vattel, *The Law of Nations;* quoted by Hall, *Christian History of the Constitution,* p. 293.
37. Vattel; ibid., p. 293.
38. Vattel; ibid., p. 294.
39. Vattel; ibid., p. 295.
40. Vattel; ibid., p. 296.

in economics rather than politics. But Smith's laissez-faire or free enterprise economics found its way into the commerce clause and the contract clause of the Constitution. His book *The Wealth of Nations* was read and believed by the founding fathers.

Smith advocated a free enterprise economy in which private individuals choose their own vocations and compete in the marketplace for jobs and profits. Government does not intervene in this economic competition except as a referee to prohibit force, fraud, monopoly, or debauchery such as pornography, obscenity, drugs, liquor, prostitution, or other forms of vice.

Adam Smith believed free competition gave people an incentive to produce more and cheaper goods and thereby raised the standard of living of the nation. Consumers choose which goods to buy based on which are of the best quality, the best price, and most suited to their needs. Buyers and sellers, employers and employees arc guided by their own self-interest in the marketplace, yet each makes decisions that benefit the entire community. The way to become rich under this system is to produce something others want and need at a price they can afford. Thus each person, looking out for his own self-interest, benefits the entire society. The more he benefits society, the more he prospers. In this way economic competition proceeds unfettered by government regulation but is guided by an "invisible hand" which causes each person, while seeking his own enrichment, to work for the common good.[41]

Smith did not give evidence of having based his economic theories directly on the Bible in *The Wealth of Nations*. However, his view of enlightened self-interest as the basic motivating force in a successful economic system is certainly consistent with the biblical view of the nature of man: "If any would not work, neither should he eat" (2 Thess. 3:10).

The founding fathers favored a free enterprise economy with minimum government regulation.

Sidney

Algernon Sidney (1622-1683) was a lieutenant-general and cavalry officer under Cromwell and the Puritan forces in the English civil war. Sidney served on the Council of the State of the Commonwealth under Cromwell's Protectorate in 1652. He was admired by republicans throughout the world and looked to as a

---

41. W. Cleon Skousen, *"Miracle of America" Study Guide* (Salt Lake City: Freemen Institute, 1981, 1984), pp. 31–32.

martyr for the cause of liberty. Sidney favored a limited monarchy over a purely republican government. He believed God had given men liberty to establish various forms of government. If men chose to establish republican governments or limited monarchies, these may not be usurped by tyrants. Rulers may exercise only such power as the people have given them, and when rulers go beyond that and usurp additional power, the people have a right to resist. Sidney insisted that the people of England had chosen to place power in the hands of Parliament and a hereditary nobility, not in an absolute monarch, and that the king's attempt to usurp authority from Parliament and the nobility was unfounded and illegitimate. He argued that political power should be apportioned according to property holdings.

Sidney was convicted and beheaded for allegedly plotting to overthrow the pro-Catholic King Charles II. His *Discourse on Government* attested to his belief in the right of resistance. The idea that free men have the God-given right to resist oppression and misrule by a tyrant was a concept the founding fathers used in forming the Declaration and Constitution.

Coke

Sir Edward Coke (1552-1634) was a predecessor of Blackstone. As Attorney General, Chief Justice of the Court of Common Pleas, and Chief Justice of the Court of King's Bench, he was an obstinate opponent of the illegal exercise of governmental authority. Throughout his legal career he championed the common law of England against encroachments of royal power. As a judge he consistently held that the king lacked constitutional authority to change or add to the common law. Attempts to buy him off with royal appointments failed and the king finally decided that the only way to silence Coke was to remove him from the bench. Coke then devoted his time to the writing of his *Institutes*. Through them he became immortal.

An American lawyer in the 1700s who could afford two reference works for his law office would first purchase Blackstone's *Commentaries* and then either Coke's *Institutes of the Laws of England* or one volume titled *Coke Upon Littleton*.

The founding fathers saw in Coke's *Institutes* the unchanging character of law, the supremacy of the law over the whims of men.

Milton

John Milton (1608-1674) was a political as well as religious figure. An expert swordsman as well as a theologian, he originally trained for a career as a clergyman but chose government work instead. As a defender of political and religious liberty, one of his early writings was a defense of freedom of the press titled "Areopagitica: A Speech of Mr. John Milton for the Liberty of Unlicensed Printing to the Parliament of England" (1644). In it he argued that the press should not be licensed.

Milton defended the right to resist illegitimate usurpation of authority. In 1649 the Parliament took power and beheaded King Charles I. At that time, Milton published a tract entitled "Tenure of Kings and Magistrates, Proving that it is lawful, and hath been held so in all ages for any who have the power, to call to account a Tyrant or wicked King, and, after due conviction, to depose and put him to death, if the ordering Magistrate have neglected to do it."[42]

Oliver Cromwell appointed Milton to his Council of State and Milton so served through Cromwell's death in 1658. Milton liked and respected Cromwell as the greatest and best man of his generation, and he generally supported Cromwell's policies. But he disagreed with Cromwell on the relationship of church and state. Whereas Cromwell held generally to the Puritan view of the holy commonwealth, Milton believed the union of church and state caused the church to become worldly, and he believed the church could truly flourish only when disestablished from the state. He put forth his position in his "Treatise on Civil Power in Ecclesiastical Causes."

His best-known works were *Paradise Lost* (1667), *Paradise Regained* (1671), and *Samson Agonistes* (1671). Shortly before he died he wrote "Of True Religion, Heresy, Schism, Toleration, and What Best Means May Be Used Against the Growth of Popery" (1673) in which he urged Protestants to tolerate each other's differing views so as to make a common cause against Roman Catholicism. He impressed American readers with his religious fervor and his dedication to personal liberty.

The Classics

Every educated man in the 1700s read the classical writings of Greek and Roman antiquity. The founding fathers frequently referred to the classics in their writings and often used Greek and Roman pseudonyms to sign their letters. Some, such as Samuel Adams, saw in the old Roman republican austerity, a picture of what America was or should be.

---

42. *Encyclopedia Britannica*, 1896, s.v. "Milton, John."

The founding fathers cited the classics illustratively rather than demonstratively.[43] They did not derive their convictions from the classical writers, nor seek to prove points by referring to them, but used them to illustrate or exemplify their arguments. The orator Cicero (106-43 B.C.) was admired for his rhetoric and his valiant but unsuccessful defense of the Roman republic against the empire. Cato the Elder (234-149 B.C.) and his great-grandson Cato the Younger (95-46 B.C.) were respected as conservative Romans who stood for austere morality and republican principles. They fought the licentiousness that accompanied the rise of absolute dictatorship under Caesar, Pompey, and Crassus.

Polybius (205-125? B.C.), the Greek historian, lived much of his life in Rome and wrote a forty-volume history of the rise of the Roman republic, five of which still exist in complete form. The founding fathers respected Polybius for his original research and impartiality. His analysis of the Roman constitution was of special interest.

Plutarch (A.D. 46-120?), wrote *Parallel Lives* which contained biographies of Greek and Roman heroes. Plutarch's writings achieved special prominence in the 1600s and 1700s because the founding fathers were inspired by the accounts of those who overthrew tyrants.

Tacitus (A.D. 56?-120?) was an orator, lawyer, senator, consul, and praetor who achieved lasting fame as an historian. His best-known works were *Annals* and *Histories* of Rome, both of which exist in incomplete form today. Tacitus was a conservative defender of the old republic. He contended that the emperors were evil and capricious despots who had sunk themselves and their nation into moral degeneration, and that the senate had become a body of sychophants who bowed to the emperor and allowed themselves and the nation to be "rushed into slavery."

Plato (428?-348? B.C.) was known for his philosophy of idealism which some of the founding fathers accepted. But his political theories, which consisted of government by philosopher-kings, communal rearing of children, etc. were rejected. Expressing the sentiment of many, John Adams wrote to Jefferson,

> I am very glad you have seriously read Plato, and still more rejoiced to find that your reflections upon him so perfectly harmonize with mine. Some 30 years ago I took upon me the severe task of

43. Zoltan Haraszti, *John Adams and the Prophets of Progress* (Cambridge: Harvard University Press, 1952).

going through all his works. With the help of two Latin translations, and one English, and one French translation, and comparing some of the most remarkable passages with the Greek, I labored through the tedious toil. My disappointment was very great, my astonishment was greater, my disgust shocking . . . His *Laws,* and his *Republic,* from which I expected most, disappointed me most.[44]

The founding fathers respected those classical writers who were believers in the old republican government, against the encroachments of imperial tyranny, and defenders of traditional morality. It is important to recognize this in order to understand that the founding fathers did not see themselves as radicals trying to overthrow the existing order to create something new. Rather, they saw themselves as conservatives defending the traditional order and the ancient rights of Englishmen against the recent encroachments of the English monarch.

So What Did They Learn?

When analyzing the sources the founding fathers read, studied, cited, and recommended to others, it becomes apparent that a number of basic themes of American republicanism have been combined from a variety of inspirations. Many of these ideas are Christian ideals which became parts of the United States Constitution. In a later chapter we will correlate specific passages of the Constitution to biblical principles.

Granted, it is difficult to synthesize the principles the founding fathers derived from their study of history and the works of some of the philosophers and theologians not only of their time but also those such as Calvin, who laid the foundation for their religious beliefs. In the chapters that follow, I believe fifteen basic principles which underlie the thinking of the founding fathers will surface. I further believe that these principles form the basic framework of the Constitution, although not all of them are expressly mentioned therein. And we will notice that these principles are either derived from, or at least compatible with, Christianity and the Bible.

1. A belief in God and his providence, by which he guides and controls the universe and the affairs of mankind.

2. A belief in and respect for revealed religion—that is, a recognition that God has revealed his truth through the Holy Scriptures.

44. John Adams to Thomas Jefferson, July 16, 1814; reprinted in *Correspondence of John Adams and Thomas Jefferson 1812–1826,* ed. Paul Wilstach (Indianapolis: Bobbs-Merrill, 1925), p. 107.

3. A belief in the God-given power of human reason to apprehend truth. While reason does not supersede revelation, it serves as an aid in the search for truth where the Scriptures are silent.

4. A belief that man is not a perfect or perfectible being, and that governmental theories must take that fact into account.

5. A belief that God has ordained human government to restrain the sinful nature of man.

6. A belief that God has established certain physical laws for the operation of the universe, as well as certain moral laws for the governance of mankind.

7. A belief that God has revealed his moral laws to man through the Scriptures (revealed or divine law) and through the law of nature, which is discoverable through human reason and the human conscience.

8. A belief that human law must correspond to the divine law and the law of nature. Human laws which contradict the higher law are invalid, nonbinding, and are to be resisted.

9. A belief that the revealed law and the law of nature form the basis for the law of nations (international law) and that this law of nations includes the right of a nation to defend itself against agressors (just warfare).

10. A belief that the revealed law and the law of nature include natural, God-given, unalienable human rights which include life, liberty, and property.

11. A belief that governments are formed by covenant or compact of the people in order to safeguard human rights.

12. A belief that governments have only such powers as are delegated to them by the people in the said covenants or compacts, and that when governments attempt to usurp powers not so delegated, they become illegitimate and are to be resisted.

13. A belief that, human nature being what it is, rulers tend to usurp more and more power if given the opportunity.

14 A belief that the best way to prevent governments from usurping power is to separate their powers and functions into legislative, executive and judicial branches.

15. A belief that, human nature being what it is, a free enterprise economy is the best way to give people an incentive to produce and develop national prosperity.

Meet the Founding Fathers

5 A Word of Introduction

able 4 lists thirteen men who have been selected as a representative sampling of the "Founding Fathers" because of the significant contributions they made in establishing the American system of government. They provide a balanced representation of Federalists and Republicans or Antifederalists as well as a geographic cross section of New England, Middle Atlantic, and Southern states.

Table 4 Statistics on the Founding Fathers

Name of Delegate	State Represented	Political Position*
John Witherspoon	New Jersey (MA)	Republican
James Madison	Virginia (S)	Federalist
George Washington	Virginia (S)	Federalist
Alexander Hamilton	New York (MA)	Federalist
John Jay	New York (MA)	Federalist
Gouverneur Morris	Pennsylvania (MA)	Federalist
Benjamin Franklin	Pennsylvania (MA)	Federalist
Thomas Jefferson	Virginia (S)	Republican
Samuel Adams	Massachusetts (NE)	Republican
John Adams	Massachusetts (NE)	Federalist
Patrick Henry	Virginia (S)	Antifederalist**
Roger Sherman	Connecticut (NE)	Republican
Charles C. Pinckney	South Carolina (S)	Republican

*These loose designations roughly reflect the political position the men held at the time of the Convention. Some of the men held different positions at various times in their lives.
**About 1792 the Antifederalists generally took the title Republican or Democratic Republican.

The Federalists favored a stronger central government. Alexander Hamilton, John Jay, and Gouverneur Morris were strong Federalists. George Washington and John Adams were moderate Federalists. While many Republicans supported the Constitution they believed it gave the central government far less power than the Federalists thought it did. Thomas Jefferson and Samuel Adams held the Republican viewpoint. Roger Sherman feared government power, and for that reason could be called a Republican. However, he was more of a Federalist on commercial matters. John Witherspoon is also best classified as a Republican. James Madison took a moderate Federalist position during the Convention and the ratification debates; afterward he gravitated toward Republicanism. Charles Cotesworth Pinckney took the Republican position as a defender of states' rights at the Convention, but later became a Federalist. Patrick Henry, the champion of liberty, opposed the Constitution because it "squinted toward monarchy," but later in life it appeared that he also became a Federalist.

The thirteen chapters which follow are not complete biographies of these men. Instead, each chapter focuses on their religious beliefs and how those beliefs affected their political thoughts and actions. To study those beliefs, it is necessary to examine their personal lives, ancestors, parents, early childhood, schooling, and any other influences which may provide insight into their religious beliefs.

Both early and recent biographies are valuable resources in gaining information about these men. Generally biographies from the early 1800s are closer to the spirit of their times and drew from sources that are no longer available. Occasionally, today historians have access to documents that were not available earlier. For that reason recent biographies often contain new information which provides unique insights. However, to avoid prejudices which often result from the biographer's affinity with the historical figure in focus, it seems most credible to let the founding fathers speak for themselves—and about each other. Their books, treatises, and speeches aid in understanding their viewpoints. In addition their private diaries and correspondence often reveal intimate thoughts of personal religious beliefs.

Were the founding fathers Christians? What were their beliefs and ideals? The answers to those questions may not always be clear.

The term *Christian* can be used in several contexts. First, it can describe someone who is "born again," or "saved," or "regenerate," a person who trusts Jesus Christ and his finished work on the cross for salvation. It is difficult to determine whether a person was "born again" from documented history alone. In some cases, as with John Jay or Patrick Henry, there is a strong personal testimony that indicates saving faith. But only God knows the heart.

The term *Christian* is also used rather loosely to denote a person whose basic doctrinal beliefs are in accord with those of Christianity but who may or may not personally trust in Christ for salvation. Such a person might be regarded as a Christian in the eyes of men even though he may not be regenerate in the eyes of God. In the chapters that follow, I use the term *Christian* largely in this sense.

And sometimes the term *Christian* is used improperly to denote a person who rejects basic fundamental doctrines of the Christian faith, but who holds generally to Christian manners and morals and a basic Christian worldview. Thomas Jefferson and Benjamin Franklin might fit into this category; the majority of the founding fathers fit into the former two.

And now, the founding fathers . . .

6 John Witherspoon

J ohn Witherspoon is best described as the man who shaped the men who shaped America. Although he did not attend the Constitutional Convention, his influence was multiplied many times over by those who spoke as well as by what was said.

Witherspoon's list of accomplishments include: chairman of the Somerset Committee of Correspondence, member of the New Jersey Senate, member of Congress, signer of the Declaration of Independence. However, his greatest contribution was as President of the College of New Jersey (since 1896 known as Princeton University). It was there he helped train the men who would become the leaders of the new nation.

John Witherspoon was born in Scotland in 1723. His father, Rev. James Witherspoon, was a Presbyterian pastor known for his piety and faithfulness.[1] Both parents had clergymen in their family lineage; his mother traced her genealogy back to John Knox. She taught John to read from the Bible by age four. Eventually he was able to recite much of the New Testament and Watt's *Psalms* and *Hymns*.[2] Home teaching followed by grammar school prepared

---

1. Varnum Lansing Collins, *President Witherspoon* (New York: Arno Press and *The New York Times*, 1969), I:8-10. Cf. Martha Lou Lemmon Stohlman, *John Witherspoon: Parson, Politician, Patriot* (Philadelphia: Westminster Press, 1897).
2. Collins, *President Witherspoon*, I:11-12; cf. Stohlman, *John Witherspoon*, p. 17.

John for the university in Edinburgh by age thirteen. In three years he earned his Master of Arts degree and spent four more years in Edinburgh preparing for the ministry. He became pastor of a Presbyterian church at Beith, Scotland, for eight years during which time he married.

At that time Scottish Presbyterianism was split between the Moderate Party and the Popular Party. The Popular Party stressed the need for more Bible-centered sermons, less emphasis on philosophy and extra-biblical matters in church services, and local control of the church. Rev. Witherspoon became the leader of the Popular Party. Around 1753 a satire on the Moderates called *Ecclesiastical Characteristics* appeared. It had been published anonymously but was immediately attributed to Witherspoon. The sixty-page pamphlet sold well, in seven editions and nine reprints. It consisted of ridicule directed toward the Moderates in the form of Maxims allegedly held by them.

Despite the controversy over *Ecclesiastical Characteristics,* Witherspoon was called to be pastor of Laigh Kirk in Paisley, Scotland, in 1757. He pastored the large church which seated 1,300 for eleven years. Paisley was known as the most intellectual community in Scotland, in which "every weaver is a politician."[3] Witherspoon's sermons at Laigh Kirk reflected his orthodox Christianity, his Calvinist zeal, and his low-church piety. He stressed salvation by grace. His sermon, "The absolute Necessity of Salvation through Christ" warned that the gospel of Jesus Christ was not to be eased or compromised. When Moderates charged that such a stern message showed that Witherspoon did not believe in Christian charity, he responded with a message titled "Inquiry into the Scripture Meaning of Charity." In it he stated that true charity includes "an ardent and unfeigned love to others and a desire of their welfare, temporal and eternal." Charity requires "the deepest concern for their dangerous state"; one who is unconcerned about the salvation of souls does not really possess Christian charity.[4] Like many Calvinists, Witherspoon believed that the truly elect give evidence of their election in their lives. For that reason he also stressed morality and good works. Using the text "By their fruits ye shall know them," he preached on "The Trial of Religious Truth by Its Moral Influence," and spoke against the theater and other practices which he regarded as worldly vices.[5] Undoubtedly

3. Stohlman, *John Witherspoon*, pp. 35-36.
4. Ibid., p. 41.
5. Ibid., p. 44; Collins, *President Witherspoon*, I:47.

Witherspoon's outspoken nature attracted opponents, but on the whole it seems he was well received.

While moderate and conservative Presbyterians battled in Scotland, their brethren in America were also engaged in controversy. The First Great Awakening of the 1740s and 1750s led to a division between the "New Lights" who stressed an experience of spiritual rebirth and the "Old Lights" who stressed orthodox doctrine and constancy of Christian life. The controversy was not actually a liberal/conservative dispute; in fact, each side suspected the other of liberal tendencies and proclaimed its own orthodoxy. The College of New Jersey tended toward the "New Light" position, with Jonathan Edwards as its president, but was not closely allied with either position. When the college needed a new president, its patrons looked to Witherspoon. His evangelical zeal made him acceptable to the "New Lights"; his emphasis on morality and Christian living made him acceptable to the "Old Lights"; and his orthodoxy appealed to both. In 1767 a delegation from the college traveled to Scotland and appealed to Witherspoon to take the position. He was interested at once, but his wife Elizabeth did not want to leave home and family to cross the ocean. Over the course of a year Elizabeth consented and in 1768 Witherspoon came to America to become president of the College of New Jersey.

Witherspoon was president of the College of New Jersey from 1768 to 1794. In those twenty-six years 478 young men graduated—about eighteen students per year. Of those 478 graduates, 114 became ministers; 13 were state governors; 3 were U.S. Supreme Court judges; 20 were Unites States Senators; 33 were U.S. Congressmen; Aaron Burr, Jr. became Vice-President; and James Madison became President.[6] Of the 55 delegates to the Constitutional Convention, 9 (one-sixth) were College of New Jersey graduates, and 6 graduated while Witherspoon was president.[7]

Rev. John Rodgers declared that Witherspoon, as president of the College of New Jersey, would "sit revered at the Head of the Presbyterian Interest already great and dayly growing in these Middle colonies. And no Man can have it more in his Power to advance the Cause of Xtian Liberty by forming the Minds of Youth to proper Sentiments on this most interesting Subject."[8]

Witherspoon's house was on the campus and next to it was a

6. Stohlman, *John Witherspoon*, p. 172.
7. Collins, *President Witherspoon*, II:229.
8. Stohlman, *John Witherspoon*, p. 70.

Presbyterian church where he preached regularly. He interacted
with his students on a daily basis.

President Witherspoon assumed both teaching responsibilities
and administrative duties. He served as Professor of Divinity[9] and
also taught other subjects. An announcement which advertised
graduate courses at the college, revealed Witherspoon's various
roles:

> . . . The President has also engaged to give Lectures twice in the
> Week, on the following Subjects (1) On Chronology and History, civil
> as well as sacred; a Branch of Study, of itself extremely useful and
> delightful, and at present in the highest Reputation in every Part of
> Europe, (2) Critical Lectures on the Scripture, with the Addition of
> Discourses on Criticism in general; the several Species of Writing,
> and the fine Arts, (3) Lectures on Composition, and the Eloquence of
> the Pulpit and the Bar. The President will also endeavour to assist
> every Student by Conversation according to the main Object, which
> he shall chuse for his own Studies; and will give Lists and Characters
> of the principal Writers on any Branch, that Students may accom-
> plish themselves, at the least Expence of Time and Labour.[10]

Along with Witherspoon's religious zeal came a keen interest in
politics. The Word of God impressed on him his civic responsibilities, and the intellectual climate of Paisley, Scotland, had quickened
his interest. Like most American Presbyterians, he was an early
advocate of independence. The College of New Jersey became a
hotbed of pro-independence sentiment. President Witherspoon approved and encouraged this sentiment, but also restrained its
excesses. He wrote to a British aristocrat in 1772:

> . . . many who in a very short time will be at the head of affairs in
> their several provinces, and I have already and shall continue to
> temper the spirit of liberty, which breathes high in their country,
> with just sentiments, not only of loyalty to our excellent sovereign, in
> which they do not seem to be defective, but with a love of order and
> an aversion to that outrage and sedition into which the spirit of
> liberty when not reined is sometimes apt to degenerate.[11]

As a Calvinist, Witherspoon was keenly aware of the need for
balance between a love of liberty and a love of order. This love for

9. Ibid., p. 74.
10. New Jersey Archives, I ser., Vol. XXVI, p. 306; quoted by Collins, *President
Witherspoon*, I:112-13.
11. Collins, *President Witherspoon*, I:141.

order prevented the architects of American independence from leading the nation down the path of anarchy, lawlessness, bloodthirstiness, and ultimate tyranny that characterized the French Revolution. Witherspoon was one who emphasized this balance.

Nevertheless, Witherspoon was a leader in the movement toward independence. His sermon of May 17, 1776, titled "The Dominion of Providence over the Passions of Men," based on Psalm 76 summarized his views. He qualified his opposition to England by saying that, "Many of their actions have probably been worse than their intentions." He declared that the cruelty and inhumanity of the British shall "finally promote the glory of God" by leading the colonists to declare independence. He called for attention to religion, declaring that "he is the best friend of American liberty who is most sincere and active in promoting true and undefiled religion and who sets himself with the greatest firmness to bear down profanity and immorality of every kind." He reminded his listeners that both duty to God and duty to country called on them to be uncorrupted patriots, useful citizens, and invincible soldiers. He concluded the sermon with, "God grant that in America true religion and civil liberty may be inseparable and that the unjust attempts to destroy the one may in the issue tend to the support and establishment of both."[12]

That word "Providence" in the title of Witherspoon's sermon and the other occasions when the founding fathers used the impersonal title "Providence" for God became one reason why many historians and theologians claim that the founders of this nation were deists rather than Christians. However, this is the definition of Providence that Hosmer cites in Samuel Johnson's *Dictionary of the English Language*, published in 1755:

PROVIDENCE- (Providentia, Latin).
          1. Foresight; timely care . . Sidney.
          2. The care of God over created beings; divine
            superintendence—Raleigh.[13]

The term *Providence* refers to God's care over men, and it is more compatible with Christianity than with deism. Witherspoon even

12. John Witherspoon, "Sermon on the Dominion of Providence over the Passions of Men," May 17, 1776; quoted and cited by Collins, *President Witherspoon*, I:197-98.

13. Samuel Johnson, *Dictionary of the English Language* (1755); quoted by William McAulay Hosmer, "Of Divine Providence in Our Declaration of Independence" (Hosmer Enterprises: P.O. Box 846, San Carlos, California 94070, 1980), pp. 14-15.

says in his sermon, "The doctrine of divine Providence is very full and complete in the sacred oracles."[14]

While Witherspoon may have kept himself a bit aloof from his colleagues, they appeared to have respected him and many listened to him preach. John Adams attended church at the College of New Jersey and wrote: "Heard Dr. Witherspoon all Day. A clear, sensible, Preacher."[15]

In 1776 Witherspoon was chosen for the Continental Congress and served as a congressional delegate from New Jersey from 1776-1782, wearing full clerical garb the entire period.[16] During his five years in Congress, he served on more than 120 committees, including the Board of War, the Committee on Secret Correspondence, or Foreign Affairs, and the Committee on Clothing for the Army.[17] His Christian commitment led him to take an active role on behalf of certain humanitarian endeavors such as "kindlier treatment of prisoners, the checking of cruelty in warfare, the better administration of military hospitals, the improvement of health and morals and therefore of discipline, in the army."[18] He was asked to draft the Thanksgiving Day proclamations and other appeals to public consciousness. He took an active role in the adoption of the Articles of Confederation, and showed great interest and ability in government finance.[19] During this period he is perhaps best known as a signer of the Declaration of Independence. Some believe the phrase "with a firm Reliance on the protection of Divine Providence" in the final sentence was his contribution.[20] Witherspoon gave himself totally to the cause of American independence; he lost two sons in the war.[21] He published an appendix to his "Dominion of Providence" sermon, titled an "Address to the Natives of Scotland residing in America," which attempted to persuade American Scotsmen to assert their "ancient rights" and support independence. The sermon and address were reprinted twice in Glasgow.[22]

14. Witherspoon, "Sermon on the Dominion of Providence," p. 2; quoted by Hosmer, "Of Divine Providence," p. 15.

15. Adams; quoted by Stohlman, *John Witherspoon*, pp. 101-2.

16. Dr. Benjamin Rush; cited by Collins, *President Witherspoon*, I:195.

17. Collins, *President Witherspoon*, II:4.

18. Ibid.

19. Ibid., II:4ff.

20. Hosmer, "Of Divine Providence," pp. 2-12; cf. Collins, *President Witherspoon*, I:217-20.

21. Stohlman, *John Witherspoon*, p. 129.

22. Collins, *President Witherspoon*, I: 223-27.

In addition, he wrote a widely circulated letter urging American pastors to support independence.[23]

In 1782, with his congressional duties finished and the war nearly over, Witherspoon returned to the College of New Jersey and continued his duties as president of the college. He remained interested in politics, and served several terms in the New Jersey state assembly. His friend, Rev. Ashbel Green, reports that as Witherspoon read the letter informing him of his daughter's death, "tears rolled down his manly cheeks, but he uttered not a word, till he had read it through. He then wiped away his tears, made a few remarks with composure, mounted his horse, and returned immediately to Tusculum."[24] In the ensuing weeks he preached sixteen successive sermons on "the doctrine and duty of submission to the will of God," all based on Luke 22:42: "Father, if thou be willing, remove this cup from me; nevertheless, not my will, but thine, be done." Despite his grief over his daughter's death, he found much to keep him busy during the following years. He worked actively on behalf of Presbyterian unity in America. Witherspoon did not attend the Constitutional Convention in 1787, but nine College of New Jersey graduates were present: William Paterson, Jonathan Dayton, David Brearley, William Churchill Houston, Gunning Bedford Jr., Luther Martin, James Madison, William Richardson Davie, and Alexander Martin.[25] Together they comprised almost one-sixth of the Convention.

In October 1789 his wife Elizabeth died. A month later Witherspoon again entered the New Jersey legislature, heading a committee to abolish the slave trade in New Jersey. At age 68, he married Ann Marshall Dill, the 24-year-old widow of one of his former students. Witherspoon was blind for three years before he died on November 15, 1794. His secretary wrote that his "descent into the grave was gradual and comparatively easy, free from any severe pain, and contemplated by himself with the calmness of a philosopher and the cheering hope of a christian."[26]

The following seven principles are reflected in Witherspoon's life and works.

1. A strong faith in God and his daily providence on behalf of men. In contrast to the deists, Witherspoon firmly believed that God controls the destiny of men and nations and intervenes actively on

---

23. Stohlman, *John Witherspoon*, p. 105.

24. Rev. Ashbel Green; quoted by Stohlman, *John Witherspoon*, p. 156.

25. Dr. M. E. Bradford, *A Worthy Company*, (Marlborough, New Hampshire: Plymouth Rock Foundation, 1982).

26. John Ramsay Witherspoon; quoted by Stohlman, *John Witherspoon*, p. 167.

their behalf. He saw Providence, not as something mechanistic as the deists did, but as a part of God's goodness through the special grace of Jesus Christ. Holding firmly to postmillennial theology, Witherspoon saw God controlling and directing history toward its culmination in Christ's rule.[27]

2. A recognition of the fact of human sin. As he explained in his "Dominion of Providence" sermon, "the corruption of our nature . . . is the foundation-stone of the doctrine of redemption. Nothing can be more absolutely necessary to true religion, than a clear conviction of the sinfulness of our nature and state."[28] He criticized those who exalted human nature;

> Men of lax and corrupt principles take great delight in speaking to the praise of human nature, and extolling its dignity, without distinguishing what it was at its first creation, from what it is in its present fallen state. But I appeal from these visionaries' reasonings to the history of all ages, and the inflexible testimony of daily experience. (C)andid attention, either to past history of present state of the world, but above all, the ravages of lawless power, out to humble us in the dust.[29]

Emphasizing that depravity is the scriptural view of man, Witherspoon stated that "the evil of sin appears from every page of the sacred oracles."[30] Sin was also evident in human history: " . . . the history of the world is little else than the history of human guilt."[31] He summarized: "nothing is more plain from scripture, or better supported by daily experience, than that man by nature is in fact incapable of recovery without the power of God specially interposed."[32]

Witherspoon held the orthodox Calvinist view of total depravity, but rejected the extreme position held by some Calvinists, that the fall totally extinguished all vestiges of the image of God in man. Anyone can cry to God for help because, "there remains so much of God written on the conscience of even the most profligate . . . ."[33] He maintained that the unregenerate "have not totally extinguished

27. Roger Schultz, "Covenanting in America: The Political Theology of John Witherspoon," Master's Thesis, Trinity Evangelical Divinity School, Deerfield, Illinois, 1985, pp.71-75, 122-23.

28. Witherspoon; quoted by Schultz, "Covenanting in America," p. 136.

29. Ibid., p. 137.

30. Witherspoon; ibid., p. 137.

31. Witherspoon; ibid., p. 137.

32. Witherspoon; ibid., p. 137.

33. Witherspoon; ibid., p. 95.

the light of natural conscience."[34] Undoubtedly referring to Romans 2:14-15, he explained that:

> It pleased God to write his law upon the heart of man at first. And the great lines of duty, however obscured by their original apostasy, are still so visible as to afford an opportunity of judging what conduct and practice is or is not agreeable to its dictates.
>
> Such authority hath natural conscience still in man that it renders those . . . inexcusable in the sight of God (Rom. 1:20-2:14). But it is of importance in the present argument to observe, that every one is able to pass a far surer judgment on the moral character of another, than his own. The pollution of the heart brings a corrupt bias on the judgment, in the man's own case . . . [w]hereas in determining the character of others, this bias is less sensibly felt.[35]

This doctrine of the depravity of man, coupled with a recognition that the law of God is written on man's conscience, led him to believe that man, while born with a tendency toward original sin, remains a responsible moral agent, capable of civic responsibility if his sinful nature is properly restrained. Witherspoon favored a government that was strong enough to restrain the sinful nature of the masses; but he also favored restraints on the government to prevent sinful rulers from becoming tyrannical and oppressive.

James Madison, called the "father of the Constitution," obtained his concept of separation of powers and checks and balances from Witherspoon's instruction at the College of New Jersey. And although Witherspoon derived the concept of separation of powers from other sources, such as Montesquieu, checks and balances seem to have been his own unique contribution to the foundation of U.S. government.

3. The absolute necessity of salvation through Christ. This idea (also one of Witherspoon's sermon titles at Paisley) remained a constant theme throughout his life. In both Scotland, and America, he called on his audience to "Fly also for forgiveness to the atoning blood of the great Redeemer. . . ."[36] He sought to "press every hearer to a sincere concern for his own soul's salvation," for in seasons of public judgment "the conscience is more open to the arrows of conviction."[37] He declared in his *Lectures on Divinity*, "Religion is the grand concern of us all . . . the salvation of our souls is the one thing needful."[38]

34. Witherspoon; ibid., pp. 95-96.
35. Witherspoon; ibid., p. 96.
36. Witherspoon; ibid., p. 104.
37. Witherspoon; ibid., p. 111.
38. Witherspoon; ibid., p. 132.

4. The need for and right to personal, political, and religious liberty. Witherspoon regarded government encroachments on such liberties as tyrannical. In keeping with Calvinism, he believed that God had ordained government, but that God had also limited the authority and function of government. Government which exceeds it authority and becomes tyrannical, must be resisted.

A few historians have suggested that Witherspoon's thinking changed when he came to America, that he became less sacred and more secular, that he relied less on the Reformers and Puritans, and more on the thinkers of the Enlightenment. Mark Noll, quoting Flower and Murphy, concludes, "It is clear that he had drunk more deeply of the Scottish Enlightenment than the [Princeton] trustees [and perhaps he himself] had supposed. . . ."[39] But, over the years, Witherspoon's thinking shows remarkable consistency. His emphasis on limited government and the rights of man finds roots in the Scottish, English, and French Calvinists like Knox, Rutherford, and Cromwell. He accepted and interacted with the Enlightenment thinkers only to the extent that their ideas were consistent with Calvinist Christianity—and their ideas were much more consistent than many acknowledge.

Witherspoon's special concern was religious liberty. Believing that government has no God-given authority to dictate to the human conscience, he warned against the "tyranny of conscience" in Catholic nations.[40] He stated that the greatest service government could render to Christianity was "to defend and secure rights of conscience in the most equal and impartial manner."[41] Witherspoon believed that religious liberty and civil liberty were inseparable and declared that "There is not a single instance in history, in which civil liberty was lost, and religious liberty preserved entire."[42] He also strongly advocated the theory of natural rights, as did nearly everyone in his day, believing those natural rights were God-given.[43] In stressing the inseparability of religious and civil liberty, he strongly defended property rights, because "If

39. Elizabeth Flower and Murray G. Murphy, *A History of Philosophy in America* (New York: Putnam's Sons, 1977), I:233; quoted in Marsden, Hatch & Noll, *The Search for Christian America* (Westchester, Illinois: Crossway, 1983), p. 91.

40. Witherspoon; quoted by Schultz, "Covenanting in America," p. 124.

41. Witherspoon; ibid., p. 124.

42. Witherspoon; ibid., p. 113.

43. Schultz, "Covenanting in America," pp. 125-26. Schultz suggests that Witherspoon's belief in natural rights may possibly be traced to Locke. This is possible, but it should be noted that Locke was in most respects an orthodox Christian.

therefore we yield up our temporal property, we at the same time deliver the conscience into bondage."[44]

Witherspoon's focus was limited government. It was based on his concept of human depravity, God-given governmental authority, God-given natural rights, limited governmental jurisdiction, and the Scottish Calvinist ideas of covenant.

5. A positive attitude toward independence. Witherspoon's pro-independence views were probably influenced by the church struggles in Scotland. A major factor that distinguished the Popular or conservative faction from the Moderate faction in Scotland, was a more faithful or literal adherence to the Scriptures. But another important issue was local versus centralized control. As leader of the Popular faction, Witherspoon fought for the right of local congregations to call their own pastors and control their own affairs. These struggles helped Witherspoon sympathize with the American colonists who wanted to control their own affairs without being subject to British control. In fact, Calvinist churches in America were models of local self-government with their congregational and presbyterian forms of government. The churches gave the colonists practical experience in self-rule and a desire to extend that self-rule to political affairs.

6. Good works and morality were the logical results of salvation by grace. In Witherspoon's view, one is saved solely by the grace of God through the atoning work of the Lord Jesus Christ on the cross. Good works and good morals are the means by which the believer shows the world that he has been saved, and give evidence of his election. His sermon at Paisley, "The Trial of Religious Truth by Its Moral Influence,"[45] clearly described his position. In his Pastoral Letter, in which he argued for independence, he also urged his audience to be diligent in morality, for immorality leads to the judgment of God. If "universal profligacy makes a nation ripe for divine judgements, and is the natural means of bringing them to ruin, reformation of manners is of the utmost necessity in our present distress."[46] Years later, in his Thanksgiving sermon, delivered after the peace treaty with England, he urged people to live for "the glory of God, the public interest of religion and the good of others," because "civil liberty cannot be long preserved without

44. Witherspoon; quoted by Schultz, "Covenanting in America," p. 113.
45. Witherspoon, "The Trial of Religious Truth by Its Moral Influence"; cited in Stohlman, *John Witherspoon*, p. 44; Collins, *President Witherspoon*, I:55
46. Witherspoon; quoted by Schultz, "Covenanting in America," p. 106.

virtue."[47] A Republic, therefore "must either preserve its virtue or lose its liberty."[48]

In Witherspoon's opinion, civic responsibility and political activism form one aspect of good works and morality. One way the elect give evidence of their election is by exercising their civic responsibilities and working for good government.

7. A strong hope that America would prosper and be blessed and used of God, as long as the new nation held to the principles of liberty and virtue. Witherspoon was postmillennial and shared the optimism of postmillennialists, but he did not appear to have perceived America as the "new Israel" or the "millennial kingdom."[49] However, he did have a deep love for America and a belief that God had a special plan for the nation. As he remarked to his friend Rev. Ashbel Green, "Don't be surprised if you see a turnpike all the way to the Pacific Ocean in your lifetime."[50]

John Witherspoon based his life and teaching on the Word of God. "The character of a Christian," he said, "must be taken from Holy Scriptures . . . the unerring standard. . . ."[51] He devoted his life to instilling the principles of Holy Scripture into the minds and souls of young men who then used those principles to shape America.

His young secretary and third cousin, John Ramsay Witherspoon, described him as having "the simplicity of a child, the humility of a patriarch and the dignity of a prince."[52] Roger Schultz's summary complements that : "[John] Adams called him a true son of liberty. So he was. But first, he was a son of the Cross."[53]

47. Witherspoon; ibid., p. 119.
48. Ibid.
49. Schultz, "Covenanting in America," p. 142.
50. Ashbel Green, *The Life of the Rev. John Witherspoon* (Princeton: Princeton University Press, reprinted 1973), p. 173; quoted by Schultz, "Covenanting in America," p. 16.
51. Witherspoon; ibid., p. 93.
52. John Ramsay Witherspoon; quoted by Stohlman, *John Witherspoon*, p. 173.
53. Schultz, "Covenanting in America," p. 149.

7 James Madison

J ames Madison is called the "Father of the Constitution." He spent over a half century in public service; a few of his positions included: the youngest delegate to the Continental Congress, signer of the Declaration of Independence, member of the Constitutional Convention, leader of the pro-Constitution forces at the Virginia Ratifying Convention, champion of religious liberty in Virginia, main author of the Bill of Rights, author of the best notes of the convention, contributing author (with Hamilton and Jay) to the Federalist Papers, Secretary of State and chief advisor to President Jefferson, two-term President of the United States during which time he was Commander-in-Chief for the War of 1812, and Rector of the University of Virginia.

No one at the Constitutional Convention was better prepared than Madison. He had worked on the Constitution of Virginia, and after extensive reading he wrote a treatise titled "The Vices of the Political System of the United States." At opening meetings of the Convention, while waiting for more delegates to arrive, the delegates present held early morning sessions during which Madison outlined the results of his studies. He and the other Virginia delegates drew up the "Fifteen Resolves" which became the basic agenda at the Convention.[1] William Pierce, a Georgia delegate to the Convention, said of Madison:

1. W. Cleon Skousen, *"Miracle of America" Study Guide* (Salt Lake City: Freemen Institute, 1981), pp. 67-68.

93

Mr. Maddison is a character who has long been in public life; but what is very remarkable every Person seems to acknowledge his greatness. He blends together the profound politician, with the scholar. In the management of every great question he evidently took the lead in the Convention, and tho' he cannot be called an Orator, he is a most agreeable, eloquent, and convincing speaker. From a spirit of industry and application which he posseses in a most eminent degree, he always comes forward the best informed Man of any point in debate. The affairs of the United States, he perhaps has the most correct knowledge of, of any Man in the Union. He has been twice a member of Congress, and was always thought one of the ablest Members that ever sat in that Council. Mr. Maddison is about 37 years of age [actually 36], a Gentleman of great modesty,—with a remarkably sweet temper. He is easy and unreserved among his acquaintances, and has a most agreeable style of conversation.[2]

Madison spoke a total of 161 times at the Constitutional Convention; only Gouverneur Morris and James Wilson spoke more frequently. He was part of the Committee on Style which determined the final wording of the Constitution, and the Committee on Postponed Matters which considered difficult and thorny questions.

Madison was born on March 16, 1751, the first of ten children of James and Eleanor Madison, Sr. Twenty-one days later he was baptized in the Episcopal Church. His father was a church vestryman and a lay delegate to the Episcopal Convention of 1776. His mother was a pious communicant in the church.

Madison's education began at home; his mother and grandmother were his first teachers. His playmates were probably the children of black slaves; this fact influenced his antislavery views years later. The Madison library, while not extensive, contained a number of volumes which probably stimulated his religious interest. Among the books were the *Holy Bible*, the *Book of Common Prayer, Gospel Mystery of Sanctification*, and *Life of Man in the Soul of God*.[3]

Starting about age 12, Madison went to school for several years under the tutelage of a Scotsman named Donald Robertson, and then under the Rev. Thomas Martin, an Episcopal minister who lived in the Madison home.[4] Madison studied Latin, Greek, arithmetic, geography, algebra, geometry, literature, French and possi-

2. William Pierce; quoted by Gaillard Hunt, *The Life of James Madison* (New York: Russell & Russell, 1902, 1968), p. 134.

3. Irving Brant, *James Madison* (Indianapolis: Bobbs-Merrill, 1941), I:56-57.

4. Ibid., I:57-58; Hunt, *Life of James Madison*, p. 11. Hunt believes most of this time was spent under Rev. Martin, while Brant believes more time was spent under Robertson.

bly Spanish under Robertson. The literary works he read probably included Virgil, Horace, Justinian's *Institutes*, Montaigne's *Essays*, Locke's *On Human Understanding*, Montesquieu's *Spirit of Laws*, Smollet's *History of England, The Imitation of Christ* by Thomas a Kempis, and others. Madison's notebook for that period contains various discussions and references to logic, astronomy, Socrates, Plato, Euclid, Fontanelle, and Locke. At one point Madison said of Robertson, "All that I have been in life I owe largely to that man."[5]

There is less information about Madison's studies under Rev. Thomas Martin, although it is believed Madison held Rev. Martin in high regard.[6] It was perhaps through fireside conversations with his father and Rev. Martin that Madison's strong pro-independence sentiments began to grow. At that time, Virginia was torn between the pro-independence views of Patrick Henry and Richard Henry Lee, and the more restrained views of George Wythe, Pendleton and others; Madison's father inclined toward Henry's position.[7]

In 1769, when Madison was 18, he enrolled in college. Rather than attending the Episcopal William and Mary College at nearby Williamsburg, Virginia, Madison was sent to a Presbyterian college, the College of New Jersey (now known as Princeton).

There are probably several factors which led Madison's Episcopal family to send him to the College of New Jersey. That College was noted for: its Christian orthodoxy, its pro-independence sentiment, and its stand for religious liberty. So it represented their views better than William and Mary. And by 1769 the Episcopal church had become largely Calvinistic and not much different from Presbyterianism in basic doctrine.

Madison came under the direct influence of the college president, Rev. Witherspoon, while attending the College of New Jersey. Witherspoon stressed divinity and theology in addition to the usual curriculum of the classics, history, philosophy, and writing and speaking of good clear English.[8] The college president seemed to have a special interest in Madison, recognizing him as a young man of great ability and dedication. The two retained their close association as they served in Congress together years later.

Madison's interest in Christianity and a career in the ministry continued throughout his studies at the College of New Jersey.

---

5. Madison; quoted by Brant, *James Madison*, I:60.
6. Hunt, *Life of James Madison*, p. 11.
7. Brant, *James Madison*, I:67.
8. Ibid., I:75.

Bishop Meade, who had been in Madison's home on one occasion, said of him,

> Mr. Madison was sent to Princeton College—perhaps through fear of the skeptical principles then so prevalent at William and Mary. During his stay at Princeton a great revival took place, and it was believed that he partook of its spirit. On his return home he conducted worship in his father's house. He soon after offered for the Legislature, and it was objected to him, by his opponents, that he was better suited to the pulpit than to the legislative hall.[9]

Madison's closest friends at college were also of a religious nature, and like Madison combined their religious interest with law and politics: William Bradford studied divinity but later chose law as a career; Samuel Stanhope Smith became a Presbyterian minister and was Witherspoon's successor as President of the College of New Jersey; John Blair Smith, a Presbyterian minister, became President of Hampden Sidney College; Caleb Wallace, ordained a minister in the Presbyterian Church, later became a lawyer and justice of the Supreme Court of Kentucky.[10]

Madison received a baccalaureate degree from the College of New Jersey on September 29, 1771. Still planning a theology career, he continued his education with graduate studies. He "remained at Princeton for another half year or so of study under Dr. Witherspoon's direction, adding a little Hebrew to his knowledge of classical languages and literature, reading in theology, and continuing his inquiries into moral philosophy and political history and thought.[11] He then returned to his family estate, Montpelier and continued theological studies. Some undated Bible study notes which appear to be from this period have been preserved. Parts of the notes are quoted from William Burkitt, *Expository Notes, with Practical Observations, on the New Testament of our Lord and Saviour Jesus Christ*. The following notes are representative.

---

9. Bishop Meade, *Old Churches, Ministers and Families of Virginia* (1872); quoted by Brant, *James Madison*, I:113. The discerning student will note that I have left off later portions of Meade's statement that Madison's interest in revival was shortlived and that he was later influenced by infidels with whom he associated. I will present and deal with these allegations later in this chapter.

10. Hunt, *Life of James Madison*, p. 15.

11. Adrienne Koch, *Madison's "Advice to My Country"* (Princeton, New Jersey: Princeton University Press, 1966), pp. 11-12.

Acts Chapter 19
Holy Ghost. have ye recd. the Holy Ghost since ye Believed. the Apostle does not mean in its Sanctifying operations, but in its miraculous Gifts v. 2d.
Spirit of Prophecy, departed (as the Jews believe) from Israel after the Death of Haggai, Zachariah & Malachi. v. 2d.
Baptizm, Christ's & John's were the same for Substance 2d.
Apostles did greater Miracles than Christ, in the matter, not manner, of them v. 11
Evil Spirits, none were, that we read of in the old Testament, bodily possessed of, but many in the New, v. 13
Conjuring Books burnt by the believing Jews & Greeks at Ephesus amounted to 50,000 pcs. of Silver; £800.
Saints fall, intimated by Alexander the Copper Smith turning Apostate. v 33
Ch.20
Sunday, why kept by the Christians, for the Sabbath v. 7
Sleepers under Gods word (at a Sermon), their wretched contempt of it. v. 9
St. Paul's travelling on foot from Troas to A-sos: an happy example for all the Ministers of Christ. v. 13.&c.
Tempt. to neglect the means for our own preservation is to Tempt God: and to trust to them is to neglect him v. 3 & c. Ch. 27. v. 31
Humility, the better any man is, the lower thoughts he has of himself v. 19
Ministers to take heed to themselves & their flock. v. 28
Believers who are in a State of Grace, have need of the word of God for their Edification and Building up therefore implies a possibility of falling v. 32
Grace, it is the free gift of God. Luke. 12. 32-v. 32
Giver more blessed than the Receiver. v 35. . . .
Gospels.
Mat. Ch 1st
Jesus is an Hebrew name and signifies a Saviour v. 1.
Christ is a Greek name and signifies Anointed. v. 1
Pollution Christ did by the power of his Godhead purify our nature from all the pollution of our Ancestors v. 5 &c
Until signifies in Scripture as much as never. v 25
Virgin Mary had no other Child (probably) but our Saviour. v. 25[12]

William C. Rives writes about Madison's theological studies:

After the manner of the Bereans he seems to have searched the Scriptures daily and diligently. . . . He explored the whole history

12. James Madison, *The Papers of James Madison*, ed. William T. Hutchinson and William M. Rachal (Chicago: University of Chicago Press), I:51-60.

and evidences of Christianity on every side, through clouds of witnesses and champions for and against, from the Fathers and schoolmen down to the infidel philosophers of the eighteenth century. No one not a professed theologian, and but few even of those who are, have ever gone through more laborious and extensive inquiries to arrive at the truth.[13]

During this period, Madison corresponded with his close college friend William Bradford. Their letters show a continuing interest in and appreciation for theology, and mutual indecision about career choices. On November 9, 1772, Madison wrote to Bradford that "a watchful eye must be kept on ourselves lest while we are building ideal monuments of Renown and Bliss here we neglect to have our names enrolled in the Annals of Heaven." He wrote his bad health of the past several months had "intimated to me not to expect a long or healthy life, yet it may be better with me after some time tho I hardly dare expect it and therefore have little spirit and alacrity to set about any thing that is difficult in the acquiring and useless in possessing after one has exchanged Time for Eternity." He commended Bradford on his choice of history and science as courses of study for that winter, and encouraged him to "season them with a little divinity now and then, which like the philosopher's stone, in hands of a good man will turn them and every lawful acquirement into the nature of itself, and make them more precious than fine gold."[14]

On June 10, 1773, Madison wrote to Bradford about the news he had received of their old college companions. He expressed warm approval of those who entered the ministry, and agreed that others were not suited for the ministry:

I received a Line or two with yours from Mrss Ervin & McPherrin who confirm I hope the fortitude & Zeal with which they enter on the ministerial Duties will procure them esteem and success. . . . Keith Debow &c I wish well but I adopt your opinion of them and had rather see them at the rustic employment you assign them than in the pulpit. Nevertheless it ought to be acknowleged that spiritual events are not limited or proportioned always to human means; yet granting this in its just extent it must be observed that the best human means should be ever employed otherwise it would look like a lazy presump-

---

13. William C. Rives, *History of the Life and Times of James Madison* (Boston: Little, Brown & Co., 1866), I:33-34.
14. Madison to William Bradford, November 9, 1772; reprinted in *Papers*, I:74-76.

tious dependance on Providence. Grier is a worthy fellow and I am pleased with his preferment; Tho' his want of Majesty and Oeconomy may be unpromising, he has integrity & Industry two very useful requisites.[15]

On August 12, 1773, Bradford wrote to Madison about his own career choice. He stated that he was considering a career as a lawyer:

Could I think myself properly qualified for the ministry I should be at no loss what choice to make. As I have always borne in mind that I was born for others as well as for myself I have always been desirous of being in that station in which I could be of most use to my fellow-creature: And in my opinion a divine may be the most useful as well as the most happy member of society. But as there are some insuperable objections to my entering that state My choice is now divided betwixt Law Physic and Merchandize. If I am rightly acquainted with my own genius it points rather to the first than to either of the others. . . . The grand objection urged against Law is, that it is prejudical to morals. It must indeed be owned that the conduct of the generallity of lawyers is very reproachable but that out noght to make their profession so as it is not the necessary consequence of it. . . . as I heard Dr. Witherspoon once observe, a man of known probity will have great weight with the Judges and his very appearing in a cause will influence them in its favour. It is then the Lawyers interest to be honest & next to the divine can there be a more useful member of society than an honest Lawyer. Can there be a nobler character than his whose business it is to support the Laws of his country & to defend the oppressed from the violence of the Oppressor; whose whole Life is spent in actions which tend to the public good, in wiping away the tear from the eye of affliction in bringing offenders to Justice or calming the fears of accused innocence?[16]

Madison commended Bradford on his choice of law but urged him to "keep the Ministry obliquely in View whatever your profession be":

15. Madison to Bradford, June 10, 1773; reprinted in *Papers*, I:88-89. Bradford had informed Madison by letter (dated May 27, 1773) that their friends Nathaniel Erwin (Irwin) and Thomas McPherrin had entered the ministry, that Robert Keith, John Debow and Moses Allen had also entered the ministry though in Bradford's opinion they were not suited for it (perhaps because they were of the rival faction at Princeton), and that James Grier, later to be ordained, was appointed as a tutor at Princeton. See *Papers*, I:85-88.

16. Bradford to Madison, August 12, 1773; reprinted in *Papers*, I:90-92.

> You forbid any recommendation of Divinity by suggesting that you
> have insuperable objections therefore I can only condole with the
> Church on the loss of a fine Genius and persuasive Orator. I cannot
> however suppress thus much of my advice on the head that you
> would always keep the Ministry obliquely in View whatever your
> profession be. . . . I have sometimes thought there could not be a
> stronger testimony in favor of Religion or against temporal Enjoy-
> ments even the most rational and manly than for men who occupy
> the most honorable and gainful departments and are rising in
> reputation and wealth, publicly to declare their unsatisfactoriness by
> becoming fervent Advocates in the cause of Christ, & I wish you may
> give in your Evidence in this way. Such Instances have seldom
> occurred, therefore they would be more striking and would be
> instead of a "Cloud of Witnesses.["]"[17]

Madison closed this letter by mentioning a scarcity of circulating
cash in Virginia which had cut prices more than half. He wrote, "I
do not meddle with Politicks but this Calamity lies so near the heart
of every friend of the Country that I could not but mention it."[18] In
just a short period of time, however, Madison devoted himself to
politics on a grand scale.

As Madison entered public life, he became just as reticent to talk
about religion as he had been to "meddle with Politicks" years
earlier. For this reason Madison is more difficult to understand and
categorize theologically, than the other founding fathers. With a
few exceptions Madison seems to have avoided the mention of God
or anything religious the rest of his life and never explained why.

Nor did he give a reason for not entering the ministry. One
historian believes it was because his soft voice made him unsuited
for a pulpit ministry in an age without microphones.[19] Others
suggest it was his frail health which was at its worst those years after
college.

Nothing in Madison's life or writings suggest that he became
disillusioned with Christianity, rejected the fundamental doctrines
of the Christian faith, or lost interest in religion. Throughout his life
Madison remained friendly and respectful toward Christianity and
toward the church.[20]

---

17. Madison to Bradford, September 25, 1773; reprinted in *Papers*, I:95–97.
18. Ibid.
19. Brant, *James Madison*, I:100.
20. Bishop Meade's statement implied that Madison's religious zeal from his College of
New Jersey days seems to have been short-lived and that Madison's "political associations
with those of infidel principles, of whom there were many in his day, if they did not actually
change his creed, yet subjected him to the general suspicion of it" (Brant, *James Madison*,
I:113). However, Brant rejects strongly the suggestion that Jefferson or others had anything

His tight-lipped silence on religion may be the result of the common belief at that time that doctrinal beliefs about religious matters were personal and private and not for public discussion.[21] Perhaps Madison believed that as a public official he had a duty to stay neutral on doctrinal matters to prevent dividing the nation. Maybe his firm belief in separation of church and state led him to refrain from public statements on matters of religion. It is likely that all three of these factors contributed to his silence.

One thing is certain: the Christian religion, particularly Rev. Witherspoon's Calvinism, influenced Madison's view of law and government.

> . . . man's innate depravity, of which Presbyterians are keenly aware, must be checked by counteracting forces; self-interest of individuals necessitates that government should limit it for the good of the whole; faction—"impulse or passion or interest adverse to the rights of other citizens or to the permanent and aggregate interest of the community," as Madison described it—separates men into groups; faction is inevitable, not removable by education, social engineering, or religion; and a workable government must recognize this. Then that government must be shaped so that one set of interests will keep other sets of interest from dominating. Checks and balances are required.[22]

Thus Dr. James H. Smylie connects Madison's political philosophy, with its import for us all, to instruction he received from the man he affectionately referred to as "the old Doctor." In his analysis of the theological background of Madison's political philosophy, Smylie claims that "With Witherspoon, Madison started from a theological rather than from an anthropological perspective. In

---

to do with changing Madison's religious beliefs. In fact, Madison seems to have been a moderating influence on Jefferson. (Brant, *James Madison*, I:272, 275ff.)

Meade (quoted by Brant, *James Madison*, I:113) gives some further reason to question Madison's orthodoxy: "I was never at Mr. Madison's but once, and then our conversation took such a turn—though not designed on my part—as to call forth come expressions and arguments which left the impression on my mind that his creed was not strictly regulated by the Bible." Unfortunately Meade's observation is limited to one visit, and he does not tell us during which period of Madison's long life that visit took place, or which subjects were discussed. That makes it difficult to know how to evaluate Meade's statement. He does add, however, that Madison never seemed hostile toward Christianity, and that he attended church.

21. Hunt, *Life of James Madison*, p. 211.

22. James H. Smylie, "Madison and Witherspoon: Theological Roots of American Political Thought," *The Princeton University Library Chronicle*, Spring 1961, pp. 118-32.

some sense Madison may be considered a lay theologian.''[23] The basic principles of law and government that remained with Madison his entire life and which he wrote into the U.S. Constitution he learned at the feet of Rev. Witherspoon.

Witherspoon's observations and beliefs on the sinfulness of man found their way into Madison's philosophy. Madison also saw that a successful government must be based on a realistic assessment of human nature. As he says in *The Federalist No. 51*:

> Ambition must be made to counteract ambition. The interest of the man must be connected with the constitutional rights of the place. It may be a reflection on human nature that such devices should be necessary to control the abuses of government. But what is government itself but the greatest of all reflections on human nature? If men were angels, no government would be necessary. If angels were to govern men, neither external or internal controls on government would be necessary. In framing a government which is to be administered by men over men, the great difficulty lies in this: you must first enable the government to control the governed; and in the next place oblige it to control itself.[24]

Madison's realization that government needs power to control the sinful urges and actions of men was based on the biblical view of the nature of man. He knew that rulers possess sinful natures and could not be trusted with too much power. Dr. M. E. Bradford says, the basic maxim of Madison's political philosophy is best summarized in his statement before the Constitutional Convention that "All men having power ought to be distrusted."[25]

Madison's conclusions of how to give government power enough to control the governed, but at the same time oblige it to control itself, are found in the Constitution of the United States.

First, he said, power must come from the people: "A dependence on the people is, no doubt, the primary control on the government; but experience has taught mankind the necessity of auxiliary precautions."[26] Government must be responsive to the will of the people through popular elections, so would-be tyrants can be voted out of office.

23. Ibid., p. 125.

24. James Madison, *The Federalist No. 51, The Federalist Papers,* ed. Clinton Rossiter (New York: Mentor Books, 1961), p. 322.

25. James Madison, remarks on the Constitutional Convention floor; quoted by M. E. Bradford, *A Worthy Company* (Marlborough, New Hampshire: Plymouth Rock Foundation, 1982), p. 147.

26. Madison, *Federalist No. 51,* p. 322.

Second, the government has only such powers as the people delegate to it through the social covenant, the Constitution. Madison emphasized that the powers of government are "derivative and limited";[27] Government has no jurisdictional authority to do anything other than that which the people have delegated to it in the Constitution. Government may not act beyond these derivative and limited powers even if a majority wants it to, because "the majority may trespass on the rights of the minority."[28]

Third, Madison believed this covenant cannot contravene the "law of nature and of nature's God."[29] The Constitution is required to respect natural law and natural rights, as are the institutions of government created by the Constitution. This is true whether a majority approves or not.

Fourth, Madison supported the separation of powers between the legislative, executive, and judicial branches of government. Each branch would have limited power to minimize the danger of abuse.

Fifth, Madison favored the *"nexus imperii"* spoken of by Witherspoon, those checks and balances by which the various branches of government are interdependent on one another. Madison and the like-minded delegates wrote checks and balances throughout the Constitution. For example, legislation must be passed by Congress, but the President can veto it, subject to being overridden by a two-thirds vote of both houses. The Supreme Court can declare acts of Congress unconstitutional, but the President appoints the members of the Court, with the advice and consent of the government. Madison and his fellow delegates knew leaders of unbridled ambition would arise. Such leaders could be more dangerous by concealing their personal ambitions (perhaps even to themselves) with expressions of dedication to the public good. In the system which Madison envisioned, such men would check each other's power out of self-interest. Congress, jealous of its own power, would check the power of an "imperial Presidency," while the President and his staff would limit the encroachments of Congress into Presidential authority in foreign affairs. In this way limited government would be preserved, and with it, human freedom.

Sixth, Madison saw the bulwark of free government in the multiplicity of interests that prevailed across America. If no one

27. Madison, "Memorial and Remonstrance", 1785; reprinted by Norman Cousins, *"In God We Trust"* (New York: Harper and Brothers, 1958), p. 309.

28. Ibid.

29. Madison, *Federalist No. 43*, p. 279.

person, or group of persons, usurped too much power, each could check the other and keep everyone under control. This "multiplicity of interests," he said, would work best if there existed in society "so many separate descriptions of citizens as will render an unjust combination of a majority of the whole very improbable, if not impracticable."[30]

Seventh, Madison advocated moderation. He exemplified moderation in both his private life and in his political relations. As an ally of Jefferson he tried to moderate Jefferson's extremes, and he pursued a moderate course throughout his own presidency. His personality seemed to bespeak moderation.

Eighth, he opposed slavery. His sense of justice and natural rights, and perhaps his fear of concentrated power of man over men, caused him to be an ardent opponent of slavery. His childhood playmates were black slaves; this also influenced his opposition to slavery. He felt close to many of his slaves, especially a young man named Billy. At one point Madison declared that "the whole Bible is against negro slavery; but that the clergy do not preach this, and the people do not see it."[31]

Yet, Madison owned over 100 slaves during his lifetime, and of those he only freed a few. He believed that because racial prejudices existed and were not likely to change, emancipation would not be practicable with the two races living together. The result would be constant unhappiness among blacks because of "the degrading privation of equal rights political or social."[32]

He believed emancipation should take place gradually, after the consent of both slave and master, with compensation to the masters and provision for the slave to make sure his condition after slavery was truly better than before. Madison favored the repatriation of the freed black population in an African country to be called Liberia. He was a lifetime member of the American Colonization Society, which had been formed in 1816 to promote that goal. At one time he served as its president.[33]

Because Madison believed the immediate emancipation of his slaves was not in their best interest, he resolved to treat his slaves as kindly as possible. In 1819 he wrote that the condition of slaves in America had greatly improved since the War of Independence.[34] In

30. Madison; quoted by Koch, *Madison's "Advice to My Country"*, p. 82.
31. Koch, *Madison's "Advice to My Country"*, p. 135.
32. Madison, 1819; quoted by Brant, *James Madison*, VI:430-31.
33. Ibid.
34. Ibid.

1865, Paul Jennings, a former slave born and raised on Madison's estate, wrote of him,

> Mr. Madison, I think, was one of the best men that ever lived. I never saw him in a passion, and never knew him to strike a slave, although he had over one hundred; neither would he allow an overseer to do it. Whenever any slaves were reported to him as stealing or "cutting up" badly, he would send for them and admonish them privately, and never mortify them by doing it before others. They generally served him very faithfully. I don't think he drank a quart of brandy in his whole life. . . . For the last fifteen years of his life he drank no wine at all.[35]

Jennings narrated an incident in which a slave greeted Madison by removing his hat in respect:

> Mr. M raised his, to the surprise of old Tom; to which Mr. M replied, "I never allow a negro to excel me in politeness." Though a similar story is told of General Washington, I have often heard this, as above, from Mr. Madison's own lips.[36]

Madison's ninth contribution to American political thought was his defense of religious liberty. In colonial Virginia the Episcopal church was the established religion, meaning that everyone had to pay taxes to support the Episcopal church. Other religions were subject to licensure and other restrictions. Madison's family was Episcopalian, but they generally supported liberty for other religions. As a youth, Madison had heard Baptist clergymen preaching from their jail cells, and the spectacle remained firmly implanted in his mind.[37] His years under Rev. Witherspoon at the College of New Jersey strengthened his belief in religious freedom. In 1774 he complained to his college friend William Bradford that the "diabolical Hell conceived principle of persecution rages among some and to their eternal Infamy the Clergy can furnish their Quota of Imps for such business." He went on to say that "There are at this [time] in the adjacent County [probably Culpepper County] not less than 5 or 6 well meaning men in close Goal [jail] for publishing their religious Sentiments which in the main are very orthodox."[38] Note Madison's outrage at the fact of persecution, and also his astonish-

---

35. Paul Jennings, *Colored Man's Reminescences of James Madison* (Brooklyn: George C. Beadle, 1865), pp. 17-18.
36. Ibid., pp. 19-20.
37. Hunt, *Life of James Madison*, p. 12.
38. Madison to Bradford, January 24, 1774; reprinted in *Papers*, I:104-6.

ment that those being persecuted are in the main "very orthodox." Madison knew what was orthodox and what was not, and he considered it outrageous that the orthodox were being persecuted.

Madison had a leading role in drafting the Virginia Constitution of 1776, and took part with Patrick Henry and others in drafting the article on religious freedom. In 1784 he opposed Patrick Henry's proposal to provide a tax for the support of teachers of the Christian religion. The next year he wrote his famous "Memorial and Remonstrance" against religious assessments which played a role in the ultimate defeat of Henry's proposal.[39] Madison saw no need for a constitutional provision protecting religious freedom at the Constitutional Convention of 1787. He believed the multiplicity of religious denominations in the United States and the rivalry between them would prevent any one denomination from establishing itself nationally over the others. But, when many people wanted a Bill of Rights, it was Madison who prepared the first draft of the First Amendment with a provision for religious liberty.

Some interpret Madison's opposition to religious establishments as evidence of his hostility to Christianity or organized religion. Actually, Madison believed religion functioned best when it was not dependent on the state for its existence or support. He wrote to his friend William Bradford, "Union of religious sentiments begets a surprizing confidence, and Ecclesiastical Establishments tend to great ignorance and Corruption; all of which facilitate the Execution of Mischievous Projects."[40] He further expressed his opinion in the "Memorial and Remonstrance":

> During almost fifteen centuries, has the legal establishment of Christianity been on trial. What have been its fruits? More or less in all places, pride and indolence in the Clergy; ignorance and servility in the laity; in both, superstition, bigotry and persecution. Enquire of the Teachers of Christianity for the ages in which it appeared in its greatest lustre; those of every sect, point to the ages prior to its incorporation with Civil policy.[41]

39. To become law, the bill had to pass three readings. It passed twice over Madison's objections; but before the third reading took place, Patrick Henry had been elected governor. With Henry out of the legislature, Madison was able to defeat the bill on its third reading.

40. Madison to Bradford, January 24, 1774; reprinted in *Papers,* I:104-6. He adds, in reference to the spirit of toleration which prevailed in Bradford's Philadelphia, "I want again to breathe your free Air. I expect it will mend my Constitution & confirm my Principles."

41. Madison, "Memorial and Remonstrance"; reprinted in Cousins, *"In God We Trust",* pp. 308–14.

Madison insisted that Christianity would flourish best without the support of the state:

> . . . the establishment proposed by this Bill is not requisite for the support of the Christian Religion. To say that it is, is a contradiction to the Christian Religion itself; for every page of it disavows a dependence on the powers of this world: it is a contradiction to fact; for it is known that this Religion both existed and flourished, not only without the support of human laws, but in spite of every opposition from them; and not only during the period of miraculous aid [the New Testament period and shortly thereafter], but long after it had been left to its own evidence, and the ordinary care of Providence: Nay, it is a contradiction in terms; for a Religion not invented by human policy, must have pre-existed and been supported, before it was established by human policy. It is moreover to weaken in those who profess this Religion a pious confidence in its innate excellence, and the patronage of its Author; and to foster in those who still reject it, a suspicion that its friends are too conscious of its fallacies, to trust it to its own merits.[42]

The "Memorial and Remonstrance," far from being an anti-Christian statement, was possibly the closest Madison came to publicly affirming Christianity. His point was that Christianity does not need the support of the state because it is not only a religion of "innate excellence" but also a religion that enjoys the "patronage of its Author." In other words, Christianity is a divinely revealed religion and pre-exists human government and is not dependent on human government. The same theme is echoed again in the Remonstrance: "Whilst we assert for ourselves a freedom to embrace, to profess, and to observe the *Religion which we believe to be of divine origin*, we cannot deny an equal freedom to those whose minds have not yet yielded to the evidence which has convinced us. If this freedom be abused, it is an offence against God, not against man: To God, therefore, not to man, must an account of it be rendered."[43]

Religious freedom is a matter of justice and fairness as well as a matter of jurisdiction. Governmental powers are "derivative and limited"; government cannot exercise jurisdiction over anything which society has not given it authority. And society is unable to give government authority over religion because society has no

42. Ibid.
43. Ibid.

authority over religion—religion is a matter between God and each individual:

> The Religion then of every man must be left to the conviction and conscience of every man; and it is the right of every man to exercise it as these [reason and conviction] may dictate. This right is in its nature an unalienable right. . . . It is the duty of every man to render to the Creator such homage, and such only, as he believes to be acceptable to him. This duty is precedent both in order of time and degree of obligation, to the claims of Civil Society. Before any man can be considered as a member of Civil Society, he must be considered as a subject of the Governor of the Universe: And if a member of Civil Society, who enters into any subordinate Association, must always do it with a reservation of his duty to the general authority; much more must every man who becomes a member of any particular Civil Society, do it with a saving of his allegiance to the Universal Sovereign. We maintain therefore that in matters of Religion, no man's right is abridged by the institution of Civil Society, and that Religion is wholly exempt from its cognizance.[44]

Madison's notes from his speech against the assessment bill in November 1784 revealed that he saw the danger that would result from a bill providing support for the Christian religion:

v. Probable effects of Bill,
 1. limited.
 2. in particular.
 3. What is Xnty? Courts of law to Judge.
 4. What edition: Hebrew, Septuagint, or Vulgate? What copy what translation?
 5. What books canonical, what apocryphal? the papists holding to be the former what protestants the latter, the Lutherans the latter what the protestants & papists ye former.
 6. In what light are they to be viewed, as dictated every letter by inspiration, or the essential parts only? Or the matter in general not the words?
 7. What sense the true one for if some doctrines be essential to Xnty those who reject these, whatever name they take are no Xn Society?
 8. Is it Trinitarianism, Arianism, Socinianism? Is it salvation by faith or works also, by free grace or by will, &c., &c.
 9. What clue is to guide (a) Judge thro' this labyright when ye question comes before them whether any particular society is a Cn society?

44. Ibid.

10. Ends in what is orthodoxy, what heresy. Dishonors christian-
    ity. panegyric on it, on our side. Decl. Rights.[45]

His point was: A bill to provide tax "for the support of the Christian
religion, or of some Christian church, denomination, or communion of Christians, or of some form of Christian worship," which
became law, would give the State of Virginia the difficult and
improper task of determining what was and was not Christian. It
would need to determine which churches to support or not support.
(For example, would Socinianism [a forerunner of Unitarianism] be
considered Christian and entitled to tax support? How about
Arianism, which taught that Christ is divine but not fully equal to
God the Father? Will the State provide tax support only for those
churches that teach salvation as by grace through faith alone, or will
the State recognize as Christian those that teach salvation by works
also? Will the State support Catholicism as being Christian?) Madison saw that such a bill would put the state in the position of
defining Christianity—which was out of the state's proper jurisdiction.

It was because Madison exalted religion that he favored religious
liberty. Since he revered the Christian religion above all others, he
wanted it to flourish in its purity, free from the corruption that
inevitably came with state support. When he introduced the First
Amendment on the floor of the House of Representatives on June 7,
1789, it read:

> The Civil Rights of none shall be abridged on account of religious
> belief or worship, nor shall any national religion be established, nor
> shall the full and equal rights of conscience be in any manner, nor on
> any pretext infringed.

The wording was changed several times in committees and on the
floor before the Congress finally agreed on the present wording:
"Congress shall make no law respecting an establishment of religion
or prohibiting the free exercise thereof. . . ."

Madison gave this explanation of the amendment's meaning
during the House debate according to Floyd's summary of the
House proceedings:

> Mr. Madison said, he apprehended the meaning of the words to be,
> that Congress should not establish *a* religion and enforce the legal
> observation of it by law, nor compel men to worship God in any

45. Madison, reprinted by Cousins, *"In God We Trust"*, pp. 302-4.

manner contrary to their conscience. Whether the words are necessary or not, he did not mean to say, but they had been required by some of the State Conventions, who seemed to entertain an opinion that under the clause of the constitution, which gave power to Congress to make all laws necessary and proper to carry into execution the constitution, and the laws under it, enabled them to make laws of such nature as might infringe the rights of conscience and establish a National Religion.[46]

Madison seems to have understood "establishment of religion" to mean setting up a particular church or denomination as the official religion of the United States.

Madison moved toward more of a separationist interpretation of church-state relations as he grew older. He recognized that religion played a vital role in preserving the strength of the nation, for

... the belief in a God All Powerful wise and good, is so essential to the moral order of the World and to the happiness of man, that arguments which enforce it cannot be drawn from too many sources nor adapted with too much solicitude to the different characters and capacities to be impressed with it.[47]

But he continued to believe that the church flourished better without the state's "help." Nevertheless, he wrote, "I must admit . . . that it may not be easy, in every possible case, to trace the line of separation, between the rights of the religious and the civil authority, with such distinctness, as to avoid collisions and doubts on unessential points!"[48]

As President, Madison pursued more of a separationist course than most other Presidents. In his inaugural address on March 4, 1809, he expressed his confidence "in the guardianship and guidance of that almighty Being, whose power regulates the destiny of nations."[49] But on February 21, 1811, he vetoed "An Act incorporating the Protestant Episcopal church in the town of Alexandria, in the District of Columbia." His reason was that incorporation was a form of licensing by which government gave churches permission to operate. Therefore, incorporation was superfluous; government has

46. I Annals, p. 730; quoted by Michael J. Malbin, *Religion and Politics: The Intentions of the Authors of the First Amendment* (Washington, D.C.: American Enterprise Institute for Public Policy Research, 1978), p. 8.

47. Madison, quoted by Smylie, "Madison and Witherspoon," p. 125.

48. Madison to Rev. Jasper Adams, 1833; quoted by Koch, *Madison's "Advice to My Country"*, p. 43.

49. Madison, Inaugural Address, March 4, 1809; quoted by Brant, *James Madison*, V:19.

no jurisdictional authority to tell churches they *can* or *cannot* operate.[50]

Congress asked President Madison to proclaim a day of prayer on two different occasions, and both times he seemed uncertain on what to do. Each time he followed his instinct for moderation and pursued a middle course of action. On July 9, 1812, he issued a proclamation to enable the religious:

> . . . societies so disposed, to offer, at one and the same time, their common vows and adorations to Almighty God, on the solemn occasion produced by the war, in which he has been pleased to permit the injustice of a foreign Power to involve these United States.[51]

In 1813 he proclaimed that "All who shall be piously disposed" were invited to give thanks and offer supplications to the Great Parent and Sovereign of the Universe, and suggested thanksgiving for the bounty of the land, the extension of arts and manufacturers, the American Constitution, and political freedom. He proposed prayers that God would bless the country's arms and aid in resisting the efforts to "degrade us on the ocean, the common inheritance of all," to inspire the enemies with moderation, justice, and accommodation, and that "we may be enabled to beat our swords into plowshares and to enjoy in peace" the rewards of honest industry and enterprise.[52]

Many complained that the first proclamation had not gone far enough. President Madison had not called on the American people to pray; he had simply proclaimed a day during which those who were so disposed could do so together. In his second proclamation he explained the reasons for such a limited proclamation:

> If the public homage of a people can ever be worthy the favorable regard of the Holy and Omniscient Being to whom it is addressed, it must be that in which those who join in it are guided only by their free choice, by the impulse of their hearts and the dictates of their consciences. [God should be given those prayers and offerings which] alone can be acceptable to Him whom no hypocrisy can deceive and no forced sacrifices propitiate.[53]

50. Madison, Legislative Veto, February 21, 1811; reprinted in Cousins, *"In God We Trust"*, pp. 317-18.

51. Madison, Proclamation, July 9, 1812; quoted in Brant, *James Madison*, VI:28.

52. Madison, Proclamation, 1813; quoted in Brant, *James Madison*, VI:198.

53. Ibid.

Madison completed his second term as President in 1817. He retired to his estate, Montpelier, and served as Rector of the University of Virginia, President of the American Colonization Society, and in other capacities. Madison died on June 28, 1836, having served his country well.

Henry Cabot Lodge described Madison as a man who spoke frequently:

> . . . never without manifesting a thorough knowledge and conveying much information to his hearers. He was eminently reasonable and practical, and although not a brilliant speaker, he was a convincing and effective leader in debate. The chief causes of his success, not only in Congress but elsewhere, were his general soundness and moderation of his views in all public questions. . . . He was candid, conscientious, just, and as a rule, high-minded. Nothing impresses one more in studying Madison's correspondence than the almost entire absence of personalities either hostile or friendly. He seems never to have undertaken to analyze character either for his own benefit or for that of his friends. He had no warm friendships apparently, except with Jefferson and Monroe, and he was equally free from bitter enemies. If not a good lover, he was still less a good hater.[54]

John Quincy Adams eulogized him on the House floor:

> Is it not a pre-eminent degree by emanations from his mind, that we are assembled here as the representatives of the people and the states of this Union? Is it not transcendentally by his exertions that we address each other here by the endearing appellations of country-men and fellow-citizens?[55]

The Father of the Constitution gave the United States a legacy that lasts to this day. James Madison's specific contributions to that legacy are those sections of the Constitution involving the separation of powers with accompanying checks and balances, and the jurisdictional view of religious freedom. His mentor, the Reverend Witherspoon, could truly be proud.

---

54. Henry Cabot Lodge, *Historical and Political Essays* (Boston: Houghton & Mifflin, 1892), p. 52.

55. John Quincy Adams, Speech to the House of Representatives, June 30, 1836; quoted by Koch, *Madison's "Advice to My Country"*, p. 158.

8 George Washington

T he U.S. Capitol has a private chapel for congressmen, one feature of which is a stained-glass window. Called "Washington's Gethsemane," the window depicts the kneeling figure of George Washington at Valley Forge, praying to God for his soldiers and his country.

The Reverend Mason Locke Weems, in his famous biography, *Life of George Washington*, first published in 1800, gives an account of what happened at Valley Forge:

> In the winter of '77, while Washington, with the American army lay encamped at Valley Forge, a certain good old friend, of the respectable family and name of Potts, if I mistake not, had occasion to pass through the woods near headquarters. Treading his way along the venerable grove, suddenly he heard the sound of a human voice, which as he advanced increased on his ear, and at length became like the voice of one speaking much in earnest. As he approached the spot with a cautious step, whom should he behold, in a dark natural bower of ancient oaks, but the commander in chief of the American armies on his knees at prayer! Motionless with surprise, friend Potts continued on the place till the general, having ended his devotions, arose, and with a countenance of angel serenity, retired to headquarters: friend Potts then went home, and on entering his parlour called out to his wife, "Sarah, my dear! Sarah! All's well! all's well! George Washington will yet prevail!"
>
> "What's the matter, Isaac?" replied she; "thee seems moved."

"Well, if I seem moved, 'tis no more than what I am. I have this day seen what I never expected. Thee knows that I always thought the sword and the gospel utterly inconsistent; and that no man could be a soldier and a Christian at the same time. But George Washington has this day convinced me of my mistake."

He then related what he had seen, and concluded with this prophetical remark—"If George Washington be not a man of God, I am greatly deceived—and still more shall I be deceived if God do not, through him, work out a great salvation for America."[1]

There are numerous other accounts of George Washington at prayer at Valley Forge. In 1832, eighty-year-old Devault Beaver

---

1. Mason Locke Weems, *The Life of George Washington; with Curious Anecdotes, Equally Honourable to Himself, and Exemplary to His Young Countrymen* (Cambridge, Massachusetts: Belknap Press of Harvard University Press, 1809 edition, reprinted 1962), pp. 181–82. This book is the first, most influential, and even today the most widely read biography of Washington. It has been enlarged and reprinted many times. Weems presents Washington as a committed Christian and relates numerous anecdotes to prove his point.

Those who wish to characterize Washington as a deist must first discredit Weems. But for all their attacks, critics have been unable to demonstrate a single clear falsehood in Weems's account. Such critics gleefully point out that Weems claimed to have been rector of Mount Vernon Parish, when in reality there was no Mount Vernon Parish. But Weems could have meant that he was rector of a parish in the Mount Vernon vicinity, and it is known that he frequently preached in the Mount Vernon area.

The claim of some critics that Weems never met Washington is refuted by Washington's own diary, in which the entry for March 3, 1787, names "The Rev. Mr. Weems" as a guest in his house.

Unfortunately Rev. Weems frequently failed to provide scholarly documentation for his statements. For example, he gives as his source for the famous cherry tree anecdote, "an aged lady, who was a distant relative, and when a girl spent much of her time in the family" (p. 9). But this does not mean the story is false. Had Weems been pressed for detail, he possibly could have provided excellent documentation. But he wrote a popular and inspirational account, probably never dreaming that his assertions would ever be challenged. At worst, Weems's anecdotes must be regarded as unsubstantiated; they have not been proven false.

The attacks on Rev. Weems and his work, and the assertion that Washington was a deist rather than a Christian, did not begin until about 1831. By this time Weems had died (1825) and was unable to speak for himself.

Rev. E. C. M'Guire came to his defense. Seeking to prove that Washington was a Christian, Rev. M'Guire wrote *The Religious Opinions and Character of Washington* in 1836. It is true, as the skeptics point out, that M'Guire often used stale or secondhand evidence. He had no choice. By this time Washington had been dead for thirty-seven years, and nearly all of those who knew him well were also dead. In relying on sources such as the daughter of a general who had served with Washington in the War, M'Guire was simply using the best evidence available at the time—and he probably had excellent sources of information since he married the daughter of Robert Lewis, Washington's nephew and private secretary.

To the charge that Weems and M'Guire, being clergymen, were biased in favor of Christianity, let it be noted that skeptics frequently show their anti-Christian bias as well. Believing that there may be considerable truth in what Weems and M'Guire have written, I have used their writings in this chapter. But I have not relied on them exclusively for any major point.

claimed to have received the account directly from Isaac Potts. Another account came from Dr. James Ross Snowden, whose father knew Potts, and yet another from Benson J. Lossing.[2] General Knox, Washington's close associate at Valley Forge was recorded as saying that Washington frequently used the grove for prayer.[3]

It is evident that Washington was a man of prayer, but it is more difficult to determine the nature of his religious convictions. Samuel Miller, a Presbyterian minister in New York City during Washington's presidency remarked that Washington displayed an "unusual, but uniform, and apparently deliberate, reticence on the subject of personal religion."[4] Bishop William White, who frequently preached before George Washington, wrote:

> I knew no man who seemed so carefully to guard against the discoursing of himself or of his acts, or of any thing pertaining to him; and it has occasionally occurred to me, when in his company, that if a stranger to his person were present, he would never have known, from any thing said by the President, that he was conscious of having distinguished himself in the eyes of the world. His ordinary behavior, although unexceptionably courteous, was not such as to encourage intrusion on what might be in his mind.[5]

Washington's silence on the subject of religion was due in part to his reserved nature. It is also possible Washington considered his religious beliefs to be a private matter. However, it is more conceivable that Washington's silence about religion came from the conviction that, as General of the Army and as President, he spoke for the entire nation and should not get entangled in doctrinal matters which could divide the nation.

Washington was a man of action rather than a man of words. But records reveal that he did express his religious convictions as a statesman and as a person.

2. William J. Johnson, *George Washington the Christian* (Milford, Michigan: Mott Media, 1919, 1976), pp. 102–7.

3. Ibid., pp. 106–7; citing Rev. E. C. M'Guire, *The Religious Opinions and Character of Washington* (1836), p. 159.

4. Samuel Miller, *The Life of Samuel Miller* (Philadelphia, 1869), I:123; quoted by Paul F. Boller, Jr., *George Washington and Religion* (Dallas: Southern Methodist University Press, 1963), p. 67.

5. William White to Colonel Hugh Mercer, Philadelphia, November 23, 1832; quoted by Boller, *George Washington and Religion*, pp. 66–67.

Washington the Statesman

Colonial America was composed of people of many religious persuasions: Puritans in the north, Episcopalians in the south, Quakers in Pennsylvania, Catholics in Maryland, Baptists in Rhode Island, Reformed in New York, and Presbyterians, Methodists, Lutherans, Unitarians, Universalists, Jews, deists, and others found throughout the nation. As General of the army and as President, Washington refused to take sides in religious disputes, and believed that the United States government should not favor any particular religious body. But he did believe religion was an essential pillar of society and that government should give aid and encouragement to religion in general, and perhaps specifically to Christianity, though not to any particular denomination.

As General of the Army, Washington worked to provide chaplains of various denominations for the Army and required his troops to attend chapel services. He deplored and prohibited gambling, drunkenness, and blasphemy. The first order he issued after he took command, July 4, 1775, read:

> The General most earnestly requires and expects a due observance of those articles of war established for the government of the army, which forbid profane cursing, swearing, and drunkenness. And in like manner he requires and expects of all officers and soldiers, not engaged in actual duty, a punctual attendance on Divine service, to implore the blessing of Heaven upon the means used for our safety and defense.[6]

He issued a similar order several weeks later, after the Continental Congress had ordered a day of fasting and prayer:

> The General orders this day to be religiously observed by the Forces under his Command, exactly in manner directed by the Continental Congress. It is therefore strictly enjoined on all Officers and Soldiers to attend Divine Service; and it is expected that all those who go to worship do take their Arms, Ammunition, and Accoutrements, & are prepared for immediate action if called upon.[7]

On other occasions he ordered or encouraged fasting, prayer, thanksgiving, or attendance at religious services. His official state-

6. Jared Sparks, *The Writings of George Washington*, (1834–7), III:491; quoted by Johnson, *George Washington the Christian*, p. 69.

7. Elizabeth Bryant Johnston, *George Washington, Day by Day* (1894); quoted by Johnson, *George Washington the Christian*, p. 70.

ments as General of the Army were filled with references to the protection and aid of the Supreme Being and reliance on Providence for the success of the nation.[8] As he resigned his commission December 23, 1783, his parting statement also expressed his dependence on God:

> ... I resign with satisfaction the appointment I accepted with diffidence, a diffidence in my abilities to accomplish so arduous a task, which, however, was superseded by a confidence in the rectitude of our cause, the support of the supreme power of the Union, and the patronage of Heaven.
>
> The successful termination of the war has verified the most sanguine expectations; and my gratitude for the interposition of Providence, and the assistance I have received from my countrymen, increases with every review of the momentous contest. . . .
>
> I consider it an indispensable duty to close this last solemn act of my official life, by commending the interests of our dearest country to the protection of Almighty God, and those who have the superintendence of them to His holy keeping.[9]

Just four years later, in 1787, Washington chaired the Constitutional Convention in Philadelphia, and in 1788 he was elected first President. When he took office in 1789, he established a tradition by adding to the proposed inaugural oath "so help me, God." In addition, his inaugural address called for "fervent supplications to that Almighty Being, who rules over the universe, who presides in the councils of nations, and whose providential aids can supply every human defect," asked for "His benediction," gave "homage to the great Author of every public and private good," declared that "every step by which [Americans] have advanced to the character of an independent nation seems to have been distiguished by some token of providential agency," warned that "the propitious smiles of Heaven can never be expected on a nation that disregards the eternal rules of order and right, which Heaven itself has ordained," and asked for the "divine blessing" of "the benign Parent of the human race."[10]

Washington did not hesitate to declare days of prayer and thanksgiving while he was in office. The first proclamation of a national day of thanksgiving, October 3, 1789, contains ideas

---

8. See Johnson, *George Washington the Christian*, pp. 68–145.
9. Sparks; quoted by Johnson, *George Washington the Christian*, p. 145.
10. Washington, First Inaugural Address, April 30, 1789; quoted by Johnson, *George Washington the Christian*, pp. 161–62.

which provide a key to Washington's understanding of church and state:

> Whereas, it is the duty of all nations to acknowledge the Providence of Almighty God, to obey his will, to be grateful for his benefits, humbly to implore his protection and favor. . . .
>
> . . . that we may then unite in most humbly offering our prayers and supplications to the great Lord and Ruler of Nations, and beseech Him to pardon our national and other transgressions; to enable us all, whether in public or private stations, to perform our several and relative duties properly and punctually; to render our national government a blessing to all the people, by constantly being a government of wise, just, and constitutional laws, discreetly and faithfully executed and obeyed; to protect and guide all sovereigns and nations (especially such as have shown kindness to us), and to bless them with good governments, peace, and concord; to promote the knowledge and practice of true religion and virtue, and the increase of science, among them and us; and, generally, to grant unto all mankind such a degree of temporal prosperity as He alone knows to be best.[11]

Washington believed that (1) good government is a blessing from God; (2) national entities as such should acknowledge, obey, thank, and pray to God; and (3) national entities should seek forgiveness from God for national transgressions as well as individual transgressions.

Another insight into Washington's views comes from a letter he wrote in response to a sermon sent to him by Rev. Joseph Buckmister, pastor of a Presbyterian or Congregational church in Portsmouth, New Hampshire. The sermon, based on Psalm 82, had been preached thirty years earlier by Rev. Benjamin Stevens, pastor of a church in Kittery, Maine. Rev. Stevens stressed that it was the will of God that men should live under some form of civil authority and "in this Sense civil Rulers are of God and his Establishment and Appointment" and are therefore entitled to such great respect that they may even be called gods, as the psalm indicates. However, they too are subject to the one true God, will be judged by him like all other men, and may even be removed by him if they are unfaithful to this calling. Washington thanked Buckmister for the sermon and assured him that it had been "duly read." He added a note

---

11. Washington, Proclamation of First National Thanksgiving, October 3, 1789; quoted by Johnson, *George Washington the Christian*, pp. 173–74.

expressing "my approbation [approval] of the doctrine therein inculcated."[12]

Washington's response to the sermon suggests he understood that (1) God desires men to live under civil authority; (2) God had established rulers over men; (3) civil rulers are therefore entitled to respect; but (4) civil rulers are subject to God; (5) civil rulers will be judged by God; and (6) civil rulers may be removed by God. This was a biblical position, and one about which Washington specifically expressed "my approbation."

Washington understood the national government's responsibility to God. He also understood the role of religion in preserving the nation. A substantial portion of his farewell address identifies and confirms that role:

> Of all the dispositions and habits which lead to political prosperity, Religion and Morality are indispensable supports. In vain would that man claim the tribute of Patriotism, who should labor to subvert these great pillars of human happiness, these firmest props of the duties of Men and Citizens. The mere Politician, equally with the pious man, ought to respect and cherish them. A volume could not trace all their connections with private and public felicity. Let it simply be asked, where is the security for property, for reputation, for life, if the sense of religious obligation desert the oaths which are the instrument of investigation in Courts of Justice? And let us with caution indulge the supposition that morality can be maintained without religion. Whatever may be conceded to the influence of refined education on minds of peculiar structure, reason and experience both forbid us to expect that national morality can prevail in exclusion of religious principle.
>
> It is substantially true that virtue or morality is a necessary spring of popular government. The rule, indeed, extends with more or less force to every species of free government. Who, that is a sincere friend to it, can look with indifference upon attempts to shake the foundation of the fabric?[13]

Washington's words about the "influence of refined education" appear to be directed to the deists, rationalists, and others who believed that man's reason alone could guide him into virtuous conduct. His warning about "attempts to shake the foundation"

---

12. Memoirs of the Long Island Historical Society, 1889, IV: 311; quoted by Johnson, *George Washington the Christian*, pp. 178–80; cf. Boller, *George Washington and Religion*, pp. 78–80.

13. Washington, Farewell Address, September 17, 1796; quoted by Johnson, *George Washington the Christian*, pp. 217–18.

seem to refer to the influence of the French Revolution, about which he felt increasing concern.[14]

Shortly after leaving the presidency, Washington expressed a similar sentiment in a more concise statement. Twenty-five clergymen from the Philadelphia area joined together and wrote Washington expressing their appreciation for his nearly half century of public service and for the remarks about religion in his farewell address. Washington thanked them for their letter, and declared that "Religion and Morality are the essential pillars of civil society."[15,16]

One point is obvious from Washington's statements regarding public recognition of God: he was careful to use terminology which would not offend any religious body.[17] Some examples are: All-Kind Providence, All-Wise and Powerful Being, Divine Author of Our Blessed Religion, Giver of Victory, God of Armies, Pure and Benign Light of Revelation, and Wonderworking Deity. The titles he used to describe God reflected most of the attributes the orthodox apply to God.

However, Washington did not totally refrain from mentioning the name of Jesus Christ or from making references to Christianity. One reference is found in a speech he delivered to the Delaware Chiefs at Washington's Middle Brook headquarters on May 12, 1779. "You will do well to wish to learn our ways of life, and above all, the religion of Jesus Christ. These will make you a greater and happier people than you are."[18] Washington used the term *Christian* on several public occasions. His order regard-

---

14. Boller, *George Washington and Religion*, p. 78.

15. Washington; quoted by Ashabel Green, *The Life of Ashabel Green, by Himself* (1849), p. 615; quoted by Boller, *George Washington and Religion*, p. 82.

16. How strange it is that the above remarks are ignored by legal scholars today, while Jefferson's metaphor about a "wall of separation between church and state" is cited repeatedly by the courts as the definitive statement of what the First Amendment means! (In fact, many Americans seem to think that phrase *is* the First Amendment!) Certainly Washington better embodied the spirit of the times than Jefferson did. Washington was chairman of the Constitutional Convention and President of the United States when the First Amendment was adopted and ratified. During all of this time Jefferson was thousands of miles away, serving as ambassador to France. Jefferson was not a delegate to the Constitutional Convention, nor a member of the Congress that adopted the First Amendment, nor a member of any state convention or legislature that ratified either. And yet his "wall of separation" metaphor, contained in a speech to a Baptist group in 1802, years after the passage of the First Amendment, is widely accepted today while Washington's words are consigned to oblivion. Why? Perhaps the radical separationists find in Jefferson's words (which they misconstrue) what they wish the First Amendment meant, rather than what the founders meant by it.

17. Boller, *George Washington and Religion*, pp. 68ff.

18. Ibid., p. 68.

ing chaplains on July 9, 1776, read: "The General hopes and trusts, that every officer and man, will endeavour so to live, and act, as becomes a Christian soldier defending the dearest Rights and Liberties of his country."[19]

Washington frequently spoke at religious gatherings as General of the Army and while he was President. He addressed, either in person or in writing, the leadership of the Dutch Reformed, Protestant Dutch, German Lutheran, United Baptist, Presbyterian, Methodist, German Reformed, Episcopal, Congregational, Swedenborgian, Quakers, United Brethren, Universalist, and Jewish meetings. He thanked these groups for their contributions to the nation, assured them of his support for religious liberty, requested their prayers before the "Throne of Grace," and promised his prayers for their endeavors. He spoke of the "pure spirit of Christianity" to the Roman Catholics of the nation. To an Episcopal gathering he declared "that Government alone can be approved by Heaven, which promotes peace and secures protection to its Citizens in every thing that is dear and interesting to them. . . ." To the Directors of the Society of the United Brethren (Moravian) for Propagating the Gospel among the Heathen he declared that U.S. Government should "co-operate, as far as the circumstances may conveniently admit, with the disinterested endeavors of your Society to civilize and christianize the Savages of the Wilderness."[20] Washington was known for his cordiality toward and respect for the clergy, and his diary reveals that he attended church regularly when the duties of his office permitted. But Washington attended a variety of churches. He was an Episcopalian so he normally attended Episcopal churches; but he also attended Presbyterian, Dutch Reformed, Luthern, and German Reformed Churches.[21] Shortly after Washington took office, the General Assembly of the Presbyterian church in the U.S.A. sent an address to him declaring that they:

> . . . esteem it a peculiar happiness to behold in our Chief Magistrate, a steady, uniform, avowed friend of the Christian religion; who has commenced his administration in rational and exalted sentiments of piety; and who, in his private conduct, adorns the doctrines of the

19. Ibid., p. 69.
20. Washington's Addresses, reproduced in Boller, *George Washington and Religion*, pp. 163–94.
21. Ibid., pp. 24–25, 29–30.

gospel of Christ; and on the most public and solemn occasions, devoutly acknowledges the government of Divine Providence.[22]

Washington would have been too modest to accept Bishop Meade's characterization of him as like "the great high priest of the nation."[23] But he did regard himself as a spiritual leader and spiritual example to the nation, and people of all denominations regarded him as such.

One aspect of his role as spiritual leader was protector of religious liberty. Washington recognized that "every person may here worship God according to the dictates of his own heart,"[24] and that "every man, conducting himself as a good citizen, and being accountable to God alone for his religious opinions, ought to be protected in worshipping the Deity according to the dictates of his own conscience."[25]

Following through on these beliefs, he ordered General Benedict Arnold:

> As the contempt of the religion of a country by ridiculing any of its ceremonies, or affronting its ministers or votaries, has ever been deeply resented, you are to be particularly careful to restrain every officer and soldier from such imprudence and folly, and to punish every instance of it. On the other hand, as far as lies in your power, you are to protect and support the free exercise of the religion of the country, and the undisturbed enjoyment of the rights of conscience in religious matters, with your utmost influence and authority.[26]

The same day he gave Arnold similar instructions in a letter:

> I also give it in charge to you to avoid all disrespect of the religion of the country, and its ceremonies. Prudence, policy, and a true Christian spirit will lead us to look with compassion upon their errors without insulting them. While we are contending for our own liberty, we should be very cautious not to violate the rights of conscience of

22. General Assembly of the Presbyterian Church in the U.S.A., May 26, 1789; quoted by Johnson, *George Washington the Christian*, p. 166.

23. Bishop Meade, *Old Churches, Ministers and Families of Virginia*, (1872), II:243; quoted by Johnson, *George Washington the Christian*, p. 219.

24. Washington; quoted by Boller, *George Washington and Religion*, p. 116.

25. Washington to the General Committee, representing the United Baptist Churches in Virginia, May 1789; quoted by Boller, *George Washington and Religion*, pp. 169–70.

26. Washington, Order dated September 14, 1775; quoted by Johnson, *George Washington the Christian*, p. 71.

others, ever considering that God alone is the judge of the hearts of men, and to Him only in this case they are answerable.[27]

To Washington, respect for religion and free exercise of religion went hand in hand. He may have been the first person to use the phrase "free exercise of religion" which is now part of the First Amendment.

Washington's insistence on religious freedom came from from his belief in God-given natural rights and God-given natural law. "The smiles of Heaven," he declared, "can never be expected on a nation that disregards the eternal rules of order and right, which Heaven itself has ordained."[28] Government is obliged by God to respect religious freedom. In speaking to the Jews of Rhode Island he referred to their "inherent natural rights," which included freedom of conscience in matters of religion.[29]

Religious liberty is a limit which God placed on rulers:

> Government being, among other purposes, instituted to protect the persons and consciences of men from oppression, it certainly is the duty of rulers, not only to abstain from it themselves, but, according to their stations, to prevent it in others.

> The liberty enjoyed by the people of these States, of worshipping Almighty God agreeably to their consciences, is not only among the choicest of their blessings, but also of their rights. While men perform their social duties faithfully, they do all that society or the state can with propriety demand or expect; and remain responsible only to their Maker for the religion, or modes of faith, which they may prefer or profess.[30]

However, Washington did not oppose government support for religion in general.

When many groups expressed a desire for a Bill of Rights to protect religious and other liberties after the Constitution was adopted, Washington declared to the Virginia Baptists that "no one would be more zealous than myself to establish effectual barriers against the horrors of spiritual tyranny, and every species of

27. Washington, Letter to Colonel Benedict Arnold dated September 14, 1775; quoted by Johnson, *George Washington the Christian*, p. 71.

28. Washington; quoted by Johnson, *George Washington the Christian*, p. 68.

29. Washington, Address to the Hebrew Congregation in Newport, Rhode Island, August 17, 1790; quoted by Boller, *George Washington and Religion*, pp. 185–86.

30. Washington to the Quakers at their yearly meeting for Pennsylvania, New Jersey, Delaware, and the western part of Maryland and Virginia, October, 1789; quoted by Boller, *George Washington and Religion*, pp. 179–80.

religious persecution."[31] This statement summarized Washington's view of the First Amendment. His choice of the metaphor *barriers* reflects Washington's military background and is especially interesting when compared with Thomas Jefferson's oft-quoted metaphor *wall of separation*. Actually, Washington's metaphor is a much better statement of what the First Amendment means, no doubt the result of his direct involvement with the Constitution and the First Amendment. He saw the First Amendment not as a prohibition of every interaction of church and state, but only those activities which constitute persecution or spiritual tyranny.

Washington believed both government and rulers are ordained by God for the ordering of society and both should acknowledge and obey God. Religion and morality are the pillars of society, so government should encourage religion. But government should avoid doctrinal disputes by not favoring one denomination over another and should protect the free exercise of religion. As Washington put it, "While just government protects all in their religious rights, true religion affords to government its surest support."[32]

In discussing the role of religion in the life of Washington as a statesman, some skeptics cite the 1797 Treaty of Tripoli as evidence that he was not a Christian. However, research into that treaty (which was negotiated in 1796 to secure safe passage for American ships through waters near the Barbary Coast of North Africa) shows it was not signed by Washington.

The copy of that treaty recently circulated is a fraud. There is also evidence that Article 11 of that treaty which stated ". . . the government of the United States of America is not in any sense founded on the Christian Religion. . . ." was actually not part of that treaty. A revised version of the Treaty of Tripoli, accepted April 17, 1806, after the U.S. went to war with Tripoli does not contain the phrase in question.

The controversy was based on false information and therefore does not relate to the debate concerning Washington's religious beliefs. For a comprehensive discussion of the Treaty of Tripoli, see appendix 1.

31. Washington to the General Committee representing the United Baptist Churches in Virginia, May 1789; quoted by Boller, *George Washington and Religion*, pp. 169–70.
32. Washington to the Synod of the Reformed Dutch Church in North America, October 1789; quoted by Boller, *George Washington and Religion*, pp. 177-78.

Washington the Man

George Washington spoke and wrote about God in general terms but remained silent about specific doctrines. His reluctance to speak brought him the label of deist. In the nineteenth century most writers assumed Washington was a Christian. Many of his contemporaries also assumed he was a Christian though a few suspected him of deism. Interestingly those of his own time who suspected him of deism were often Christians who hoped he would more openly speak out for the doctrines of their faith. Today, those who call him a deist are frequently the skeptics who see his silence as the absence of Christian beliefs.

The argument for deism then and now is based on his silence. There is no written evidence that Washington was a deist. He never claimed to be a deist. Records show that he was a mason, but the masons cannot be called a deist organization; people of all faiths belong to masonry. And masonry had a very limited influence on Washington. He wrote to Rev. G. W. Snyder in 1798 that far from "Presiding over the English lodges in this country" as Snyder supposed, he had not been in a masonic lodge "more than once or twice within the last thirty years."[33]

Washington's upbringing, actions and words indicate that he was a Christian.

His Upbringing

George was born February 22, 1732, the eldest son of Augustine and Mary Washington (Augustine also had children by his first wife). Later, August and Mary had a daughter named Betty. Both of George's parents came from a long line of churchmen.[34]

August planned to send George to Appleby Grammar School in England, the same school which he attended as a child. However, August died at age forty-nine, when George was eleven, so George received most of his education at home. Before August died he instilled in George many of the precepts and principles he learned at Appleby, which included academics and obedience based on the Bible. Wilbur describes an example of August Washington's teaching techniques:

33. Washington to G. W. Snyder, 1798; quoted by John C. Fitzpatrick, ed., *The Writings of George Washington from the Original Manuscript Sources, 1745-1799* (Washington, D.C.: U.S. Govt. Printing Office, 1931-1944), XXXVI:453; quoted by Victor L. Smith, "An Analysis of the Religious Beliefs of George Washington," Senior Paper Submitted to History Department, Dr. David Poteet, Oral Roberts University, Tulsa, Oklahoma, 1982, p. 51.

34. Johnson, *George Washington the Christian*, p. 17.

In teaching his children August had a quiet way of employing a simple practical illustration to explain his meaning and to drive home the lesson. For example, one day George lost his temper and blurted out an unwarranted, extreme remark because his sister Betty did not understand something he was trying to teach her. The quiet, kindly little girl was hurt, and started to cry.

By the time that father August had grasped the situation George was very sorry for what he had done.

With some deliberateness August cut two branches from a bush, then said, "Here are two branches that I have cut from this bush. I want each of you to take a branch and break it into two separate sticks."

In a moment each child had two halves, each one frayed at the point where it had been broken.

"George," August then said, "can you put your two pieces back together, just as they were before you broke them?"

George put the frayed ends of his sticks together, but realized at once the hopelessness of the task.

"Betty, can you put your stick back together, make it as good as new?"

The little girl put the ends together and then ruefully shook her head. "No, Father," she said, "I can't."

"You both agree," said August, "that you can't put them together. I can't either. No human being can. No matter how much we may wish to do so, we can never put the pieces back together. We cannot undo what we have done."

Then he went on. "These sticks illustrate a very important lesson. Just before I asked you to break them, George lost his temper and said something for which he is now very sorry.

"He wishes, oh so deeply, that he could somehow bring back those words, and *un*say them. But no matter how sorry you may be George, you cannot recall those harsh, unwarranted terms. The words are something like the stick. It is broken into two parts and the two parts can never be put back together.

"One of the rules that I learned at Appleby Grammar School fits our problem very well. It was a simple one, 'Think before you speak.'

"Another Appleby rule also applies. It was 'Speak no injurious words, either in jest or in earnest.'"

August didn't need to say more.[35]

Here is another recorded example of August Washington's teaching:

George's size and strength were often commented on by well-

35. Ibid., pp. 63–64.

meaning friends and neighbors. When such a thing happened Father August made a later comment like, "George, we are all very pleased that you are big and strong. But while you also, can be pleased, you should realize that you have no reason to preen yourself about it. My father was a big man. He passed on to me an unusually fine, powerful body. The Lord has seen fit to pass it on to you. You have not achieved it by your own thinking or working. It is entirely a gift from others.

"The same would be true," Father went on, "if someone should tell you, or your sister Betty, that you are handsome, have beautiful hair, or fine eyes, or a nice mouth. You have no cause to assume credit for any of these things. They are all a gift from your parents and your grandparents.

"But if someone should say, 'George is a very well-behaved boy!', 'How obedient and thoughtful George is!', or 'How considerate Betty is!', 'How helpful both George and Betty are!' If someone made comments like these, then the situation would be very different. Then you could be proud and somewhat satisfied because you, yourself, had created a situation that brought deserved praise."[36]

It appears August Washington was an honest, hardworking, God-fearing family man who was close to nature and used nature to teach his children.[37] As a church vestryman, August probably attended church regularly and took his family with him.[38] George appears to have been very close to his father, but their relationship was broken off by the father's death at age forty-nine on April 12, 1743, when George was eleven years old. Physicians diagnosed the cause of death as gout, but some scholars today believe it may have been a heart attack. On his deathbed August gave George and the rest of his family this testimony:

> I thank God that in all my life I never struck a man in anger; for had I done so I am sure (so great is my strength) that I would have killed my antagonist. Then his blood, at this awesome moment, would lie heavily on my soul. As it is, I die at peace with all mankind.[39]

George, who had idolized his father, missed him greatly, even though his older half-brothers Lawrence and Austin took him under their wing and supervised his studies. Evidence of his longing for his

---

36. Ibid., pp. 77–78.

37. Nathaniel Wright Stephenson and Waldo Hillary Dunn, *George Washington* (London: Oxford University Press, 1940), pp. 27–28.

38. William H. Wilbur, *The Making of George Washington* (Caldwell, Id.: 1970, 1973), p. 43.

39. August Washington, quoted by Wilbur, p. 92.

father is found in a book which became the property of George on his father's death. In the book, *Short Discourse on the Common Prayer* by Rev. Thomas Comber, the names of August and Mary Washington are inscribed in their own handwriting. In that book George carefully wrote his father's name nine times, and also the monograms "AW." As Wilbur says, "Young George certainly had no intention of leaving a message for posterity; he wasn't thinking of others, he was communing with his dead father."[40] Wilbur adds,

> It seems logical to conclude that the little book of Discourses was particularly precious to George. The signatures of both his father and his mother are on the front flyleaf; it is quite certain that his mother had read passages from it to the children many times; and his father had assigned George reading lessons in it on many occasions. His father's signature certainly helped to bring back the dead man's presence.
>
> Rev. Thomas Comber's *Discourses* may well have been the first grown-up book that George ever owned. This gave it added importance in his eyes and increased the effect that it had on the development of his character.[41]

Obviously young George carefully studied the eight-page discourse on the Lord's Prayer and other gems of wisdom contained in this book. No doubt these Discourses reminded George of his father and also helped to shape his religious beliefs. These excerpts are an indication of the material discussed: [Sins of uncleanness are] "punished by the laws of God and man" [because] "they defile both soul and body"; "no sin more early or easily steals on unwary youth," "destroys families," [and] "destroys the strength and takes away the courage of the bravest men."

[The Lord's Prayer is] "the epitome of the Gospel . . . containing our persuasion of God's love, our desire of his honor, our subjection to his authority, our submission to his will, our dependence on his providence; our need of his mercy to pardon former offences and of His Grace to keep us from future sins; and of both to deliver us from the punishment of us all." According to Wilbur, "Reverend Comber's little book expresses much of George Washington's religion. He was never interested in theological questions; he had

40. Wilbur, p. 96.
41. Ibid.

absolute faith in the omnipotent power of God. Washington's religion was one of complete and quiet trust in his Creator."[42]

George's mother, Mary Washington, also influenced his religious beliefs. The family belonged to the Church of England and George was baptized into the church on April 22, 1732. Mary was a pious woman. She frequently read the Bible and other religious books to George. A well-worn and much-marked copy of *Contemplations: Moral and Divine* by Sir Matthew Hale was found in Washington's library after his death. It bore the inscription "Mary Washington."[43]

Mary Washington was devoted to her son, and he returned that devotion. Her last words to George shortly before her death at age eighty-two showed that she believed God had a special plan for George in his new position as President:

> And you will see me no more. My great age, and the disease which is fast approaching my vitals, warn me that I shall not be long in this world. I trust in God that I may be somewhat prepared for a better. But go, George, fulfill the high destinies which Heaven appears to have intended for you; go, my son, and may that Heaven's and a mother's blessing be with you always.[44]

Lawrence Washington, George's half-brother, took over much of the responsibility for George's schooling after the death of August. Wilbur describes Lawrence as "a man of high ideals and solid religious beliefs, well above the average Virginian of his day in these qualities," who shared with George not only the Greek and Roman heroes but the Old Testament as well.

Perhaps at Lawrence's insistence, George made a habit of copying things that were important to him. One of the things he copied was a series of maxims commonly called "Hawkins' Rules." The rules, which both August and Lawrence Washington learned at

42. Wilbur, p. 98. Several of George's notebooks from school days have been preserved. In one is the entry: "If you can't find it in the Book of Ezekiel, look in Israel" (Israel was the name commonly used at that time for the first five books of the Old Testament), p. 126. When he was thirteen, he either composed or copied a hymn which begins: "Assist me, Muse divine, to sing the Morn,/On Which the Saviour of Mankind was born. W. Herbert Burk, *Washington's Prayer* (1907), p. 12; quoted by Johnson, *George Washington the Christian*, p. 21.

43. Sir Matthew Hale, *Contemplations: Moral and Divine* (London, 1695); John N. Norton, *Life of General Washington*, (1870), p. 34; cited by Johnson, *George Washington the Christian*, pp. 19–20.

44. Benson J. Lossing, *The Pictorial Field-Book of the Revolution* (1860), II:220; quoted by Johnson, *George Washington the Christian*, p. 157.

Appleby Grammar School in England, consisted of admonitions to practice self-restraint, modesty, and consideration for others.

Washington's youthful piety is revealed in the prayers found in a twenty-four page manuscript book, titled "Daily Sacrifice." The booklet was found in April 1891 among a collection of Washington's papers. The manuscript is the actual handwriting of George Washington at about the age of twenty; but it is uncertain whether Washington composed the prayers himself or copied them from another source. He cites no source and no source has been found to date, so it is likely that he composed them. However, even if they are copied it is significant that he considered the lengthy prayers worth copying. These Sunday prayers were used by Washington at age 20:

Sunday Morning

Almighty God, and most merciful father, who didst command the children of Israel to offer a daily sacrifice to thee, that thereby they might glorify and praise thee for thy protection both night and day; receive, O Lord, my morning sacrifice which I now offer up to thee; I yield thee humble and hearty thanks that thou has preserved me from the dangers of the night past, and brought me to the light of this day, and the comforts thereof, a day which is consecrated to thine own service and for thine own honor. Let my heart, therefore, Gracious God, be so affected with the glory and majesty of it, that I may not do mine own works, but wait on thee, and discharge those weighty duties thou requirest of me; and since thou art a God of pure eyes, and wilt be sanctified in all who draw near unto thee, who doest not regard the sacrifice of fools, nor hear sinners who tread in the courts, pardon, I beseech thee, my sins, remove them from thy presence, as far as the east is from the west, and accept of me for the merits of thy son Jesus Christ, that when I come into thy temple, and compass thine altar, my prayers may come before thee as incense; and as thou wouldst hear me calling upon thee in my prayers, so give me grace to hear thee calling on me in thy word, that it may be wisdom, righteousness, reconciliation and peace to the saving of my soul in the day of the Lord Jesus. Grant that I may hear it with reverence, receive it with meekness, mingle it with faith, and that it may accomplish in me, Gracious God, the good work for which thou has sent it. Bless my family, kindred, friends and country, be our God & guide this day and for ever for his sake, who lay down in the Grave and arose again for us, Jesus Christ our Lord, Amen.

Sunday Evening

O most Glorious God, in Jesus Christ my merciful and loving father, I acknowledge and confess my guilt, in the weak and imperfect performance of the duties of this day. I have called on thee for pardon and forgiveness of sins, but so coldly and carelessly, that my prayers are become my sin and stand in need of pardon. I have heard thy holy word, but with such deadness of spirit that I have been an unprofitable and forgetful hearer, so that, O Lord, tho' I have done thy work, yet it hath been so negligently that I may rather expect a curse than a blessing from thee. But, O God, who art rich in mercy and plenteous in redemption, mark not, I beseech thee, what I have done amiss; remember that I am but dust, and remit my transgressions, negligences & ignorances, and cover them all with the absolute obedience of thy dear Son, that those sacrifices which I have offered may be accepted by thee, in and for the sacrifice of Jesus Christ offered upon the cross for me; for his sake, ease me of the burden of my sins, and give me grace that by the call of the Gospel I may rise from the slumber of sin into the newness of life. Let me live according to those holy rules which thou has this day prescribed in thy holy word; make me to know what is acceptable in thy sight, and therein to delight, open the eyes of my understanding, and help me thoroughly to examine myself concerning my knowledge, faith and repentance, increase my faith, and direct me to the true object Jesus Christ the way, the truth and the life, bless, O Lord, all the people of this land, from the highest to the lowest, particularly those whom thou hast appointed to rule over us in church & state. continue thy goodness to me this night. These weak petitions I humbly implore thee to hear accept and ans. for the sake of thy Dear Son Jesus Christ our Lord, Amen.

Age 20, 1752[45]

It is unknown whether additional pages have been lost or if the prayers were never completed.[46] The prayers show the recognition of Jesus Christ as the Son of God, "my only saviour," whose blood was shed on the cross "for me," respect for God's "holy word," a desire to be more like Jesus, a recognition of personal sin, a desire to be delivered from the "cunning of the devil, or deceitfulness of sin," acknowledgement of need for the "means of Grace," prayers for the rulers of church and state, and watchfulness for the "coming of the Lord Jesus" and the time when "the trumpet shall sound, and the dead shall arise and stand before the judgment seat. . . ." These are the sentiments of an orthodox Christian.

---

45. W. Herbert Burk, *Washington's Prayer* (1907), pp. 87–95; quoted by Johnson, *George Washington the Christian*, pp. 24–35.

46. Burk, *Prayers*, pp. 87–95; quoted in Johnson, *George Washington the Christian*, p. 35.

His Actions

Loren P. Beth, a noted liberal constitutional scholar, claims that George Washington was not a church member.[47] He is wrong.

There is documented proof that Washington was a member of the Truro Parish of the Anglican (Episcopal) Church; he was a vestry-man of the church, and served as church warden.[48] The old vestry book of Pohick Church, part of Truro Parish, contains this entry: "At a Vestry held for Truro Parish, October 25, 1762, ordered, that George Washington, Esq. be chosen and appointed one of the Vestry-men of this Parish, in the room of William Peake, Gent. deceased."[49] Washington was required to take an oath of office, since as a vestryman he also exercised civic functions. This is noted in early court records:

> At a Court held for the County of Fairfax, 15th February, 1763— George Washington, Esq. took the oaths according to Law, repeated and subscribed the Test and subscribed to the Doctrine and Discipline of the Church of England in order to qualify him to act as a Vestryman of Truro Parish.[50]

Washington's signed oath was found on a leaf of the church record of Pohick:

> I, A B, do declare that I will be conformable to the Doctrine and Discipline of the Church of England, as by law established.
>
> 1765. May 20th—Thomas Withers Coffer, Thomas Ford, John Ford.
>
> 19th August—Geo. Washington, Daniel M'Carty, ...[51]

The Church of England, while not as strict as the Congregational or Puritan churches, nevertheless held to the orthodox Christian view of the Trinity, the Divinity of Jesus Christ as the Second Person of the Trinity, the efficacy of the atonement on the cross, and the sinfulness of man. A deist or Unitarian could not in good conscience sign such a statement.

47. Loren P. Beth, *The American Theory of Church and State* (Gainesville, Florida: University of Florida Press, 1958), p. 73.

48. W. M. Clark, *Colonial Churches* (1907), p. 113; cited by Johnson, *George Washington the Christian*, pp. 51–52.

49. Clark; quoted by Johnson, *George Washington the Christian*, p. 49.

50. Ibid., pp. 49–50.

51. Lossing, *Field-Book*, II:215; quoted by Johnson, *George Washington the Christian*, p. 50.

Vestry meetings were held at various churches within the parish ranging from seven to twenty miles from Washington's home. Vestry records show Washington attended meetings regularly.[52] His diary also reflects his presence at the meetings, as well as faithful though not unfailing attendance at church services throughout his life. Occasionally weather or his public office duties prevented him from going to church. Church involvement during that period took a major portion of the day, given the distances traveled and modes of transportation. When Washington was unable to attend church he conducted services at home.[53]

Records show that Washington also drew plans for a new church building at Pohick and contributed money for the building project. He also contributed to other churches which he attended.[54]

The fact that Washington sometimes abstained from communion while he was President and possibly on other occasions, causes many historians to question his faith. Bishop White, of the Episcopal Church in Philadelphia, claimed that Washington did not receive communion while attending his church during his presidency.[55]

Other accounts establish that Washington did at times receive communion. Major Popham, who served under Washington during the War, wrote to Mrs. Jane Washington on March 14, 1839:

In a conversation with the Reverend Doctor Berrian, a few days since, he informed me that he had lately paid a visit to Mount Vernon, and that Mrs. Washington had expressed a wish to have a doubt removed from her mind, which had long oppressed her, as to the certainty of the General's having attended the communion while residing in the city of New York subsequent to the Revolution. As nearly all the remnants of those days are now sleeping with their fathers, it is not very probable that at this late day an individual can be found who could satisfy this pious wish of your virtuous heart except the writer. It was my great good fortune to have attended St. Paul's Church in this city with the General during the whole period of his residence in New York as President of the United States. The pew of Chief-Justice Morris was situated next to that of the President, close to whom I constantly sat in Judge Morris's pew, and I am as confident as a memory now laboring under the pressure of fourscore

52. Ibid., p. 51.
53. Ibid.
54. Clark and Norton; cited by Johnson, *George Washington the Christian*, p. 55.
55. William White to Colonel Hugh Mercer, Philadelphia, August 15, 1835; quoted by Boller, *George Washington and Religion*, p. 33. It might be noted that Bishop White supervised several churches and could not have observed Washington every Sunday.

years and seven can make me, that the President had more than once—I believe I may say often—attended at the sacramental table, at which I had the privilege and happiness to kneel with him. And I am aided in my associations by my elder daughter, who distinctly recollects her grandmamma—Mrs. Morris—often mentioned that fact with great pleasure.[56]

In an 1855 letter, General S. H. Lewis claimed General Porterfield, the brigade-inspector under Washington, told him:

General Washington was a pious man, and a member of your church (Episcopal). I saw him myself on his knees receive the sacrament of the Lord's Supper in _____ Church, in Philadelphia.

He specified the time and place. My impression is that Christ Church was the place, and Bishop White, as he afterward was, the minister. This is, to the best of my recollection, an accurate statement of what I heard from General Porterfield on the subject.[57]

There is also an account of Washington taking communion with Presbyterians while encamped at Morristown.

While the American army, under the command of Washington, lay encamped at Morristown, New Jersey (winter of 1776-7), it occurred that the service of the communion (then observed semi-annually only) was to be administered in the Presbyterian church of that village. In a morning of the previous week the General, after his accustomed inspection of the camp, visited the house of the Rev. Doctor Jones (Johnes), then pastor of the church, and, after the usual preliminaries, thus accosted him:

"Doctor, I understand that the Lord's Supper is to be celebrated with you next Sunday. I would learn if it accords with the canon of your church to admit communicants of another denomination?"

The Doctor rejoined, "Most certainly; ours is not the Presbyterian table, General, but the Lord's table; and we hence give the Lord's invitation to all his followers, of whatever name."

The General replied, "I am glad of it; that is as it ought to be; but, as I was not quite sure of the fact, I thought I would ascertain it from yourself, as I propose to join with you on that occasion. Though a member of the Church of England, I have no exclusive partialities."

56. Major Popham to Mrs. Jane Washington, New York, March 14, 1839; quoted by Johnson, *George Washington the Christian*, pp. 189–90.

57. General S. H. Lewis, to Rev. Mr. Dana, Alexandria, Virginia, December 14, 1855; quoted by Johnson, *George Washington the Christian*, pp. 194–95.

The Doctor reassured him of a cordial welcome, and the General was found seated with the communicants the next Sabbath.[58]

Bishop Meade, who was Bishop of Virginia from 1829-1862 offers one insight into why Washington occasionally abstained from communion. He suggests that in Washington's day there was a "most mistaken notion, too prevalent both in England and America, that it was not so necessary in the professors of religion to communicate at all times, but that in this respect persons might be regulated by their feelings" and circumstances. He adds, "Into this error of opinion and practice General Washington may have fallen, especially at a time when he was peculiarly engaged with the cares of government and a multiplicity of engagements, and when his piety may have suffered some loss thereby."[59] William Dunlap, Canon of Washington Cathedral, suggested that "Washington entertained such a vivid appreciation of the grace received through participating in the sacrament of the Lord's Supper as to warrant his refraining from participating in it when circumstances or temperament led him to believe he was not through preparation of mind and heart in the proper condition for its reception."[60] But Trevelyan probably summarizes it best: "Washington always had his reasons for what he did, or left undone; but he seldom gave them; and his motive for abstaining from the sacrament was not a subject on which he would be inclined to break his ordinary rule of reticence."[61]

Many have questioned Washington's communion practices, but few doubt that he was a man of prayer. Many accounts establish that he and his wife, Martha, engaged in regular private devotions. George Washington Parke Custis, George and Martha's grandson whom they later adopted, relates Washington's tearful prayer at the bedside of his dying stepdaughter.[62] Custis adds, "Throughout the war, as it was understood in his military family, he gave a part of

58. Rev. Samuel H. Coxe, quoted by David Hosack, M.D., *Memoir of DeWitt Clinton* 1829, p. 183; quoted by Johnson, *George Washington the Christian*, pp. 87–88.

59. Meade; quoted by Johnson, *George Washington the Christian*, p. 197.

60. William Dunlap; quoted by Edward Slater Dunlap, *George Washington as a Christian and Churchman* (Washington, D.C., 1932), p. 10; quoted by Boller, *George Washington and Religion*, p. 35.

61. Sir George Trevelyan, *The American Revolution* (1908), III:309; quoted by Johnson, *George Washington the Christian*, p. 98.

62. George Washington Parke Custis, *Recollections and Private Memoirs of Washington*, ed. Benson J. Lossing (1860), p. 21; cited by Johnson, *George Washington the Christian*, pp. 60–61; see also Norton, *Life of Washington*, p. 123.

every day to private prayer and devotion."[63] Cornelius Doremus, with whose family General Washington lived for part of the winter of 1781 in Pequannock, New Jersey, stated that his bedroom was directly over that of Washington's and that he often heard Washington's voice in prayer.[64] General Robert Porterfield related that he once found General Washington on his knees in morning devotions. General Porterfield mentioned this to General Hamilton who informed him that this was Washington's regular habit.[65] Numerous other accounts of Washington in prayer exist.

Washington's prayer habits also included table grace. He would ask a clergyman to lead in prayer if one was present. If not, he led in prayer. On one occasion at Mount Vernon, Washington asked a clergyman to lead in prayer and then, apparently out of habit, proceeded to say the grace. Martha interrupted, "My dear, you forgot that you had a clergyman dining with you today." Washington then replied pleasantly, "My dear, I wish clergymen and all men to know that I am not a graceless man."[66]

Besides declaring days of prayer and fasting, as General and as President, Washington fasted himself. For example, his diary entry for June 1, 1774, reads, "Went to church, and fasted all day."[67]

Although Washington kept his religious beliefs to himself, he lived the life of a pious Christian. He attended church regularly, served as a church officer, took communion except for one and possibly two periods of his life, prayed and held devotions both publicly and privately, fasted, and was at all times respectful toward God and Christianity. Years after Washington's death Rev. Lee Massey, rector of the parish which included Mount Vernon from 1765 into the 1770s, wrote:

> I never knew so constant an attendant on church as Washington. And his behavior in the house of God was ever so deeply reverential that it produced the happiest effects on my congregation, and greatly assisted me in my pulpit labors. . . .

63. Custis; quoted by Johnson, *George Washington the Christian*, p. 131.

64. Mrs. C. M. Kirkland; cited by Johnson, *George Washington the Christian*, p. 131.

65. Meade; quoted by Johnson, *George Washington the Christian*, pp. 130–31.

66. William B. Sprague, *Annals of the American Pulpit* (New York, 1859-69), III:440; quoted by Boller, *George Washington and Religion*, p. 37.

67. Washington, Diary, June 1, 1774; quoted by Johnson, *George Washington the Christian*, p. 62.

No company ever withheld him from church. I have often been at Mount Vernon on the Sabbath morning when his breakfast table was filled with guests, but to him they furnished no pretext for neglecting his God, and losing the satisfaction of setting a good example. For, instead of staying at home, out of false complaisance to them, he used constantly to invite them to accompany him.[68]

His Words

Some questions are still troubling: Why wasn't Washington more outspoken about his Christian faith? Was he a deist? If he truly was a Christian, why wouldn't he say so?

In some ways he did. Even if the secondhand accounts of Weems and others are discounted, there remain noteworthy references to Christian beliefs.

J. B. Buckley, writing in 1896, explained Washington's reticence about his beliefs by saying that it "was not then, and is not now the habit of Christian men to mention the name of Christ in correspondence upon general subjects."[69] Observing Christians in various walks of life accentuates the fact that some Christians witness more with words, others more by deeds.

Washington's position of national leadership may have led to his reluctance to speak out on doctrinal issues. A letter he wrote to Brigadier-General Nelson on August 20, 1778, reflects that mentality:

> The hand of Providence has been conspicuous in all this, that he must be worse than an infidel that lacks faith, and more than wicked that has not gratitude enough to acknowledge his obligations. But it will be time enough for me to turn preacher when my present appointment ceases; and therefore I shall add no more on the doctrine of Providence.[70]

Even privately, Washington appears to have disliked doctrinal disputes. He called such disputes "the most inveterate and distressing" of all the "animosities which have existed among mankind." He hoped policies of religious toleration would reconcile "Christians of every denomination so far that we should never again see their religious disputes carried to such a pitch as to endanger the

---

68. Rev. Lee Massey; quoted by Johnson, *George Washington the Christian*, p. 546.

69. J. B. Buckley, "Washington as a Christian and a Communicant," *Independent*, February 19, 1898, p. 206; quoted by Boller, *George Washington and Religion*, p. 75.

70. Washington to Brig. Gen. Nelson, August 20, 1778; quoted by Johnson, *George Washington the Christian*, pp. 119–20.

peace of society.''[71] As for himself, he declared, ''. . . in politics, as in religion, my tenets are few and simple. . . .''[72]

Washington did express distinct religious sentiments which identify him as a Christian. The prayers he penned as a young man of about twenty indicate his Christian commitment; at least once he referred to Jesus Christ. On June 8, 1783, Washington sent a circular letter to the governors of the thirteen states from his headquarters in Newburgh, New York. He closed that letter with a prayer that God would:

> . . . most graciously be pleased to dispose us all, to do Justice, to love mercy, and to demean ourselves with that Charity, humility, and pacific temper of mind, which were the Characteristicks of the Divine Author of our blessed Religion, and without an humble imitation of whose example in these things, we can never hope to be a happy Nation.[73]

The characteristics he listed—charity, humility, pacific temper—identify the ''Divine Author'' as Jesus Christ. By referring to Jesus Christ as the ''Divine Author of our blessed Religion,'' Washington implied his belief in the divinity of Jesus Christ; this set him apart from the deists and Unitarians of his day. Concerning this passage, Washington's biographer, Henry Cabot Lodge declared categorically, ''Washington either believed in the divinity of Christ or when he wrote those words he deliberately stated something which he did not believe.''[74] In other words, if Washington was a deist he must have been a liar and a hypocrite as well!

That same circular letter also contained an interesting insight into Washington's view of the Bible. In the letter he refers to the ''pure and benign light of Revelation.'' Washington believed religious truth was revealed by God in his Holy Word. This set Washington apart from the deists and rationalists who rejected divine revelation and

71. Washington to Sir Edward Newenham, October 20, 1792; quoted by Johnson, *George Washington the Christian*, p. 211.

72. Washington to Dr. James Anderson, December 24, 1795; quoted by Boller, *George Washington and Religion*, p. 92.

73. Washington, Circular Letter to Governors, June 8, 1783; quoted in Boller, *George Washington and Religion*, p. 71. On page 76 Boller makes an interesting observation. Noting the tendency of deists of the day like Thomas Paine to refer to Jesus as ''an amiable and virtuous man,'' Boller notes the absence of such references in Washington's writings: ''. . . nowhere in Washington's letters does there appear a humanistic reference, direct or implied, to Jesus and his teachings.'' Perhaps the argument from silence can cut both ways!

74. Henry Cabot Lodge, Letter to *New York Daily Tribune*, May 26, 1902; quoted by Boller, *George Washington and Religion*, p. 72.

believed that man comes to religious truth and other truth through the power of human reason.

In some notes which Washington wrote in preparation for one of his public addresses, he referred to "The blessed Religion revealed in the word of God. . . ."[75] He did not use those notes, but they indicate that he regarded the Bible as the Word of God and that he considered the revelation of the Bible to be the source of our religious beliefs and principles.

Other historical records show that Washington ordered Bibles and prayer books for his two stepchildren ages eight and six in 1761. Washington's name headed the list of subscribers to the "Self-Interpreting Bible" of John Brown, a Scottish Presbyterian, when that work was published in 1792.[76] In 1795 Washington acknowledged receipt of a Bible, and considered that Bible important enough to bequeath to his friend Bryan Lord Fairfax.[77]

It also appears that Washington believed in original sin. His speech notes made reference to "human depravity,"[78] and his order of March 6, 1776, called for a day of fasting, prayer, and humiliation "to implore the Lord and Giver of all victory to pardon our manifold sins and wickedness."[79]

On several occasions Washington expressed belief in life after death. Shortly after his stepdaughter Martha Custis died on June 19, 1773, Washington wrote, "The sweet, innocent girl entered into a more happy and peaceful abode than she had met with in the afflicted path she had hitherto trod."[80] When his mother died in 1789 he wrote a letter to his sister in which he thanked God that their mother had had a long and healthy life, and declared that "Under these considerations, and the hope that she is translated to a happier place, it is the duty of her relatives to yield due submission to the decrees of the Creator."[81] In a letter to Secretary of War James McHenry, Washington expressed the hope shortly before his death "that no reproach may attach itself to me, when I have taken my departure for the land of Spirits."[82]

75. Washington; quoted by Boller, *George Washington and Religion*, p. 41.

76. Marion Simms, *The Bible in America* (New York, 1936), p. 132.

77. Washington, Last Will and Testament, July 9, 1799; cited by Boller, *George Washington and Religion*, p. 40.

78. Washington; quoted by Boller, *George Washington and Religion*, p. 41.

79. Washington, Order dated March 6, 1776; quoted by Johnson, *George Washington the Christian*, p. 77.

80. Paul Leicester Ford, *The True George Washington* (1903), p. 29.

81. Washington to Betty Lewis, 1789; quoted by Johnson, *George Washington the Christian*, p. 172.

82. Washington to James McHenry, March 25, 1799; quoted by Boller, *George Washington and Religion*, p. 112.

Washington's last days revealed more of his faith and courage but little more of his doctrine. As he lay dying at the age of sixty-seven, he said to his physician, "Doctor, I die hard, but I am not afraid to go."[83] A little later he asked his secretary, Tobias Lear, to have him decently buried and not to bury him until he had been dead for three days; when Lear said he understood, Washington replied, " 'Tis well."[84] The adopted grandson George Washington Parke Custis wrote, "In that last hour, prayer was not wanting at the throne of grace. Close to the couch of the sufferer, resting her head upon that ancient book, with which she had been wont to hold pious communion a portion every day for more than half a century, was the venerable consort [Mrs. Washington] absorbed in silent prayer."[85]

M'Guire adds that once or twice in those last hours Washington was heard to say, "I should have been glad, had it pleased God, to die a little easier, but I doubt not it is for my good."[86]

Did Washington embrace Christianity? His adopted daughter thought so. Nelly Custis was Martha Washington's granddaughter, and when Nelly's father died, George and Martha Washington adopted her and she lived in their home for twenty years. In 1833 she wrote to the historian Jared Sparks, expressing indignation that anyone would question Washington's Christianity:

> ... General Washington had a pew in Pohick Church, and one in Christ Church at Alexandria. He was very instrumental in establishing Pohick Church, and I believe subscribed largely. His pew was near the pulpit. . . .
>
> He attended the church at Alexandria when the weather and roads permitted a ride of ten miles. In New York and Philadelphia he never omitted attendance at church in the morning, unless detained by indisposition. . . . No one in church attended to the service with more reverential respect. My grandmother, who was eminently pious, never deviated from her early habits. She always knelt. The General, as was then the custom, stood during the devotional parts of the service. On communion Sundays he left the church with me, after the blessing, and returned home, and we sent the carriage back for my grandmother.

83. Sparks; quoted by Johnson, *George Washington the Christian*, p. 232; cf. Boller, *George Washington and Religion*, p. 113.

84. Franklin B. Hough, *Memorials of the Death of Washington* (1865); quoted by Johnson, *George Washington the Christian*, pp. 233-34; cf. Boller, *George Washington and Religion*, p. 113.

85. Custis; quoted by Johnson, *George Washington the Christian*, pp. 234–35.

86. M'Guire; quoted by Johnson, *George Washington the Christian*, p. 233.

It was his custom to retire to his library at nine or ten o'clock, where he remained an hour before he went to his chamber. He always rose before the sun, and remained in his library until called for breakfast. I never witnessed his private devotions. I never inquired about them. I should have thought it the greatest heresy to doubt his firm belief in Christianity. His life, his writings, prove that he was a Christian. He was not one of those who act or pray, "that they may be seen of men." He communed with his God in secret.

My mother resided two years at Mount Vernon, after her marriage with John Parke Custis, the only son of Mrs. Washington. I have heard her say that General Washington always received the sacrament with my grandmother before the Revolution. When my aunt, Miss Custis, died suddenly at Mount Vernon, before they could realize the event, he knelt by her and prayed most fervently, most affectingly, for her recovery. Of this I was assured by Judge Washington's mother, and other witnesses.

He was a silent, thoughtful man. He spoke little generally; never of himself. I never heard him relate a single act of his life during the war. I have often seen him perfectly abstracted, his lips moving, but no sound was perceptible. I have sometimes made him laugh most heartily from sympathy with my joyous and extravagant spirits. I was, probably, one of the last persons on earth to whom he would have addressed serious conversation, particularly when he knew that I had the most perfect model of female excellence ever with me as my monitress, who acted the part of a tender and devoted parent, loving me as only a mother can love, and never extenuating or approving in me what she disapproved in others. She never omitted her private devotions, or her public duties; she and her husband were so perfectly united and happy that he must have been a Christian. She had no doubts, no fears for him. After forty years of devoted affection and uninterrupted happiness, she resigned him without a murmur into the arms of his Saviour and his God, with the assured hope of eternal felicity. Is it necessary that any one should certify, "General Washington avowed himself to *me* a believer in Christianity"? As well may we question his patriotism, his heroic, disinterested devotion to his country. His mottoes were, "Deeds, Not Words"; and "For God and My Country."

> With sentiments of esteem,
> I am,
> Nelly Custis[87]

---

87. Nelly Custis to Jared Sparks, February 26, 1833; quoted by Johnson, *George Washington the Christian*, pp. 242–45.

The observations and conclusions of Nelly Custis were virtually the unanimous opinion of those who knew Washington.[88] Chief Justice John Marshall, Washington's biographer, associate, ally, and personal friend, wrote, "Without making ostentatious professions of religion, he was a sincere believer in the Christian faith, and a truly devout man."[89] Washington's fellow Virginian James Madison said that he did

> . . . not suppose that Washington had ever attended to the arguments for Christianity, and for the different systems of religion, or in fact that he had formed definite opinions on the subject. But he took these things as he found them existing, and was constant in his observance of worship according to the received forms of the Episcopal Church in which he was brought up.[90]

The evidence of George Washington's Christian character is perhaps best summarized by Jared Sparks, whose twelve-volume collection of Washington's writings made him the best-informed biographer of Washington in the nineteenth century (1834-1837):

> A Christian in faith and practice, he was habitually devout. His reverence for religion is seen in his example, his public communications, and his private writings. He uniformly ascribed his successes to the beneficent agency of the Supreme Being. Charitable and humane, he was liberal to the poor and kind to those in distress. As a husband, son, and brother, he was tender and affectionate. . . .[91]
>
> If a man spoke, wrote, and acted as a Christian through a long life, who gave numerous proofs of his believing himself to be such, and who was never known to say, write or do a thing contrary to his professions, if such a man is not to be ranked among the believers of Christianity, it would be impossible to establish the point by any train of reasoning. . . .

88. Johnson cites an impressive list of contemporaries and later historians who considered Washington a Christian. The only exception among his contemporaries appears to have been Bishop White and two of his associates. White declared with regret in 1832 that he could not recall "any fact which would prove General Washington to have been a believer in the Christian revelation" except for his "constant attendance on Christian worship." But the statement is made thirty-three years after Washington's death, and while White was bishop over several churches in the Philadelphia one of which Washington attended during his presidency, the extent to which Bishop White had personally conversed with Washington or was familiar with his writings is uncertain. (Boller, *George Washington and Religion*, p. 89).

89. John Marshall, *The Life of George Washington*, (1804-7), II:445; quoted by Johnson, *George Washington the Christian*, p. 260.

90. After-Dinner Anecdotes of James Madison, Excerpts from Jared Sparks' Journal for 1829-31," *Virginia Magazine of History and Biography*, LX (April 1952), p. 263.

91. Sparks; quoted by Johnson, *George Washington the Christian*, p. 261.

After a long and minute examination of the writings of Washington, public and private, in print and in manuscript, I can affirm that I have never seen a single hint or expression from which it could be inferred that he had any doubt of the Christian revelation, or that he thought with indifference or unconcern of that subject. On the contrary, whenever he approaches it, and, indeed, whenever he alludes in any manner to religion, it is done with seriousness and reverence.[93]

93. Sparks; quoted by Johnson, *George Washington the Christian*, p. 261.

9 Alexander Hamilton

T|he picture many people have of Hamilton is a man consumed by personal ambition as well as a man who worshiped power. But Hamilton's life reveals much more: a superb lawyer, a patriot who loved his country and loved liberty, and a man with strong Christian convictions.

The following three points summarize Hamilton's philosophy. First, he believed in God-given natural law and God-given natural rights. About age seventeen he was writing pamphlets arguing the patriots' cause of independence. In "The Farmer Refuted," printed in 1775, he wrote:

> The sacred rights of mankind are not to be rummaged for among old parchments or musty records. They are written, as with a sunbeam, in the whole volume of human nature, by the hand of the Divinity itself, and can never be erased or obscured by mortal power.[1]

He added that, "Good and wise men, in all ages . . . have supposed that the Deity, from the relations we stand in to Himself, and to each other, has consitituted an eternal and immutable law, which is indispensably obligatory upon all mankind, prior to any human institutions whatever."[2] As authority for this proposition, Hamilton

1. Alexander Hamilton, "The Farmer Refuted", 1775; quoted by Nathan Schachner, *Alexander Hamilton* (New York: Barnes & Co., 1946, 1961), p. 38.
2. Hamilton, "The Farmer Refuted," 1775; quoted by Saul K. Padover, *The Mind of Alexander Hamilton* (New York: Harper, 1958), p. 430.

cited Sir William Blackstone's dictum that the law of nature "which, being coeval with mankind, and dictated by God himself, is, of course, superior in obligations to any other. It is binding all over the globe, in all countries, and at all times. No human laws are of any validity, if contrary to this; and such of them as are valid derive all their authority, mediately, or immediately, from this original."[3] He further quotes Blackstone for the proposition that "the first and primary end of human laws, is to maintain and regulate these absolute rights of individuals."[4]

Hamilton emphasized his commitment to individual liberty, natural rights, and natural law throughout his life. Late in life he argued the famous Croswell case in which a New York newspaperman was prosecuted for publishing libelous criticism of Jefferson. Under the common law, truth was not a defense to libel, but Hamilton contended that truth was a defense under the law of God, and even the common law is invalid if it seeks to "repeal or impair this law of God, for by his eternal laws it is inherent in the nature of things."[5] A divided court sustained the lower court conviction, but in response to Hamilton's plea the New York legislature passed a law declaring truth to be a defense to libel.

Second, Hamilton was convinced of the sinful nature of mankind. His belief in original sin was central to his political philosophy, although he often expressed it in more secular terms. On June 22, 1787, at the Constitutional Convention he stated:

> Take mankind in general, they are vicious—their passions may be operated upon. . . . Take mankind as they are, and what are they governed by? Their passions. There may be in every government a few choice spirits, who may act from more worthy motives. One great error is that we suppose mankind more honest than they are. Our prevailing passions are ambition and interest; and it will be the duty of a wise government to avail itself of those passions, in order to make them subservient to the public good.[6]

He wrote to James A. Bayard in 1802, "Nothing is more fallacious than to expect to produce any valuable or permanent results in political projects by relying merely on the reason of men. Men are

---

3. Sir William Blackstone; quoted by Padover, *Mind of Hamilton*, p. 80.

4. Ibid., pp. 80-81.

5. Hamilton; quoted by Forrest McDonald, *Alexander Hamilton* (New York: W. W. Norton & Co., 1979), p. 358.

6. Hamilton, Remarks to Constitutional Convention, June 22, 1787; quoted by Padover, *Mind of Hamilton*, p. 430.

rather reasoning than reasonable animals, for the most part governed by the impulse of passion."[7]

Hamilton believed man's self-interest is highly localized. "It is a
known fact in human nature, that its affections are commonly weak
in proportion to the distance or diffusiveness of the object. . . A man
is more attached to his family than to his neighborhood, to his
neighborhood than to the community at large."[8]

In terms of government Hamilton believed this meant, "We must
take man as we find him, and if we expect him to serve the public
[we] must interest his passions in doing so. A reliance on pure
patriotism had been the source of many of our errors,"[9] for, "The
science of policy is the knowledge of human nature."[10] Or as he said
to Richard Harrison in 1793:

> Till the millennium comes, in spite of all our boasted light and
> purification, hypocrisy and treachery will continue to be the most
> successful commodities in the political market. It seems to be the
> destined lot of nations to mistake their foes for their friends, their
> flatterers for their faithful servants.[11]

In other words, the true political scientist does not expect of people
more than they are capable of doing or giving. He recognizes people
for what they are, basically self-interested and prone to sin, and
seeks to harness that self-interest and channel it toward the public
good by such means as the profit motive (Hamilton was a careful
reader of Adam Smith). In Hamilton's view, utopian societies in
which men are expected to act out of altruistic motives are formulas
for disaster. He said, "I have found that constitutions are more or
less excellent as they are more or less agreeable to the natural
operation of things."[12]

Third, Hamilton's basic view of natural law, natural rights, and
human nature led him to fear the masses. Unchecked democracy, in
his view, would lead to mobocracy, and ultimately to tyranny.

7. Hamilton, Letter to James A. Bayard, April 1802; quoted by Padover, *Mind of
Hamilton*, pp. 430-31.

8. Hamilton, *The Federalist* No. 17.

9. Hamilton, Remarks to Constitutional Convention, June 22, 1787; quoted by Padover,
Mind of Hamilton, p. 428.

10. Ibid., p. 432.

11. Hamilton, Letter to Richard Harrison, January 5, 1793; quoted by Padover, *Mind of
Hamilton*, p. 432.

12. Hamilton, Remarks to New York Ratification Convention, June 21, 1788; quoted by
Padover, *Mind of Hamilton*, p. 422.

It has been observed, by an honorable gentleman, that a pure democracy, if if were practicable, would be the most perfect government. Experience has proved that no position in politics is more false than this. The ancient democracies, in which the people themselves deliberated, never possessed one feature of good government. Their very character was tyranny; their figure, deformity. When they assembled, the field of debate presented an ungovernable mob, not only incapable of deliberation, but prepared for every enormity.[13]

He recognized the dangers in giving power to rulers as well as to the masses. He said at the Constitutional Convention, "Give all power to the many and they will oppress the few. Give all power to the few and they will oppress the many. Both, therefore, ought to have the power that each may defend itself against the other."[14] Hamilton believed the solution was somewhere between democracy and monarchy, or, as he put it in *The Federalist* No. 9, a "confederate republic." In this confederate republic, (a) power would be divided between federal and state governments and separated among the various branches of government;[15] (b) the functions of government would be to provide the nation's necessities, procure the true happiness of the nation, and fortify the nation against external attack;[16] (c) the rights of the people would be safeguarded through

13. Ibid., p. 423.

14. Hamilton, Remarks to Constitutional Convention; in Arthur H. Vandenberg, *The Greatest American, Alexander Hamilton* (New York: G. P. Putnam's Sons, 1921), pp. 118-19.

15. McDonald, pp. 57-62.

16. Ibid., pp. 53-57. McDonald attributes Hamilton's concept of the functions of government largely to the reading of Vattel, whose classic *The Law of Nations* was published in 1758. McDonald says concerning the nation's happiness:

The second object of good government, "to procure the true happiness of the Nation," bore no relation to the selfish concept of "doing one's own thing" that unthinking moderns might regard as the meaning of the phrase "pursuit of happiness" in the Declaration of Independence. Indeed, it was the antithesis of self-indulgence or hedonism. On the part of the state, it entailed rigorous instruction of the people in good citizenship and the arts and sciences, both practical and "polite," and the cultivation of religious piety within the limits of the right to liberty of conscience. On the part of the individual, it entailed love of country and rigorous attention to the duty of making oneself as virtuous, moral, and useful a member of society as possible. The matter provided "an infallible criterion, by which the nation may judge of the intentions of those who govern it. If they endeavour to render the great and the common people virtuous, their views are pure and upright; and you may rest assured that they solely aim at the great end of government, the happiness and glory of the nation." On the other hand, if they corrupted the morals of the common people with permissiveness, thus spreading "a taste for luxury, effeminacy, a rage for licentious pleasures . . . beware, citizens! beware of those corruptors! They only aim at purchasing slaves in order to exercise over them an arbitrary sway." [The quote is from Vattel's *Law of Nations*, Book 1, Chapter 11, paras. 110-24, pp. 47-55]. Hamilton's public life and the way he reared his children demonstrated that he shared Vattel's view of what constituted "true" happiness.

the supremacy of law and legal procedure and be subject to the protections of trial by jury and judicial review; and (d) the operation of government would be in the hands of the professional and propertied classes.

Hamilton was under no illusion that the wealthy and educated were any less sinful than the rest of the populace. He told the New York ratifying convention:

> It is a harsh doctrine that men grow wicked in proportion as they . . . enlighten their minds . . . The difference . . . consists, not in the quantity but kind of vices, which are incident to the various classes; and here the advantage of character belongs to the wealthy. Their vices are probably more favorable to the prosperity of the state, than those of the indigent, and partake less of moral depravity. . . .[17]

Given these presuppositions, Hamilton's policies are understandable. Hamilton's background reveals that the ideas which led him to advocate a strong central government and a national bank came from his early religious training.

Hamilton was born and raised on the island of Nevis, in the West Indies. The exact date of his birth is uncertain; Hamilton once said it was January 11, 1757.[18] His mother Rachel Lavine was a French Huguenot who was living with James Hamilton, a Scotsman seeking his fortune in the West Indies. In 1763, a year after Alexander's brother James Jr. was born, James Hamilton left Rachel and went to other islands in the West Indies. In 1768 Rachel died, leaving Alexander, age eleven, and James, age six. Hamilton remembered his mother "with inexpressible fondness, and often spoke of her as a woman of superior intellect, highly cultivated, of elevated and generous sentiments, and of unusual elegance of person and manner."[19]

McDonald writes that early in life Hamilton was exposed to three varieties of Calvinism—the Scottish through his father, the French through his mother, and the Dutch through Henry Cruger. Cruger was a Dutch businessman who employed Alexander as an apprentice clerk when he was twelve years old. Two years later when Cruger became ill and sailed to New York for medical treatment, he chose Alexander Hamilton to manage his affairs. At age fourteen,

---

17. Hamilton, New York Ratification Convention, June 21, 1788; quoted by Padover, *Mind of Hamilton*, p. 429.

18. In this chapter I will use the 1757 date in all computations of age.

19. Hamilton's son; quoted by Robert Henderickson, *Hamilton I (1757-1789)* (New York: Mason/Charter, 1976), p. 19.

Hamilton was running an international business. The letters he wrote to Henry Cruger reflect an amazing business knowledge. One letter to his father which he wrote at age fifteen stands out not only for its dramatic expression but also for its theological content. It is a letter dated September 6, 1772, describing a great hurricane that ravaged the islands:

Honoured Sir:

I take up my pen just to give you an imperfect account of the most dreadful hurricane that memory or any records whatever can trace. . . .

My reflections and feelings on this frightful and melancholy occasion are set forth in the following self-discourse. Where now, Oh! vile worm, is all thy boasted fortitude and resolution? What is become of thy arrogance and self-sufficiency? Who dost thou tremble and stand aghast? How humble, how helpless—how contemptible you now appear. And for why? The jarring of the elements—this discord of clouds? Oh, impotent, presumptious fool! How darest thou offend that omnipotence, whose nod alone were sufficient to quell the destruction that hovers over thee, or crush thee into atoms? See thy wretched helpless state and learn to know thyself. Despise thyself and adore thy God. . . . let the sun be extinguished, and the heavens burst asunder—yet what have I to dread? My staff can never be broken—in omnipotence I trust.

He who gave the winds to blow and the lightnings to rage—even him I have always loved and served—his precepts have I observed— his commandments have I obeyed—and his perfections have I adored. He will snatch me from ruin—he will exalt me to the fellowship of Angels and Seraphs, and to the fulness of never ending joys. . . .

Hark! Ruin and confusion on every side—Tis thy turn next; but one short moment—even now—Oh Lord help—Jesus be merciful!

But see, the Lord relents, He hears our prayers—The lightning ceases—the winds are appeased—the warring elements are reconciled, and all things promise peace—The darkness is dispelled—and drooping nature revives at the approaching dawn. Look back. Oh, my soul—look back and tremble—Rejoice at thy deliverance, and humble thyself in the presence of thy deliverer.

Yet hold, Oh vain mortal! check thy ill-timed joy. Art thou so selfish as to exult because thy lot is happy in a season of universal woe? Hast thou no feelings for the miseries of thy fellow creatures, and art thou incapable of the soft pangs of sympathetic sorrow?— Look around thee and shudder at the view. See desolation and ruin wherever thou turnest thine eye. See thy fellow-creatures pale and lifeless; their bodies mangled—their souls snatched into eternity— unexpecting—alas! perhaps unprepared! . . .

Oh distress unspeakable—my heart bleeds —but I have no power to solace! Oh ye, who revel in affluence, see the afflictions of humanity, and bestow your superfluity to ease them. Say not, we have suffered also, and withhold your compassion. What are your sufferings compared to these? Ye have still more than enough left.— act wisely—Succour the miserable and lay up a treasure in Heaven. . . .[20]

It appears from this letter that Rachel Levine adequately provided for the spiritual and academic needs of her children. Rachel was a member of St. John's Anglican Church. Hendrickson suggests that Alexander was especially awed by the Anglican Order for the Burial of the Dead over his mother's body at her funeral. "I am the resurrection and the life, saith the Lord: he that believeth in me, though he were dead, yet shall he live: . . . we brought nothing into this world, and it is certain we can carry nothing out." Hendrickson notes that Hamilton observed Episcopalian [Anglican] forms of worship all his life, though he never became an official communicant in any church.[21]

Hamilton's Calvinist zeal and support for American freedom were learned from the Reverend Hugh Knox, a Calvinist, scholar, local Presbyterian minister, and schoolmaster under whom Hamilton studied. Knox recognized and encouraged the piety and the genius he saw in Hamilton. Knox was also a strong advocate of American independence, having studied and earned his theology degree at the College of New Jersey. While Hamilton was active in the War of Independence, Knox wrote him many encouraging letters.[22] Through Knox, Hamilton acquired most of his early thought, theology, and academic training. He also received considerable home instruction especially in reading and writing French from his mother and her relatives. As a young child he was taught by a Jewish schoolmistress and learned to recite the Ten Commandments in Hebrew.[23]

Rev. Knox believed that a young man of Hamilton's genius should receive a college education, and when Hamilton showed him his "Hurricane letter," Knox took action. He raised funds from others on the island who admired young Hamilton and arranged for

20. Margaret Esther Hall, *The Hamilton Reader* (New York: Oceana, 1957), pp. 33-36.
21. Hendrickson, Vol. I, p. 17.
22. Broadus Mitchell, *Alexander Hamilton: Youth to Maturity 1755-1788* (New York: MacMillan, 1957), pp. 32-33; see also the other authors cited herein.
23. Broadus Mitchell, *Alexander Hamilton: A Concise Biography* (New York: Oxford, 1976), p. 11; Schachner, *Alexander Hamilton*, p. 17.

him to be sent to America.[24] Alexander made the trip in the autumn of 1772, arrived in Boston in October, remained a few days, and undoubtedly observed the strong sentiment for independence in Boston. Hamilton then journeyed to New York, where he delivered letters of introduction from Rev. Knox to two Presbyterian friends, Knox's old teacher Dr. John Rodgers and Rev. John Mason. They sent Alexander to a Presbyterian academy in nearby Elizabethtown, New Jersey, headed by Elias Boudinot and William Livingston.

Hamilton was approximately fifteen when he arrived at the Elizabethtown Academy. He already had a wealth of knowledge and experience. In addition to knowing some French and Hebrew he had a basic knowledge of Latin, theology, and the classics. His business experience with Cruger helped him understand mathematics and economics, and gave him confidence in dealing with ship captains, planters, merchants, lawyers, slaves, and suppliers. But his goal was to attend the College of New Jersey (Princeton), and the entrance requirements for admission included the ability to write Latin prose, translate Virgil, Cicero, and the Greek gospels, and to possess a commensurate knowledge of Latin and Greek grammar.[25]

Two people greatly influenced Hamilton at Elizabethtown Academy. Alexander lived in the home of William Livingston, a retired lawyer and teacher, staunch Presbyterian, and supporter of the cause of independence. Alexander probably learned much of his polemic skill and straightforward writing style from Livingston. Elias Boudinot was like a foster father to Hamilton, according to Broadus Mitchell. Boudinot was an attorney who "had a theological preoccupation that must either put one on his knees or make him a rebellious blasphemer."[26] He became the first president of the American Bible Society.[27] Boudinot was a good-hearted man who supported Presbyterianism and independence, and Hamilton loved him greatly. Throughout Hamilton's professional life Boudinot remained his companion.

At Elizabethtown Academy Hamilton grew both spiritually and academically. He translated some of Homer's *Iliad*, composed the prologue and epilogue for a play, and carefully wrote out a set of

24. Mitchell, *Youth to Maturity*, pp. 33-35.

25. Ibid., p. 43.

26. Ibid., p. 48; see also Broadus Mitchell, *Alexander Hamilton: The National Adventure 1788-1804* (New York: MacMillan, 1962), p. 59.

27. Hendrickson, Vol. I, p. 584 n. 3.

notes, quotations, and paraphrases of the first three chapters of Genesis and chapters 1-13 of Revelation.[28]

By the end of 1773 Hamilton finished his studies at Elizabethtown and wanted to go to the College of New Jersey, the alma mater of Rev. Knox and the citadel of Presbyterianism. He interviewed with President Witherspoon, but insisted that he be admitted immediately (mid-year) and be allowed to advance as fast as his abilities would allow. Witherspoon was unable to persuade the admissions office to grant such an exceptional request.[29] So Hamilton attended King's College in New York, an Anglican institution loyal to the British Crown. King's College did not appear to radically change Hamilton's views, but it might have led him toward greater respect for authority. For despite Hamilton's political and religious differences, he became a loyal friend of the president of King's College, Myles Cooper. On May 10, 1775, an angry revolutionary mob gathered outside Dr. Cooper's house and threatened to tar and feather him or worse. Hamilton and his roommate Robert Troup diverted the crowd and made it possible for Cooper to escape. Cooper showed his gratitude by publishing a poem in *Gentleman's Magazine of London* in which he referred to Hamilton, without naming him, as "a heaven-directed youth":

> Stanzas Written on the Evening of the 10th of May, 1776
> By an Exile from America
>
> The mob was at the gate
> When straight, a heaven-directed youth,
> Whom oft my lessons led to truth,
>
> And honour's sacred shrine,
> Advancing quick before the rest
> With trembling tongue my ear addresst,
>
> Yet sure in voice divine,
> Awake! Awake! The storm is high, —
> This instant rouse,—this instant fly,—
> The next may be too late. . . .[30]

However, during the same period of time Hamilton was writing pro-independence pamphlets and working for independence. "The Farmer Refuted" was written while Hamilton was at King's College.

---

28. Ibid., p. 45.
29. Ibid., p. 50.
30. Myles Cooper, *Gentleman's Magazine of London;* quoted by Hendrickson, Vol. I, p. 55.

Nor did King's College negatively affect Hamilton's Calvinist faith. His roommate and lifelong friend Robert Troup writes that young Alexander "was attentive to public worship, and in the habit of praying upon his knees both night and morning. . . . I have lived in the same room with him for some time, and I have often been powerfully affected by the fervor and eloquence of his prayers. He had read many of the polemical writers on religious subjects, and he was a zealous believer in the fundamental doctrines of Christianity. . . . I confess that the arguments with which he was accustomed to justify his belief, have tended in no small degree to confirm my own faith in revealed religion."[31]

Hamilton got along well at King's College despite his political and theological differences. His name does not appear on any lists of disciplinary measures taken against students during that time.[32] He did well academically, participated in the debating society, and completed his studies in 1775. His published speeches from that period reflect that he read Grotius, Pufendorf, Locke, Montesquieu, Blackstone, Hobbes, Berlamaqui, Postlethwaite Hume, and others.

On March 14, 1776, Hamilton, at age nineteen, was commissioned as captain of the New York provincial artillery company. He was noted for his bravery in leading men into battle, and he trained his troops so well that his company "drew all eyes by the disciplined appearance of its ranks and the brisk, soldierly stride of its men."[33] Around March 1, 1777, General Washington promoted him to Lieutenant Colonel and made him his personal aide-de-camp. In that capacity Hamilton handled much of Washington's personal correspondence and was among Washington's closest personal advisors.

Hamilton's military service placed him in contact with two people who profoundly affected his life. One was Aaron Burr, who became his lifelong enemy. The other was Elizabeth Schuyler, who became his wife. She was the daughter of a Dutch Reformed family in upstate New York; her father a planter, politician, and military figure became Hamilton's close friend and ally. Elizabeth is described as a loving and faithful companion. Alexander and Elizabeth had eight children. She survived Alexander by fifty years, dying at age ninety-seven. When she died a tiny bag was found hanging around her neck containing scraps of love letters Alexander had written. She devoted much of later years to preserving her

31. Robert Troup; quoted by Hendrickson, Vol. I, p. 51.
32. Ibid., p. 52.
33. Schachner, *Alexander Hamilton*, p. 54.

husband's papers and memories. Elizabeth, being of the Dutch Reformed variety of Calvinism, complemented Hamilton's devotion to Calvinist Christianity. Broadus Mitchell describes her as, "Loyal, sincere, and unselfish, she was the right helpmeet for a man of genius. Her religious devotion was a grateful ingredient in the storms and sorrows they suffered together."[34]

In 1781 Hamilton resigned as Washington's aide-de-camp. Hamilton began to study law in 1782, and later the same year he became a delegate to the Continental Congress. In 1784 his passionate belief in the need for law, order, and procedure caused him to vehemently protest the refusal of the New York legislature to restore confiscated loyalist property. He was also instrumental in establishing the Bank of New York.

Hamilton was convinced of the inadequacy of the Articles of Confederation and in 1786 served as a delegate to the Annapolis Convention where he drafted a resolution calling for a constitutional convention, to expand the powers of the general government. In 1787 he served in the New York State Assembly and was also a delegate to the Constitutional Convention, where he was elected a member of the committee on standing rules.

His one major speech at the Convention on June 22, 1787, called for a more centralized government. He left the Convention shortly after that speech and returned to New York.

Hamilton was frustrated because under the rules each state was allowed only one vote at the Convention, that vote to be cast as the majority of the state's delegates wished. Since New York's two other delegates held strongly to the Antifederalist position, Hamilton consistently found his own state's vote being cast against his personal position. He hoped to work through influential men outside the Convention to sway the delegates. On July 10, because they felt the Convention was leaning too much to the Federalist position, the remaining two New York delegates also left the Convention. At Washington's request Hamilton returned.

As a delegate to the New York ratifying convention, and although federalists were a small minority at that convention, Hamilton succeeded in persuading the convention to ratify the Constitution by a 30-27 vote. In 1789 President Washington appointed Hamilton Secretary of the Treasury. In this position Hamilton helped form a national bank and establish a national Mint, headed by his old friend Elias Boudenot, and expanded the powers of the federal government.

34. Mitchell, *A Concise Biography*, p. 79.

Hamilton said little about his religious beliefs throughout this period of his life. He apparently continued to attend Anglican services, and for the most part remained a devoted family man. His public and private correspondence contained only an occasional "May God bless you" and similar references. But nothing even suggestive of the "Hurricane letter" appears at this time.

Two things are certain. First, he never renounced the theology he held as a youth. Second, the political principles which were based on his Calvinistic theology—God-given natural law and natural rights, the threat to natural law and natural rights posed by the sinful nature of man, and the need for strong government power coupled with firm law and procedure to restrain the sinful nature of man—formed the basis of his entire political career. His Christian conscience led him to oppose slavery, possibly because of the condition of the slaves he saw in the West Indies. Early in life Hamilton declared that it is our "Christian duty" not to submit to slavery; in 1785 he was a founding member of the Society for Promoting the Manumission of Slaves. In 1786 he introduced a petition in the New York legislature urging an end of the slave trade.[35]

Hamilton became more outspoken about his Christian faith. One factor which revived his faith was the French Revolution. France, he declared, was "the most flagitious, despotic, and vindictive government that ever disgraced the annals of mankind." Referring to "the disgusting spectacle of the French Revolution," he insisted that Americans could never indulge "so frightful a volcano of atheism, depravity, and absurdity . . . so hateful an instrument of cruelty and bloodshed. . . ."[36]

Hamilton was concerned that the atheism and lawlessness of France might spread to the United States. He became convinced that the Christian religion provided a much-needed moral restraint on the people, inducing them to civic virtue.

A family tragedy also renewed Hamilton's sense of his personal need for Christianity. He was close to all eight of his children, but his oldest son Philip was his brightest. However, in November 1801 Philip was killed in a duel which resulted from an argument he had with an Antifederalist lawyer who had criticized Alexander's policies.[37] Hamilton wrote about his son's death to Gouverneur Morris on February 12, 1802:

35. Hendrickson, Vol. I, p. 569.
36. Hamilton; quoted in Schachner, *Alexander Hamilton*, p. 375.
37. Ibid., pp. 407-8.

My loss is indeed great. The brightest as well as the eldest hope of my family has been taken from me. You estimated him rightly. He was a fine youth. But why should I repine? It was the will of heaven, and he is now out of reach of the seductions and calamities of a world full of folly, full of vice, full of danger—of least value in proportion as it is best known. I firmly trust also, that he has safely reached the haven [of eternal repose] and felicity.[38]

In 1802 Hamilton laid out plans for the establishment of the "Christian Constitutional Society." This would consist of a national organization with state and local chapters which would distribute literature, engage in charitable activities such as aid to immigrants, and promote the two factors which stabilize and give order and meaning to American society, the Christian religion and the rule of law under the Constitution.[39] However, his plans did not come to fruition.

Hamilton felt that John Adams did not have the qualifications for a president. In spite of Hamilton's opposition, Adams was elected. Then Hamilton directed his efforts toward discrediting Adams, making it impossible for Adams to be reelected. But Thomas Jefferson and Aaron Burr, the two likely candidates to succeed Adams, were even more unsatisfactory to Hamilton. He finally indicated a preference for Jefferson who was elected.

The continuous political disputes and disagreements between Burr and Hamilton continued to grow and fester. When Burr sought the governorship of New York, Hamilton denounced him as a dangerous man. Burr was defeated. In an exchange of letters Burr challenged Hamilton to a duel, and despite the efforts of many friends to forestall it, Hamilton accepted.

The duel was scheduled for July 11, 1804. At age forty-seven, Hamilton prepared for the duel as though he fully expected to die; he had determined not to fire at Burr.

Hamilton abhorred the thought of dueling partly out of religious conviction, and perhaps in part in reflection on Philip's death. Under the unwritten code of the day it was unmanly for him to run away from the challenge; his personal pride would not allow it. Nor could he apologize for or retract his remarks because he was

38. Richard B. Morris, *Alexander Hamilton and the Founding of the Nation* (New York: Dial Press, 1957), p. 601; quoting letter of Hamilton to Gouverneur Morris, February 12, 1802.
39. Hamilton, Letter to James Bayard, April 1802; cited by Mitchell, *The National Adventure*, pp. 513-14.

thoroughly convinced Burr was an evil and dangerous man. Hamilton's only solution was to enter the duel and die with honor.

Three days before the duel, Hamilton wrote his last will and testament:

> In the name of God, Amen.
> . . . Though, if it should please God to spare my life, I may look for a considerable surplus out of my present property; yet if he should speedily call me to the eternal world, a forced sale, as is usual, may possibly render it insufficient to satisfy my debts. I pray God that something may remain for the maintenance and education of my dear wife and children. . . . —Though conscious that I have too far sacrificed the interests of my family to public avocations, and on this account have the less claim to burthen my children, yet I trust in their magnanimity to appreciate, as they ought, this my request. In so unfavorable an event of things, the support of their dear mother, with the most respectful and tender attention, is a duty all the sacredness of which they will feel. Probably her own patrimonial resources will preserve her from indigence. But in all situations they are charged to bear in mind that she has been to them the most devoted and best of mothers. . . .[40]

A few days before the duel Hamilton wrote to his friend Nathaniel Pendleton,

> . . . I was certainly desirous of avoiding this interview [term used for duel] for the most cogent reasons:
> (1) My religious and moral principles are strongly opposed to the practice of duelling, and it would ever give me pain to be obliged to shed the blood of a fellow-creature in private combat forbidden by the laws.
> (2) My wife and children are extremely dear to me, and my life is of the utmost importance to them in various views.
> (3) I feel a sense of obligation towards my creditors; who, in case of accident to me by the forced sale of my property, may be in some degree sufferers. I did not think myself at liberty as a man of probity lightly expose them to this hazard.
> (4) I am conscious of no ill will to Col. Burr, distinct from political opposition, which, as I trust, has proceeded from pure and upright motives.
> Lastly, I shall hazard much and can possibly gain nothing by the issue of this interview. . . .

40. Last Will and Testament of Alexander Hamilton; quoted by Morris, *Hamilton and the Founding of the Nation*, p. 609.

. . . As well, because it is possible that I may have injured Col. Burr, however convinced myself that my opinions and declarations have been well-founded, as from my general principles and temper in relation to similar affairs, I have resolved, if our interview is conducted in the usual manner, and it pleases God to give me the opportunity, to reserve and throw away my first fire, and I have thoughts even of reserving my second fire, and thus giving a double opportunity to Col. Burr to pause and reflect. It is not, however, my intention to enter into any explanations on the ground. Apology from principle, I hope, rather than pride, is out of the question. . . .[41]

Hamilton also confided this intent to his friend Rufus King, because King had told Hamilton that "any man of ordinary understanding" could see that Hamilton "owed it to his family and the rights of self-defense to fire at his antagonist."[42]

On July 10, the day before the duel, Hamilton wrote to his wife:

This letter, my dear Eliza, will not be delivered to you, unless I shall first have terminated my earthly career, to begin, as I humbly hope, from redeeming grace and divine mercy, a happy immortality. If it had been possible for me to have avoided the interview, my love for you and my precious children would have been alone a decisive motive. But it was not possible, without sacrifices which would have rendered me unworthy of your esteem. I need not tell you of the pangs I feel from the idea of quitting you, and exposing you to the anguish I know you would feel. Nor could I dwell on the topic, lest it should unman me. The consolations of religion, my beloved, can alone support you; and these you have a right to enjoy. Fly to the bosom of your God, and be comforted. With my last idea I shall cherish the sweet hope of meeting you in a better world. Adieu, best of wives—best of women. Embrace all my darling children for me.[43]

The evening before the duel, his thoughts turned to the West Indies, his mother, and her family. He wrote again to his wife:

My beloved Eliza:
Mrs. Mitchell [Hamilton's mother's sister] is the person in the world to whom, as a friend, I am under the greatest obligation. I have not hitherto done my duty to her. But resolved to repair my omission to

---

41. Hamilton to Nathaniel Pendleton; quoted by Padover, *Alexander Hamilton*, pp. 48-50.

42. Rufus King; quoted by John C. Miller, *Alexander Hamilton: Portrait in Paradox* (New York: Harper, 1959), p. 572.

43. Hamilton, Letter to Elizabeth Hamilton, July 10, 1804; quoted by Padover, *Alexander Hamilton*, p. 50.

her as much as possible, I have encouraged her to come to this country, and intend, if it shall be in my power, to render the evening of her days comfortable. But if it shall please God to put this out of my power, and to enable you hereafter to be of service to her, I entreat you to do it, and to treat her with the tenderness of a sister. This is my second letter. The scruples of a Christian have determined me to expose my own life to any extent, rather than subject myself to the guilt of taking another. This much increases my hazards, and redoubles my pangs for you. But you had rather I should die innocent than live guilty. Heaven can preserve me, and I humbly hope will; but, in the contrary event, I charge you to remember that you are a Christian. God's will be done! The will of a merciful God must be good. Once more, Adieu, my darling, darling wife.[44]

The duel took place early the next morning on a plateau called Weehawken on the New Jersey side of the Hudson River (Ironically, Hamilton and others had succeeded in having the practice of dueling outlawed in New York.)[45] Burr fired immediately, and the shot struck Hamilton's right side and fractured a rib. Hamilton's pistol discharged, apparently due to a reflexive clenching of the hand upon being hit; the shot went wild. The unconscious Hamilton was taken back across the river for treatment. Halfway across he revived and said, "Pendleton knows . . . I did not intend to fire at him."[46]

Hamilton laid in agony for thirty-one hours before he died. The Rev. Benjamin Moore, the Episcopal Bishop, immediately went to Hamilton's bedside. Hamilton requested communion, but at first Bishop Moore refused—some say because of the sin of dueling, others because Hamilton was not a confirmed member of the Episcopal Church. When Bishop Moore left for a short time Dr. Mason of the Dutch Reformed Church ministered to him. He also refused communion because his denomination prohibited giving the sacrament privately. He comforted Hamilton by explaining that communion was only a sign of salvation and that he could be saved through repentance. Hamilton answered that he knew that it was only a sign but he wanted it. They spoke of the sin of dueling, and Hamilton confessed, "It was always against my principles. I used every expedient to avoid the interview; but I have found, for some time past, that my life must be exposed to that man. I went to the field determined not to take his life." He clasped his hands toward heaven and declared with emphasis, "I have a tender reliance on

44. Ibid, p. 51.
45. Miller, *Portrait in Paradox*, p. 573.
46. Schachner, *Alexander Hamilton*, p. 429.

the mercy of the Almighty, through the merits of the Lord Jesus Christ.''

Bishop Moore returned that afternoon. Hamilton explained that he had intended to join the church for some time, that he had repented of his sins, that he had forgiven Burr, and that he would testify against dueling if he survived. The Bishop agreed to administer the sacrament, and Hamilton received the communion with unmistakable gratitude.[47]

That night Hamilton slept fitfully, but the next day he began sinking. His wife, seven children, and other relatives were with him in his final hours. He died the following afternoon, July 12, 1804. It is said that the bullet that killed Alexander Hamilton also killed Aaron Burr, because from that point on Burr was ruined politically. Also, public horror over Hamilton's death did much to eliminate the practice of dueling in America.

Alexander Hamilton's political achievements are well known. Nicholas Murray Butler lists the five greatest nation-builders in American history as George Washington, Alexander Hamilton, John Marshall, Daniel Webster, and Abraham Lincoln.[48] The French statesman Talleyrand remarked, ''I consider Napoleon, Fox and Hamilton the three greatest men of our epoch, and without hesitation I award the first place to Hamilton.''[49] Chancellor James Kent, one of the best-known judges in American history, considered Hamilton the greatest lawyer he had ever known.[50] Fisher Ames, a delegate to the Constitutional Convention, paid a tribute to Hamilton shortly after his death, that well summarizes Hamilton's career: ''[he] had not made himself dear to the passions of the multitude by condescending . . . to become their instrument . . . it was by . . . loving his country better than himself, preferring its interest to its favor, and serving it, when it was unwilling and unthankful, in a manner that nobody else could, that he rose, and the true popularity, the homage that is paid to virtue, followed him.''[51]

47. Mitchell, *The National Adventure*, pp. 536-37. Mitchell cites the following early authorities: William Coleman, ed., *A Collection of Facts and Documents, relating to the Death of . . . Alexander Hamilton* (New York: Hopkins & Seymour, 1804), pp. 50-55; Allen McLane Hamilton, *Intimate Life of Alexander Hamilton* (New York: Scribner, 1910), pp. 404-6.

48. Nicholas Murray Butler, ''Address at the Unveiling of the Statue of Alexander Hamilton in the City of Paterson, New Jersey'', May 30, 1907; reprinted by Hall, *The Hamilton Reader*, pp. 9-20.

49. Talleyrand, quoted by Hon. Chauncey M. Depew, ''Address at the Unveiling of the Statue of Alexander Hamilton'' in Central Park, New York, November 22, 1880; reprinted by Hall, *The Hamilton Reader*, pp. 21-29.

50. Schachner, *Alexander Hamilton*, p. 347; see also pp. 180, 415-17.

51. Fisher Ames; quoted by Mitchell, *The National Adventure*, p. 542.

10 John Jay

Norman Cousins calls John Jay the "father of American conservatism."[1] Richard Hildreth believed that Jay was "one of the three granite pillars of America's political greatness;" the three which also included Washington and Hamilton constituted "a trio not to be matched, in fact, not to be approached in our history, if, indeed, in any other."[2] John Jay's son, William Jay described him as, "a rare but interesting picture of the Christian patriot and statesman."[3]

At age twenty-nine John Jay was the youngest delegate to the 1774 Continental Congress. Because he possessed both sound judgment and wisdom he was selected to prepare a draft of the United States' address which asked Great Britain for redress of grievances.[4] Jay supported the War of Independence although his conservative nature hoped for a reconciliation with England until about 1778. He served as Chief Justice of the Supreme Court of New York during the war; while in that position he fulfilled various mission assignments for the United States. After helping to complete

1. Norman Cousins, *"In God We Trust": The Religious Beliefs and Ideas of the American Founding Fathers* (New York: Harper & Brothers, 1958), p. 358.

2. Richard Hildreth [19th-century Federalist historian]; quoted by Frank Monaghan, *John Jay: Defender of Liberty* (Indianapolis: Bobbs-Merrill, 1935, 1972), p. ix.

3. William Jay, *The Life of John Jay, with Selections from His Correspondence* (New York: Harper, 1833), I:463.

4. Cousins, *"In God We Trust"*, p. 358.

the peace treaty with England which ended the war, Congress made him Secretary of Foreign Affairs.

Jay did not attend the Constitutional Convention, but strongly supported ratification. Jay, along with Alexander Hamilton and James Madison, wrote the *Federalist Papers* which explained the principles of the Constitution and were instrumental in securing the ratification of the Constitution. The *Papers* are regarded as the best exposition of the principles of the Constitution ever written. Jay's abilities as a statesman led President Washington to appoint him the first Chief Justice of the United States Supreme Court. As Chief Justice, Jay strengthened the power of the federal courts by upholding the right of a citizen of one state to sue another state government in the Supreme Court.[5] He strengthened the sovereignty of the United States in international affairs by holding that the federal courts could rule in favor of the Swedish and American owners of a ship which the French government claimed to have lawfully captured.[6] He also negotiated Jay's Treaty of 1794 which averted war with England by obtaining their agreement to: evacuate outposts in western America, compensate Americans for spoil in the amount of more than $10 million, and continue uninterrupted commerce with America.

From 1795 to 1801 Jay was Governor of New York. He was recognized for his honesty, his refusal to appoint or dismiss officials because of political affiliation, and his devotion to his duties. The reforms Jay sought included: the revision of the criminal law to eliminate the death penalty for everything but major crimes, humane treatment of prisoners, abolition of slavery, and "An Act to prevent the profanation of the Sabbath."[7]

Jay retired from public life in 1801 at the age of fifty-seven, but later served several terms as president of the American Bible Society. He died May 17, 1829, at the age of eighty-four.

Jay's ancestors were French Huguenots [Calvinist Protestants] who fled France because of religious persecution. John Jay wrote an unfinished account of his ancestors which is quoted by his son: "Thus by divine Providence every member of the family was rescued from the rage and reach of persecution and enabled to preserve a portion of prosperity more than adequate to their actual necessities."[8]

5. *Chisholm v. Georgia*, 2 U.S. 419, 2 Dallas 419 (1793); opinion by Justice Iredell, Chief Justice Jay joining.

6. *Glass v. Sloop Betsy*, 3 U.S. 6, 3 Dallas 6 (1794); opinion by Chief Justice Jay.

7. Monaghan, *John Jay*, pp. 408-11; William Jay, *Life of John Jay*, I:401-2.

8. John Jay; quoted by William Jay, *Life of John Jay*, I:3-6.

John Jay was born in New York City December 12, 1745, the eighth of ten children. When he was a small child a small-pox epidemic swept through New York City, a brother and sister were blinded by it, so the family moved to a better environment in the countryside.

William Jay says of his father's home life:

> . . . seldom have parents been so loved and reverenced as they were by him. Both father and mother were actuated by sincere and fervent piety; both had warm hearts and cheerful tempers; and both possessed, under varied and severe trials, a remarkable degree of equinamity. But in other respects they differed widely. He possessed strong masculine sense, was a shrewd observer and admirable judge of men; resolute, persevering, and prudent; and affectionate father, a kind master, but governing all under his control with absolute sway. She had a cultivated mind and fine imagination; mild and affectionate in her temper and manners, she took delight in the duties as well as the pleasures of domestic life; while a cheerful resignation to the will of Providence, during many years of sickness and suffering, bore witness to the strength of her religious faith. So happily did these various dispositions harmonize together, that the subject of this memoir often declared, that he had never, in a single instance, heard either of his parents use towards the other an angry or unkind word.[9]

John's mother taught him the basics of English and Latin. When he was between six and seven years old his father wrote of him, "Johnny is of a very grave disposition, and takes to learning exceedingly well. He will soon be fit for grammar school."[10] And at age eight John was sent to grammar school at nearby New Rochelle, New York, where he was taught by Rev. Mr. Stoope, pastor of the combined Episcopal and French church. New Rochelle was made up almost entirely of French Huguenots, and John learned their ways and became fluent in French.

John enrolled in King's College at age fourteen. A basic entrance requirement at the college was to "give a rational account of the Latin and Greek grammars," read the first three of Tully's *Select Orations* and the first three books of the *Aeneid*, and translate the first ten chapters of St. John's Gospel from Greek into Latin.[11] The school followed a rigorous regimen and enforced strict rules against "Drunkenness, Fornication, Lying, Theft, Swearing, Cursing, or

9. Ibid., I:11.
10. Peter Jay; ibid., I:11.
11. Monaghan, *John Jay*, p. 26.

any other scandalous immorality" including cock-fighting, card-playing, dice and "Dilapidations of the College."[12] His studies included Greek, Latin, rhetoric, and the works of such writers as Grotius, Ossian, Seneca, Aristotle, Livy, Isocrates, Plutarch, Cicero and Locke.[13] He was one of two students selected to give the salutatory addresses on graduation day, May 22, 1764.[14]

John pursued a law career and from 1764-1768 studied in the law offices of Benjamin Kissam of New York; he was then admitted to the bar. His law practice was successful, and led into an equally successful career as a politician and statesman. Throughout both professions, Jay remained committed to the Christian principles he learned during childhood.

Jay always seemed conscious of God's sovereign hand at work in human affairs and in his own life. He repeatedly referred to the "beneficient care of heaven," in delivering his family from religious persecution in France.[15] He saw God's hand at work in the conflicts between the United States and Great Britain. His address at the New York Convention, which called for the support of the Declaration of Independence, was filled with references to biblical figures such as Nebuchadnezzar, Jacob, and Esau. He compared America to Israel and stated that God would not bless America's cause unless it was true to him:

> Even the Jews, those favourites of Heaven, met with frowns, when they forgot the smiles of their benevolent Creator. By tyrants of Egypt, of Babylon, of Syria, and of Rome, they were severely chastised; and those tyrants themselves, when they had executed the vengeance of Almighty God, their own crimes bursting on their own heads, received the rewards justly due to their violation of the sacred rights of mankind.
>
> You were born equally free with the Jews. . . .[16]

Jay insisted that America forsake selfish vice and trust in God:

> Let a general reformation of manners take place—let universal charity, public spirit, and private virtue be inculcated, encouraged, and practiced. Unite in preparing for a vigorous defence of your

12. Ibid., p. 26.

13. Ibid., pp. 27-28; William Jay, *Life of John Jay*, I:13.

14. Monaghan, *John Jay*, pp. 30-31; William Jay, *Life of John Jay*, I:14-15. The accounts differ slightly. Jays says his father gave the address in Latin; Monaghan cites a contemporary account that says it was in English.

15. John Jay; quoted by William Jay, *Life of John Jay*, I:8.

16. John Jay, Address to New York Convention, December 23, 1776; ibid., I:52.

country, as if all depended on your own exertions. And when you have done all things, then rely upon the good Providence of Almighty God for success, in full confidence that without his blessings, all our efforts will inevitably fail.[17]

He concluded that independence was part of God's plan for bringing the gospel to the Western world, and that God would give success to the cause of independence if Americans trusted God:

The holy gospels are yet to be preached to these western regions; and we have the highest reason to believe that the Almighty will not suffer slavery and the gospel to go hand in hand. It cannot, it will not be.[18]

Jay was also conscious of God's hand in his own life. He realized that God accomplishes his will through human beings. In the spring of 1794 Jay knew that he might be used by God and traveled to England to negotiate a treaty. He realized this would entail a long separation from his family and wrote to his wife:

If it should please God to make me instrumental to the continuation of peace, and in preventing the effusion of blood and other evils and miseries incident to war, we shall both have reason to rejoice. Whatever may be the event, the endeavour will be virtuous, and consequently consolatory. Let us repose unlimited trust in our Maker; it is our business to adore and to obey. My love to the children.

> With very sincere and tender affection,
> I am, my dear Sally, ever yours,
> John Jay[19]

Jay trusted God's plan even in the face of tragedy. Several days after his daughter's death in 1818 he wrote:

The removal of my excellent daughter from the house of her earthly, to the house of her Heavenly Father, leaves me nothing to regret or lament on *her* account. Her absence is, nevertheless, a privation which I feel very sensibly, both on my own account and that of her affectionate brothers and sisters. I hope we shall be favored with grace to derive consolation from the reflection that her departure was ordered by infinite wisdom and goodness, and that this temporary separation will terminate in a perpetual reunion.[20]

17. Ibid., I:55.
18. Ibid., I:56.
19. John Jay to Sally Jay, April 15, 1794; quoted by William Jay, *Life of John Jay*, I:311.
20. John Jay to Rev. Samuel F. Jarvis, May 4, 1818; ibid. I:451.

His last will and testament recounted the hand of God in his life:

> Unto Him who is the author and giver of all good, I render sincere and humble thanks for his merciful and unmerited blessings, and especially for our redemption and salvation by his beloved Son. He has been pleased to bless me with excellent parents, with a virtuous wife, and with worthy children. His protection has accompanied me through many eventful years, faithfully employed in the service of my country; and his providence has not only conducted me to this tranquil situation, but also given me abundant reason to be contented and thankful. Blessed be his holy name. While my children lament my departure, let them recollect that in doing them good, I was only the agent of their Heavenly Father, and that he never withdraws his care and consolations from those who diligently seek him.[21]

Norman Cousins says Jay accepted "the literal truth of the Bible."[22] Monaghan agrees, saying:

> Jay believed the Bible. He knew every word of it to be completely and literally true. His immense faith buoyed him up in every misfortune. His quiet piety and radiant serenity impressed themselves upon all his children. When Peter Augustus, his eldest son, died in 1843 he likewise admonished his children in these last words: "My children, read the Bible and believe it."[23]

In his address to the American Bible Society in 1822 he spoke of the "original, and subsequent fallen, state of man, his promised redemption from the latter, and the institution of sacrifices having reference to it" as being well-known to those who lived before the flood. He mentions Noah in a way which shows he accepted Noah as an actual historical person. He spoke of the confusion of tongues at Babel and God leading Abraham out of the City of Ur into a new land as literal historical events.[24] As president of the American Bible Society, Jay wrote to Rev. S. S. Woodhull, the Society's secretary, that God is the "Author and giver of the gospels."[25]

---

21. John Jay, Last Will and Testament; ibid. I:519-20.
22. Cousins, *"In God We Trust"*, p. 360.
23. Monaghan, *John Jay*, p. 428.
24. John Jay to American Bible Society, May 9, 1822; quoted by Cousins, *"In God We Trust"*, pp. 373-76.
25. John Jay to Rev. S. S. Woodhull, December 7, 1821; quoted by William Jay, *Life of John Jay*, I:454.

Jay trusted the truth of Scripture because he believed it was the inspired Word of God:

> Our Redeemer commanded his apostles to preach the Gospel to every creature: to that end it was necessary that they should be enabled to understand and to preach it correctly, and to demonstrate its Divine origin and institution by incontestible proofs. The Old Testament, which contained the promises and prophesies respecting the Messiah, was finished at a period antecedent to the coming of our Saviour, and therefore afforded no information nor proof of his advent and subsequent proceedings. To qualify the apostles for their important task, they were blessed with the direction and guidance of the Holy Spirit, and by him were enabled to preach the Gospel with concordant accuracy, and in divers languages: they were also embued with power to prove the truth of their doctrine, and of their authority to preach it, by wonderful and supernatural signs and miracles.

These supernatural signs and miracles of the apostolic era, then, were God's way of giving authority to his apostles as they proclaimed the gospel. But God led them to write the New Testament in a way which required both divine inspiration and inerrancy:

> A merciful Providence also provided that some of these inspired men should commit to writing such accounts of the Gospel, and of their acts and proceedings in preaching it, as would constitute and establish a *standard* whereby future preachers and generations might ascertain what they ought to believe and to do; and be thereby secured against the danger of being misled by the mistakes and corruptions incident to tradition. The Bible contains these writings, and exhibits such a connected series of the Divine revelations and dispensations respecting the present and future state of mankind, and so amply attested by internal and external evidence, that we have no reason to desire or expect that further miracles will be wrought to confirm the belief and confidence which they invite and require.[26]

Jay based his faith on the Book which he believed was inspired by God Himself.

In 1823 he addressed the American Bible Society and spoke of "making known the Holy Scriptures, and inculcating the will of their Divine and merciful Author, throughout the world. . . ."[27] Jay

---

26. John Jay to American Bible Society, May 12, 1825; ibid., I:510-15; Cousins, *"In God We Trust"*, pp. 381-84.

27. John Jay to American Bible Society, May 8, 1823; quoted by Cousins, *"In God We Trust"*, p. 378.

shared his understanding of the gospel in an 1824 address to the American Bible Society. He stressed the need to share the gospel with the world, because "a great proportion of mankind are ignorant of the revealed will of God":

> By conveying the Bible to people thus circumstanced we certainly do them a most interesting act of kindness. We thereby enable them to learn, that man was originally created and placed in a state of happiness, but, becoming disobedient, was subjected to the degradation and evils which he and his posterity have since experienced. The Bible will also inform them, that our gracious Creator has provided for us a Redeemer, in whom all the nations of the earth should be blessed—that this Redeemer has made atonement "for the sins of the whole world," and thereby reconciling the Divine justice with the Divine mercy, has opened a way for our redemption and salvation; and that these inestimable benefits are of the free gift and grace of God, not of our deserving, nor in our power to deserve. The Bible will also animate them with many explicit and consoling assurances of the Divine mercy to our fallen race, and with repeated invitations to accept the offers of pardon and reconciliation.[28]

At about age eighty-two, Jay was stricken with a terminal disease and again commended the Bible to his family:

> Always reserved in the expression of his religious feelings, he made no remarks on his situation; but throughout the day his spirits appeared to be unusually raised, and he conversed with cheerfulness and animation on ordinary topics. He was urged by one of the family to tell his children on what foundation he now rested his hopes, and from what source he drew his consolation. "They have the BOOK," was his concise, but expressive reply.[29]

John Jay believed in Jesus Christ as the divine Savior of the world. He accepted the plan of redemption and salvation found in Scripture and as it was taught by orthodox Protestantism. He did not go out of his way to debate religious matters, but he was not ashamed to claim Jesus Christ as his Savior. He wrote concerning his visit to France:

> During my residence there, I do not recollect to have had more than two conversations with atheists about their tenets.
> I was at a large party, of which were several of that description.

28. John Jay to American Bible Society, May 13, 1824; ibid., pp. 378-81.
29. William Jay, *Life of John Jay*, I:458; cf. Monaghan, *John Jay*, p. 435.

They spoke freely and contemptuously of religion. I took no part in the conversation. In the course of it, one of them asked me if I believed in Christ. I answered that I did, and that I thanked God that I did. Nothing further passed between me and them or any of them on that subject.[30]

Jay relied on faith in Jesus Christ and eternal life at the death of his wife:

In may of 1802 Mrs. Jay began to fail rapidly, and on the twenty-eighth, with her husband and children at her bedside, she died. In that tragic hour Jay remained calm. When he saw that death had claimed her he at once led his children into the adjoining room, took up the family Bible and turned to the fifteenth chapter of First Corinthians. His eyes glistened but his voice was firm: "Now if Christ be preached that he rose from the dead, how say some among you that there is no resurrection of the dead? But if there be no resurrection of the dead, then is Christ not risen: and if Christ be not risen, then is our preaching vain, and your faith also is vain. . . . Behold I shew you a mystery; We shall not all sleep, but we shall all be changed, . . . and the dead shall be raised incorruptible. . . . So when this corruptible shall have put on incorruption, and this mortal shall have put on immortality, then shall be brought to pass the saying that is written; Death is swallowed up in victory. . . ." He closed the book and looked out upon the hills that sloped away to the westward. In his mind's eye he beheld the promised reunion with his Sally and his beloved parents—such a scene as William Blake gazed upon when he drew his "Family Reunited in Heaven."[31]

John Jay lived the Christian faith. Monaghan puts it simply: "He excelled in good works."[32] He helped to keep a number of children in schools in Westchester County, and although he was not wealthy, he frequently gave to people who were in need. Dr. A. H. Stevens spoke about a visit to the Jays' home in 1816:

I recall the scene in the family parlor, the venerable Patriarch and his children, and the household within his gates, uniting in thanksgiving, confession and prayer. Sir, it was more like Heaven upon earth than

---

30. John Jay to John Bristed, April 23, 1811; quoted by Cousins, pp. 364-65.
31. Monaghan, *John Jay*, p. 428. One might compare the death of his brother Peter Jay in 1813. A committed Christian, Peter said to John, "I am going fast—through the mercies of my Saviour, I shall receive everlasting life and happiness in less than two days." William Jay, *Life of John Jay*, I:450.
32. Monaghan, *John Jay*, p. 429.

anything I ever witnessed or conceived. It was worth more than all the sermons I ever listened to.[33]

In 1816 Jay's daughter Ann wrote to her brother Peter Augustus of their father, "In him we see verified many of the promises of scripture to those who love & fear God. Surely the end of this man is peace."[34]

Jay believed the Christian faith should affect people's view of politics, and that pastors should speak out against that which is morally repugnant:

> Although the mere expediency of public measures may not be a proper subject for the pulpit, yet, in my opinion, it is the right and duty of our pastors to press the observance of all moral and religious duties, and to animadvert on every course of conduct which may be repugnant to them. . . .[35]

In the same letter he wondered "whether our religion permits Christians to vote for infidel rulers" and concluded that was a question which deserved more consideration. He suggested that "what the prophet said to Jehoshaphat about his attachment to Ahab" [2 Chr 19:2: "Shouldest thou help the ungodly, and love them that hate the Lord?"] might help answer the question.[36]

Jay's application of Scripture and theology to current problems is found in a letter he wrote in 1818 to John Murray, a Quaker who genuinely respected him. Murray and Jay disagreed on the question of war and pacifism, and in the letter Jay outlined his position on the subject.

Jay first noted that the Bible places certain "institutions" or regulations on war; and if the Bible regulates war, it must approve war if conducted according to those regulations.

Then he spoke of moral or natural law which was "given by the Sovereign of the universe to all mankind . . . Being founded by infinite wisdom and goodness on essential right, which never varies, it can require no amendment or alteration." Certain positive ordinances of God, such as circumcision, are of limited obligation,

---

33. Alfred H. Partridge, *Memorial of . . . William Jay* (1960), pp. 13-14; quoted in Monaghan, *John Jay*, p. 430.

34. Ann Jay to Peter Augustus Jay, 1816; ibid., p. 430.

35. John Jay to Jedidiah Morse, January 1, 1813; quoted by Cousins, *"In God We Trust"*, pp. 363-64.

36. Ibid.

and others such as the Sabbath were changed by the Lord of the Sabbath. But basic moral law, including the punishment for murder, has not changed.

Jay notes Murray's objection, that the law was given by Moses, but the law of Moses is superseded by a more perfect system, the gospel of Jesus Christ. Jay responds:

> It is true that the law was given by Moses, not however in his individual or private capacity, but as the agent or instrument, and by the authority of the Almighty. The law demanded exact obedience, and proclaimed: "Cursed is every one that continueth not in all things which are written in the book of the law to do them." The law was inexorable, and by requiring *perfect* obedience, under a penalty so inevitable and dreadful, operated as a schoolmaster to bring us to Christ for *mercy*.
>
> Mercy, and grace, and favour, did come by Jesus Christ; and also that truth which verified the promises and predictions concerning him, and which exposed and corrected the various errors which had been imbibed respecting the Supreme Being, his attributes, laws, and dispensations.

Jesus Christ did not abrogate the moral law in bringing mercy and grace. He corrected certain misunderstandings of the law, such as who is our neighbor; but he left the moral law intact:

> Our Saviour himself assures us that he came not to destroy the law and the prophets, but to fulfill; that whoever shall do and teach the commandments, shall be called great in the kingdom of heaven; that it is easier for heaven and earth to pass, than title of the law to fail. This certainly amounts to a full approbation of it. Even after the resurrection of our Lord, and after the descent of the Holy Spirit, and after the miraculous conversion of Paul, and after the direct revelation of the Christian dispensation to him, he pronounced this memorable encomium on the law, viz.: "The law is *holy,* and the commandments *holy, just,* and *good.*"

Jay explained that the lex talionis, or law of like punishment, gives civil rulers the authority to punish criminals, but does not give private citizens the right to take vengeance on their enemies:

> It is true that one of the *positive* ordinances of Moses, to which you allude, did ordain retaliation or, in other words, a tooth for a tooth. But we are to recollect that it was ordained, not as a rule to regulate the conduct of private individuals toward each other, but as a legal penalty or punishment for certain offences. Retaliation is also

manifest in the punishment prescribed for murder—life for life. Legal punishments are adjusted and inflicted by the law and magistrate, and not by unauthorized individuals. These and all other positive laws or ordinances established by Divine direction, must of necessity be consistent with the moral law. It certainly was not the design of the law or ordinance in question, to encourage a spirit of personal or private revenge. On the contrary, there are express injunctions in the law of Moses which inculcate a very different spirit, such as these: "Thou shalt not avenge, nor bear any grudge against the children of thy people; but thou shalt love thy neighbor as thyself." "Love the stranger, for ye were strangers in Egypt." "If you meet the enemy's ox or his ass going astray, thou shalt surely bring it back to him," etc., etc.

Jay concluded that the moral law can never be violated with the approval of God, and "as the moral law is incorporated in the Christian dispensation, I think it follows that the right to wage *just* and *necessary* war is admitted, and not abolished, by the gospel." In answer to Murray's inquiry whether there ever was a just war, Jay cites the war of David with his rebellious son Absalom:

That war was caused by, and proceeded from, "the lusts" of Absalom, and was horribly wicked. But the war waged against him by David was not caused by, nor did it proceed from, "the lusts" of David, but was right, just, and necessary. Had David submitted to be dethroned by his detestable son, he would, in my opinion, have violated his moral duty and betrayed his official trust.

Jay cited Luke 22:36 ["He that hath no sword, let him sell his garment, and buy one"] and other passages. He also explained the "two kingdoms" concept in clear terms consistent with Lutheran and Calvinist theology:

The gospel appears to me to consider the servants of Christ as having two capacities or character, with correspondent duties to sustain and fulfil.

Being subjects of his *spiritual* kingdom, they are bound in that capacity to fight, pursuant to his orders, with *spiritual* weapons, against his and their spiritual enemies.

Being also subjects and partakers in the rights and interests of a temporal or worldly state or kingdom, they are in that capacity bound, whenever lawfully required, to fight with weapons in just and necessary war, against the *worldly* enemies of that state or kingdom.

He emphasized that because of the fallen sinful nature of man enemies would inevitably arise.

> The depravity which mankind inherited from their first parents, introduced wickedness into the world. That wickedness rendered human government necessary to restrain the violence and injustice resulting from it. To facilitate the establishment and administration of government, the human race became, in the course of Providence, divided into separate and distinct nations. Every nation instituted a government, with authority and power to protect it against domestic and foreign aggressions.

The sinful nature of man necessitates and justifies two types of warfare: "one against domestic malefactors; the other against foreign aggressors. The first being regulated by the law of the land; the second by the law of nations; and both consistently with the moral law."

He concluded that the "swords into plowshares" passage does not refer to the present but to the millennium in which Christ shall rule:

> I nevertheless believe, and have perfect faith in the prophecy, that the time will come when "the nations will beat their swords into plough-shares, and their spears into pruning-hooks; when nation shall not lift up sword against nation, neither shall they learn war any more." But does not this prophecy clearly imply, and give us plainly to understand, that in the *meanwhile*, and *until* the arrival of that blessed period, the nations will not beat their swords into plough-shares, nor their spears into pruning-hooks; that nation will not forbear to lift up sword against nation, nor cease to learn war?
>
> It may be asked, Are we to do nothing to hasten the arrival of that happy period? Literally no created being can either accelerate or retard its arrival. It will not arrive sooner nor later than the appointed time.
>
> But whatever may be the time or the means adopted by Providence for the abolition of war, I think we may, without presumption, conclude that mankind must be prepared and fitted for the reception, enjoyment, and preservation of universal permanent peace, before they will be blessed with it. Are they as yet fitted for it? Certainly not. Even if it was practicable, would it be wise to disarm the good before "the wicked cease from troubling?" By what other means than arms and military force can unoffending rulers and nations protect their rights against unprovoked aggressions from within and from without? Are there any other means to which they could recur, and on the

efficacy of which they could rely. To this question I have not yet heard, nor seen, a direct and precise answer.[37]

Jay saw the establishment of civil government as necessary for the imposition of punishment on wrongdoers, and the waging of just war. He believed natural law and natural rights were closely related, and included the right to own property and enter into contracts.[38] All of these were part of the law of God. By identifying such relationships it is evident that John Jay's Christian faith governed both his public and private life.

Jay was not a narrow partisan of denominationalism. He appeared narrow in 1774, when the Continental Congress proposed that sessions open with prayer. Jay felt that there would be too much diversity with the various denominations present for that to work. However, despite his views, an Episcopalian chaplain was appointed.[39]

Jay's perspective broadened as his Christian faith deepened. The Episcopal Church to which he belonged, taught the doctrine of apostolic succession—only those whose ordination could be traced back to the apostles were ministers of God. Jay did not agree. He asked,

If it be asked, whether the ministers of the Calvinistic and of certain other churches are of apostolic succession, it is answered by all our bishops and clergy that they are not. . . .

Who is there among us that can be prepared to declare, in solemn prayer, and in such positive and unqualified terms, that none but Episcopalian ministers have any part or lot in this important promise? Who is there that can be certain that the apostles, as to that promise, were not considered as the representatives of all who should become sincere and pious converts to, and believers in, the doctrines which they were sent to publish and to teach? . . . Great, indeed, must be the confidence and hardihood of those advocates for this construction of the promise who can, without hesitation, deny that our blessed Redeemer was with those non-Episcopalian ministers and congregations amounting to several hundred thousands, who for his sake endured all the varieties and rigors of persecution. If the great Captain of our Salvation was not with them, how and by whom were they enabled to meet and sustain such trials so firmly, to resist

37. John Jay to John Murray, April 15, 1818; quoted by Cousins, *"In God We Trust"*, pp. 365-73.

38. John Jay, *The Federalist No. 2; The Federalist Papers*, ed. Clinton Rossiter (New York: Mentor Books, 1961), pp. 37 ff.

39. Cousins, *"In God We Trust"*, p. 360.

the adversary so resolutely, and to fight the good fight of faith so triumphantly?[40]

Perhaps working with people of different denominations through the American Bible Society helped broaden his perspective. He told the Society in 1824:

> It is well known, that both cathedrals and meeting-houses have heretofore exhibited individuals who have been universally and justly celebrated as real and useful Christians; and it is also well known, that at present not a few, under similar circumstances and of similar characters, deserve the like esteem and commendation. As *real* Christians are made so by Him without whom we "can do nothing," it is equally certain that He receives them unto His family, and that in *His* family mutual love and uninterrupted concord never cease to prevail. There is no reason to believe or suppose that this family will be divided into separate classes, and that separate apartments in the mansions of bliss will be allotted to them according to the different sects from which they had proceeded.
>
> These truths and considerations direct our attention to the *new* commandment of our Saviour, that his disciples "do love one another." . . .[41]

This certainly does not mean Jay ever compromised his fundamental principles, or that he denied the centrality of Jesus Christ as the only and essential way of salvation. Jay recognized, perhaps most clearly later in life, that all who trust Jesus Christ for salvation are part of Christ's true church. He was able to accept differences of opinion among Christians, shown by the closing of his letter to the pacifist Quaker John Murray, "We differ in opinion, and, I am persuaded, with equal sincerity."[42]

Jay believed in religious liberty like the other founding fathers. He recognized that state control of the church tended to suppress church growth and church strength, and that "Since the rights of man and the just limits of authority in Church and State have been more generally and clearly understood, the Church has been less disturbed by that zeal which 'is not according to knowledge'; and liberal sentiments and tolerant principles are constantly enlarging

---

40. John Jay, Letter to the Corporation of Trinity Church; ibid., pp. 385-88.

41. John Jay to American Bible Society, May 13, 1824; quoted by William Jay, *Life of John Jay*, I:509.

42. John Jay to John Murray, April 15, 1818; quoted by Cousins, *"In God We Trust"*, pp. 365-73.

the sphere of their influence."[43] His support for religious liberty and his political creed were based on the will of God, the author and guarantor of all human rights. In 1826, at the age of eighty, he told the Committee of the Corporation of the City of New York, "The most effectual means of securing the continuance of our civil and religious liberties is, always to remember with reverence and gratitude the source from which they flow."[44]

43. John Jay to American Bible Society, May 13, 1824; ibid., pp. 378-81.
44. John Jay to Committee of the Corporation of the City of New York, June 29, 1826; quoted by William Jay, *Life of John Jay*, I:457-58.

11 Gouverneur Morris

If George Washington represents the spirit which called the Constitution together; and James Madison represents the ideas contained in the Constitution; then Gouverneur Morris represents the letter of the Constitution. Morris spoke on the Convention floor 173 times, more than any other delegate. As head of the Committee on Style, he drafted and was then responsible for most of the wording of the Constitution.

Morris was born to a prominent family January 31, 1752, in Morrisania, New York. He was fond of sports as a child and was educated in a French Huguenot school in New Rochelle, New York. He then attended King's College (now Columbia), studied for the bar, and began to practice law at age nineteen. At age twenty-four he lost a leg in an accident, and his wooden leg was his distinguishing feature throughout his life.

Morris served in the New York Assembly 1775-1777, during which time he, along with John Jay and Robert R. Livingston, drafted a constitution for New York. He served in the Continental Congress 1777-1779, but was defeated for reelection because as an opponent of lawlessness, he was suspected of being pro-British. He then settled in Philadelphia to practice law, and in 1780 Robert Morris (no relation) chose him as assistant superintendent of finance for the American War of Independence, a post he held until 1785.

In 1787 the state of Pennsylvania chose him as a delegate to the

Constitutional Convention, where he was a leading advocate of a strong central government. He favored a president elected for life, senators with life tenure chosen by the President, and independence and life tenure for appellate judges. He also opposed slavery, declaring, "I will never concur in upholding domestic slavery. It is the curse of heaven on the States where it prevails."[1] Morris supported ratification of the Constitution, although he felt it failed to give the federal government enough authority.

President Washington sent Morris to France in 1789, and later named him U.S. Minister to France. Morris detested French morals and was thoroughly disgusted by the French Revolution, but positively represented American interests while serving there. He was the only foreign minister to remain in France during the Reign of Terror. On several occasions his house in France was searched and he was arrested once for not having a "citizen card" in his possession; each time he protested and eventually received a surly apology from the French government. He tried to shelter the French aristocracy and was unsuccessful in arranging for the King and Queen to escape. As a result, the revolutionary French government "feared and disliked" Morris.[2] When Washington's administration became disgusted with "Citizen" Genet (French minister to the U.S.) and demanded his recall, the French government retaliated by demanding that the U.S. recall Gouverneur Morris in 1794. Morris spent the next four years traveling throughout Europe, and returned to Morrisania, New York, in 1798.

In 1800 New York elected Morris to the United States Senate to fill an unexpired term. He served until 1803. As a Federalist Morris was critical of the Jefferson administration, but supported the Louisiana Purchase, perhaps as a means of reducing French influence in the Western Hemisphere. He also encouraged the plans for the Erie Canal, something he had suggested twenty years earlier. Despite his overall low view of human nature, he had great faith in the United States of America. Morris showed keen foresight in many ways; his prediction of American greatness was almost prophetic: "The proudest empire in Europe is but a bauble compared to what America *will* be, *must* be, in the course of two centuries, perhaps of one!"[3]

Morris opposed the War of 1812, calling it an "unjust war." He felt that the United States was giving aid and comfort to France by

---

1. Gouverneur Morris; quoted by Henry Cabot Lodge, *Historical and Political Essays* (New York: Houghton & Mifflin, 1892), p. 84.
2. Lodge, *Essays*, p. 104
3. Morris, 1801; quoted by Lodge, *Essays*, p. 113 (emphasis original).

going to war with Britain, and that this was an affront to "Christian civilization."[4] He urged New York and New England to secede from the Union and form a new confederation; he argued that secession was constitutional based on his experience at the Constitutional Convention.[5]

Faith in God

Gouverneur Morris had a deep and abiding faith in a God who intervenes in world affairs. This faith distinguishes Morris from the deists with their belief in an absentee God. Speaking to the New York Assembly about American relations with Britain shortly before the Declaration of Independence, Morris declared "Providence has kindly interfered so far for our preservation."[6] An April 17, 1778, letter to his mother shows his faith in God and his willingness to be part of God's plan:

> I look forward serenely to the course of events, confident that the Fountain of supreme wisdom and virtue will provide for the happiness of his creatures. . . .
> Whenever the present storm subsides, I shall rush with eagerness into the bosom of private life, but while it continues, and while my country calls for the exertion of that little share of abilities, which it has pleased God to bestow on me, I hold it my indispensable duty to give myself to her.[7]

He also expressed a faith in God in letters he wrote to George Washington, a man Morris greatly admired, "I hope in God, my dear Sir, that you may long continue to preside."[8] In 1793 he expressed the hope that Washington would seek reelection, "It will be time enough for you to have a successor, when it shall please God to call you from this world's theater."[9]

---

4. Morris; quoted by M. E. Bradford, *A Worthy Company: Brief Lives of the United States Constitution* (Marlborough, New Hampshire: Plymouth Rock Foundation, 1982), p. 92.

5. Morris, "Address to the People of the State of New York"; cited by Bradford, *A Worthy Company*, p. 92.

6. Morris, Speech to New York Congress, ca. 1776; quoted by Jared Sparks, *The Life of Gouverneur Morris, with Selections from His Correspondence and Miscellaneous Papers* (Boston: Gray and Bowen, 1832), I:106.

7. Morris, letter to mother, April 17, 1778; quoted by Sparks, *Life of Morris*, I:157–58.

8. Morris to George Washington, January 24, 1789; quoted by Sparks, *Life of Morris*, II:88.

9. Morris to George Washington, June 25, 1793; quoted by Sparks, *Life of Morris*, II:335.

When Morris' sister's child passed away, he consoled his sister with faith in God:

> His bounty is as unbounded as His power! Confiding in the one, be resigned to the other; and accepting with gratitude what it may please Him to give, surrender with respectful obedience what He shall think proper to take away. O God! thy will be done.[10]

Morris was asked what he predicted for immoral, revolution-torn France, and he replied grimly, "Guerre, famine, peste (war, famine, pestilence)", then added, "I pray God the prediction be not fully accomplished."[11] He saw God's hand at work in the defeat of Napoleon by Czarist Russia: "The signal victories of Russia (over France) demand our thanks to Almighty God, by whose Providence they are ordered."[12] He expressed confidence in God's goodness and intervention on the behalf of the French refugees in Dresden, Germany:

> . . . This ground of hope in the kindness of that Being, who is to all his creatures an indulgent father. . . .
>
> O God! it is thy wisdom which hath ordained, and thy hand which heavily hath inflicted this blow, consistent most surely with those just decrees, which we may not presume to measure, nor ever dare to know, but yet we know, for we feel, that thy mercy will season to those, who suffer them, the sharpness of these afflictions. Yes, we feel! and it is this consciousness, which, precious and paramount to all reasoning, has diffused through the whole human race, and impressed in the heart of each individual, the same conviction of his own existence, and the existence of God. Yes, we feel! and it is in the strict accordance between our finest feelings, and the principles of the religion we profess, that this stands demonstrated by their evidence to be of divine origin.[13]

Late in life Morris declared that "The Almighty will work out his wise ends by means of human folly,"[14] recognizing that God uses the foolish things of this world for his glory (1 Cor 1:18-31). He also

---

10. Morris to Ephemia Ogden, June 23, 1793; quoted by Sparks, *Life of Morris*, III:44.

11. Morris to David Humphreys, June 5, 1793; quoted in Sparks, *Life of Morris*, II:323.

12. Morris to Harrison Gray Otis, April 29, 1813; quoted in Sparks, *Life of Morris*, III:288.

13. Morris, Diary, August 19, 1796; quoted in Sparks, *Life of Morris*, I:435.

14. Morris to Timothy Pickering, October 17, 1814; reprinted in Sparks, *Life of Morris*, III:313.

thanked God for his blessings and concluded, "I descend towards the grave full of gratitude to the Giver of all good."[15]

Madame de Damas, a close friend, wrote:

> If instead of a simple error, an opinion is ventured in his presence offensive to religion, good morals, or sound political principles, it is no longer a regard for truth alone, it is the passion of virtue, the ardor for justice, the love of humanity, which inflames his generous soul. . . .
>
> The idea of a Deity is always present, the habit of contemplating him in his works, of imitating his goodness, of submitting to his will, with that calm resignation which arises from a belief that God can will nothing but what is good; such is the fountain from which his soul derives a confidence full of serenity, a boundless charity, and a hope. . . .[16]

Jesus Christ

It is difficult to determine what Gouverneur Morris thought of Jesus Christ, since Jesus is seldom mentioned in his correspondence. Bradford states that Morris was an Episcopalian, and at that time the Episcopal Church had an orthodox view of the Trinity and Jesus Christ. Absent some evidence to the contrary, we may assume that Morris agreed with the doctrine of the church to which he belonged.

A reference to Christ does appear in his writings. In 1785 Morris opposed a proposal to abolish the charter of the Bank of North America which the Pennsylvania State Assembly was considering. Morris thought the action would violate commitments made by the state:

> How can we hope for public peace and national prosperity, if the faith of governments so solemnly pledged can be so suddenly violated? If private property can be so lightly infringed? Destroy this prop, which once gave us support, and where will you turn in the hour of distress? To whom will you look for succor? By what promises or vows can you hope to obtain confidence? This hour of distress will come. It comes to all, and the moment of affliction is known to Him alone, whose divine providence exalts or depresses states and kingdoms. Not by the blind dictates of arbitrary will. Not by a tyrannous and despotic mandate. But in proportion to their obedience or disobedience of his just and holy laws. It is he who

15. Morris, 1809; quoted by Lodge, *Essays*, p. 112.
16. Madame de Damas; reprinted in Sparks, *Life of Morris*, I:508–9.

commands us that we abstain from wrong. It is he who tells you, "do unto others as ye would that they should do unto you."[17]

The "Him" who "exalts or depresses . . . kingdoms," who ordains "just and holy laws," and "who commands us to . . . abstain from wrong," is clearly God. The statement, "do unto others," is a quotation from Jesus Christ (Mt 7:12; Lk 6:31). The same pronoun is used for Jesus Christ and God. It appears that Morris did equate Jesus Christ with God.

The Bible

Morris did not clearly state his view of the Scriptures. But his writings frequently contain biblical allusions which indicate a familiarity with the Bible. He refers to the rod of Aaron in Egypt swallowing up the others; he mentions that a certain burden is easy and yoke is light, he hopes that a certain person might remember his creator in the days of his youth, he speaks of the trumpets of Joshua; he speaks of "peace in our time, O Lord!"; he hopes foreign nobles will keep their estates in the western territories because where a man's treasure is, there will his heart be also; they who live by the sword will die by the sword; people will not listen because if they hear not Moses and the prophets, neither will they be persuaded, though one rose from the dead; and he refers to a "den of robbers."[18]

In an 1811 letter to John Murray, Jr., he referred to the "Holy Writings."[19] And in 1813 he wrote to David B. Ogden, "to which I reply, in the language of Holy Writ, thou shalt not do evil that good may come of it."[20] Morris recognized special revelation—something the deist denied.

Gouverneur Morris held a low view of human nature, as did most Americans of his day. He had no naive views of human goodness or human perfectability. And yet, human nature was not totally bad; it contained elements of both good and bad: "There is always a counter-current in human affairs, which opposes alike both good and evil. Thus the good we hope is seldom obtained, and the evil we fear is rarely realized."[21]

17. Morris, "An Address on the Bank of North America," Pennsylvania State Assembly, 1785; reprinted in Sparks, *Life of Morris*, III:465.

18. Sparks, *Life of Morris*, II:61, 120, 245; III:160, 203, 213, 251, 372.

19. Morris to John Murray, Jr., September 22, 1811; reprinted in Sparks, *Life of Morris*, III:270.

20. Morris to David B. Ogden, April 5, 1813; reprinted in Sparks, *Life of Morris*, III:287.

21. Morris, 1803; quoted by Lodge, *Essays*, p. 111.

Morris, like many pessimists, had an excellent sense of humor which is revealed in his mild ridicule of Jefferson's faith in human goodness:

> It is the fashion with those discontented creatures called Federalists, to say that our President [Jefferson] is not a Christian; yet they must acknowledge that, in true Christian meekness, when smitten on one cheek he turns the other, and by his late appointment of Monroe has taken especial care that a stone which the builders rejected should become the first of the corner. These are his works; and for his faith, it is not a grain of mustard; but the full size of a pumpkin, so that while men of mustard-seed faith can only move mountains, he finds no difficulty in swallowing them. He believes, for instance, in the perfectability of man, the wisdom of mobs, and moderation of Jacobins He believes in payment of debts by diminution of revenue, in defense of territory by reduction of armies, and in vindication of rights by the appointment of ambassadors.[22]

A strong government was necessary, Morris believed, to restrain man's evil tendencies. However, the type of government a particular nation should have varied. The French, for example, were not capable of the same type of government as the Americans. Morris explained, "They (the French) want an American constitution, with the exception of a King instead of a President, without reflecting that they have not American citizens to support that constitution."[23]

Morris anticipated as early as 1789 that the French Revolution would lead to "probable tyranny."[24] And the reason for his pessimism was the low morals of the French people:

> The materials for a revolution in this country (France) are very indifferent. Everybody agrees that there is an utter prostration of morals; but this general proposition can never convey to an American mind the degree of depravity. It is not by any figure of rhetoric, or force of language, that the idea can be communicated. A hundred anecdotes, and a hundred thousand examples, are required to show the extreme rottenness of every member. There are men and women who are greatly and eminently virtuous. I have the pleasure to number many in my acquaintance; but they stand forward from a background deeply and darkly shaded. It is however, from such crumbling matter, that the great edifice of freedom is to be erected

22. Morris, 1803; quoted by Lodge, *Essays*, p. 110.
23. Morris to George Washington, July 3, 1789; quoted by Lodge, *Essays*, p. 92.
24. Morris, Diary, September 16, 1789; reprinted in Sparks, *Life of Morris*, I:323.

here. Perhaps, like the stratum of rock, which is spread under the whole surface of their country, it may harden when exposed to the air; but it seems quite as likely that it will fall and crush the builders.
. . . there is one fatal principle which pervades all ranks. It is a perfect indifference to the violation of engagements. Inconstancy is so mingled in the blood, marrow, and very essence of this people, that when a man of high rank and importance laughs to day at what he seriously asserted yesterday, it is considered as in the natural order of things. Consistency is a phenomenon. Judge, then, what would be the value of association, should such a thing be proposed, and even adopted. The great mass of the common people have no religion but their priests, no law but their superiors, no morals but their interest. These are the creatures who, led by drunken curates, are now in the high road a la liberte, and the first use they make of it is to form insurrections everywhere for the want of bread.[25]

From various letters and diary entries it is evident that Morris deplored the immorality of the French people. He viewed the French Revolution as a monstrosity, built on a false foundation and therefore doomed to tragic failure. His views of the French Revolution give insight into his thinking. His vivid descriptions of the all-pervasive disregard for human life and rampant lawlessness clearly demonstrate the depths of savagery to which a revolution can sink, if it is not based on true principles of divine law.

Morris recognized France's central problem as the lack of sound religious principles. He wrote to Jefferson from Paris, "The open contempt of religion, also, cannot but be offensive to all sober minded men."[26] He wrote to Thomas Pinckney that "Since I have been in this country, I have seen the worship of many idols, but little of the true God." He hoped for a constitution as "the principle means, under Divine Providence, of extending the blessings of freedom." But he doubted this would be forthcoming, "because I do not yet perceive that reformation of morals without which liberty is but an empty sound."[27]

Morris wished the best possible government for the French nation despite his objections to French morality. However, he believed that the American constitutional republic would not work in France.

25. Morris to George Washington, April 29, 1789; reprinted in Sparks, *Life of Morris*, II:68–69.
26. Morris to Thomas Jefferson, December 21, 1792; reprinted in Sparks, *Life of Morris*, II:255.
27. Morris to Thomas Pinckney, December 3, 1792; reprinted in Sparks, *Life of Morris*, II:248.

While Morris believed the nature of government must vary according to the character of its people, he also spoke about the absolute principles of the law of nature and the law of nations. He insisted that "the tranquility and liberty of nations can only be sustained upon the basis of justice."[28]

He believed those principles apply differently in different situations. A system of government that would work for a highly religious and moral people (as Morris thought the Americans to be) would not work in an immoral society like France.

And because principles vary from country to country Morris believed that, "The true object of a great statesman is to give to any particular nation the kind of laws which is suitable to them, and the best constitution which they are capable of."[29]

Morris believed that nations must learn the supremacy of law before they can govern themselves. Otherwise, they are easily exploited by demagogues and led into radical causes. He wrote to Robert R. Livingston, "The engine by which a giddy population can be most easily wrought on to do mischief, is their hatred of the rich."[30] He said of American proposals for a constitution, "Give the votes to the people who have no property, and they will sell them to the rich"—or else vote themselves the possessions of those more prosperous.[31]

Societies need education and training before they are ready for self-government, and they must learn to revere laws above the whims of men, even majorities. He wrote in 1789 from France,

> . . . in free governments the laws being supreme, and the only supreme, there arises from that circumstances a spirit of order, and a confidence in those laws for the redress of all injuries, public or private. The sword of justice is placed in the hands of a constitutional magistrate and each individual trembles at the idea of wresting it from his grasp, lest the point shall be turned upon his own bosom, or that of his friend. In despotic governments the people, habituated to behold everything bending beneath the weight of power, never possess that power for a moment without abusing it. Slaves, driven to despair, take arms, execute vast vengeance, and then sink back to their former condition of slaves. In such societies the patriot, the melancholy patriot, sides with the despot, because anything is better

28. Morris, "Notes on the Form of a Constitution for France," uncertain date; reprinted in Sparks, *Life of Morris*, III:481.

29. Morris, 1798; quoted by Lodge, *Essays*, p. 108.

30. Morris to Robert R. Livingston, October 10, 1802; reprinted in Sparks, *Life of Morris*, III:172.

31. Morris, quoted and cited by Bradford, *A Worthy Company*, p. 91.

than a wild and bloody confusion. Those, therefore, who form the sublime and godlike idea of rescuing their fellow creatures from a slavery, they have long groaned under, must begin by instruction, and proceed by slow degrees, must content themselves with planting the tree, from which posterity is to gather the fruit.[32]

In saying that law is supreme, Morris meant people are to place law on such a pedestal that all respect it, and no one is in a position to exploit or manipulate it to his own advantage. Neither majorities nor minorities nor rulers nor commoners will be able to change law without careful deliberation. Judges are to interpret and apply the law without regard to whether they will be reelected or reappointed. Morris favored life tenure for appellate judges, because "Those who are charged with the important duties of administering justice, should, if possible, depend only on God."[33]

Morris stated, in his notes suggesting a constitution for France, that religion plays a major role in educating people for self-government:

> Religion is the only solid basis of good morals; therefore education should teach the precepts of religion, and the duties of man toward God.
>
> These duties are, internally, love and adoration; externally, devotion and obedience; therefore provision should be made for maintaining divine worship as well as education.
>
> But each one has a right to entire liberty as to religious opinions, for religion is the relation between God and man; therefore it is not within the reach of human authority.[34]

Morris proposed each district in France have a Council of Education and Worship, formed and headed by the local bishop and other ecclesiastical and educational authorities, and that the state collect tithes for education and worship. He also proposed a legislature of ninety senators, twenty of whom were to be bishops and other church authorities.[35]

Morris probably recognized that this type of church establishment, while suitable to France, would not work in the United States. It is interesting that Morris believed state funding and

32. Morris, "Observations on Government, Applicable to the Political State of France," July, 1789; reprinted by Sparks, *Life of Morris*, II:465.

33. Morris, Speech Prepared for the King of France; reprinted in Sparks, *Life of Sparks*, II:506.

34. Morris, "Notes on the Form of a Constitution for France," uncertain date; reprinted by Sparks, *Life of Morris*, III:483.

35. Ibid., III:488, 490–91.

maintenance of divine worship and education, and "entire liberty of religious opinions" could co-exist.

Morris died November 6, 1816, living long enough to see the restoration of the Bourban dynasty in France.

It is impossible to say for certain that Gouverneur Morris was a Christian. He did not clearly express himself on religious doctrines. He did display faith in a God who is active in human affairs. He belonged to a church which affirmed the Triune God and the divine authority of the Bible; his public statements on those subjects are in accord with that position. His view of the nature of man recognized human sinfulness, his political beliefs were formed around that view of human nature. And he saw religion and morality as essential prerequisites for a free society. He definitely formed his political philosophy around a biblical worldview.

12 Benjamin Franklin

Asecular Puritan! That title perhaps best fits Benjamin Franklin. He combined so many interests and traits that he is a difficult person to classify. He served as a printer's apprentice, printer, publisher, and editor during his eighty-four years. His scientific mind led to many discoveries: the armonica, the Franklin stove, and bifocals. His observations on geology, continental drift, climate changes, and elephants in the Arctic were well known. His kite experiment with lightning was so famous that Jefferson said Franklin's name would be venerated "so long as the thunder of heaven shall be heard or feared."[1]

Franklin's interests went beyond science. He was an eminent philosopher and thinker and founder of the American Philosophical Society. His *Autobiography* is the most widely read in the world. His practical, but profound sayings in *Poor Richard's Almanac* have impressed millions. He served as a military commander, delegate to the Continental Congress, signer of the Declaration of Independence, U.S. Minister to England and later France, Governor of Pennsylvania, and delegate to the Constitutional Convention. Carl Van Doren concludes Franklin's 782-page biography by describing him as "a harmonious human multitude."[2]

1. Thomas Jefferson to Jonathan Williams, July 3, 1796; quoted by Andrew M. Allison, W. Cleon Skousen, and M. Richard Maxfield, *The Real Benjamin Franklin* (Salt Lake City, Utah: The Freeman Institute, 1982), p. 233.

2. Carl Van Doren, *Benjamin Franklin* (New York: Viking Press, 1938), p. 782.

Benjamin Franklin the son of Josiah Franklin, a Congregationalist, was born in Boston on January 17, 1706; and despite the stormy winter weather, he was carried across the street the same day to be baptized in the Old South Church. The Franklin home was frequently the scene of prayer meetings,[3] psalmsinging,[4] and other religious activity.

Benjamin learned to read at an early age; he found much religious literature in his father's library. He says in his *Autobiography* that "I do not remember when I could not read."[5] I "was put to the grammar-school at eight years of age, my father intending to devote me, as the tithe of his sons, to the service of the Church. . . . My uncle Benjamin [a clergyman], too, approved of it, and proposed to give me all his short-hand volumes of sermons, I suppose as a stock to set up with, if I would learn his character."[6] Franklin had two years of formal education in grammar school before he returned home to assist his father in his business as a "tallow-chandler" and "sope-boiler."

Franklin says he "had been religiously educated as a Presbyterian."[7] In fact, his home church in Boston was Congregational, but as a young man he moved to Philadelphia, and Presbyterians in Philadelphia were the foremost spokesmen for Calvinism—just as the Congregationalists were the foremost spokesmen for Calvinism in Boston. (Writing in Philadelphia, Franklin naturally referred to the Congregationalists as Presbyterians, a term his local readers would understand.)

Cotton Mather, the famous Calvinist theologian, was frequently the preacher at the Congregational Church his family attended in Boston. Franklin did not accept all of Mather's stern Calvinist doctrines, but he admired Mather,[8] shared his faith in God, and learned much of Mather's ethical system. Franklin was impressed with Mather's emphasis on the Puritan work ethic.[9] Throughout his life Franklin expressed in secular terms what Rev. Mather stressed in terms of Calvinist theology. Whitney Griswold says that Franklin:

---

3. Ibid., p. 5.

4. Allison et al., *The Real Benjamin Franklin*, p. 7.

5. Benjamin Franklin, *Autobiography*, 1771–75; reprinted Garden City, New York: Garden City Publishing Co., Inc., 1916), p. 13.

6. Franklin, *Autobiography*, p. 13. By "tithe" he means that he was the tenth son and 13th child; by "character" he means his system of shorthand.

7. Franklin, *Autobiography II*, (1784); reprinted in *Franklin's Autobiographical Writings*, ed. Carl Van Doren (New York: Viking Press, 1945), p. 624.

8. Whitney Griswold, "Two Puritans on Prosperity," in *Benjamin Franklin and the American Character*, ed. Charles R. Sanford. (Boston: D.C. Heath & Co., 1955), p. 44.

9. Ibid., pp. 43–44.

. . . subscribed to a system of ethics identical to Cotton Mather's. In his life Franklin was a Deist, if not an out-and-out agnostic; in his writings, he was the soul of Puritanism. Why was this?

To be sure, Franklin had been born a Puritan in Puritan society. In childhood he heard his father admonish him over and over again on the inestimable value of all the Puritan virtues. But neither heredity nor environment can wholly account for Dr. Franklin. Was there some spiritual kinship, then, some intellectual contact with Puritan philosophers? Franklin himself says there was. The books which he precociously read numbered among them Pilgrim's Progress, Plutarch, and the works of Daniel Defoe. But it was from none of these that the spark of Franklin's Puritanism flashed. If we are to take him at his word, we must consider rather a small volume entitled *Essays to Do Good* by the Reverend Cotton Mather. This, he says in the *Autobiography*, "perhaps gave me such a turn of thinking that had an influence on some of the principle future events of my life." And in 1784, from the terminus of his great career, he wrote Cotton Mather's son renewing the acknowledgment. The *Essays* had given him "such a turn of thinking, as to have an influence on my conduct through life, for I have always set a greater value on the character of a *doer of good*, than on any other kind of reputation; and if I have been, as you seem to think, a useful citizen, the public owes the advantage of it to that book."[10]

Griswold says "it would be interesting" to lay the texts of Mather's *Essays* and Franklin's *Autobiography* side by side, so much is the former reflected in the latter."[11] Like Mather, Franklin attributed to the Lord his rise from poverty to affluence, and emphasized the virtues of temperance, silence, order, resolution, frugality, industry, sincerity, justice, moderation, cleanliness, tranquility, chastity, and humility. Elsewhere Franklin stressed the responsibility to be charitable.

Franklin was brought up in a Christian home, taught from the Bible, attended church regularly, and was indoctrinated in the Calvinist religion. He loved the hymns of Issacs Watts;[12] his favorite author was John Bunyan of *Pilgrim's Progress*. As a young child, he expected to enter the ministry.

But Franklin began to depart from the orthodox faith during his teens. He says in his *Autobiography*:

10. Ibid., p. 45.
11. Ibid., p. 46.
12. Melvin H. Buxbaum, *Benjamin Franklin and the Zealous Presbyterians* (University Park: Pennsylvania State University Pres, 1975), p. 66.

My parents had early given me religious impressions, and brought me through my childhood piously in the Dissenting way. But I was scarce fifteen, when, after doubting by turns of several points, as I found them disputed in the different books I read, I began to doubt of Revelation itself. Some books against Deism fell into my hands; they were said to be the substance of sermons preached at Boyle's Lectures. It happened that they wrought an effect on me quite contrary to what was intended by them; for the arguments of the Deists, which were quoted to be refuted, appeared to me much stronger than the refutations; in short, I soon became a thorough Deist.[13]

Elsewhere he mentions that reading the writings of Shaftesbury and Collins led him to "become a real doubter in many points of our religious doctrine."[14]

Franklin became an apprentice printer to his brother James at about age twelve. The two became embroiled in a controversy with the clergy over the practice of inoculation against smallpox. The clergy favored inoculation, while the scientific community opposed it; the Franklins sided with the scientists.[15] During the same period, Franklin anonymously wrote the famous Silence Dogood letters which appeared in his brother's newspaper, the *New England Courant*. Silence Dogood appeared as a widow of a clergyman, a religious woman, but very opposed to the bigotry and hypocrisy of the Calvinist or Puritan community in which she lived.[16] Franklin exposed his anti-Calvinist feelings in these letters and in other ways, becoming somewhat controversial in the community. At one point he stated that the Calvinists were "so zealous for the Confession, that they seem to give it Preference to the Holy Scriptures."[17] This indicated that his hostility was not necessarily directed against religion or Christianity as a whole. He claimed that his "indiscreet disputations about religion began to make me pointed at with horror by good people as an infidel and an atheist."[18] Partly for this reason, he left Boston and moved to Philadelphia at age seventeen.

He worked for a printer in Philadelphia and eventually became a printer, publisher, editor, and author. These ventures were so successful that by age forty he could retire and devote himself to

13. Franklin, *Autobiography*, pp. 110–11.
14. Ibid., p. 29.
15. Buxbaum, *Benjamin Franklin*, p. 48.
16. Ibid., pp. 47–76.
17. Ibid., p. 103.
18. Franklin, *Autobiography*, p. 39.

civic projects. However, his rebellion against his Calvinistic roots continued throughout these years. He seldom attended church, and had problems with "that hard-to-be governed passion of youth that hurried me frequently into intrigues with low women that fell in my way."[19] As a young man he developed a pantheistic form of religion, believing that God is in nature.[20] Some historians suggest that Franklin doubted immortality during this period, though he himself denies that. Franklin also joined freemasonry, rising to the rank of master mason, and was more influenced by masonic thinking than the other founding fathers. However, as mentioned earlier and as Van Doren also notes, "Freemasonry in America had been social and local, with little influence in politics."[21]

Franklin's basic problem with the Calvinists during these years was that they believed in revelation and he placed his ultimate faith in human reason. As Fay says, "The antinomy between reason and holy revelation was brutally made clear to him by these [deist] philosophers and by his companions. Like them, he had chosen reason, but more than they he had kept a hold on a simple natural belief; he always remained faithful to that religion which the sun and beasts of the earth continually proclaim and for which the human soul is eternally seeking."[22] Franklin confirms that throughout this period of his life "Revelation had indeed no weight with me."[23]

However, God's hand was not totally removed from Franklin's life during this time. He says in his second *Autobiography*:

> I had been religiously educated as a Presbyterian; and tho' some of the dogmas of that persuasion, such as the eternal decrees of God, election, reprobation, etc., appeared to me unintelligible, others doubtful, and I early absented myself from the public assemblies of the sect, Sunday being my studying day, I never was without some religious principles. I never doubted, for instances, the existence of the Deity; that he made the world, and govern'd it by his Providence; that the most acceptable service of God was doing good to man; that our souls are immortal; and that all crime will be punished, and virtue rewarded, either here or hereafter. These I esteem'd the essentials of every religion; and, being to be found in all the religions we had in our country, I respected them all, tho' with different

---

19. Franklin; quoted by Allison et al., *The Real Benjamin Franklin*, p. 39.
20. Bernard Fay, *Franklin, the Apostle of Modern Times* (Boston: Little, Brown & Co., 1929), pp. 91–93; cf. Van Doren, *Benjamin Franklin*, p. 51.
21. Van Doren, *Benjamin Franklin*, p. 656.
22. Fay, *Franklin*, p. 44.
23. Franklin, *Autobiography*, p. 112.

degrees of respect, as I found them more or less mix'd with other
articles, which, without any tendency to inspire, promote, or confirm
morality, serv'd principally to divide us, and make us unfriendly to
one another. This respect to all, with an opinion that the worst had
some good effects, induc'd me to avoid all discourse that might tend
to lessen the good opinion another might have of his own religion;
and as our province increas'd in people, and new places of worship
were continually wanted, and generally erected by voluntary contribution, my mite for such purpose, whatever might be the sect, was
never refused.[24]

Franklin's autobiographies reveal that during this period he held a
basic faith in God, and although he did not accept some of the basic
doctrines of Calvinism, he did believe that Calvinism and other
Christian systems were of great social value because they gave
people an incentive to live good, moral, virtuous lives. He was
willing to encourage people to be faithful to their religious beliefs
and was willing to support those religions financially, even though
he could not accept their theology intellectually.

Franklin eventually began to see the value in orthodox Christianity and to doubt the value of deism. After admitting that at one point
in his life he had become a "thorough Deist," Franklin continues:

My arguments perverted some others, particularly Collins and Ralph;
but, each of them having afterwards wrong'd me greatly without the
least compunction, and recollecting Keith's conduct towards me
(who was another free-thinker), and my own towards Vernon and
Miss Read, which at times gave me great trouble, I began to suspect
that this doctrine, tho' it might be true, was not very useful.[25]

In other words, Christianity provided incentives for men to live
moral lives, with its promises of eternal rewards and punishments,
and deism did not. Franklin preferred that men live by Christianity
even though it be objectively false, than by deism even though it be
objectively true.

He acknowledged that God must be something more than the
God of the deists who does not actively intervene in human affairs.
Here Franklin can be identified as a theist; one who believes in a
more personal God who relates to man in history. God preserved
Franklin from the potentially tragic consequences of his own foolish
actions during his years of immorality:

24. Van Doren, *Autobiographical Writings*, p. 624.
25. Franklin, *Autobiography*, p. 111.

And this persuasion, with the kind hand of Providence, or some guardian angel, or accidental favourable circumstances and situations, or all together, preserved me, thro' this dangerous time of youth, and the hazardous situations I was sometimes in among strangers, remote from the eye and advice of my father, without any willful gross immorality or injustice, that might have been expected from my want of religion.[26]

Two people influenced Franklin as he began his new life in Philadelphia. Franklin lived with and worked for a French Protestant printer named Keimer. He was a maverick in religious matters, but a biblicist who wore his beard at full length because of Leviticus 19:27 and kept the seventh day as the Sabbath. Franklin and Keimer discussed religion extensively, and for the most part agreeably.[27] Franklin also lived with and had conversations about religion with an elderly Catholic family.[28]

Franklin became convinced of the importance of virtue and morality in public and private life while living in Philadelphia. He did not believe in divine revelation, but he acknowledged that certain moral laws and principles applied to all mankind. He "entertain'd an opinion that, though certain actions might not be bad *because* they were forbidden by it [revelation], or good because it *commanded* them, yet probably these actions might be forbidden *because* they were bad for us, or commanded *because* they were beneficial to us, in their own natures, all the circumstances of things being considered."[29] In other words, Franklin adopted a form of theistic utilitarianism. He viewed God as the author of ethical values, but believed that God authored them for utilitarian purposes. For example, God had in fact forbidden certain things, but he had forbidden them because they were bad for people.

With this in mind, Franklin set forth a "Plan for Attaining Moral Perfection." He catalogued the virtues which he considered necessary or desirable, and described them:

1. TEMPERANCE.
   Eat not to dullness; drink not to elevation.
2. SILENCE.
   Speak not but what may benefit others or yourself; avoid trifling conversation.

26. Ibid., pp. 112–13.
27. Ibid., pp. 69–71.
28. Ibid., pp. 91–94.
29. Ibid., p. 112.

3. ORDER.
   Let all your things have their places; let each part of your
   business have its time.
4. RESOLUTION.
   Resolve to perform what you ought; perform without fail what
   you resolve.
5. FRUGALITY.
   Make no expense but to do good to others or yourself; i.e., waste
   nothing.
6. INDUSTRY.
   Lose no time; be always employ'd in something useful; cut off all
   unnecessary actions.
7. SINCERITY.
   Use no hurtful deceit; think innocently and justly; and, if you
   speak, speak accordingly.
8. JUSTICE.
   Wrong none by doing injuries, or omitting the benefits that are
   your duty.
9. MODERATION.
   Avoid extreams; forbear resenting injuries so much as you think
   they deserve.
10. CLEANLINESS.
    Tolerate no uncleanliness in body, cloaths, or habitation.
11. TRANQUILLITY.
    Be not disturbed at trifles, or at accidents common or
    unavoidable.
12. CHASTITY.
13. HUMILITY.
    Imitate Jesus and Socrates.[30]

Franklin was determined to practice each of these virtues, so he
worked on them one at a time. He resolved to "give a week's strict
attention to each of the virtues successively,"[31] and prepared a table
to evaluate his performance each day.[32] He started with enthusiasm
and optimism but left the plan with mixed results:

I was surpris'd to find myself so much fuller of faults than I had
imagined; but I had the satisfaction of seeing them diminish. . . . My
scheme of Order gave me the most trouble . . . my faults in it vexed
me so much, and I made so little progress in amendment, and had
such frequent relapses, that I was almost ready to give up the
attempt, and content myself with a faulty character in that re-

30. Ibid., pp. 147–49.
31. Ibid., p. 151.
32. Ibid.

spect. . . . But, on the whole, tho' I never arrived at the perfection hld
been so ambitious of obtaining, but fell far short of it, yet I was, by
the endeavour, a better and a happier man. . . . In reality there is,
perhaps, no one of our natural passions so hard to subdue as pride.
Disguise it, struggle with it, beat it down, stifle it, mortify it as much
as one pleases, it is still alive, and will every now and then peep out
and show itself; you will see it, perhaps, often in this history; for, even
if I could conceive that I had compleatly overcome it, I should
probably be proud of my humility.[33]

The virtues Franklin mentions are consistent with those Christianity identifies and with those preached by Cotton Mather. The
orthodox Christian will recognize a "justification by works" in
Franklin's plan for moral perfection. He expressed no need for
God's grace to help him overcome his faults; he was going to do it
by his diligent self-effort. Buxbaum claims Franklin despised the
doctrine of justification by faith.[34] Franklin acknowledges, "tho' my
scheme was not wholly without religion, there was in it no mark of
any of the distinguishing tenets of any particular sect." He wanted
his plan for moral perfection to be acceptable to all denominations.[35] His sister Jane Mecom apparently expressed concern that
Ben had abandoned the doctrine of justification by faith. However,
he denied that, writing to her:

. . . You express yourself as if you thought I was against Worshipping
of God, and believed Good Works would merit Heaven; which are
both Fancies of your own, I think, without Foundation.—I am so far
from thinking that God is not to be worshipped, that I have compos'd
and wrote a whole Book of Devotions for my own Use: And I imagine
there are few, if any, in the World, so weake as to imagine, that the
little Good we can do here, can *merit* so vast a Reward hereafter.
There are some Things in your New England Doctrines and Worship,
which I do not agree with, but I do not therefore condemn them, or
desire to shake your Belief or Practice of them. [He then cites
Jonathan Edwards for the proposition that an evil tree cannot bear
good fruit, and therefore good works must emanate from a person
whose life is right with God.][36]

---

33. Ibid., pp. 155–64.
34. Buxbaum, *Benjamin Franklin*, p. 102.
35. Franklin, *Autobiography*, p. 160.
36. Benjamin Franklin to Jane Mecom, July 28, 1743; reprinted in *The Letters of
Benjamin Franklin & Jane Mecom*, ed. Carl Van Doren (London: Princeton University Press,
1950), p. 38.

Apparently Franklin succeeded in clearing up his sister's doubts about his eternal salvation. In 1788, forty-five years later, she wrote to him that "Blessed be God you have never discovered any thing but the Pleasure of doing good, & Heaven has blessed you in the deed." She expressed confidence that Ben would enjoy a "Blessed State to all Eternity where my Dear Brother we shall meet. . . ."[37]

On another occasion Franklin expressed his need for the grace of God:

> By Heaven we understand a state of happiness, infinite in degree, and eternal in duration; I can do nothing to deserve such rewards; he that for giving a draught of water to a thirsty person should expect to be paid with a good plantation, would be modest in his demands compared with those who think they deserve Heaven for the little good they do on earth. Even the mixed, imperfect pleasures we enjoy in this world are rather from God's goodness than our merit; how much more such happiness of Heaven. For my own part I have not the vanity to think I deserve it, the folly to expect it, nor the ambition to desire it; but content myself in submitting to the will and disposal of that God who made me, who has hitherto preserved and blessed me, and in whose Fatherly goodness I may well confide, that he will never make me miserable, and that even the afflictions I may at any time suffer shall tend to my benefit.[38]

Franklin's love/hate relationship with Calvinism is difficult to explain. He was not a regular church member, but he contributed to the support of the Presbyterian Church and others as well as maintained his own church pew. He helped establish the academy in Philadelphia, and he wanted religion taught there; he opposed using lotteries to finance it,[39] and objected to Anglican control, wanting it to remain open to Presbyterians.[40] He had his daughter baptized, and in letters to his daughter in 1764 he wrote:

> Go constantly to church, whoever preaches. The act of devotion in the common prayer book is your principal business there, and if properly attended to, will do more towards amending the heart than sermons generally can do. For they were composed by men of much greater piety and wisdom, than our common composers of sermons can pretend to be; and therefore I wish you would never miss the

37. Jane Mecom to Benjamin Franklin, November 11, 1788; reprinted in ibid., p. 316.
38. Benjamin Franklin, 1753; quoted by Albert Henry Smyth, ed., *The Writings of Benjamin Franklin* (New York: The Macmillan Company, 1905-7), III:144.
39. Buxbaum, *Benjamin Franklin*, p. 173.
40. Ibid., pp. 153–84.

prayer days; yet I do not mean you should despise sermons, even of
the preachers you dislike, for the discourse is often much better than
the man, as sweet and clear waters come through very dirty earth. I
am the more particular on this head, as you seemed to express a little
before I came away, some inclination to leave our church, which I
would not have you do.[41]

The year before he wrote to his wife, "You spent your Sunday very
well, but I think you should go oftener to church."[42] He gave
fatherly advice to a youthful admirer, Catherine Ray, "Be a good
girl and don't forget your catechism. Go constantly to meeting—or
church—till you get a good husband; then stay at home, and nurse
the children, and live like a Christian."[43]

It seemed that Franklin gradually returned to the piety of his
early youth. But he had not returned to Calvinism. However,
a somewhat unorthodox Presbyterian preacher in Philadelphia
named Hemphill did attract Franklin's attention:

Among the rest, I became one of his constant hearers, his sermons
pleasing me, as they had little of the dogmatical kind, but inculcated
strongly the practice of virtue, or what in the religious stile are called
good works. Those, however, of our congregation, who considered
themselves as orthodox Presbyterians, disapprov'd his doctrine, and
were join'd by most of the old clergy, who arraign'd him of
heterodoxy before the synod, in order to have him silenc'd. I became
his zealous partisan, and contributed all I could to raise a party in his
favour, and we combated for him awhile with some hopes of
success.[44]

When the synod charged Hemphill with heresy for preaching
justification by works, Franklin countered that Hemphill was promoting virtue instead of harping on dull and irrelevant points of
official doctrine.[45] Franklin accused the synodical commission with
treating Hemphill in an un-Christian manner. The commission
charged that Hemphill had encouraged his listeners to rely on
reason and live according to nature; Franklin insisted that Hemphill
meant that Christ had come to earth to help men return to their

41. Franklin to daughter, 1764; quoted by Smyth, *Writings*, IV:286; quoted by Allison et
al., *The Real Benjamin Franklin*, pp. 312–13.

42. Franklin to wife, 1763; quoted by Smyth, *Writings*, IV:202; quoted by Allison et al.,
The Real Benjamin Franklin, p. 313.

43. Franklin to Catherine Ray, 1755; quoted by Smyth, *Writings*, III:288; quoted by
Allison et al., *The Real Benjamin Franklin*, p. 313.

44. Franklin, *Autobiography*, p. 178.

45. Buxbaum, *Benjamin Franklin*, p. 95.

initial state of perfection and God had given men laws which are designed to promote human best interest. This, Franklin said, was perfectly consistent with the Gospel.[46] The commission charged that Hemphill taught that men did not need to be converted. Franklin argued that Hemphill meant that the true evidence of conversion was not "spiritual pangs and convulsions" but consistent good works.[47] The commission charged that Hemphill had taught that Cornelius was saved by good works; Franklin insisted that Hemphill said only that Cornelius's good works "disposed God to give him a miraculous revelation of the Gospel."[48] Franklin published several articles in the *Gazette* defending Rev. Hemphill and comparing the commission to the Inquisition. However, Rev. Hemphill was convicted of heterodoxy and was censured and suspended. Buxbaum suggests that Franklin's main reason for defending Hemphill was to exploit the controversy for the purpose of attacking his old enemies the Calvinists: "Here," Buxbaum says, "as elsewhere in his dealings with Calvinism, he is less concerned with arriving at truth than at making his opponents contemptible."[49] The issue did concern biblical interpretation, and Franklin's defense was not only an attack on orthodoxy but also an attempt to demonstrate that Rev. Hemphill's teachings were for the most part consistent with orthodox Christianity.

Whatever his personal feelings about Calvinism, Franklin used his publishing house to print Calvinistic writings. Among the books published by Franklin were *Distinguishing Marks of a Work of the Spirit of God* by Jonathan Edwards (1742), *Soul-Saving Gospel Truths* by Increase Mather (1743), *The New England Psalter*, and John Wesley's *Collection of Psalms and Hymns* (1747). He also published various secular, scientific, and classical works.[50]

Franklin's attitude toward Calvinism and Presbyterianism changed as he grew older. Perhaps the greatest blow Franklin suffered in his lifetime was the death of his four-year-old son, Francis Folger Franklin, affectionately called "Franky":

> In 1736 I lost of my sons, a fine boy of four years old, by the small-pox, taken in the common way. I long regretted bitterly, and still regret that I had not given it to him by inoculation. This I mention for the sake of parents who omit that operation, on the

46. Ibid., pp. 98–99.
47. Ibid., p. 99.
48. Ibid., pp. 101–2.
49. Ibid., p. 101.
50. Van Doren, *Benjamin Franklin*, pp. 103, 116.

supposition that they should never forgive themselves if a child died under it; my example showed that the regret may be the same either way, and that, therefore, the safer should be chosen.[51]

Thirty-six years later, Franklin wrote to his sister that he still had tender feelings about Franky "whom to this day I cannot think of without a sigh."[52]

In assessing the spiritual impact of Franky's death on his father, we should remember the earlier controversy over smallpox inoculation. The New England clergy favored inoculation while the scientific community opposed it. As believers in the Enlightenment, young Franklin and his brothers had sided with the scientists.

But the clergy had been right, and the scientists had been wrong—and Franklin's failure to inoculate his son may have contributed to young Franky's death. Did this shake Franklin's faith in science and reason, and increase his respect for the clergy and revelation? Possibly.

Franklin's other son William became Governor of New Jersey, and unlike his father was a royalist. Ben Franklin took his son's support for the British during the War of Independence as personal desertion. "Nothing has ever hurt me so much and affected me with such keen sensations," he said, "as to find myself deserted in my old age by my only son; and not only deserted, but to find him taking up arms against me in a cause wherein my good fame, fortune, and life were all at stake."[53] It became necessary for William to flee to England and the two only partially reconciled late in life. The dispute was partly religious: William had become thoroughly Anglican and tried to exert state control over the College of New Jersey (which Witherspoon and the Presbyterians successfully resisted), while Ben Franklin, a supporter of independence, worked more closely with the Presbyterians.[54]

The Presbyterians, with their Calvinist view of limited government and the duty to resist tyranny, were among the nation's strongest supporters of independence. So indirectly, the War of Independence brought Franklin closer to Calvinism.

The Great Awakening of the 1740s, also led Franklin closer to Presbyterianism. Humanly speaking, the preaching of two great men, George Whitefield and Jonathan Edwards, aided this religious

51. Franklin, *Autobiography*, p. 183.

52. Franklin to Jane Mecom, January 13, 1772; reprinted in Van Doren, *Letters*, p. 135.

53. Benjamin Franklin to William Franklin August 16, 1784; quoted in Smyth, *Writings*, IX:252–53; quoted by Allison et al., *The Real Benjamin Franklin*, p. 245.

54. See generally Buxbaum, *Benjamin Franklin*, pp. 178–84.

revival. Franklin was impressed with Whitefield, a Calvinist and fundamentalist, who strongly stressed the biblical themes of sin and salvation. Buxbaum suggests that Franklin supported Whitefield because the Calvinist clergy opposed him.[55] But Franklin was also impressed by Whitefield's faith, sincerity, and ability to motivate people to change their lives for the better:

> In 1739 arrived among us from Ireland the Reverend Mr. Whitefield, who had made himself remarkable there as an itinerant preacher. He was at first permitted to preach in some of our churches; but the clergy, taking a dislike to him, soon refus'd him their pulpits, and he was oblig'd to preach in the fields. The multitudes of all sects and denominations that attended his sermons were enormous, and it was matter of speculation to me, who was one of the number, to observe the extraordinary influence of his oratory on his hearers, and how much they admir'd and respected him, notwithstanding his common abuse of them, by assuring them they were naturally half beasts and half devils. It was wonderful to see the change soon made in the manners of our inhabitants. From being thoughtless or indifferent about religion, it seem'd as if all the world were growing religious, so that one could not walk thro' the town in an evening without hearing psalms sung in different families of every street.[56]

Even Franklin was not immune to Whitefield's appeal. Whitefield was soliciting contributions for an orphan house in Georgia, but Franklin had reservations:

> I did not disapprove of the design, but, as Georgia was then destitute of materials and workmen, and it was proposed to send them from Philadelphia at a great expense, I thought it would have been better to have built the house here, and brought the children to it. This I advis'd; but he was resolute in his first project, rejected my counsel, and I therefore refus'd to contribute. I happened soon after to attend one of his sermons, in the course of which I perceived he intended to finish with a collection, and I silently resolved that he should get nothing from me. I had in my pocket a handful of copper money, three or four silver dollars, and five pistoles in gold. As he proceeded I began to soften, and concluded to give the coppers. Another stroke of his oratory made me asham'd of that, and determin'd me to give the silver; and he finish'd so admirably, that I empty'd my pocket wholly into the collector's dish, gold and all.[57]

55. Ibid., p. 145.
56. Franklin, *Autobiography*, pp. 191–92.
57. Ibid., p. 194.

Franklin's support for the evangelist also took other forms. Buxbaum claims that for that period Franklin's *Gazette* carried more then six times as many favorable news items about Whitefield as any other newspaper in America. However, as time went on the *Gazette's* coverage became less favorable.[58] Franklin's *Autobiography* indicates no such cooling. He says, "Ours was a mere civil friendship, sincere on both sides, and lasted to his death."[59] He adds that while some questioned Whitefield's use of money, he did not: "I, who was intimately acquainted with him (being employed in printing his Sermons and Journals, etc.), never had the least suspicion of his integrity, but am to this day decidedly of opinion that he was in all his conduct a perfectly honest man; and methinks my testimony in his favour ought to have the more weight, as we had no religious connection."[60]

Note the phrase, "no religious connection." Neither man was deceived about the spiritual gulf between them. Franklin wrote that Whitefield "us'd, indeed, sometimes to pray for my conversion, but never had the satisfaction of believing that his prayers were heard."[61] Whitefield's concern for Franklin's spiritual state is evident in what he wrote:

> I find that you grow more famous in the learned world. As you have made pretty considerable progress in the mysteries of electricity, I would now humbly commend to your diligent unprejudiced study the mystery of the new-birth. It is a most important, interesting study, and when mastered, will richly answer and repay you for all your pains. One at whose bar we are shortly to appear, hath solemnly declared, that without it, "we cannot enter the kingdom of heaven."[62]

There is nothing to confirm that Franklin undertook that study of the new birth, or that he personally experienced the new birth in Christ. But there is indication that his beliefs changed over his life-span of eighty-four years. Born and raised a Puritan Calvinist, Franklin rebelled in his teens and became a "thorough deist."

58. Buxbaum, *Benjamin Franklin*, pp. 143–44.
59. Franklin, *Autobiography*, pp. 195–96.
60. Ibid., p. 195.
61. Ibid., p. 195.
62. George Whitefield to Benjamin Franklin, August 1752; quoted by Buxbaum, *Benjamin Franklin*, p. 150.

Seeing the way deists lived their lives led him to conclude that deism, if it was true, had little social utility. As a result he supported Christianity because it gave people an incentive to live better lives. His hostility toward Calvinism gradually abated for uncertain reasons, perhaps clue to the inoculation factor, the influence of Whitefield, and his association with Calvinists in the War of Independence. His personal beliefs slowly moved away from deism and toward Christianity, although he may never have embraced the Christian faith. He became reconciled toward his former enemies, the Calvinists, in later life. At age seventy-three he wrote to his daughter that her son Ben, who was with him in Paris, was going to be sent to a Presbyterian school in Switzerland: "Ben, if I should live long enough to want it, is like to be another comfort to me. . . . As I intend him for a Presbyterian as well as a republican, I have sent him to finish his education at Geneva."[63] And he wrote of that Presbyterian stronghold Scotland that, "did not strong connexions draw me elsewhere, I believe Scotland would be the country I shall choose to spend the remainder of my days in."[64]

No framer of the Constitution has been more widely charged with sexual promiscuity than Franklin. But in fact, except for the "intrigues with low women that fell in my way" during his teenage years, the charges are unsubstantiated. Historians, forgetting that it was Franklin's habit to ignore public censure, have made much of the fact that he never tried to refute the attacks.

William Franklin, the Governor of New Jersey, is widely assumed to have been Franklin's illegitimate son. But in fact, William's parentage has not been determined. Various stories speculating his true identity exist. But the most likely explanation is that William Franklin was the natural son of Benjamin and Deborah Franklin. Deborah had been married to John Rogers, but this marriage was probably invalid because he also had a wife living in England. Furthermore, other unproven reports indicated that Rogers had died in the West Indies. Under these circumstances it was impossible for Ben and Deborah to enter into a formal marriage ceremony, so they probably entered into a common-law marriage.[65] At any rate, William was welcomed into the Franklin household and raised

63. Benjamin Franklin to his daughter Sally, 1779; quoted by Buxbaum, *Benjamin Franklin*, p. 220. Compare Franklin's letter to Jane Mecom, April 22, 1779: ". . . I have last week sent Benny to Geneva, where there are as good Schools as here, & where he will be educated a Republican and a Protestant, which could not be so conveniently done at the Schools in France." Reprinted in Van Doren, *Letters*, p. 191.

64. Franklin to Lord and Lady Kames: quoted by Van Doren, *Benjamin Franklin*, p. 282.

65. Allison et al., *The Real Benjamin Franklin*, pp. 45–48.

as a natural son. In addition Franklin supposedly had an illegitimate daughter named Judith Osgood. But Lopez and Herbert explain that:

> In 1770, Franklin's close associate John Foxcroft married Judith Osgood in England. Franklin gave away the bride and referred to her thereafter as his "daughter" because he had acted as surrogate father at the wedding, by no means an unusual practice. Many were the women he would call wife or daughter throughout his life, in a teasing or affectionate manner without suspecting, of course, that anybody would take him literally, then or later.[66]

Other stories of Franklin's immoral activities relate to numerous illicit affairs he allegedly had with French ladies at age seventy and older while serving as U.S. Minister to France. In keeping with French custom Franklin returned their embraces and kisses with obvious relish, which offended the stern Massachusetts Puritan John Adams. But Franklin, as a result, was loved by the French in a way that John Adams never was. Franklin spent time with Madame Brillon, a vivacious young woman, and with Madame Helvetius, an equally vivacious elderly woman. On one occasion Madame Brillon played chess with Franklin while sitting in her covered bath. They called each other "Papa" and "Daughter." The evidence of his relationships with these women indicates a flirtatious manner that may have exceeded the bounds of wisdom or propriety. Anything beyond that is pure (or impure) conjecture.

Lopez and Herbert confirm that there is no shred of evidence that Franklin had affairs with French women. "In that age of diaries and memoirs not a single Parisienne ever boasted that she had captured the famous *philosophe*."[67] Donovan agrees "There is not one iota of evidence in history to justify this image. True, Franklin liked women, and many women adored Franklin. . . . He spent much time in their company, and some of his most interesting writing is in correspondence with female friends. But there is nothing to indicate that his relations with any of them were other than gallant and intellectual."[68] Van Doren also denies that Franklin was a "lively lecher in France" and explains:

> The long life of all his affectionate friendships helps to define them.

66. Claude-Anne Lopez and Eugenia W. Herbert, *The Private Franklin: The Man and His Family* (New York: W. W. Norton & Co., Inc., 1975), pp. 26–27.

67. Lopez and Herbert, *The Private Franklin*, p. 274.

68. Frank Donovan, ed., *The Benjamin Franklin Papers* (New York: Dodd, Mead & Co., 1962), p. 235.

Without the brevity of ordinary lust, or the perseverance of obsession, they had a general warmth which, while no doubt sexual in origin, made them strong, tender, imaginative, and humorous beyond the reach of mere desire, with its hard, impersonal appetite. Always a person himself, Franklin treated every woman as if she were a person too, and made her feel more truly one than ever. Because he loved, valued, and studied women, they were no mystery to him, and he had no instinctive fear of them. Statesman and scientist, profoundly masculine, he took women into account as well as any other force of nature.[69]

Franklin was influenced by both the Puritans and the deist, but neither can wholly claim him. Identifying the basics of Franklin's faith reveals that his beliefs rest somewhere between the two.

1. *Faith in God.* Ben Franklin, the so-called deist, was the delegate who called for prayer on June 28, 1787, when the Constitutional Convention was on the verge of breaking up.

In this situation of this assembly, groping, as it were, in the dark to find political truth, and scarce able to distinguish it when presented to us, how has it happened, Sir, that we have not hitherto once thought of humbly applying to the Father of Lights to illuminate our understandings? In the beginning of the contest with Britain, when we were sensible of danger, we had daily prayers in this room for the divine protection. Our prayers, Sir, were heard—and they were graciously answered. . . .

I have lived, Sir, a long time; and the longer I live, the more convincing proofs I see of this truth, that *God governs in the affairs of men.* And if a sparrow cannot fall to the ground without his notice, is it probable that an empire can rise without his aid? We have been assured, Sir, in the sacred writings that "except the Lord build the house, they labor in vain that build it." I firmly believe this; and I also believe that, without his concurring aid, we shall succeed in this political building no better than the builders of Babel. . . .

I therefore beg leave to move that, henceforth, prayers imploring the assistance of heaven and its blessings on our deliberations be held in this assembly every morning before we proceed to business, and that one or more of the clergy of this city be requested to officiate in that service.[70]

The motion for opening the sessions with prayer every morning was

69. Van Doren, *Benjamin Franklin*, pp. 639, 653–54.
70. Benjamin Franklin, June 28, 1787; quoted by Smyth, *Writings*, IX:600–1; quoted by Allison et al., *The Real Benjamin Franklin*, pp. 258–59.

not acted on because the Convention lacked funds to pay a clergyman, and because the delegates were afraid that news of outside clergymen coming to assist in services would start rumors that dissension was breaking out in the Convention. But the speech reveals that eighty-one year-old Franklin had drastically changed his beliefs since he had been a teenage deist. For his central, italicized statement that "God governs in the affairs of men" violates the cardinal tenet of deism, that God does not actively intervene in human affairs. Franklin's references to God hearing and answering prayers, to "sacred writings," to "Babel," and to the fall of sparrows, demonstrates that Franklin took Scripture seriously.

Franklin's concept of God is different from the Puritans. In his view God is less stern, more genial:

> I conceive for many reasons that He is a good Being, and as I should be happy to have so wise, good, and powerful a Being my friend, let me consider in what manner I shall make myself most acceptable to Him. Next to the praise resulting from and due to His wisdom, I believe He is pleased and delights in the happiness of those He has created; and since without virtue man can have no happiness in this world, I firmly believe He delights to see me virtuous, because He is pleased when He sees me happy. And since He has created many things which seem purely designed for the delight of man, I believe He is not offended when He sees his children solace themselves in any manner of pleasant exercises and innocent delights; and I think no pleasure innocent that is to man hurtful. I love Him therefore for His Goodness, and I adore Him for His Wisdom.[71]

Given this view of God, it is fitting that the first fast day in Pennsylvania was proposed in 1748 by Benjamin Franklin. He drew up the proclamation declaring that "it is the duty of mankind on all suitable occasions to acknowledge their dependence on the Divine Being" and praying that "Almighty God would mercifully interpose and still the rage of war among the nations and put a stop to the effusion of Christian blood . . . [that] He would take this province under His protection, confound the designs and defeat the attempts of its enemies, and unite our hearts and strengthen our hands in every undertaking that may be for the public good, and for our defence and security in this time of danger."[72]

2. *Jesus Christ.* On March 9, 1790, at age eighty-four, Franklin

---

71. Benjamin Franklin, *Articles of Belief and Acts of Religion,* 1728; quoted by Van Doren, *Benjamin Franklin,* p. 81.
72. Franklin, 1748; quoted in Van Doren, *Benjamin Franklin,* p. 188.

answered a letter from Ezra Stiles, President of Yale, in which Stiles asked "the opinion of my venerable friend concerning Jesus of Nazareth."[73]

> As to Jesus of Nazareth, my opinion of whom you particularly desire, I think his system of morals and his religion, as he left them to us, the best the world ever saw or is likely to see; but I apprehend it has received various corrupting changes, and I have, with most of the present dissenters in England, some doubts as to his divinity; though it is a question I do not dogmatize upon, having never studied it, and think it needless to busy myself with it now, when I expect soon an opportunity of knowing the truth with less trouble. I see no harm, however, in its being believed, if that belief has the good consequence, as probably it has, of making his doctrines more respected and more observed; especially as I do not perceive that the Supreme takes it amiss, by distinguishing the unbelievers of his government of the world with any peculiar marks of his displeasure.[74]

Franklin expressed that he had "some doubts as to his divinity." A thorough deist would have no such "doubts"; he would totally reject the divinity of Christ. Franklin indicates that he is uncertain about the question, and is waiting to (hopefully) see God face to face so he can learn the truth of the matter firsthand. Furthermore, Franklin has no objection to others believing in the divinity of Christ, since it probably makes Christ's doctrines more respected and observed.

3. *The Bible.* Franklin gave no clear indication of his view of the inspiration of Scripture, but expressed great respect for its wisdom: "As the Scriptures are given for our reproof, instruction and warning, may we make a due use of this example, before it be too late!"[75] At the Constitutional Convention he referred to the Scriptures as the "sacred writings." Franklin respectfully quoted the Bible throughout his life and treated it with respect.

4. *Natural Law.* Franklin was a firm Newtonian;[76] he believed in fixed, absolute, and unchanging natural laws of science. He also believed in natural, God-given moral laws for the governance of human affairs. As early as 1747, twenty nine years before the

73. Ezra Stiles to Franklin; quoted by Van Doren, *Autobiographical Writings*, p. 783.

74. Franklin to Ezra Stiles, March 9, 1790; quoted by Van Doren, *Autobiographical Writings*, p. 784.

75. Franklin; quoted in Smyth, *Writings*, II:340.

76. Paul W. Conner, *Poor Richard's Politicks: Benjamin Franklin and His New American Order* (New York: Oxford University Press, 1965), pp. 173–74.

Declaration of Independence, Franklin wrote of the "great command of nature and nature's God."[77]

5. *Morality.* Franklin was a moralist; his morality was like Cotton Mather's and the Puritans, though he expressed it in more secular terms. He seemed to make it in part a matter of self-effort rather than divine help. He believed morality and virtue were necessary for personal happiness and well-being; but also essential to the nation:

> The moral character and happiness of mankind, are so interwoven with the operations of government, and the progress of the arts and sciences is so dependent on the nature of our political institutions, that it is essential to the advancement of civilized society to give ample discussion to these topics.[78]

Franklin once declared, "Let me add that only a virtuous people are capable of freedom. As nations become corrupt and vicious, they have more need of masters."[79] Perhaps for this reason Franklin late in life expressed concern about the French Revolution (though he did not live to see its full horrors) and prayed for the King of France.[80]

6. *Man.* Franklin began his prayer speech before the Constitutional Convention by saying, "The small progress we have made . . . is, methinks, a melancholy proof of the imperfection of the human understanding."[81] In 1788 he said that in political affairs:

> . . . each man has his particular private interest in view. That as soon as a party has gained its general point, each member becomes intent upon his particular interest; which, thwarting others, breaks that party into divisions, and occasions more confusion.
>
> That few in public affairs act from a mere view of the good of their country, whatever they may pretend; and, though their actings bring real good to their country, yet men primarily considered that their own and their country's interest was united, and did not act from a

77. Franklin, "The Speech of Polly Baker, *Gentleman's Magazine*, April 1747; reprinted in Van Doren, *Benjamin Franklin*, p. 154.

78. Franklin to Lord James, January 1, 1769; quoted by Conner, *Poor Richard's Politicks*, p. 107.

79. Franklin, 1789; quoted by Smyth, *Writings*, X:50; quoted by Allison et al., *The Real Benjamin Franklin*, p. 393.

80. Franklin, 1785; quoted by Smyth, *Writings*, IX: 321; quoted by Allison et al., *The Real Benjamin Franklin*, p. 422.

81. Franklin, Speech to Constitutional Convention; quoted by Allison et al., *The Real Benjamin Franklin*, p. 258.

principle of benevolence. That fewer still, in public affairs, act with a view to the good of mankind.[82]

Franklin believed that the few good men who existed should unite:

There seems to me at present to be great occasion for raising a United Party for Virtue, by forming the virtuous and good men of all nations into a regular body, to be governed by suitable good and wise rules, which good and wise men may probably be more unanimous in their obedience to, than common people are to common laws.

I at present think that whoever attempts this aright, and is well qualified, cannot fail of pleasing God and of meeting with success.[83]

7. *Eternal Life.* Franklin believed in eternal life.[84] He stressed that eternity was a time of rewards and punishments for good and evil conduct, but also claimed that no one could earn eternal life by works alone. Possibly Franklin believed eternal life was a gift from God, but during eternity men will experience rewards and punishments based on their conduct. A 1728 epitaph Franklin had prepared for himself, which was never used, affirmed his faith in the resurrection unto eternal life as seen through the eyes of a printer:

The body of
B. Franklin, printer
(Like the cover of an old book,
Its contents torn out
And stripped of its lettering and gilding),
Lies here, food for worms.
But the work shall not be lost;
For it will (as he believed) appear once more
In a new and more elegant edition,
Revised and corrected
By the Author.[85]

8. *Balance.* "Moderation in all things" seems to have been Franklin's credo. He tried to find a middle ground in morality, in religion, in politics, in everything he did. He tried to work out a balance between all aspects of life.

At the Constitutional Convention Franklin emphasized the practical. His values were to some extent utilitarian. He spoke several

---

82. Franklin, 1788; quoted by Smyth, *Writings*, I:339; quoted by Allison et al., *The Real Benjamin Franklin*, p. 449.

83. Ibid.

84. See generally, Van Doren, *Autobiographical Writings*, pp. 642, 670.

85. Ibid., p. 29.

times on the Convention floor, once urging that the President not be paid a salary, once opposing the veto power. It was Franklin who moved that the Constitution be ratified by the Convention. Later he expressed the belief that the Convention had been guided by God in producing the Constitution.[86]

86. Franklin, 1788; quoted in Smyth, *Writings*, IX:702; quoted in Allison et al., *The Real Benjamin Franklin*, p. 343.

13 Thomas Jefferson

eligious Beliefs

The name Thomas Jefferson is primarily associated with the Declaration of Independence, but he is also known for the phrase "wall of separation between church and state."[1] Jefferson's religious convictions aroused strong disputes during his time, which have continued to be the subject of scholarly debate in modern times.

Jefferson was strongly attacked for his religious beliefs when he ran for President against John Adams in 1800. One of the most powerful attacks came from Rev. William Linn, a Dutch Reformed

---

1. Thomas Jefferson, "Address to the Danbury Baptists, 1802"; quoted by Arthur Frommer, *The Bible in the Public Schools* (New York: Liberal Press, 1963), p. 19. Speaking to a Baptist audience, it seems likely that Jefferson intentionally referred to the words of an earlier Baptist leader, Roger Williams:

> ". . . when they have opened a gap in the hedge or wall of separation between the garden of the church and the wilderness of the world, God hath ever broke down the wall itself, removed the candlestick, and made His garden a wilderness, as at this day. And that therefore if He will eer please to restore His garden and paradise again, it must of necessity be walled in peculiarly unto Himself from the world . . ." (quoted by Lynn R. Buzzard and Samuel Ericsson, *The Battle for Religious Liberty* [Elgin, Illinois: David C. Cook, 1982], p. 51).

Williams meant that the church must be protected from the state. In contrast, Jefferson's words have been interpreted to mean that the state must be protected from the church! (See also pp. 242–45.)

minister in New York City. In the pamphlet *Serious Considerations on the Election of a President,* Linn asked, "Does Jefferson ever go to church? How does he spend the Lord's day? Is he known to worship with any denomination of Christians?" Linn continued:

> Let the first magistrate to be a professed infidel, and infidels will surround him. Let him spend the sabbath in feasting, in visiting or receiving visits, in riding abroad, but never in going to church; and to frequent public worship will become unfashionable. Infidelity will become the prattle from the highest to the lowest condition in life, and universal desoluteness will follow. . . .
>
> Will you then, my fellow-citizens, with all this evidence . . . vote for Mr. Jefferson? . . . As to myself, were Mr. Jefferson connected with me by the nearest ties of blood, and did I owe him a thousand obligations, I would not, and could not vote for him. No; sooner than stretch forth my hand to place him at the head of the nation "Let mine arms fall from my shoulder blade, and mine arm be broken from the bone."[2]

John Adams, Jefferson's opponent, was much more orthodox in his Christian faith;[3] Adams's wife, Abigail, joined the attack, charging that Jefferson was a deist: "Can the placing at the head of the nation two characters known to be Deists be productive of order, peace, and happiness?"[4]

But supporters came to Jefferson's defense. Tunis Wortman wrote the pamphlet *A Solemn Address to the Christians and Patriots upon the Approaching Election of a President of the United States,* in which he declared, "That the charge of deism . . . is false, scandalous and malicious—That there is not a single passage in the Notes on Virginia, or any of Mr. Jefferson's writings, repugnant to Christianity; but on the contrary, in every respect, favourable to it."[5] Dewitt Clinton also defended Jefferson by declaring, "we have the strongest reasons to believe that he is a real Christian." Clinton said, "I feel persuaded that he is a believer" and "I feel happy to hail him a Christian." He continued with:

2. Rev. William Linn, "Serious Considerations on the Election of a President"; quoted by Saul K. Padover, *Jefferson: A Great American's Life and Ideas* (New York: Mentor Books, 1942, 1970), pp. 116–17.

3. Fawn M. Brodie, *Thomas Jefferson: An Intimate History* (New York: Bantam Books, 1974, 1981), p. 341.

4. Abigail Adams: quoted by Brodie, *Thomas Jefferson,* p. 444.

5. Tunis Wortman, "A Solemn Address to the Christians and Patriots upon the Approaching Election of a President of the United States"; quoted by Padover, *A Great American,* pp. 117–18.

And let me add . . . that he has for a long time supported out of his own private revenues, a worthy minister of the Christian church—an instance of liberality not to be met with in any of his rancorous enemies; whose love of religion seems principally to consist in their unremitted endeavors to degrade it into a handmaid of faction.[6]

Two issues pinpointed in the debate deserve special mention. First, no one questioned the propriety of inquiry into a presidential candidate's religious beliefs. Second, should a deist be president was not the issue. No one argued that. The question was whether Jefferson was a deist or a Christian. No one debated that a presidential candidate's religious beliefs were strictly a personal matter.

The debate about Jefferson's beliefs continues today. Ralph Ketcham declares without proof in *The Encyclopedia of Philosophy* that Jefferson was "not deeply interested in religion" and that he "accepted the conventional deism of his day."[7] Evangelical Christian scholars Peter Marshall and David Manuel label Jefferson an unbeliever and conclude that "what Jefferson was really calling for was an end to Christianity."[8] Noll, Hatch, and Marsden present little proof for their conclusions, which suggest that Jefferson and others "had found in God what they most admired in men."[9] John Whitehead too questions Jefferson's beliefs.[10] But Dickinson Adams takes a different position. He acknowledges that Jefferson started with the critical, questioning attitude of the Enlightenment. But he adds that "unlike many other adherents of the Enlightenment, especially those in France, Jefferson's rationalism led him ultimately to an affirmation of faith rather than a rejection of religious belief."[11]

As in previous discussions pertaining to the religious beliefs of the founding fathers, Thomas Jefferson's writings and scholarly comments will be consulted to help determine his religious beliefs.

The discussion begins with Jefferson's formative years.

---

6. DeWitt Clinton, "A Vindication of Thomas Jefferson, against the Charges Contained in a Pamphlet Entitled 'Serious Considerations';" quoted by Padover, *A Great American*, p. 118.

7. *The Encyclopedia of Philosophy*, s.v. "Jefferson, Thomas."

8. Peter Marshall and David Manuel, *The Light and the Glory* (Old Tappan, New Jersey: Fleming H. Revell, 1977), pp. 350–51.

9. Mark A. Noll, Nathan O. Hatch, and George M. Marsden, *The Search for Christian America* (Westchester, Illinois: Crossway Books, 1983), pp. 74ff.

10. John W. Whitehead, *The Separation Illusion* (Milford, Michigan: Mott Media, 1977).

11. Dickinson Adams, ed., *Jefferson's Extracts from the Gospels* (Princeton: Princeton University Press, 1983), p. 3.

Jefferson's Early Life

Thomas Jefferson was born in 1743 on a farm about five miles east of Charlottesville, in Albemarle County, Virginia. Padover describes the Jefferson family as "hard-working, God-fearing, and affectionate."[12] He says that Jefferson loved and admired his father but rarely mentioned his mother;[13] however, Major Spalding relates that "Mr Jefferson's mother was a Randolph, and he acknowledged that he owed every thing to her rearing."[14] Jefferson's father was an avid reader, owning sets of Shakespeare, Swift, and Pope. He taught Thomas to read and write and was probably responsible for instilling in Thomas a love for learning. Padover writes:

> The father also set his impressionable boy an example of vigorous physical out-of-doors life. Thomas learned to ride, to shoot, to paddle a canoe on the Rivanna, and to hunt deer and turkey. His lean young body grew to marvelous health and endurance.
>
> Tom did not ride and shoot and canoe only; he also studied diligently. His education consisted of the typical classical curriculum of the period.
>
> Tom mastered languages, both classical and modern, with great ease. He read Homer in his canoe trips down the Rivanna and Virgil while lying under an oak tree.[15]

Jefferson wrote of his father's friendliness, generosity, and strength of character, but little is written about his father's beliefs. He did instill in Thomas a firm faith in God, a strong sense of moral obligation, a love for the outdoors (Jefferson's love for nature and the rural life did much to shape his religious and political philosophy), an appreciation and capacity for hard work, and a love for classical learning.

When Thomas was fourteen years old his father died. At age sixteen, Thomas enrolled in William and Mary College at nearby Williamsburg, Virginia. Many of the professors at William and Mary were ministers of the gospel, among them Rev. Thomas Dawson the

---

12. Padover, *A Great American*, p. 10.
13. Ibid.
14. Major Spalding: quoted by Elizabeth F. Ellet, *The Women of the American Revolution* (1849); reprinted in Verna M. Hall, *The Christian History of the American Revolution* (San Francisco: Foundation for American Christian Education, 1975, 1982), p. 74.
15. Padover, *A Great American*, p. 11.

college president, Rev. Emanuel Jones of the Indian school, Rev. Thomas Robinson of the grammar school, Rev. William Preston who taught moral philosophy, Rev. John Camm who taught theology, and Rev. Richard Graham who taught natural philosophy. Perhaps because of his love for classical learning, Jefferson seemed attracted to three men who were not clergymen. One was Dr. William Small, a Scotsman and friend of Erasmus Darwin (Charles Darwin's grandfather), who became Jefferson's professor and close personal friend. He taught Jefferson a pattern of "liberal thinking stripped of orthodoxy"[16] and, as Jefferson confessed, "probably fixed the destinies of my life."[17] The second was George Wythe, founder of America's first law school who became a signer of the Declaration of Independence, and a delegate to the Constitutional Convention. He taught Jefferson his love for classical learning and thinking and influenced his faith in republican government. Jefferson wrote of him, "In his philosophy he was firm, and neither troubling, nor perhaps trusting, anyone with his religious creed, he left the world to the conclusion, that that religion must be good which could produce a life of such exemplary virtue."[18]

The third was Francis Fauquier, the acting governor of Virginia, with whom Wythe, Small, and Jefferson frequently dined. Fauquier contributed to Jefferson's understanding of government, law, and philosophy. It is believed that Fauquier was a disciple of Lord Shaftesbury, who stressed that religion is a private personal matter that has no place in public affairs.[19] These men did not teach Jefferson any specific doctrines or ideas, but they shared with him ways of thinking and looking at the world.

Three other men (Sir Francis Bacon, Sir Isaac Newton, and John Locke) became Jefferson's philosophical idols. He never met them, yet he tried to reflect their beliefs. These three were mentioned in a letter from Jefferson to Benjamin Rush.[20] Each man of this "trinity" made a unique contribution to Jefferson's thought. Ketcham summarizes their influence:

16. Ibid., p. 14.

17. Thomas Jefferson; quoted by ibid., p. 14.

18. Thomas Jefferson, 1820; quoted by Saul K. Padover, *The Complete Jefferson, Containing His Major Writings, Published and Unpublished, Except His Letters* (New York: Duell, Sloan & Pearce, 1943), pp. 927–28.

19. Sharon Lynn Hughes, "The Formal Education of Thomas Jefferson," paper presented for Legal History, O. W. Coburn School of Law, Oral Roberts University, Tulsa, Oklahoma, 1984, p. 4.

20. Letter to Dr. Benjamin Rush from Thomas Jefferson, 1811; quoted by M. Richard Maxfield, K. DeLynn Cook, and W. Cleon Skousen, *The Real Thomas Jefferson* 2nd ed. (Washington, D.C.: National Center for Constitutional Studies, 1981, 1983), pp. 467–68.

He accepted Bacon's empiricism and emphasis on the role of reason in improving society. From Newton he acquired his view that the universe was harmonious, governed by law, and amenable to human investigation. Locke enunciated the political implications of these viewpoints and was, for Jefferson, the pre-eminent philosophical guide.[21]

Modern scholars frequently ignore the fact that while these men accepted some of the rationalistic premises of the Enlightenment, each of them remained basically committed and orthodox Christians.[22]

Most often one's theology shapes his or her philosophy. But in Jefferson's case the opposite appears to be true, his philosophy shaped his theology. His strong emphasis on the role of reason created a barrier which prevented him from accepting the full truth of Christian doctrine. Dickinson Adams explains Jefferson:

> The precise details and chronology are still somewhat obscure, but it seems clear that at some point during the 1760s Jefferson experienced a religious crisis in the course of which he rejected his ancestral Anglican creed and embraced instead a vaguely defined natural religion. This religious transformation was apparently caused by Jefferson's inability "from a very early part of my life" to accept the central Christian doctrine of the Trinity owing to the "difficulty of reconciling the ideas of Unity and Trinity" in the godhead. His rationalism led him, in the words of a contemporary Virginian, to repudiate "as falsehoods things unsusceptible of strict demonstration." Having rejected the dogma of the Trinity as a logical absurdity that could not be reconciled with human reason, Jefferson then subjected the rest of Christianity to the test of rational analysis and concluded that its basic doctrines were simply unacceptable to an enlightened man living in the eighteenth century. "The person who becomes sponsor for a child, according to the ritual of the church in which I was educated," he later explained in declining a French friend's request that he serve as godfather to his son, "makes a solemn profession, before god and the world, of faith in articles, which I had never sense enough to comprehend, and it has always appeared to me that comprehension must precede assent."[23]

It was rationalism which led Thomas Jefferson to reject orthodox Christianity early in his life (Jefferson was in his late teens or early

21. *The Encyclopedia of Philosophy*, s.v. "Jefferson, Thomas."
22. See chapter 4 for a discussion of the Christian basis of the thinking of Bacon, Newton, and Locke.
23. Adams, *Extracts*, p. 5.

twenties when this religious crisis took place. In the 1790s, when Jefferson was in his late forties or early fifties, he had another change of heart and became much more favorably disposed toward Christianity.) What Luther and others could not understand by human reason, they could affirm by faith in God's revelation; however, Jefferson could not. Noll, Hatch, and Marsden say that, "Thomas Jefferson, the author of the Declaration, especially repudiated the idea of subordinating his thought to biblical principles."[24] Jefferson expressed faith in reason in many statements, including the following:

> Reason and free inquiry are the only effectual agents against error.[25]
>
> I hope that we have not labored in vain, and that our experiment will still prove that men can be governed by reason.[26]
>
> Every man's reason [is] his own rightful umpire. The principle, with that of acquiescence in the will of the majority, will preserve us free and prosperous as long as they are sacredly observed.[27]
>
> Truth and reason are eternal. They have prevailed. And they will eternally prevail; however, in times and places they may be overborne for a while by violence, military, civil, or ecclesiastical.[28]

Jefferson's faith in the power of human reason to work for human good was not as complete as that of other Enlightenment thinkers. A person must have faith in people's ability and willingness to employ reason correctly and be governed by it to have absolute faith in human reason. Jefferson was realistic enough to recognize (perhaps he was influenced by the biblical view of sin) that people are not always good and are not always governed by reason. He wrote in 1781:

> Let us too give this experiment fair play, and get rid, while we may, of those tyrannical laws. It is true, we are as yet secured against them by the spirit of the times. I doubt whether the people of this country would suffer an execution for heresy, or a three years' imprisonment for not comprehending the mysteries of the Trinity. But is the spirit of the people an infallible, a permanent reliance? Is it government? Is

24. Noll et al, *Christian America*, pp. 129–30.
25. Thomas Jefferson, Notes on Virginia; quoted by Albert Ellery Bergh, ed., *The Writings of Thomas Jefferson* (Washington: The Thomas Jefferson Memorial Association, 1907), 2:221 (1782).
26. Thomas Jefferson, Letter to George Mason, 1791; quoted by Paul Leicester Ford, ed., *The Writings of Thomas Jefferson* (New York: G. P. Putnam's Sons, 1892–99); 5:275.
27. Thomas Jefferson, 1814; quoted in Bergh, *Writings*, 14:136.
28. Thomas Jefferson, 1810; quoted in Bergh, *Writings*, 12:361.

this the kind of protection we receive in return for the rights we give up? Besides, the spirit of the times may alter, will alter. Our rulers will become corrupt, our people careless. A single zealot may commence persecution, and better men be his victims. It can never be too often repeated, that the time for fixing every essential right on a legal basis is while our rulers are honest, and ourselves united. From the conclusion of this war we shall be going down hill. It will not then be necessary to resort every moment to the people for support. They will be forgotten, therefore, and their rights disregarded. They will forget themselves, but in the sole faculty of making money, and will never think of uniting to effect a due respect for their rights. The shackles, therefore, which shall not be knocked off at the conclusion of this war, will remain on us long, will be made heavier and heavier, till our rights shall revive or expire in a convulsion.[29]

Jefferson's point was that people are not always wise or virtuous; rather, they go through comparatively good and bad periods of history. The best way to safeguard liberty is by making good laws to protect liberty while people are so disposed, and hopefully these laws will restrain the enemies of liberty during bad periods of history. Jefferson's recognition of the limitations of human nature was one reason he opposed kings and dictators, benevolent or otherwise. He knew the evil tendencies in men would eventually come to the forefront and cause rulers to suppress the populace. In his first inaugural address he said, "Sometimes it is said that man cannot be trusted with the government of himself. Can he, then, be trusted with the government of others? Or have we found angels in the forms of kings to govern him? Let history answer this question."[30]

Jefferson placed a great deal of faith in the power of human reason to discover truth and facilitate responsible self-government. His faith in reason undergirds his entire theology and philosophy of life and government.

Jefferson's view of God, man, Jesus Christ, the Bible, Christianity, the church, and other matters must be examined in light of his basic presuppositions.

29. Thomas Jefferson, "Notes on the State of Virginia," 1781; reprinted in Padover, *The Complete Jefferson*, p. 676.
30. Thomas Jefferson, First Inaugural Address, March 4, 1801; quoted by ibid., p. 385.

Jefferson's View of God

All of my evidence and research indicates that Jefferson never questioned the existence of God. His most famous work, the Declaration of Independence, contains many references to God:

> . . . the separate and equal Station to which the Laws of Nature and of Nature's God entitle them . . .
> . . . all Men are created equal, that they are endowed by their Creator with certain unalienable Rights . . .
> . . . appealing to the Supreme Judge of the World for the Rectitude of our Intentions . . .
> . . . with a firm Reliance on the Protection of divine Providence . . .

Jefferson's faith in human reason did not hinder his belief in God. He argued that reason and rational proof aids a person in coming to understand God. As he wrote to John Adams in 1823:

> Indeed I think that every Christian sect gives a great handle to Atheism by their general dogma that, without a revelation, there would not be sufficient proof of the being of a god. . . . I hold (without appeal to revelation) that when we take a view of the Universe, in its parts general or particular, it is impossible for the human mind not to perceive and feel a conviction of design, consummate skill, and indefinite power in every atom of its composition. The movements of the heavenly bodies, so exactly held in their course by the balance of centrifugal and centripetal forces, the structure of our earth itself, with its distribution of lands, waters and atmosphere, animal and vegetable bodies, examined in all their minutest particles, insects mere atoms of life, yet as perfectly organized as man or mammoth, the mineral substances, their generation and uses, it is impossible, I say, for the human mind not to believe that there is, in all this, design, cause and effect, up to an ultimate cause, a fabricator of all things from matter and motion, their preserver and regulator while permitted to exist in their present forms, and their regenerator into new and other forms. We see, too, evident proofs of the necessity of a superintending power to maintain the Universe in its course and order. Stars, well known, have disappeared, new ones have come into view, comets, in their incalculable courses, may run foul of suns and planets and require renovation under other laws; certain races of animals are become extinct; and, were there no restoring power, all existences might extinguish successively, one by one, until all should be reduced to a shapeless chaos. So irresistible are these evidences of an intelligent and powerful Agent that, of the infinite numbers of men who have existed thro' all time, they have believed, in the proportion of a

million at least to Unit, in the hypothesis of an eternal pre-existence
of a creator, rather than in that of self-existent Universe. Surely this
unanimous sentiment renders this more probable than that of the few
in the other hypothesis.[31]

Jefferson firmly believed in God, but he could not accept the
Christian concept of the Trinity. As Dickinson Adams says:

> The cornerstone of Jefferson's religion was an unswerving com-
> mitment to monotheism. He firmly believed in the existence of one
> God, who was the creator and sustainer of the universe and the
> ultimate ground of being. . . . There was one thing about the godhead
> of which Jefferson was certain, however: the one true God that man
> was obliged to worship and adore was not the triune deity of
> orthodox Christianity. Jefferson had nothing but scorn for the
> traditional doctrine of three persons in one God. He rejected it as a
> contradiction in terms, regretted it as a relapse into polytheism, and
> scoffed at it as the "hocus-pocus phantasm of a god like another
> Cerberus with one body and three heads." Of all the alleged
> corruptions of Christianity, this was the one he denounced with the
> greatest feeling and frequency.[32]

Jefferson's rejection of the Trinity is found throughout his writings. He wrote to John Adams in 1813:

> It is too late in the day for men of sincerity to pretend they believe in
> the Platonic mysticisms that three are one, and one is three; and yet
> the one is not three, and the three are not one; to divide mankind by
> a single letter into ὁμοὄθσιαης and ὁμοιοθσιαης.[33] [This refers to the
> Arian controversy which culminated in the Council of Nicea in A.D.
> 325. The orthodox party, led by Athanasius, held that Christ was of
> the same substance as the Father, and therefore, used the Greek term
> *homoousios*, meaning same substance. Arius and his party used the
> term *homoiousios*, meaning Christ was of a similar (not same)
> substance with the Father. The Council of Nicea adopted the view of
> Athanasius and incorporated into the Nicene Creed the phrase,
> "being of one substance with the father."]

He wrote in 1813 to William Canby:

> Of all the systems of morality ancient or modern which have come

31. Thomas Jefferson, Letter to John Adams, April 11, 1823; reprinted by Adams,
Extracts, pp. 410–11.

32. Ibid., pp. 39–40.

33. Thomas Jefferson, Letter to John Adams, August 22, 1813; reprinted by ibid., p. 347.

under my observation, none appear to me so pure as that of Jesus. He who follows this steadily need not, I think, be uneasy, altho' he cannot comprehend the subtleties and mysteries erected on his doctrines by those who, calling themselves his special followers and favorites, would make him come into the world to lay snares for all understandings but theirs. These metaphysical heads, usurping the judgment seat of god, denounce as his enemies all who cannot perceive the Geometrical logic of Euclid in the demonstrations of St. Athanasius that three are one, and one is three; and yet that the one is not three, nor the three one.[34]

In 1816 he urged Francis Adrian Van der Kemp to undertake further study in this area:

Ridicule is the only weapon which can be used against unintelligible propositions. [Note: Given Jefferson's faith in reason, why cannot reason be used?] Ideas must be distinct before reason can act upon them; and no man ever had a distinct idea of the trinity. It is the mere Abracadabra of the mountebanks calling themselves the priests of Jesus.[35]

He wrote Timothy Pickering in 1821:

When we shall have done away with the incomprehensible jargon of the Trinitarian arithmetic, that three are one, and one is three, when we shall have knocked down the artificial scaffolding, reared to mask from view the simple structure of Jesus, when, in short, we shall have unlearned every thing which has been taught since his day, and got back to the pure and simple doctrines he inculcated, we shall then be truly and worthily his disciples: and my opinion is that if nothing had ever been added to what flowed purely from his lips, the whole world would at this day have been Christian.[36] [Note the faith in human reason.]

Jefferson best illustrates his belief that human reason and trinitarianism cannot be reconciled and that human reason must prevail over trinitarianism in an 1822 letter to James Smith:

In fact the Athanasian paradox that one is three, and three but one is

34. Jefferson, Letter to William Canby, September 18, 1813; reprinted by ibid., pp. 349–50.

35. Jefferson, Letter to Francis Adrian Van der Kemp, July 30, 1816; reprinted by ibid., pp. 374–75.

36. Jefferson, Letter to Timothy Pickering, February 27, 1821; reprinted by ibid., pp. 402–3.

so incomprehensible to the human mind that no candid man can say
he has any idea of it, and how he can believe what presents no idea.
He who thinks he does only deceives himself. He proves also that
man, once surrendering his reason, has no remaining guard against
absurdities the most monstrous, and like a ship without a rudder is
the sport of every wind. With such persons gullability which they call
faith takes the helm from the hand of reason and the mind becomes
a wreck.[37]

Jefferson's rejection of trinitarianism placed him in agreement
with the deists and unitarians of his day. He agreed with the deists,
unitarians, and Christians in believing that God was the Creator of
all things including man, and in believing that God had established
certain physical and moral laws by which the universe and human
society were to be governed.[38]

However, Jefferson rejected the deist belief that God created the
universe, established certain scientific principles and laws by which
the universe operates, and now takes no active role in the affairs of
mankind and does not work actively in the universe except possibly
through the continuing effect of the laws of nature which he placed
in operation.[39]

In contrast, Jefferson believed that God was the Sustainer as well
as the Creator of the universe. Jefferson was convinced that the
universe could not operate according to previously established laws
on its own; its continued efficacy required the superintending and
guiding power of Providence:

> We see, too, evident proofs of the necessity of a superintending
> power to maintain the Universe in its course and order. . . . were
> there no restoring power, all existences might extinguish succes-
> sively, one by one, until all should be reduced to a shapeless chaos.[40]

Not only is God actively involved in sustaining and restoring the
universe (cf. Col 2:17); he is also actively involved in human affairs.
Jefferson recognized God as the source of human life, human
liberty, and human rights. He stated in the Declaration of Independence, all men "are endowed by their Creator with certain unalien-

37. Jefferson, Letter to James Smith, December 8, 1822; reprinted by ibid., pp. 408–9.
38. See footnote 31.
39. *Lutheran Cyclopedia*, s.v. "Deism." "System of belief which holds either that the
universe is a self-sustained mechanism from which God withdrew immediately after creation
or that God is still active in the universe, but only through the laws of nature."
40. Thomas Jefferson, Letter to John Adams, April 11, 1823; reprinted by Adams,
Extracts, pp. 410–11.

able Rights, that among these are Life, Liberty, and the pursuit of Happiness."

In his "Declaration of the Causes and Necessity for Taking Up Arms" he echoed a similar theme:

> We . . . most solemnly, before God and the world, declare that . . . the arms we have been compelled to assume, we will use with perseverence, exerting to their utmost energies all those powers which our Creator hath given us, to preserve that liberty which He committed to us in sacred deposit.[41]

Jefferson reflected this view in two other statements:

> The God who gave us life gave us liberty at the same time; the hand of force may destroy but cannot disjoin them.[42]
>
> Can the liberties of a nation be thought secure when we have removed their only firm basis, a conviction in the minds of the people that these liberties are . . . the gift of God? That they are not to be violated but with His wrath?[43]

God gives rights and liberties; and he also actively intervenes in human society to work his will. This recognition separates Jefferson from the deists. One statement in particular demonstrates Jefferson's conviction, "We are not in a world ungoverned by the laws and the power of a Superior Agent. Our efforts are in His hand, and directed by it, and He will give them their effect in His own time."[44]

Jefferson believed God imparts his wisdom to guide people and nations:

> May that Infinite Power which rules the destinies of the universe lead our councils to what is best, and give them a favorable issue for your peace and prosperity.[45]
>
> I join in addressing Him whose Kingdom ruleth over all, to direct the administration of affairs to their own greatest good.[46]
>
> I shall need . . . the favor of that Being in whose hands we are, who led our forefathers, as Israel of old, from their native land, and

41. Jefferson, "Declaration of the Causes and Necessity for Taking Up Arms," 1775; quoted by Maxfield et al., *The Real Thomas Jefferson*, p. 403.

42. Jefferson, "Summary View of the Rights of British America," 1774; quoted by ibid., p. 523.

43. Jefferson, "Notes on Virginia," 1781, 1782; quoted by ibid., p. 523.

44. Jefferson, 1815; quoted by ibid., p. 404.

45. Jefferson, First Inaugural Address, 1801; quoted in ibid., p. 403.

46. Jefferson, 1801; quoted in ibid., p. 403.

planted them in a country flowing with all the necessaries and
comforts of life; who has covered our infancy with His providence,
and our riper years with His wisdom and power; and to whose
goodness I ask you to join with me in supplications, that He will so
enlighten the minds of your servants, guide their councils, and
prosper their measures, that whatsoever they do shall result in your
good, and shall secure to you the peace, friendship, and approbation
of all nations.[47]

These are not the words of a deist. Nor would a deist speak of
submission to God and thankfulness to God the way Jefferson did:

> Whatever is to be our destiny, wisdom as well as duty dictates that
> we should acquiesce in the will of Him whose it is to give and take
> away, and be contented in the enjoyment of those (loved ones) who
> are still permitted to be with us.[48]
>
> While we devoutly return thanks to the beneficient Being who has
> been pleased to breathe into (our sister nations) the spirit of concil-
> iation and forgiveness, we are bound with peculiar gratitude to be
> thankful to Him that our own peace has been preserved.[49]

Jefferson saw God as the Creator and Sustainer of the universe,
the source of human rights and liberties, and the Supreme Being
who rules and overrules in human affairs. God leads nations "as
Israel of old," breathing into nations "the spirit of conciliation and
forgiveness," giving men material comforts, wisdom, and power.
Accordingly men are to pray to him, thank him, and submit to his
will.

Jefferson did not consider God a morally indifferent being.
Rather, God is a beneficient being who seeks the good of people and
nations: "Providence . . . delights in the happiness of man here and
his greater happiness hereafter."[50] But God is not indiscriminate
with goodness and beneficence; He is a God of justice who punishes
wrongs. Jefferson recognized God as the author of human rights
which "are not to be violated but with his wrath." Jefferson
continued, speaking of American black slavery:

> Indeed I tremble for my country when I reflect that God is just: that
> his justice cannot sleep for ever: that considering numbers, nature
> and natural means only, a revolution of the wheel of fortune, and

47. Jefferson, Second Inaugural Address, 1805; quoted in ibid., pp. 403–4.
48. Jefferson, Letter to John Page, 1804; quoted in ibid., p. 404.
49. Jefferson, First Annual Message to Congress, 1801; quoted in ibid., p. 404.
50. Jefferson, First Inaugural Address, 1801; quoted in ibid., p. 455.

exchange of situation (between slaves and masters), is among possible events: that it may become probable by supernatural interference! The Almighty has no attribute which can take sides with us in such a contest.[51]

Jefferson believed that God executes his judgment and his justice in this world by means of his ruling and overruling providence. God also judges men in eternity, as will be demonstrated later.

Jefferson's View of Jesus Christ

Jefferson's reason compelled him to reject the Trinity; he could not accept Jesus Christ as the Son of God, the Second Person of the Godhead. But he had great respect for the person, life, and teachings of Jesus the man.

At one point Jefferson said Jesus was only "a man, of illegitimate birth, of a benevolent heart, enthusiastic mind, who set out without pretensions to divinity, ended in believing them, and was punished capitally for sedition by being gibbetted according to the Roman law."[52]

But Jefferson's later writings show respect for Jesus:

His system of morality was the most benevolent and sublime probably that has been ever taught, and consequently more perfect than those of any of the ancient philosophers. . . . (He was) the most innocent, the most benevolent, the most eloquent and sublime character that ever has been exhibited to man.[53]

(I consider) the moral precepts of Jesus as more pure, correct, and sublime than those of the ancient philosophers; yet I do not concur with him (the author of a recent sermon) in the mode of proving it. He thinks it necessary to libel and decry the doctrines of the philosophers; but a man must be blinded, indeed, by prejudice who can deny them a great degree of merit. I give them their just due, and yet maintain that the morality of Jesus as taught by himself, and freed from the corruptions of latter times, is far superior. Their philosophy went chiefly to the government of our passions, so far as respected ourselves, and the procuring of our own tranquility. In our duties to others they were short and deficient. They extended their cares scarcely beyond our kindred and friends individually, and our

51. Jefferson, "Notes on the State of Virginia," 1781, 1782; quoted by Brodie, *Thomas Jefferson*, pp. 199–200.

52. Jefferson, Letter to Peter Carr, August 10, 1787; quoted by Adams, *Extracts*, p. 7.

53. Jefferson, Letter to Dr. Joseph Priestley, 1803; quoted in Maxfield et al., *The Real Thomas Jefferson*, p. 495.

country in the abstract. Jesus embraced with charity and philanthropy our neighbors, our countrymen, and the whole family of mankind. They confined themselves to actions; he pressed his sentiments into the region of our thoughts, and called for purity at the fountainhead.[54]

Jefferson was impressed with two attributes of Jesus' philosophy (1) his wider concept of duty to mankind as a whole, and (2) his emphasis on purity of thought in addition to purity of action.

Jefferson explained how Jesus differed from the Jews:

His system of morals . . . if filled up in the style and spirit of the rich fragments he left us, would be the most perfect and sublime that has ever been taught by man. . . . 1. He corrected the deism of the Jews, confirming them in their belief of one only God, and giving them juster notions of His attributes and government. 2. His moral doctrines relating to kindred and friends were more pure and perfect than those of the most correct of the philosophers, and greatly more so than those of the Jews; and they went far beyond both in inculcating universal philanthropy, not only to kindred and friends, to neighbors and countrymen, but to all mankind, gathering all into one family under the bonds of love, charity, peace, common wants, and common aids. . . . 3. The precepts of philosophy, and of the Hebrew code, laid hold of actions only. He pushed his scrutinies into the heart of man, erected his tribunal in the region of his thoughts, and purified the waters at the fountainhead. 4. He taught emphatically the doctrines of a future state, which was either doubted or disbelieved by the Jews, and wielded it with efficacy as an important incentive, supplementary to the other motives to moral conduct.[55]

His view of Jesus was greatly influenced by two contemporary men. The first was Henry St. John, Viscount Bolingbroke, a British Tory leader and writer. Bolingbroke convinced Jefferson that the Bible was not inspired and that the miracles Jesus supposedly worked were "equivocal at best, such as credulous superstitious persons, and none else, believed. . . ."[56] Bolingbroke stressed that Jesus' system of belief and practice was neither perfect nor complete, and the partial, unjust, and cruel God of the Old Testament was not a true picture of the real God.[57] Dickinson Adams says, "It is evident from random comments in Jefferson's writings that these selections

54. Jefferson, 1803; quoted in ibid., p. 495.
55. Jefferson, Letter to Dr. Benjmain Rush, 1803; quoted in ibid., pp. 495–96.
56. Bolingbroke; cited by Adams, *Extracts*, p. 6.
57. Ibid., pp. 6–7.

from Bolingbroke's works accurately reflect his own considered opinion of Christianity before the late 1790s.''[58]

Later, Dr. Joseph Priestley, an English chemist and Unitarian theologian, had an even greater influence on Jefferson. While Bolingbroke led Jefferson to reject traditional Christianity, Priestley led him to accept and respect Jesus as a person and teacher. Priestley argued that orthodox Christian doctrine was not the teaching of Jesus but was added later. Dickinson Adams summarizes Priestley's position:

> There was but one God, and he had given Jesus the special mission of revealing his true nature to the world and of teaching men how to lead virtuous lives on earth so that they would be rewarded rather than punished in the life to come. Jesus was not a member of the godhead, nor did he ever claim to be. Nevertheless, God signified his approval of Jesus' teachings by enabling him to perform miracles and to rise from the dead, thereby making him the greatest moral teacher who had ever lived. As a result, mankind was obliged to worship the one true God and to follow the moral teachings of Jesus. Virtually everything else in orthodox Christianity—doctrines like the Trinity, the atonement, and original sin, as well as devotional practices like the veneration of relics and saints—was a corruption of the primitive purity of the Christian message and had to be discarded to restore Christianity to its pristine simplicity and thus make it acceptable to modern men, who were otherwise inclined to reject it as a mass of superstitions.[59]

For the most part Jefferson accepted Priestley's position—except for the contention that Jesus performed miracles and rose from the dead. Remember that Jefferson believed that the laws of nature did not change or allow for exceptions. Priestley "persuaded him that Jesus had never laid claim to divinity, which to him made Jesus more credible as a great moral teacher.''[60]

Jefferson developed two writings which were reconstructions or abridgements of the Bible as a result of his devotion to the person and teachings of Jesus. The first, "The Philosophy of Jesus," written around 1803, has been lost in its original form but has been largely reconstructed from surviving portions of copies. "The Life and Morals of Jesus" was written around 1820 and also consists of a

58. Ibid., p. 7.
59. Ibid., p. 15.
60. Ibid., p. 15.

compilation of Bible verses with many of the miraculous elements edited out.[61]

Jefferson attributed Jesus' sense of divine mission to him being brought up among a superstitious people who regarded the "fumes of the most disordered imaginations . . . as special communications of the deity."[62] Foremost in Jefferson's personal creed was the unity of God, followed closely by the moral teachings of Jesus.

Jefferson's View of the Bible

Jefferson studied the Bible diligently; he read it in English, French, Latin, and Greek. But he did not regard it as the inspired Word of God.

He could not accept any kind of revelation that contradicted or transcended reason, so he rejected the portions of the Bible which spoke of the miraculous and did not include them in his compilations of Bible verses: "The Philosophy of Jesus" and "The Life and Morals of Jesus." His view of the Bible was similar to Bultmann's "demythologization" a century and a half later.

Jefferson foreshadowed the liberal higher critics of the nineteenth and twentieth centuries in other ways. He believed the Gospels were first written down many years after the death of Jesus by the "most unlettered of men" and that they were further corrupted as time passed by "those who pretend to be his special disciples."[63] However, Jefferson did believe the Gospels contained the basic teachings of Jesus in reasonably accurate form.

Jefferson cautiously recommended the Bible as a book for serious study. He wrote in "Notes on the State of Virginia":

Instead, therefore, of putting the Bible and Testament into the hands of the children at an age when their judgments are not sufficiently matured for religious inquiries, their memories may here be stored with the most useful facts from Grecian, Roman, European and American history. The first elements of morality too may be instilled into their minds. . . .[64]

He advised one of his nephews to read the Bible "as you would read Livy or Tacitus."[65] He recommended the Bible under the heading of

61. Ibid., pp. 26–28, 37–39.
62. Jefferson, Letter to William Short, August 4, 1820; quoted by ibid., p. 41.
63. Ibid., p. 23.
64. Jefferson, "Notes on the State of Virginia," 1781, 1782; reprinted by Padover, *The Complete Jefferson*, p. 667.
65. Jefferson, Letter to Peter Carr, August 10, 1787; quoted by Adams, *Extracts*, p. 7.

"History" rather than "Religion" in a letter to Robert Skipworth.[66] In 1825 he expressed his opinion concerning the Book of Revelation:

> It is between 50 and 60 years since I read it, and I then considered it as merely the ravings of a Maniac, no more worthy, nor capable of explanation than the incoherences of our own nightly dreams. I was therefore well pleased to see, in your first proof-sheet, that it was said to be not the production of St. John, but of Cerinthus, a century after the death of that Apostle. Yet the change of the Author's name does not lessen the extravagances of the composition, and come they from whomsoever they may, I cannot so far respect them as to consider them as an allegorical narrative of events, past or subsequent. There is not coherence enough in them to countenance any suite of rational ideas. You will judge therefore from this how impossible I think it is that either your explanation, or that of any man in the heavens above, or on the earth beneath, can be a correct one. What has no meaning admits no explanation. And pardon me if I say, with the candor of friendship, that I think your time too valuable, and your understanding of too high an order, to be wasted on these paralogisms. You will perceive, I hope, also that I do not consider them as revelations of the supreme being, whom I would not so far blaspheme as to impute to him a pretension of revelation, couched at the same time in terms which, he would know, were never to be understood by those to whom they were addressed.[67]

The previous statement was directed only to the Book of Revelation, not to the entire Bible. Rather than diminishing his appreciation for the Bible, it is more likely that Jefferson thought the Book of Revelation was not really part of the original canon of Scripture. However, perhaps Jefferson's true feelings and values were displayed at the death of his daughter in 1804. Padover relates Jefferson's reactions to this personal tragedy:

> His beautiful young daughter Maria, a brilliant and gifted girl whose aim in life had been to be worthy of her father, fell gravely ill. In the spring the anxious father hurried to Monticello to be at her bedside. He came just in time. Maria's death at twenty-six was a merciless blow to her father. Jefferson, now sixty-one and with only one surviving child, was shaken as he had not been since his wife's death. For hours after the young woman died, the stricken President stayed

66. Jefferson, Letter to Robert Skipworth, August 3, 1771; cited by ibid., p. 7.
67. Jefferson, Letter to Alexander Smyth, January 17, 1825; reprinted by ibid., pp. 415–16.

in his room with a Bible in his hand. Once again he was alone with
his soul in the presence of death.[68]

Jefferson's View of Man

Jefferson did not accept the Calvinist view of the total depravity
of man. Instead, he believed that man had some basic goodness,
some basic ability to apprehend and respond to that which is true
and good, though he also recognized man's ability to choose evil.

However, he did ascribe this basic goodness to God. "It shews
how necessary was the care of the Creator in making the moral
principle so much a part of our constitution as that no errors of
reasoning or of speculation might lead us astray from its observance
in practice."[69] He also believed this goodness was not limited to
Christians, or to believers in God:

> If we did a good act merely from the love of god, and a belief that it
> is pleasing to him, whence arises the morality of the Atheist? It is idle
> to say as some do, that no such being exists. We have the same
> evidence of the fact as of most of those we act on, to wit, their own
> affirmations, and their reasonings in support of them.[70]

Jefferson emphasized that God plants basic moral sense in every
man, with a few defective souls as exceptions, and gives preachers
and teachers the responsibility of cultivating and correcting this
moral sense:

> The creator would indeed have been a bungling artist, had he
> intended man for a social animal, without planting in him social
> dispositions. . . . When it is wanting we endeavor to supply the defect
> by education, by appeals to reason and calculation, by presenting to
> the being so unhappily conformed other motives to do good, and to
> eschew evil; such as the love, or the hatred or rejection of those
> among whom he lives and whose society is necessary to his happi-
> ness, and even existence; demonstrations by sound calculation that
> honesty promotes interest in the long run; the rewards and penalties
> established by the laws; and ultimately the prospects of a future state

68. Padover, *A Great American*, pp. 149–50.
69. Jefferson, Letter to Thomas Law, June 13, 1814; reprinted by Adams, *Extracts*,
p. 355.
70. Ibid.

of retribution for the evil as well as the good done while here. These are the correctives which are supplied by education, and which exercise the functions of the moralist, the preacher and legislator: and they lead into a course of correct action all those whose depravity is not too profound to be eradicated.[71]

Jefferson's belief in the liberty of conscience accompanied this view of man's basic reasonability. His famous words are inscribed on his tombstone: "I have sworn upon the altar of god eternal hostility against every form of tyranny over the mind of man."[72] The words were taken from a letter he wrote to Benjamin Rush in 1800. In the Bill for Establishing Religious Freedom which Jefferson presented to the Virginia Assembly on June 13, 1779, he stated:

> Well aware that the opinions and belief of men depend on their own will, but follow involuntarily the evidence proposed to their minds; that Almighty God hath created the mind free, and manifested his supreme will that free it shall remain by making it altogether insusceptible of restraint; that all attempts to influence it by temporal punishments, or burthens, or by civil incapacitations, tend only to beget habits of hypocrisy and meanness, and are a departure from the plan of the holy author of our religion, who being lord both of body and mind, yet choose not to propagate it by coercions on either, as was in his Almighty power to do, but to exalt it by its influence on reason alone. . . .[73]

Jefferson actually wrote into law many of the basic premises of his own religion—that the mind is free, contrary to the predestinarian beliefs of the Calvinists; and that men come to religious truth through reason alone, not through divine revelation—under the guise of disestablishing religion.

He believed in the human soul. Unlike many Christian theologians, Jefferson believed that the soul was composed of some form of matter—even God and the angels are composed of some form of matter:

> To talk of immaterial existences is to talk of nothings. To say that the human soul, angels, god, are immaterial, is to say they are nothings, or that there is no god, no angels, no soul. I cannot reason otherwise: but I believe I am supported in my creed of materialism by Locke, Tracy, and Stewart. At what age of the Christian church this heresy

71. Ibid., p. 357.
72. Jefferson, Letter to Benjamin Rush, September 23, 1800; reprinted by ibid., p. 320.
73. Padover, *The Complete Jefferson*, p. 946.

of immaterialism, this masked atheism, crept in, I do not know. But a heresy it certainly is. Jesus taught nothing of it. He told us indeed that "God is a spirit," but he has not defined what a spirit is, nor said that it is not matter. And the ancient fathers generally, if not universally, held it to be matter: light and thin indeed, an etherial gas, but still matter.[74]

Although the soul is composed of matter, it survives death. Jefferson believed in immortality and in a final judgment. He wrote to the son of a friend, "Adore God. Reverence and cherish your parents. Love your neighbor as yourself. Be just. Be true. Murmur not at the ways of Providence. So shall the life into which you have entered be the Portal to one of eternal and ineffable bliss."[75] Jefferson believed this final judgment to be one of works/righteousness. He wrote to William Canby, "I believe . . . that he who steadily observes those moral precepts in which all religions concur, will never be questioned, at the gates of heaven, as to the dogmas in which they all differ."[76] He wrote to Maria Cosway, a close friend from his days in Paris, "The religion you so sincerely profess tells us we shall meet again; and we have all so lived as to be assured it will be in happiness."[77]

Jefferson's other writings indicate that faith may also have a role in final judgment. He wrote to Charles Thomson:

These are the absurdities into which those run who usurp the throne of god, and dictate to him what he should have done. May they, with all their metaphysical riddles, appear before that tribunal with as clean hands and hearts as you and I shall. There, suspended in the scales of eternal justice, faith and works will shew their worth by their weight.[78]

His words to his namesake combine faith and works, "Adore God. . . . Love your neighbor as yourself" seem to resolve the problem.

74. Jefferson, Letter to John Adams, August 15, 1820; reprinted by Adams, *Extracts*, p. 400.

75. Jefferson, Letter to Thomas Jefferson Smith, February 21, 1825; reprinted by ibid., pp. 40–41.

76. Jefferson, Letter to William Canby, September 18, 1813; reprinted by ibid., p. 350.

77. Jefferson, Letter to Maria Cosway; quoted by Padover, *A Great American*, pp. 178–79.

78. Jefferson, Letter to Charles Thomson, January 29, 1817; reprinted by Adams, *Extracts*, p. 384.

Jefferson's View of the Church

Jefferson has been portrayed as an enemy of the church and preachers. He had little patience with those who were more concerned with doctrinal matters than in preaching and living the moral precepts of Jesus. He believed the church and preachers had distorted the pure and simple teachings of primitive Christianity.

He was especially hostile toward the Calvinists and their doctrines. He wrote about Calvin to John Adams:

> I can never join Calvin in addressing his god. He was indeed an Atheist, which I can never be; or rather his religion was Daemonism. If ever man worshipped a false god, he did. The being described in his 5 points is not the God whom you and I acknowledge and adore, the Creator and benevolent governor of the world, but a daemon of malignant spirit. It would be more pardonable to believe in no god at all, then to blaspheme him by the atrocious attributes of Calvin.[79]

In a letter to William Short:

> The Presbyterian clergy are loudest, the most intolerant of all sects, the most tyrannical, and ambitious; ready at the word of the lawgiver, if such a word could be now obtained, to put the torch to the pile, and to rekindle in this virgin hemisphere the flames in which their oracle Calvin consumed the poor Servetus, because he could not find in his Euclid the proposition which has demonstrated that three are one, and one is three, nor subscribe to that of Calvin that magistrates have a right to exterminate all heretics to Calvinistic creed.[80]

In 1802, when he was preparing his address to the Danbury Baptists (in which he uttered the much-misunderstood phrase "wall of separation between church and state"), Jefferson wrote to Attorney General Levi Lincoln, "I know it will give great offense to the New England clergy; but the advocate of religious liberty is to expect neither peace nor forgiveness from them."[81] On another occasion Jefferson acknowledged that the "half reformation of Luther and Calvin did something towards a restoration of his (Christ's) genuine doctrines," but added that "Calvinism has introduced into the

79. Jefferson, Letter to John Adams, April 11, 1823; reprinted by ibid., p. 410.
80. Jefferson, Letter to William Short, April 13, 1820; reprinted by ibid., p. 393.
81. Jefferson, Letter to Levi Lincoln, January 1, 1802; quoted by Frommer, *The Bible in the Public Schools*, p. 19.

Christian religion more new absurdities than its leader had purged it of old ones."[82]

But elsewhere Jefferson insisted that he was not an enemy of the church, only of religious intoleration. After writing Benjamin Rush that he had "sworn on the altar of god eternal hostility against every form of tyranny over the mind of man," he added, "But this is all they have to fear from me."[83] Jefferson's oldest grandson and namesake, Thomas Jefferson Randolph, wrote an intimate account of his grandfather's life and character. After acknowledging Jefferson's hostility toward the abuses and perversions of Christianity, he said:

> He was regular in his attendance (at) church, taking his prayer book with him. He drew the plan of the Episcopal church in Charlottesville, was one of the largest contributors to its erection, and contributed regularly to the support of its minister. I paid, after his death, his subscription of $200 to the erection of the Presbyterian church in the same village. A gentleman of some distinction calling on him and expressing his disbelief in the truths of the Bible, his reply was, "Then, sir, you have studied it to little purpose."
>
> He was guilty of no profanity himself, and did not tolerate it in others. He detested impiety, and his favorite quotation for his young friends, as a basis for their morals, was the 15th psalm of David.
>
> He did not permit cards in his house; he knew no game with them.[84]

In summary, Jefferson was critical of religious intolerance, preoccupation with dogma, and other religious abuses, but he approved of Christianity's positive influence on society as a whole. Dr. Benjamin Rush helped to persuade Jefferson that Christianity was a bulwark on which republican government could rest. This probably contributed to Jefferson's increasing approval of the Christian religion.[85] Shortly after becoming President he said, "(The) Christian religion, when divested of the rags in which (the clergy) have inveloped it, is a religion of all others most friendly to liberty, science and the freest expansions of the human mind."[86]

Jefferson's estimation of the value of religion was basically utilitarian. He judged religion on its usefulness to society not on the

---

82. Jefferson, Letter to Salma Hale, July 26, 1818; quoted by Adams, *Extracts*, p. 385.
83. Jefferson, Letter to Benjamin Rush, September 23, 1800; reprinted by ibid., p. 320.
84. Thomas Jefferson Randolph, undated letter (perhaps written during the 1850s) to biographer Henry S. Randall; reprinted in Maxfield et al., *The Real Thomas Jefferson*, p. 321.
85. Adams, *Extracts*, pp. 18–19.
86. Jefferson, Letter to Moses Robinson, March 23, 1801; reprinted by ibid., pp. 324–25.

basis of its objective truth. He wrote to Miles King in 1814, "I must ever believe that religion substantially good which produces an honest life, and we have been authorized by one, whom you and I equally respect, to judge of the tree by its fruit."[87] Dickinson Adams suggests that Jefferson's growing appreciation for Christianity in the 1790s may have been caused in part by his growing conviction that Christianity could serve as a moral basis for the nation.[88] But Jefferson's religious affections should not be limited to utilitarianism or national good.

Finally, Jefferson emphasized personal conscience rather than religious actions because he did not fully appreciate the effect religious beliefs had on an individual's actions or on society as a whole. He believed that religion was a private matter between man and God so he saw no reason for government to regulate that belief. As he put it:

> . . . our rulers can have no authority over such natural rights, only as we have submitted to them (in a social compact). The rights of conscience we never submitted, we could not submit. We are answerable for them to our God. The legitimate powers of government extend only to such acts as are injurious to others. But it does me no injury for my neighbor to say there are twenty gods, or no God. It neither picks my pocket nor breaks my leg.[89]

Rev. William Linn, Jefferson's outspoken critic, responded:

> Let my neighbor once persuade himself that there is no God, and he will soon pick my pocket, and break not only my leg but my neck. If there be no God, there is no law, no future account; government then is the ordinance of man only, and we cannot be subject for conscience sake.[90]

Jefferson began to appreciate the relationship of Christianity and morality and republican government in the 1790s. It is likely Jefferson modified his earlier 1781 viewpoint. However, his distinction between conscience and action and the right of government to regulation remained a shallow and poorly thought out concept.

---

87. Jefferson, Letter to Miles Kings, September 26, 1814; reprinted by ibid., p. 360.

88. Ibid., pp. 16–19.

89. Jefferson, "Notes on the State of Virginia," 1781, 1782; reprinted by Padover, *The Complete Jefferson*, p. 675.

90. Rev. William Linn; quoted by Adams, *Extracts*, p. 11.

Was Jefferson a Christian?

If we accept the definition of an orthodox Christian as one who believes it is impossible to saved except through faith in the substitutionary atonement of the Son of God on Calvary's cross, it would be difficult to characterize Thomas Jefferson as a Christian. It is unlikely that he would so characterize himself, given that definition.

Jefferson probably did not consider himself a Christian before the 1790s. He identified Christianity with the doctrines which he disagreed with and wanted no part of orthodox Calvinism. Jefferson began to change as he understood Priestley's liberalized version of Christianity and learned the value of the Christian faith from Dr. Benjamin Rush. Dickinson Adams says:

> . . . by presenting him with a demystified form of Christianity that comported with his rationalistic world view, Priestley made it possible for Jefferson to regard himself as a genuine Christian and launched him on the quest for the authentic teachings of Jesus that was to lead in time to the "Syllabus" and "The Philosophy of Jesus."[91]

In this sense it was possible for Jefferson to declare in 1816:

> . . . I am a real Christian, that is to say, a disciple of the doctrines of Jesus, very different from the Platonists, who call me infidel, and themselves Christians and preachers of the gospel, while they draw all their characteristic dogmas from what its Author never said nor saw.[92]

Dickinson Adams says that "an analysis of the elements of his Christian faith reveals that there was both more to it than those who emphasize his rationalism have conceded and less than those who stress his religiousness have admitted."[93]

The study of Jefferson's Christian faith or lack thereof is hindered by the fact that he considered innermost religious beliefs to be a private matter:

> I have ever thought religion a concern purely between our God and our consciences, for which we were accountable to Him and not to the priests. I never told my own religion, nor scrutinized that of

---

91. Adams, *Extracts*, p. 16.
92. Jefferson, Letter to Charles Thomson, January 9, 1815; reprinted by ibid., p. 365.
93. Ibid., p. 39.

another. I never attempted to make a convert nor wished to change another's creed. I have ever judged of the religion of others by their lives, . . . for it is in our lives, and not from our words, that our religion must be read. By the same test the world must judge me.[94]

Jefferson's grandson makes a similar statement:

Of his peculiar religious opinions, his family knew no more than the world. If asked by one of them his opinion on any religious subject, his uniform reply was that it was a subject each was bound to study assiduously for himself, unbiased by the opinions of others. It was a matter solely of conscience; after thorough investigation, they were responsible for the righteousness, but not the rightfulness, of their opinions. (He believed) that the expression of his opinion might influence theirs, and he would not give it!

He held it to be an invasion of the freedom of religious opinion to attempt to subject the opinions of any man to the ordeal of public judgment; he would not submit to it in his own case, nor sanction it in another. He considered that religious opinions should be judged by the fruits they produced—if they produced good men, they must be good.[95]

Padover says that as Jefferson approached death, "He read a great deal, especially the Greek dramatists (in the original) and the Bible."[96] Jefferson's grandson, who was with him in his last hours stated:

Upon being suddenly aroused from sleep by a noise in the room, he asked if he had heard the name of Mr. Hatch mentioned—the minister whose church he attended. On my replying in the negative he observed, as he turned over, "I have no objection to seeing him, as a kind and good neighbor." The impression made upon my mind at the moment was that, his religious opinions having been formed upon mature study and reflection, he had no doubts upon his mind, and therefore did not desire the attendance of a clergyman; I have never since doubted the correctness of the impression then taken.[97]

94. Jefferson, 1816; quoted in Maxfield et al, *The Real Thomas Jefferson*, p. 602.
95. Thomas Jefferson Randolph, Letter to Henry S. Randall; reprinted in ibid., pp. 321–22.
96. Padover, *A Great American*, p. 184.
97. Thomas Jefferson Randolph; reprinted in Maxfield et al., *The Real Thomas Jefferson*, p. 332.

Perhaps the statement, "I am of a sect by myself, so far as I know,"[98] best summarizes the mystery of what Jefferson really believed in his heart.

The Interrelationship of Church and State

Jefferson had greater faith in the ability of the common man to participate in government than most of the other founding fathers— because he believed man was a rational creature. He had fewer reservations about majority rule than other leaders of his time.

Jefferson also had faith in the ability of the common man to govern himself and conduct his own affairs without government interference. "That government governs best which governs least," he said. He strongly supported a bill of rights to protect the individual from government oppression.

Jefferson strongly favored individual liberty in religion. His philosophy of church/state relations is best summarized in his opening words of the Virginia Bill of Rights: "Almighty God hath created the human mind free." Jefferson enacted into statute his own belief about God, creation, and man with those words; and debased the Calvinist view of total depravity, unconditional election, and irresistible grace. He believed man had the capacity to reason for himself toward an understanding of God and the universe, and was convinced man did not need the state to point him in the direction of holiness.

Jefferson's 1802 address to the Danbury Baptists contains his best-remembered statement about church/state relations. ". . . I contemplate with solemn reverence that act of the whole American people which declared that their legislature should 'make no law respecting an establishment of religion, or prohibiting the free exercise thereof,' thus building a *wall of separation between Church and State.*" [emphasis added][99] Observations about Jefferson's "wall of separation" metaphor reveal:

1. Its importance is greatly overrated. The courts often cite the metaphor as the definitive interpretation of the meaning of the First Amendment; many Americans think the phrase is part of the Amendment itself. (The phrase "separation of church and state" appears nowhere in the Constitution or Bill of Rights.) Jefferson made the statement in 1802, thirteen years after Congress passed

98. Jefferson; quoted in ibid.; p. 602.

99. Thomas Jefferson, "Address to the Danbury Baptists, 1802"; quoted by Frommer, *The Bible and the Public Schools*, p. 19.

the First Amendment. Jefferson was not a delegate to the 1787 Constitutional Convention, nor was he a member of Congress in 1789, nor was he a member of any state legislature or ratifying convention at any time relevant to the passage of the First Amendment; he was serving as U.S. Minister to France throughout this time. Jefferson's view should not be considered definitive. Washington's metaphor about the need to "establish effectual barriers against the horrors of spiritual tyranny and every species of religious persecution,"[100] is more timely (1789, the same year the First Amendment was passed by Congress) and was uttered by the most respected man in America at that time.

2. Since Jefferson was speaking to a Baptist group (as was Washington), he possibly borrowed the metaphor from an earlier Baptist leader, Roger Williams, who wrote:

> . . . when they have opened a gap in the hedge or *wall of separation between the garden of the church and the wilderness of the world,* God hath ever broke down the wall itself, removed the candlestick, and made his garden a wilderness, as at this day. And that therefore if He will eer please to restore His garden and paradise again, it must of necessity be walled in peculiarly unto Himself from the world. . . .[101] [emphasis added]

According to Williams, the "wall of separation" was to protect the "garden of the church" from the "wilderness of the world." Today the metaphor has been stood on its head, and the wall is thought to protect the state from the church.

3. The phrase is misunderstood. Jefferson probably used the term *state* in the generic sense to refer to the federal government. He did not mean the states were to be separated from religion. In his second inaugural address he said:

> In matters of religion I have considered that its free exercise is placed by the Constitution independent of the powers of the General Government. I have therefore undertaken on no occasion to prescribe the religious exercise suited to them, but have left them, as the Constitution found them, under the direction and discipline of the church or state authorities acknowledged by the several religious societies.[102]

100. Washington to the Committee representing the United Baptist Churches in Virginia, May 1789; quoted by Paul Boller, Jr., *George Washington and Religion* (Dallas: Southern Methodist University Press, 1963), pp. 169–70.

101. Roger Williams; quoted by Buzzard and Ericsson, *The Battle for Religious Liberty*, p. 51.

102. Thomas Jefferson, Second Inaugural Address; quoted by Whitehead, *The Separation Illusion*, p. 89.

Jefferson wrote to a clergyman in 1808:

> I consider the government of the United States as interdicted by the Constitution from intermeddling with religious institutions, their doctrines, discipline, or exercises. This results not only from the provision that no law shall be made respecting the establishment or free exercise of religion, but from that also which reserves to the states the powers not delegated to the United States. Clearly, no power to prescribe any religious exercise, or to assume authority in religious discipline, has been delegated to the general government.[103]

This indicates that Jefferson understood the "wall" to exempt the church from the jurisdiction of the federal government, because under the social compact, the federal government had never been delegated any such authority. It did not mean the states and the churches could not interact with one another. It is interesting that Jefferson opposed nationally-sponsored days of prayer as President, but supported state-sponsored days of prayer as governor of Virginia.

Another interesting fact: In 1803 President Jefferson recommended that Congress pass a treaty with the Kaskaskia Indians which provided, among other things, a stipend of $100 annually for seven years from the Federal treasury for the support of a Catholic priest to minister to the Kaskaskia Indians. This and two similar treaties were enacted during Jefferson's administration—one with the Wyandotte Indians and other tribes in 1806, and one with the Cherokees in 1807. In 1787, another act of Congress ordained special lands "for the sole use of Christian Indians" and reserved lands for the Moravian Brethren "for civilizing the Indians and promoting Christianity." This was renewed in 1796 with a new law entitled "An Act regulating the grants of land appropriated for Military services and for the Society of the United Brethren, for propagating the Gospel among the Heathen." Congress extended this act three times during Jefferson's administration and each time he signed the extension into law. Citing these and other facts, Professor Robert Cord concludes, "These historical facts indicate that Jefferson . . . did not see the First Amendment and the Establishment Clause requiring 'complete independence of religion and government.'"[104]

Jefferson was a believer in "the Laws of Nature and of Nature's God," and looked to the Creator and his laws as the source of all

---

103. Thomas Jefferson, *Jefferson's Writings*, Monticello, ed. (1905), IX:428–30.
104. Robert L. Cord, *Separation of Church and State: Historical Fact and Current Fiction* (New York: Lambeth Press, 1982), p. 45.

rights. Human rights are the gift of God, so their realization and enjoyment cannot be separated from God. Jefferson believed in religious liberty because religious liberty was part of the law of God. The words engraved on the Jefferson Memorial echo that belief. "The God who gave us life, gave us liberty at the same time. . . . Can the liberties of a nation be secure when we have removed their only firm basis, a conviction in the minds of the people that those liberties are the gift of God?"

Conclusions

The following nine points can be concluded about Jefferson's beliefs:

1. Thomas Jefferson was neither a deist nor an orthodox Christian; his views best conform to the Unitarians of his day.

2. Jefferson had faith in the power of human reason to apprehend truth and govern the affairs of men.

3. Jefferson's concept of God was monotheistic; he rejected trinitarianism as contrary to human reason. He regarded God as the Creator and Sustainer of the universe, as the author of natural and moral laws, as the giver of human rights and liberties, and as the beneficial and just judge of the universe who actively guides, superintends, and intervenes in human affairs.

4. Jefferson did not believe in Jesus Christ as the Son of God or as the Second Person of the Godhead, but he respected Jesus as the world's greatest example and teacher of morals.

5. Jefferson rejected the Bible as the inspired Word of God. He believed the Bible contained basic moral teachings of Jesus, but also believed it contained much which had been written later and which had to be rejected as false and contrary to reason.

6. Jefferson believed God created man as a free and rational creature; therefore no church or government may coerce human volition or interfere with liberty of conscience.

7. His emphasis on human freedom and human reason led him to oppose the predestination doctrines and theocratic practices of the Calvinists. Jefferson's belief that Jesus was originally monotheistic and that trinitarianism had been created later by the church, led him to oppose clergymen who were so concerned about church doctrine and church practice that they neglected the pure and simple moral teachings of Jesus. Jefferson eventually saw the value of Christianity for the nation and the individual; he attended church, gave to the support of several churches, and lived a pious life.

8. Jefferson rejected orthodox Christianity earlier in his life. In the 1790s he understood Christianity in terms of following the moral teachings of Jesus; in that respect he considered himself a Christian.

9. Jefferson believed religion was a private matter between a man and his God. Consequently he was reluctant to offer his opinion on certain religious doctrines. For this reason it is difficult to confirm what Jefferson actually believed.

14 Samuel Adams

S amuel Adams is known as the "Father of the American Revolution"; he is also called the "Last of the Puritans."

Samuel Adams never became President, but he was much more famous and respected in Europe than his cousin John who became the nation's second president.[1]

Jefferson said of Samuel Adams, "I always considered him as more than any other member [in Congress] the fountain of our important measures."[2] Of the preparation of his first inaugural address Jefferson said, "In meditating the matter of that address, I often asked myself, is this exactly in the spirit of the patriarch of liberty, Samuel Adams?"[3]

Modern authorities recognize Adams's contribution to American independence. *Encyclopedia Britannica* declares that "Samuel Adams did more than any other American to arouse opposition against English rule in the Colonies."[4] *World Book Encyclopedia* acknowledges that "He became the leading speaker in the cause of

1. Page Smith, *John Adams* (Garden City: Doubleday, 1962), I:367.
2. Jefferson to Samuel Adams, 1801; reprinted by Paul Leicester Ford, ed., *The Writings of Thomas Jefferson* (New York: G. P. Putnam's Sons, 1892–99), 8:38; quoted by Andrew M. Allison, M. Richard Maxfield, K. DeLynn Cook, and W. Cleon Skousen, *The Real Thomas Jefferson* (Washington, D.C.: National Center for Constitutional Studies, 1983), p. 341.
3. Jefferson, 1819; quoted by ibid., pp. 341–42.
4. *Encyclopedia Britannica: Macropaedia: Knowledge in Depth*, s.v. "Adams, Samuel."

American independence."[5] Both sources recount his exploits as head of the patriots in Boston, as organizer of pro-independence groups, as founder of the committees of correspondence, as probable instigator of the Boston Tea Party. They recognize his role in Massachusetts' legislature from 1765-1774, in the Continental Congress from 1774-1781, as a delegate to Massachusetts' Constitutional Convention in 1780 and in Massachusetts' convention for ratification of the U.S. Constitution, and his service as Lieutenant Governor of Massachusetts 1789-1793 and Governor from 1794-1797. They recognize that he played a crucial role in the ratification of the U.S. Constitution because at first he opposed Massachusetts' ratification but finally agreed to support the Constitution when the Federalist forces promised a Bill of Rights.

These sources make no mention of the role of religion in the life and philosophy of Samuel Adams. Yet religion—more specifically, Puritan Christianity—was the chief impetus for everything Samuel Adams did. John C. Miller captures the real Samuel Adams:

> Sam Adams never forgot those stirring days during the Great Awakening when George Whitefield "thundered in the Pulpit against Assemblies & Balls" and New Englanders seemed to turn the clock back to the time of Winthrop and Cotton. The glimpse Adams caught of "Puritanism" in 1740 had profound influence upon his later career. It became one of his strongest desires to restore Puritan manners and morals to New England: in his eyes, the chief purpose of the American Revolution was to separate New England from the "decadent" mother country in order that Puritanism might again flourish as it had in the early seventeenth century. Adams hoped to do by means of a political revolution what George Whitefield had done through a religious awakening. Puritanism was his goal: revolution his method of attaining it.[6]

Samuel Adams was born September 16, 1722. His father, a prosperous beer manufacturer, was a pillar and deacon of the Congregational Church—a combination which was accepted at the time. Deacon Adams, as he was known, had a reputation as a "godly man."[7]

Samuel attended the Boston Latin School, where he learned

5. *World Book Encyclopedia*, s.v. "Adams, Samuel."
6. John C. Miller, *Sam Adams: Pioneer in Propaganda* (Stanford: Stanford University Press, 1936, 1960), p. 85.
7. William V. Wells, *The Life and Public Services of Samuel Adams* (1865), III:427–28; cited by Miller, *Sam Adams*, p. 4.

Greek and Latin, and at age fourteen he enrolled in Harvard College. His parents hoped he would enter the ministry, but as Miller says, "Sam's morals were good and he was seldom missing from the family pew on Lord's Days, yet he showed little interest in theology or metaphysics."[8]

The First Great Awakening sparked Sam's interest in spiritual things. Miller describes how the Awakening affected Harvard:

> . . . While he [Samuel Adams] was at Harvard College, the Great Awakening swept over the country and Harvard became "a new Creature" filled with devout young men who had experienced the "New Birth." George Whitefield was welcomed in New England as "an Angel of God and Messenger of Jesus Christ," and there were few students at Cambridge able to resist his hot gospeling. Harvard again became a citadel of righteousness and the clergy exulted over "the sweet Work going on at Cambridge." When Whitefield first visited the college he was dismayed by the laxity he found: tutors did not pray with their pupils and their favorite theologian was Tillotson, whom Whitefield declared "knew less of Christianity than Mahomet." But after the religious awakening of 1740, it was said that only "Voices of Prayer and Praise" were to be heard in students' rooms and Tillotson and Clark were cast aside for Flavel and the Mathers. Indeed, the piety of the college became so formidable that even "divers gentlemen's Sons" who came to Harvard prepared to spend four years in sloth and pleasure were suddenly seized with remorse and became so "zealous for Christ's Cause as to devote themselves entirely to Studies of Divinity." In Boston, where the Congregational clergy had for many years past seen the Devil making long strides, the Great Awakening brought about a "Week of Sabbaths": taverns, dancing schools, and assemblies "which have always proved unfriendly to serious Godliness" were deserted for prayer meetings and sermons, and religious conversation became "almost fashionable." At every opportunity, Whitefield put "a Damp upon Polite Diversions" and beseeched his hearers to shun the snares Satan had laid for them in fashionable dress. His exhortations produced startling changes in Boston. Young men and women cast off their finery and walked along the fashionable Boston Mall, built in imitation of St. James's Park in London, wearing the sombre dress seen in the heydey of Puritanism.[9]

Miller suggests that the effects of this Awakening upon New

---

8. Ibid., p. 4.
9. Ibid., pp. 6–7.

England were short-lived; but he acknowledges that its effect upon Samuel Adams was profound and permanent.

Samuel's father initially stirred his son's interest in politics. Deacon Adams served as a tithingman, constable, assessor, selectman, and representative at the General Court of Massachusetts. His greatest influence was exercised through the Boston Caucus Club, a group of citizens who met informally and planned and decided the affairs of the community. Miller relates that "Bostonians nominally decided their concerns in the town meeting, but under Deacon Adams, and still more under his son and successor in the leadership of the Caucus Club, the political bosses laid their plans and thoroughly cut and dried all the town's important business long before the citizens met in the town meeting—there usually to do as the Caucus Club bid. During the eighteenth century, the Caucus Club became so powerful that Sam Adams turned it into a revolutionary machine and with its aid made himself 'Dictator' of Boston"[10] Deacon Adams's political involvement took place before independence was a serious consideration, but was a strong advocate of the rights of the colonies. He was frequently asked to draw up declarations of grievances against England. Miller adds:

> Deacon Adams made his house a gathering place for Boston politicians, from petty "bosses" to such leaders as Elisha Cooke, "the greate Darling of his Country" and standard bearer of the Massachusetts Country Party. When the Crown demanded a fixed salary from the Massachusetts General Court for the royal governors, Elisha Cooke and Deacon Adams led the colony's resistance, with the result that the King and the governor were worsted in the struggle. Sam's biographers have supposed that he was allowed to sit at Elisha Cooke's feet; if so, no rebel could have had better schooling. Governor Jonathan Belcher, who certainly had no reason to love Cooke, said he had "a fixt enmity to all kingly government" and "endeavoured, to poyson the Minds of His Countreymen, with his republican notions, in order to assert the Independency of New England"—the accusation later brought against Sam Adams by the royal governors of Massachusetts.[11]

Deacon Adams was interested in religion, politics, and business; Samuel was only interested in religion and politics. Perhaps for that reason Samuel's early attempts at business failed; he never became a wealthy man. He earned a meager salary as a tax collector for

---

10. Ibid., p. 8.
11. C. K. Shipton, *Sibley's Harvard Graduates*, IV, 352–54; cited by ibid., p. 9.

many years, an office which he ineptly filled because of his sympathetic nature. But Samuel actively pursued his religious and political interests and often combined the two. Miller says,

> He never overlooked an opportunity to give a religious flavor to his political activities. During crises in the struggle between the House of Representatives and the royal governor, Adams set aside days of fasting and prayer to 'seek the Lord'; and by this means he gave the American Revolution the character of a moral and religious crusade. No patriot leader had greater success than Sam Adams in convincing New Englanders that if they tamely surrendered their liberty to the British government, their religion was certain to be swallowed up by 'Popery' or Episcopacy.[12]

Adams received inspiration from the early Puritans, and took his illustrations from the ancient Romans. He studied Roman literature at Harvard and was convinced that the early Roman republic and early Puritan New England shared many of the same virtues—piety, morality, austerity, industry, modesty, and thrift. He believed that contemporary New England was departing from those virtues just as latter-day Rome had done, and with the same disastrous results. Miller summarizes Samuel's thinking:

> In Adams's mind, a Roman Senator would have quickly made himself at home in seventeenth-century Puritan New England because Rome and New England were spiritually built upon common ground. Adams became known as the 'Cato' of the American Revolution because from youth to old age he preached the necessity of returning to an earlier and simpler way of life: his first revolt was against materialism and his first hatreds were against those whom he believed hostile to the rebirth of the Puritan or 'Old Roman' spirit in New England.[13]

Adams avoided and condemned luxury, indolence, and licentiousness throughout his life; when he was elected to the Continental Congress his friends had to purchase a suitable set of clothes for him.

He was at times suspected of being a "leveller" who wanted to abolish property rights and redistribute wealth, but he emphatically declared that was not the case. In 1768 he declared that redistribution of income and property was as objectionable as giving the King

---

12. Ibid., pp. 84–85.
13. Ibid., p. 19.

and Parliament absolute power over the colonists' money. Adams asserted with John Locke that private property is a God-given natural right and a chief purpose of government is to protect property rights.[14] "The utopian schemes of leveling and a community of goods are as visionary and impracticable as those which vest all property in the Crown. [These ideas] are arbitrary, despotic, and, in our government, unconstitutional"[15] Adams is sometimes accused of radicalism, but he always insisted that he had no intention of fomenting newfangled revolutionary principles; he only wanted to revive the "ancestorial Spirit of Liberty."[16] He based his defense of liberty on time-honored principles of natural law, under which neither the king nor the Parliament had authority over the colonies.[17]

Adams's skills lay in propaganda and organization at the grass-roots level. His leadership of the Boston Caucus is typical, but his organizational genius is displayed through the establishment of Committees of Correspondence, through the Sons of Liberty, and many other activities as Miller reveals:

> He was never more angelic than when singing hymns in Dr. Checkley's meetinghouse, where he displayed "an exquisite ear for music, and a charming voice." But Adams found a way of turning even this talent to politics. He organized singing societies among Boston mechanics at which, Tories complained, more revolutionaries were produced than songbirds, because Adams presided over the meetings and "embraced such Opportunities to ye inculcating Sedition, 'till it had ripened into Rebellion."[18]

Adams did not hesitate to invoke religious themes as he propagandized for American independence. He compared the situation to Cromwell's time in England, which he regarded with great favor, and he accused his Tory opponents of "popery" repeatedly and once declared that Tory governor Thomas Hutchison venerated royal instruction "as ever a poor deluded Catholic reverenc'd the decree of Holy Father at Rome."[19]

His opponents used similar language. When Adams managed to win John Hancock, the wealthiest and perhaps most influential man

---

14. Ibid., p. 317.
15. Adams; quoted by W. Cleon Skousen, *The Making of America* (Washington, D.C.: The National Center for Constitutional Studies, 1985), p. 219.
16. Miller, *Sam Adams*, p. 85.
17. Ibid., pp. 86, 90, 243, 267.
18. Ibid., p. 84.
19. Samuel Adams, *Boston Gazette*, April 1, 1771; quoted by ibid., p. 232.

in New England, over to the cause of independence, the Tories declared that he had seduced Hancock "in the same Manner that the Devil is represented seducing Eve, by a constant whispering at his Ear."[20] They accused him of using religion for political purposes. Governor Hutchinson said Adams made religion a "stalking horse," and others said he had "a religious Mask ready for his Occasions; he could transform his self into an Angel of Light with the weak Religionist, & with the abandoned he would disrobe his self."[21] Adams was willing to make common cause with unbelievers for political purposes and he was a cunning politician who at times seemed to believe the ends justify the means. He sincerely believed in the ends he sought to accomplish.

Samuel Adams served in the Continental Congress and was a signer of the Declaration of Independence. He was reluctant to give George Washington command over the American forces in the war, because Washington lacked the military stature of an Oliver Cromwell and Samuel would have preferred a general from New England. In the end both Samuel and John Adams supported Washington, although Samuel would have preferred Washington to pursue a more aggressive strategy as commander in chief.

Adams had faith that God would make the United States into a great nation. In 1768 he declared that America was a great empire that would soon give its laws to England,[22] and in 1772 he argued that "providence will erect a mighty empire in America" while Britain will be "sunk into obscurity and contempt."[23] He did not entirely share John Adams's fear of the masses. When Massachusetts prepared to draft a new constitution in 1780, Samuel Adams favored a single-house legislature while John Adams favored three houses.

Samuel Adams's main contribution to the 1780 Massachusetts Constitution was Article III which dealt with religion. Under the royal charter, most citizens were required to pay taxes for the support of the Congregational Church; Baptists, Quakers, and Anglicans were exempted. Article III stated that members of each denomination were to pay taxes for the support of their own ministers. Those who did not belong to churches or who belonged to churches too small to support a minister, were to pay taxes to the

20. Peter Oliver, *Origin and Progress of the American Rebellion* (1781), Egerton MSS., Gay Transcripts, Massachusetts Historical Society, 68; quoted by ibid., p. 100.

21. Ibid., p. 84.

22. Ibid., p. 311.

23. Samuel Adams, *Boston Gazette*, August 24, 1772; November 2, 1772; cited by ibid., p. 311.

Congregational Church. New religious bodies appearing in Massachusetts after 1780 were required to wage a costly legal battle to win legal recognition. Despite opposition, Adams's provision became part of the 1780 Constitution and remained in effect until 1833.[24]

Samuel Adams believed all law comes from God and human law should conform to the revealed law of God as found in nature and in the Scriptures. He wrote under the heading, "The Rights of the Colonists as Christians":

> These may be best understood by reading—and carefully studying the institutes of the great Lawgiver and head of the Christian Church: which are to be found clearly written and promulgated in the New Testament—
>
> By the Act of the British Parliament commonly called the Toleration Act, every subject in England Except Papists etc was restored to, and re-established in, his natural right to worship God according to the dictates of his own conscience. And by the Charter of this Province it is granted ordained and established (that it is declared as an original right) that there shall be liberty of conscience allowed in the worship of God, to all christians except Papists, inhabiting or be resident within said Province or Territory. Magna Charta itself is in substance but a constrained Declaration, or proclamation, and promulgation in the name of King, Lord, and Commons of the sense the latter had of their original inherent, indefeazible natural Rights, and also those of free Citizens equally perdurable with the other. That great author that great jurist, and even that Court writer Mr. Justice Blackstone holds that his recognition was justly obtained of King John sword in hand: and peradventure it must be one day sword in hand again rescued from total destruction and oblivion.[25]

Adams continued to put down tendencies toward frivolity, luxury, and excess after the war, but was somewhat disappointed. Miller explains:

> The chief obstacle to the return of Puritanism, he believed, was the old aristocracy which, by setting the people an example of high living and loose morals, had attempted to destroy their "Sense of true Religion & Virtue, in hopes thereby the more easily to carry their Point of enslaving them." As one of the first fruits of the Revolution, Adams anticipated the resurrection of "that Sobriety of Manners,

24. Samuel Eliot Morison, *The Struggle over the Adoption of the Constitution of Massachusetts, Massachusetts Historical Society Proceedings*, L (1917), 317, 379; cited by ibid., pp. 357–58.
25. Samuel Adams, *The Writings of Samuel Adams*, ed. Harry Alonzo Cushing (New York: Octagon Books, Inc., 1968), II:355–56.

that Temperance, Frugality, Fortitude and other manly Virtues which were once the Glory and Strength of my much lov'd native Town.''... In Sam Adams's eyes, the American Revolution was to do far more than establish an independent state: it was to purify society, revolutionize manners and morals, and pave the way for another Puritan Age. Its most important consequences were to be felt in Boston, where another "Christian Sparta" would rise and where "Old Puritans" and "Romans" would restore to the metropolis its fame as a refuge for the virtuous.[26]

Governor Hancock made some efforts to restore Christian morality to Massachusetts, but did not go nearly as far as Adams wanted, and was largely unsuccessful at that. Adams wrote, "I am greatly concerned for my dear native Town, lest after having stood foremost in the Cause of Religion and Liberty she lose her Glory."[27]

As a delegate to the Massachusetts ratifying convention, Adams initially opposed the Constitution, but when the Federalists promised a Bill of Rights, he supported ratification.

Adams served as Lieutenant Governor under Hancock from 1789 to 1793, and was elected Governor of Massachusetts upon Hancock's death. He served as governor until 1797. During those years Samuel Adams held the most powerful position in the nation except that of the President because of the awesome powers given to the governor by the 1780 Massachusetts Constitution.

As governor Samuel Adams continued to express his Christian faith and belief in Puritan millennialism, by issuing the following fast proclamation on March 20, 1797:

And as it is our duty to extend our wishes to the happiness of the great family of man, I conceive that we cannot better express ourselves than by humbly supplicating the Supreme Ruler of the world that the rod of tyrants may be broken into pieces, and the oppressed made free; that wars may cease in all the earth, and that the confusions that are and have been among the nations may be overruled by promoting and speedily bringing on that holy and happy period when the kingdom of our Lord and Saviour Jesus Christ may be everywhere established, and all people everywhere willingly bow to the septre of Him who is Prince of Peace.[28]

26. Miller, *Sam Adams*, pp. 359–60.

27. Samuel Adams, *Massachusetts Historical Society Proceedings*, XLIII, 333; quoted by ibid., p. 364.

28. Samuel Adams, Fast Proclamation, March 20, 1797; quoted in Wells, *Samuel Adams*, II:365–66.

His refusal to suppress unruly mobs and condemn the French Revolution aroused public antagonism. Adams saw France as a kindred enemy of England, and he looked on the nations which opposed France as a league of "Tyrant Kings to exterminate those rights and liberties which the Gracious Creator has granted to man."[29] His opposition to England, his love of liberty, and his role as a rebel blinded him to the evils and excesses of the French Revolution, even though the French concept of liberty differed widely from his own. Adams had been cast in the role of resisting authority his whole life and found it impossible to take the other side. His strong republican principles led him to oppose his Federalist cousin's bid for the presidency; he supported Thomas Jefferson instead. He sought to become a presidential elector in the 1796 election between John Adams and Jefferson, but was defeated because Massachusetts was John Adams's home state. After that defeat he announced that he would not seek reelection as governor, and in 1797 he retired from public life.

In later years Adams was afflicted with palsy which left him unable to write; his final years saw him in broken health. John Adams hoped that he would be spared the fate of his cousin Samuel, "a grief and distress to his family, a weeping, helpless object of compassion for years."[30] Adams's Christian faith remained constant to the end. His last known correspondence was a rebuke to Thomas Paine on November 30, 1802:

> When I heard you had turned your mind to a defence of infidelity, I felt myself much astounded and more grieved, that you had attempted a measure so injurious to the feelings and so repugnant to the true interest of so great a part of the citizens of the United States. The people of New England, if you will allow me to use a Scripture phrase, are fast returning to their first love. . . .[31]

Adams died in 1803 at the age of eighty-one, a consistent republican to the end. Buried in the Old Granary Burying Ground where "old Endicott lies," Miller concludes, "Sam Adams was at last among the Puritans."[32]

---

29. Miller, *Sam Adams*, p. 400.
30. *The Works of John Adams*, X, 100; quoted by ibid., p. 400.
31. Wells, *Samuel Adams*, II:372–73.
32. Ibid., p. 400.

15 John Adams

J ohn Adams's scholarship, along with his insight and blunt honesty, made him one of the most interesting and perceptive commentators of his era. His diaries, correspondence, and personal notes are filled with valuable information about the personalities, ideas, and events of that period. The only other President as highly regarded for his scholarship was Jefferson. While Jefferson's mind was closed to possibility of revelation, Adams's was open to both Christianity and Enlightenment thinking. Adams's July 16, 1814, letter to Jefferson shows the breadth of his knowledge:

> I am very glad you have seriously read Plato; and still more rejoiced to find that your reflections upon him so perfectly harmonize with mine. Some thirty years ago I took upon me the severe task of going through all his works. With the help of two Latin translations and one English and one French translations, and comparing some of the most remarkable passages with the Greek, I labored through the tedious toil. My disappointment was very great, my astonishment was greater, and my disgust was shocking.[1]

One historian calls him "Honest John Adams."[2] However,

1. Adams to Jefferson, July 16, 1814; reprinted in *Correspondence of John Adams and Thomas Jefferson 1812–1826*, ed. Paul Wilstach (Indianapolis: Bobbs-Merrill, 1925), p. 109.
2. Gilbert Chinard, *Honest John Adams* (Boston: Little, Brown & Co., 1933, 1961).

Adams lacked Lincoln's tact and diplomacy, and often spoke in ways which earned him enemies rather than friends.

Adams's character is frequently discussed, but the Puritan religion that formed it is often forgotten. John Adams was raised and then remained a Puritan his entire life. As a faithful churchgoer and stern moralist, he stood for decency, honesty, and hard work, and expected the same of others. He may have questioned some of the specific doctrines of Christianity in his later years (he lived to be 91) but he remained a friend and supporter of organized religion in general and Christianity in particular, and was an implacable foe of those who attacked religion. He regarded Thomas Paine as an "insolent Blasphemer of things sacred and a transcendent Libeller of all that is good," and declared that "It is indeed a disgrace to the moral Character and the Understanding of this Age, that this worthless fellow should be believed in any thing. But Impudence and Malice will always find Admirers."[3]

John Adams was born in Braintree (later renamed Quincy), Massachusetts, on October 30, 1735.[4] His ancestors had come from Braintree, England, a strong center of Puritanism.[5] His father was a church deacon and also held several civil offices. Adams describes him as "the honestest Man I ever knew."[6] John's father acquired a good education, largely through self-study, particularly borrowing books from the pastor's library.[7] John Adams's boyhood friend and schoolmate was John Hancock who later became President of the Continental Congress. Young Hancock's father was the preacher at the church the Adamses attended. As a child John Adams was sent to grammar schools to learn Latin, Greek, and the classics in preparation for the ministry. John always enjoyed sports, games, and the outdoors. Once when he protested against going to school his father replied:

3. John Adams, *Diary and Autobiography of John Adams*, ed. L. H. Butterfield (Cambridge, Massachusetts: The Belknap Press of Harvard University Press, 1962), IV:5–6 (autobiography covering 1777). Elsewhere in his autobiography Adams mentions the belief that Paine's pamphlets were of major importance in the War for Independence, but he says, "I doubted it at the time and have doubted it to this day." He also mentions writings of Paine which contain a "ridiculous" argument from the Old Testament for independence. When he confronted Paine with his objections, he says, Paine laughed and expressed contempt for the Old Testament and said he derived his ideas from Milton (ibid., III:330–34).

4. Under the "Old Style" calendar in use at the time his birthday was October 19; under the "New Style" Gregorian calendar adopted in 1752, his birthday was October 30.

5. Page Smith, *John Adams* (Garden City: Doubleday, 1962, 1963), II:714.

6. Adams, *Autobiography*, III:256.

7. Chinard, *Honest John Adams*, p. 9.

What would you do Child? Be a Farmer. A Farmer? Well I will shew you what it is to be a Farmer. You shall go with me to Penny ferry tomorrow Morning and help me get Thatch. I shall be very glad to go Sir.—Accordingly next morning he took me with him, and with great good humour kept me all day with him at Work. At night at home he said Well John are you satisfied with being a Farmer. Though the Labour had been very hard and very muddy I answered I like it very well Sir. Ay but I don't like it so well: so you shall go to School today.[8]

Adams learned to love books and scholarship, but never forgot his love for farming: Throughout his life he retained and managed his farm property near Braintree, naming his farm "Montezillo." He explained that, "Mr. Jefferson lives at Monticello the lofty Mountain. I live at *Montezillo* a little Hill."[9] He lived in Braintree and was actively engaged in farming, when his career responsibilities permitted. He often longed to be back on the farm when he was involved in the turmoils of national and international affairs.

Religion had an important role in Adams's development. The family attended church regularly, and used the Bible extensively at home.[10] John's father taught him to read before sending him to school. At grammar school Adams studied *The New England Primer*, which was based on Puritan theology. It taught the alphabet with such verses as "In Adams Fall/We sinned all" for A, on to "Zebediah served the Lord." As Smith says,

In unison John and his schoolmates recited the somber verses:

> There is a dreadful fiery hell,
> Where wicked ones must always dwell;
> There is a heaven full of joy,
> Where goodly ones must always stay;
> To one of these my soul must fly,
> As in a moment, when I die.

In an age when the mortality rate among growing children was very high, they repeated:

> In the burying place may see,
> Graves shorter there than I;
> From death's arrest no age is free,
> Young children too must die:
> My God, may such an awful sight
> Awakening be to me.

8. Adams, *Autobiography*, III:257–58.
9. Ibid., III:248; citing letter of Adams to Richard Rush, November 24, 1814.
10. Chinard, *Honest John Adams*, p. 9.

The *Primer* offered young John Adams a "dialogue between Christ, Youth and the Devil," in which God addresses the bad child with these words:

> Thou hast thy God offended so,
> Thy soul and body I'll divide:
> Thy body in the grave I'll hide,
> And thy dear soul in Hell must lie
> With Devils to Eternity. . . .
> Thus end the days of woeful youth,
> Who won't obey or mind the truth;
> Nor hearken to what preachers say,
> But do their parents disobey:
> They in their youth go down to Hell,
> Under eternal wrath to dwell.
> Many don't live out half their days,
> For cleaving unto sinful ways.[11]

Many youth of that day did not pay attention to these warnings. Smith says:

> There was in Braintree, as in other rural towns close to the compelling sexuality of the barn- and farmyard, an almost tangible sensuality. The tides of physical desire rose in the boys and girls as they rose in the farm stock. Many yielded, some reluctantly, restrained by the fear of Calvin's devil or the more practical outcome of illicit love-making, others gladly and heedlessly in animal rut.[12]

Adams also faced these temptations:

> Imaginative, lively, quick and handsome, John had a particular fondness for girls and they, in turn, responded to him. The junior gallant had an expressiveness of face and speech that charmed the village belles. From the age of ten he made numerous conquests or fell victim himself to bright eyes and appealing smiles. Moreover, as he entered his early teens he revealed a precocious masculinity, a latent sexual vigor, that attracted members of the opposite sex. At the same time he was well aware of the dangers as well as the delights of feminine proximity. His parents had most solemnly instructed him in the practical morality that must guide his relations with the females of Braintree.[13]

In Adams's *Autobiography* he states that his young romances were "all modest and virtuous Girls and always maintained this Character through Life. No Virgin or Matron ever had cause to blush at the

11. *New England Primer;* quoted by Smith, *John Adams,* I:11.
12. Ibid., I:10.
13. Ibid., I:10.

sight of me, or to regret her Acquaintance with me. . . . My Children may be assured that no illegitimate Brother or Sister exists or ever existed."[14] Adams explained that his parents "held every Species of Libertinage in such Contempt and Horror," and that he was convinced that they were right, since he saw the bad effects of libertinism in other countries (undoubtedly referring to France). He added that "The Happiness of Life depends more upon Innocence in this respect, than upon all the Philosophy of Epicurus, or of Zeno without it. . . . Happiness is lost forever if innocence is lost, at least until a Repentance is undergone so severe as to be an overballance to all the gratifications of Licentiousness. Repentance itself cannot restore the Happiness of Innocence, at least in this Life."[15]

In 1751, at the age of fifteen, John entered Harvard College. Harvard required a strict regimen which included regular daily prayers and Scripture reading at 6:00 AM, followed by breakfast, classes at 8:00 AM, more classes and study throughout the day, evening prayers at 5:00 PM. Saturdays were always set aside for theology studies, consisting of exposition of Scripture by President Holyoke, memorizing works of dogmatic theology, and students taking turns reading passages of Scripture and expounding the meaning before the other students. At the same time, Harvard was becoming a center for theological liberalism, and immorality was common. But Adams studied hard and avoided serious difficulties. His diary reveals regular church attendance and careful interest in the sermon content:

10 June 1753 Sunday. At Colledge a clear morning. Heard Mr. Appleton expound those words in I. Cor. 12 Chapt. 7 first verses, and in the afternoon heard him preach from those words in 26 of Matthew 41 verse, watch and pray that ye enter not into temptation.

17 June 1753 Sunday. At Colledge, sunshiny-morning, heard Mr. Appleton expound those words in I. Cor. 12 Chap. from 7, to the end of 11 verse, in the afternoon heard him preach from the first Psalm, and first verse.

24 June 1753 Sunday. At Colledge, a Cloudy morning, heard Mr. Cotton of New-town vociferate from the 19. of Proverbs 2nd verse. In the afternoon, from those words in the 37th. Psalm and 4th verse, Delight thyself in the Lord and he shall give thee thy Desires.[16]

14. Adams, *Autobiography*, III:260–61.
15. Ibid., III:261.
16. John Adams, *The Earliest Diary of John Adams*, ed. L. H. Butterfield (Cambridge, Massachusetts: The Belknap Press of Harvard University Press, 1966), pp. 43, 44, 47.

Adams was selected to be one of the commencement speakers at graduation in July 1755. The Reverend Thaddeus Maccarty of Worcester, Massachusetts, attended the commencement exercises in search of a schoolmaster for his town. He heard Adams speak and was so impressed by Adams's earnestness and eloquence that he hired John on the spot. Adams had gone to Harvard intending to study for the ministry, but decided to take some time away from college to prepare himself for advanced theological studies. It appears he was an effective schoolmaster, using praise as well as punishment and using as his basic text the *New England Primer* in which he had been taught. He wrote that he imagined his classroom as a miniature kingdom: "I have several renowned generals but three feet high, and several deep-projecting politicians in petticoats; I have others catching and dissecting flies, accumulating remarkable pebbles, cockle shells, etc., with as ardent curiosity as any virtuoso in the Royal Society."[17]

John Adams continued to show strong interest in Christianity during his two years as schoolmaster in Worcester. He frequently had discussions with a lawyer named James Putnam, who had been influenced greatly by deism. In debates with Adams, Putnam argued that religion was mere delusion, that the apostles were "a company of enthusiasts," and that there was no future state of reward or punishment. Adams forcefully defended orthodox Christianity, believing that Putnam secretly wanted to have his own skepticism overthrown so he could also believe.[18]

Adams liked and admired Rev. Maccarty. Adams attended church faithfully while in Worcester, hearing Rev. Maccarty as well as others preach.[19] Maccarty was one of the "New Lights" who were influenced by revival preachers such as George Whitefield and Jonathan Edwards.[20] Maccarty and Adams frequently talked at mealtime, and he undoubtedly influenced Adams's thinking. Adams's diary entries show that religion was on his mind a great deal:

Wednesday, 17 March 1756. A fine morning. Proceeded on my Journey towards Braintree. Stop'ed at Josiah Adams's. Baited at Clarks of Medway. Dined at Clarks of Medfield. Stopd to see Mr. Haven of Dedham, who told me very civilly that he supposed I took my faith on Trust from Dr. Mayhew, and added that he believed the

17. Adams; quoted by Smith, *John Adams*, I:25.
18. Ibid., I:27–28.
19. Adams, *Diary*, I:1–40.
20. Smith, *John Adams*, I:27.

doctrine of the satisfaction of J[esus] C[hrist] to be essential to Christianity, and that he would not believe this satisfaction, unless he believed the Divinity of C[hrist]. Mr. Balch was there too, and observed that he would not be a Christian if he did not believe the Mysterys of the Gospel. That he could bear with an Arminian, when, with Dr. Mayhew, they denied the Divinity and Satisfaction of J[esus] C[hrist] he had no more to do with them. That he knew not what to make of Dr. Mahhews two discourses upon the Expected Dissolution of all Things. They gave him an Idea of a Cart whose wheels want'd greazing. . . . He added farther that Arminians, however stiffly they maintain their opinions in health, always, he takes notice, retract when they come to Die, and chose to die Calvinists.

Sunday, 24 April 1756. Astronomers tell us, with good Reason, that not only all the Planets and Satellites in our Solar System, but all the unnumbered Worlds that revolve around the fixt Starrs are inhabited, as well as this Globe of Earth. If this is the Case all Mankind are no more in comparison of the whole rational Creation of God, than a point to the Orbit of Saturn. Perhaps all these different Ranks of Rational Beings have in a greater or less Degree, committed moral Wickedness. If so, I ask a Calvinist, whether he will subscribe to this Alternative, "either God almighty must assume the respective shapes of all these different Species, and suffer the Penalties of their Crimes, in their Stead, or else all these Being[s] must be consigned to everlasting Perdition?" Heard Mr. Maccarty. Spent the Evening at the Colonels.

Monday, 25 April 1756. The Reflection that I penned Yesterday, appears upon the review to be weak enough. For 1st. we know not that the Inhabitants of other Globes have sinned. Nothing can be argued in this manner, till it is proved at least probable that all those Species of rational Beings have revolted from their rightful Sovereign.—When I examine the little Prospect that lies before me, and find an infinite variety of Bodies in one Horizon of perhaps two milles diameter, how many Millions of such Prospects there are upon the Survace of this Earth, how many millions of Globes there are within our View, each of which has as many of these prospects upon its own surface as our Planet—great! and marvellous are thy works!

Thursday, 28 April 1756. Fast day. Heard Mr. Maccarty. Spent the Evening at Putnams. Our proper Business in this Life is, not to accumulate large Fortunes, not to gain high Honours and important offices in the State, not to waste our Health and Spirits in Pursuit of the Sciences, but constantly to improve our selves in Habits of Piety and Virtue. Consequently, the meanest Mechanick, who endeavours in proportion to his Ability, to promote the happiness of his fellow men, deserves better of Society, and should be held in higher Esteem than the Greatest Magistrate, who uses his power for his own Pleasures or Averice or Ambition.

Friday, 29 April 1756. A hazy, dull Day. Reading Milton. That man's Soul, it seems to me, was distended as wide as Creation. His Power over the human mind was absolute and unlimited. His Genius was great beyond Conception, and his Learning without Bounds. I can only gaze at him with astonishment, without comprehending the vast Compass of his Capacity.

Wednesday, 25 October 1758. . . . in the Evening I went to ask Mr. Thatcher's Concurrence with the Bar. Drank Tea and spent the whole Evening, upon original sin, Origin of Evil, the Plan of the Universe, and at last, upon Law.[21]

Adams began to have reservations about his plans to study for the ministry while in Worcester. Perhaps he began to think his talents lay in the fields of law and politics, or maybe he developed some questions about certain doctrines of Calvinism—though he remained firmly committed to Christianity. One disadvantage he found in living in Worcester was that Sundays were sacrificed "to the Frigid performances" of disciples of "Frigid John Calvin."[22] But back in college problems concerning doctrinal disputes and the mistreatment of clergymen left other doubts in Adams's mind. He wrote in his *Autobiography*:

. . . a Controversy was carried on between Mr. Bryant the Minister of our Parish and some of his People, partly on Account of his Principles which were called Arminian and partly on Account of his Conduct, which was too gay and light if not immoral. Ecclesiastical Councils were called and sat at my Fathers House. Parties and their Accrimonies arose in the Church and Congregation, and Controversies from the Press between Mr. Bryant, Mr. Niles, Mr. Porter, Mr. Bass, concerning the five Points [presumably the five points of Calvinism]. I read all these Pamphlets and many other Writings on the same Subject and found myself involved in difficulties beyond my Powers of decision. At the same time, I saw such a Spirit of Dogmatism and Bigotry in Clergy and Laity, that if I should be a Priest I must take my side, and pronounce as positively as any of them, or never get a Parish, or getting it must soon leave it. Very strong doubts arose in my mind, whether I was made for a Pulpit in such times, and I began to think of other Professions. I perceived very clearly, as I thought, that the Study of Theology and the pursuit of it as a Profession would involve me in endless Altercations and make my Life miserable, without any prospect of doing any good to my fellow Men.[23]

21. Adams, *Diary*, I:14–15, 22, 23, 55. These passages are but representative of many others.

22. Adams to Nathan Webb, 1 September 1755; quoted in ibid., p. 37.

23. Adams, *Autobiography*, III:262.

After teaching for two years Adams decided to pursue law. In doing so he emphasized that he was not forsaking his obligations as a Christian. He said in his diary, ". . . I set out with firm Resolutions I think never to commit any meanness or injustice in the Practice of Law. The Study and Practice of Law, I am sure does not dissolve the obligations of morality or of Religion. And altho the Reason of my quitting Divinity was my Opinion concerning some disputed Points, I hope I shall not give Reason of offense to any in that Profession by imprudent Warmth."[24]

Adams pursued law by studying such legal works as Justinian, Gilbert, Blackstone and Coke, Bacon, and Bolingbroke, under the tutorship of attorney James Putnam. But he continued his spiritual development by following his resolution to "rise with the sun and to study the Scriptures, on Thursday, Friday, Saturday, and Sunday mornings, and to study some Latin author the other 3 mornings."[25]

He completed his preparation for the bar in 1758 and returned to Braintree to practice law and farm. His law practice kept him busy in both Braintree and Boston. During this time he became interested in politics, and met and married Abigail Smith. They began their courtship in 1762 and were married October 25, 1764.

Abigail profoundly influenced her husband's life. The daughter of a minister, Abigail was an attractive, vivacious and intelligent woman. She was interested in literature, philosophy, and current affairs. John and Abigail were frequently separated by his service to his country in England, France, and Philadelphia. Their correspondence during those periods gives one of the best pictures of life and thought of that period.

Abigail was a strong Christian with a strong faith in the providence of God, who faithfully attended church. She frequently used biblical allusions in her correspondence. She compared the defense of the nation to Nehemiah's rebuilding of the walls of Jerusalem;[26] she compared America's situation to the time when "a Righteous few might have saved from the impending Wrath of an offended deity the Ancient cities of Sodom and Gomorrah;"[27] she compared

---

24. Adams, *Diary*, I:43.

25. Ibid., I:35.

26. Abigail Adams to John Adams, June 25, 1775; reprinted in *The Book of Abigail and John: Selected Letters of the Adams Family 1762–1784*, ed. L. H. Butterfield (Cambridge, Massachusetts: Harvard University Press, 1975), pp. 92–93.

27. Abigail Adams to Elbridge Gerry, July 20, 1781; reprinted in Butterfield, *Abigail and John*, pp. 292–94.

her husband's work for the nation to that of Moses and Elijah, and made references to Noah's ark and other biblical accounts. She wrote to Jefferson that she and her daughter had heard Handel's *Messiah* at Westminster Abbey and described it as so sublime beyond description" that she could easily imagine that she was among angels listening to a heavenly choir."[28] When Jefferson was elected President instead of her husband in 1800, her greatest reservation was that "he [either Jefferson or Burr] is not a believer in the Christian system."[29]

Abigail stressed Christian morality, and wrote to her son John Quincy Adams that she would rather see him dead than "an immoral, profligate or graceless child."[30]

John Adams, influenced by his friends Josiah Quincy, James Otis, and his second cousin Samuel Adams, became interested in politics as a strong partisan of the American cause against the British. He served on town committees and joined a lawyers' group in Boston which studied legal history and theory. In 1765 he published "A Dissertation of Canon and Feudal Law" in installments in the *Boston Gazette*. In this series he established the existence of an American legal tradition, attempted to develop American pride and patriotism, and expressed objections to the Stamp Act. The dissertation's beginning, which is frequently quoted, was left out of the *Gazette*. "I always consider the settlement of America with reverence and wonder, as the opening of a grand scene and design in Providence for the illumination of the ignorant, and the emancipation of the slavish part of mankind over the earth."[31] Additional letters to the *Gazette* on the British Constitution and American rights followed the dissertation. In 1766 Adams was elected a selectman for Braintree. In 1768 he wrote instructions for the British representatives to the General Court for their protest of Britain's seizure of John Hancock's sloop *Liberty*, and successfully defended Hancock in admiralty court against smuggling charges connected with *Liberty*. In 1769 he again wrote instructions for the Boston representatives to the General Court, this time protesting the presence of British troops and the growing power of admiralty courts. In 1769 he defended a case involving colonial rights. The British navy had a practice of "impressing" seamen—taking men

---

28. Abigail Adams to Thomas Jefferson, June 6, 1785; quoted in Smith, *John Adams*, II:631.

29. Abigail Adams to Mary Cranch, February 3, 1801; quoted in ibid., II:1061.

30. Abigail Adams to John Quincy Adams, June, 1778; quoted in ibid., I:409.

31. John Adams, "Dissertation on the Canon and Feudal Law"; quoted by Chinard, *Honest John Adams*, p. 48.

against their will and forcing them to serve as sailors. The British ship *Rose* had stopped the American ship *Pitt* for the purpose of impressing some of the crew into service for the British navy, four of the *Pitt* crewmen resisted and in the scuffle Lieutenant Henry Gibson Panton of the *Rose* was killed with a harpoon. Adams defended the *Pitt* crewmen, arguing that impressment was against the law of nature and the law of nations and violated the rights of American colonists. Adams's fame increased when he won an acquittal on the grounds of justifiable homicide.

The most famous and controversial case of his career was the "Boston Massacre" in 1770. The incident began with a young Boston boy throwing snowballs at a British soldier. The soldier handled him roughly, and a hostile crowd gathered. The soldier called for help, and six more soldiers arrived under the command of Captain Preston. The mob grew, and engaged in insults, threats, and shoving, until the soldiers began firing, killing five and injuring six others. The soldiers were charged with murder.

Adams was a partisan of the colonists' cause and had previously protested the use of British troops in Boston. But, this time Adams believed the soldiers acted in self-defense and should not be hanged as murderers. Adams and Josiah Quincy defended the British soldiers when no other Boston lawyer would. Adams's defense aroused the wrath of many of his patriot friends, but he consoled himself and defended his action by quoting a passage from a book by the Marquis de Beccaria, "If, by supporting the rights of mankind, and of invincible truth, I shall contribute to save from the agonies of death one unfortunate victim of tyranny, or of ignorance equally fatal, his blessing and tears of transport will be a sufficient consolation to me for the contempt of all mankind."[32]

Adams and Quincy secured the acquittal of Captain Preston and six of his men through careful jury selection (keeping Bostonians off the jury) and skillful use of the law and evidence. The remaining two soldiers were convicted of manslaughter, branded on the hand, and then dismissed. Some of the patriots resented Adams's role in the defense, but most including Sam Adams did not. In addition, Adams had endeared himself to the rich merchants of the area by his defense of law and order; as a result he had the best law practice in Boston. The incident probably impressed on his mind even further the need for supremacy of law and the dangers of mob rule—no matter whose side the mob is on.

---

32. Marquis de Beccaria; quoted by ibid., p. 61.

In 1773 and 1774 Adams was elected a member of the Massachusetts Council, but his election was negated both times because of
his patriot sentiments, first by Governor Hutchinson, then by
Governor Gage. In June 1774 he was elected as a Massachusetts
delegate to the Continental Congress.

Adams served on numerous committees while in Congress,
including the committee to draft a declaration of independence; he
also made the principal speech in favor of the resolution for
independence. But he did not neglect spiritual matters during this
time. He attended church regularly and often attended two different
churches on Sundays. His diary entry for Sunday, September 4,
1774 reads:

> Went to the Presbyterian Meeting and heard Mr. Sprout in the
> forenoon. He uses no Notes—don't appear to have any. Opens his
> Bible and talks away. Not a very numerous, nor very polite Assem-
> bly. . . .
>
> Went in the Afternoon to Christ Church, and heard Mr. Coombs.
> This is a more noble Building, and a genteeler Congregation. The
> Organ and a new Choir of Singers, were very musical. Mr. Coombs
> is celebrated here as a fine Speaker. He is sprightly, has a great deal
> of Action, speaks distinctly. But I confess, I am not charmed with his
> oratory. His Style was indifferent, His Method, confused. In one
> word, his composition was vastly inferiour to the ordinary sermons of
> our How, Hunt, Chauncey, Elliot, and even Stillman. Mr. Mifflin
> spent the Sunday Evening with Us, at our Lodgings.[33]

September 11, 1774, Adams records attending the Presbyterian
services again and having the "Opportunity of seeing the Custom of
the Presbyterians in administering the Sacrament," which he
describes in detail. That evening "Reed, Cushing and I strolled, to
the Moravian Evening Lecture where we heard soft, sweet Music
and a dutchified english Prayer and Preachment."[34]

On Sunday, October 23, 1774, he heard a message that may have
contributed to his appreciation for religious freedom:

> Heard Mr. Piercy, at Mr. Sprouts. He is Chaplain to the Countess
> Huntington. Comes recommended to Mr. Cary of Charlestown, from
> her, as a faithful servant of the Lord. No Genius—no Orator.
>
> In the Afternoon I went to the Baptist Church and heard a trans
> Alleganian—a Preacher, from the back Parts of Virginia, behind the

33. Adams, *Diary*, II:122.
34. Ibid., II:131–32.

Allegany Mountains. He preached an hour and a half. No Learning—No Grace of Action or Utterance—but an honest Zeal. He told us several good Stories. One was, that he was once preaching in Virginia and said that those Ministers who taught the People that Salvation was to be obtained by good Works, or Obedience, were leading them to ruin. Next Day, he was apprehended, by a Warrant from a Magistrate, for reviling the Clergy of the Church of England. He asked for a Prayer Book and had it. Turned to the 18 or 20th Article, where the same sentiment is strongly expressed. He read it to the Magistrate. The Magistrate as soon as he heard it, dash'd the Warrant out of his Hand, and said sir you are discharged.

In the Evening I went to the Methodist Meeting and heard Mr. Webb, the old soldier, who first came to America, in the Character of Quarter Master under Gen. Braddock. He is one of the most fluent, eloquent Men I ever heard. He reaches the Imagination and touches the Passions, very well, and expresses himself with great Propriety. The Singing here is very sweet and soft indeed. The first Musick I have heard in any Society, except the Moravians, and once at Church with the organ.[35]

But Adams missed the Congregational churches of New England. He wrote in his diary October 9, 1774:

Phyladelphia with all its Trade, and Wealth, and Regularity is not Boston. The Morals of our People are much better, their Manners are more polite, and agreeable—they are purer English. Our Language is better, our Persons are handsomer, our Spirit is greater, our Laws are wiser, our Religion is superior, our Education is better. We exceed them in every Thing, but in a Markett, and in charitable public foundations.[36]

He expressed similar thoughts the same day in a letter to Abigail:

This Day I went to Dr. Allisons Meeting in the Forenoon and heard the Dr.—a good discourse upon the Lords Supper. This is a Presbyterian Meeting. I confess I am not fond of the Presbyterian Meetings in this Town. I had rather go to Church. We have better Sermons, better Prayers, better Speakers, softer, sweeter Musick, and genteeler Company. And I must confess, that the Episcopal Church is quite as agreeable to my Taste as the Presbyterian. They are both Slaves to the Domination of the Priesthood. I like the Congregational Way best—next to that the Independent.[37]

35. Ibid., II:156.
36. Ibid., II:149–50.
37. John Adams to Abigail Adams, October 9, 1774; reprinted in Butterfield, *Abigail and John*, pp. 78–79.

Adams expressed his distaste for Presbyterian services, but when no Congregational churches were available, he most often attended Presbyterian churches,—perhaps because Presbyterianism was closest to Congregationalism in doctrine.

Religion also played an important role in the affairs of the Continental Congress. Rev. Witherspoon, a delegate from New Jersey, occasionally preached. Adams wrote of Witherspoon in his diary for February 17, 1777: "Yesterday, heard Dr. Witherspoon upon redeeming Time. An excellent Sermon. I find that I understand the Dr. better, since I have heard him so much in Conversation, and in the Senate."[38] Occasionally prayers were expressed in the congress and its committees; Adams records on September 10, 1774, that the reading of prayers by Mr. Duche in subcommittee had had a "very good effect."[39] Throughout this time Adams seemed conscious of the possibility that Providence had a special role for him in history:

> For myself, I own I tremble at the Thought of an Election. What will be expected of me? What will be required of me? What Duties and Obligations will result to me, from an Election? What Duties to my God, my King, my Country, my Family, my Friends, myself? What Perplexities, and Intricacies, and Difficulties shall I be exposed to? What Snares and Temptations will be thrown in my Way? What Self denials and Mortifications shall I be obliged to bear?
>
> If I should be called in the Course of Providence to take a Part in public Life, I shall Act a fearless, intrepid, undaunted Part, at all Hazards—tho it shall be my Endeavour likewise to act a prudent, cautious and considerate Part. . . .
>
> But I was not sent into this World to spend my days in Sports, Diversions and Pleasures.
>
> I was born for Business; for both Activity and Study. I have little Appetite, or Relish for any Thing else.
>
> I must double and redouble my Diligence. . . .[40]

As independence drew near, Adams likened himself to Moses in a letter to Abigail:

> Is it not a saying of Moses, "Who am I, that I should go in and out before this great people?" When I consider the great events which are passed, and those greater which are rapidly advancing, and that

38. Adams, *Diary*, II:259.
39. Ibid., II:131.
40. Ibid., II:82.

I may have been instrumental in touching some springs and turning some small wheels, which have had and will have such effects, I feel an awe upon my mind which is not easily described.[41]

Providence did have plans for John Adams: In 1777 Congress chose him to be a joint commissioner to France, serving with Benjamin Franklin and Arthur Lee. He sailed for France in February 1778, taking his ten-year-old son John Quincy; they arrived in March.

The French people's elegance and graciousness and enjoyment of life impressed Adams. But as a staunch New England Congregationalist he was shocked and dismayed by the decadence of French morals. Their idleness, their disregard for the Sabbath, their irreligion disturbed him greatly—it disturbed him even more that his fellow minister, Benjamin Franklin was so beloved by the French because he so readily tolerated and accepted French ways. Adams describes a conversation with "M. M." [presumably a Mr. Marbois]:

All Religions are tolerated in America, said M. M., and the Ambassadors have in all Courts a Right to a Chappell in their own Way. But Mr. Franklin never had any.—No said I, laughing, because Mr. F. had no—I was going to say, what I did not say, and will not say here. I stopped short and laughed.—No, said Mr. M., Mr. F. adores only great Nature, which has interested a great many People of both Sexes in his favour.—Yes, said I, laughing, all the Atheists, Deists and Libertines, as well as the Philosophers and Ladies are in his Train—another Voltaire and Hume.—Yes said Mr. M., he is celebrated as the great Philosopher and the great Legislator of America.—He is said I a great Philosopher, but as a Legislator of America he has done very little. It is universally believed in France, England and all Europe, that his Electric Wand has accomplished all this Revolution but nothing is more groundless. He has [done] very little. It is believed that he made all the American Constitutions, and their Confederation. But he made neither. He did not even make the Constitution of Pennsylvania, bad as it is.[42]

Adams wrote of Franklin on another occasion saying, "That He was a great Genius, a great Wit, a great Humourist and a great Satyrist, and a great Politician is certain. That he was a great Phylosopher, a great Moralist and a great Statesman is more questionable."[43]

41. John Adams to Abigail Adams, May 17, 1776; quoted by Chinard, *Honest John Adams*, p. 96.

42. Adams, *Diary*, II:391.

43. Adams, *Autobiography*, IV:69. Franklin for his part said of Adams, "I am persuaded that he means well for his Country, is always an Honest man, often a wise one, but sometimes, and in some things, absolutely out of his sense." Franklin to Robert R. Livingston, July 22, 1783; quoted in Adams's *Diary* I:lxix.

Probably nothing about France shocked Adams more than the brazen immorality of French women: their revealing dress, their ribald sense of humor, their extramarital affairs, and the boldness with which they discussed sexual matters in public. In his *Autobiography* Adams stated that the strength of a nation rests to a large extent on the morality of its women. He said that men are likely to be lax in morals and women must set the moral tone of society:

> From all that I had read of History of Government, of human life and manners, I had drawn this Conclusion, that the manners of Women were the most infallible Barometer, to ascertain the degree of Morality and Virtue in a Nation. All that I have since read and all the observations I have made in different Nations, have confirmed me in this opinion. The Manners of Women, are the surest Criterion by which to determine whether a Republican Government is practicable, in a Nation or not. The Jews, the Greeks, the Romans, the Swiss, the Dutch, all lost their public Spirit, their Republican Principles and habits, and their Republican Forms of Government, when they lost the Modesty and Domestic Virtues of their Women. . . .
>
> The foundations of national Morality must be laid in private Families. In vain are Schools Accademies and universities instituted, if loose Principles and licentious habits are impressed upon Children in their earliest years. The Mothers are the earliest and most important Instructors of youth. . . . The Vices and Examples of the Parents cannot be concealed from the Children. How is it possible that Children can have any just Sense of the sacred Obligations of Morality or Religion if, from their earliest Infancy, they learn that their Mothers live in habitual Infidelity to their fathers, and their fathers in as constant Infidelity to their Mothers.[44]

Adams pointed out that French Catholics regard marriage as a sacrament of the Church, and consequently their disregard for marriage vows constitutes disrespect for religion as well. "Besides the Catholic Doctrine is, that the Contract of marriage is not only a civil and moral Engagement, but a Sacrament, one of the most solemn Vows and Oaths of Religious devotion. Can they then believe Religion and Morality too any thing more than a Veil, a Cloak, an hypocritical Pretext, for political purposes of decency and Conveniency."[45] According to Adams, French immorality concerned eternal laws of God, and had a direct bearing on politics and

44. Adams, *Autobiography*, IV:123; cf. Smith, *John Adams*, I:404.
45. Ibid.

government. He believed that republican institutions could only flourish among virtuous people. He declared concerning the U.S. Constitution in 1789, "Our constitution was made only for a moral and religious people. It is wholly inadequate for the government of any other."[46] Adams was convinced that republican government would never work in France, and he opposed the French Revolution long before many Americans were aware of its excesses. He expressed concern about what would happen to "a republic of thirty million atheists," because fiery spirits and demagogues would assume dominance and the French would end up with "no equal laws, no personal liberty, no property, no lives."[47] He wrote to Brand-Hollis, an admirer of the French Revolution, "I hereby promise and assure you, that you will live to see that I am precisely right."[48] When the French Revolution had degenerated into a debacle of anarchy and bloodletting, Adams declared, "All that astonished me in the whole Revolution was that all the disasters which overwhelmed the empire and destroyed the repose of Europe were not foreseen and foretold by every man of sense in Europe,"[49] and that even primitive man had a better government than that of Revolutionary France.[50]

French religion disturbed Adams almost as much as French irreligion. Adams found Roman Catholicism contrary to his doctrine and practice as a New England Puritan. In Philadelphia he attended a Catholic church, and then wrote to Abigail:

This afternoon, led by Curiosity and good Company I strolled away to Mother Church, or rather Grandmother Church, I mean the Romish Chapell. Heard a good, short, moral Essay upon the duty of Parents to their Children, founded in Justice and Charity, to take care of their Interests temporal and spiritual. This Afternoons Entertainment was to me, most awfull and affecting. The poor Wretches, fingering their Beads, chanting Latin, not a Word of which they

46. John Adams, 1789; quoted in *War on Religious Freedom* (Virginia Beach, Virginia: Freedom Council, 1984), p. 1.

47. Adams to Dr. Price, April 19, 1790; quoted by Smith, *John Adams*, II:786.

48. Adams to Brand-Hollis, June 11, 1780; quoted by ibid., II:786.

49. John Adams, 1812, handwritten comments on the margin of his copy of Mary Wolls' book *Historical and Moral View of the Origin and Progress of the French Revolution*; reprinted in Zoltan Haraszti, *John Adams and the Prophets of Progress* (Cambridge, Massachusetts: Harvard University Press, 1952), p. 204.

50. John Adams, handwritten note on the margin of his copy of Marquis de Condercet's *Outlines of an Historical View of the Progress of the Human Mind*; reprinted in ibid., p. 242.

understood, their Pater Nosters and Ave Maria's. Their holy Water—
their Crossing thselves perpetually—their Bowing to the Name of
Jesus, wherever they hear it—their Bowings, and Kneelings, and
Genuflections before the Altar. The Dress of the Priest was rich with
Lace—his Pulpit was Velvet and Gold. The Altar Piece was very
rich—little Images and Crucifixes about—Wax Candles lighted up.
But How shall I describe the Picture of our Saviour in a Frame of
Marble over the Altar at full Length upon the Cross, in the Agonies,
and the Blood dropping and streaming from his Wounds.[51]

Adams was impressed with the beauty of the music; he stated that
the choir sang "most sweetly and exquisitely." But rather than
leading people to God, he saw it as bewitching, "Here is every Thing
which can lay hold of the Eye, Ear and Imagination. Every Thing
which can charm and bewitch the simple and ignorant. I wonder
how Luther ever broke the spell."[52]

Adams expressed his disapproval of Catholicism years before, in
his 1765 "Dissertation on Canon and Feudal Law." He opposed the
use of Canon Law in America because it was "framed, by the
Romish Clergy, for the Aggrandisement of their own order."
According to Adams the Catholic clergy had:

> . . . found Ways to make the World believe that God had entrusted
> them with Keys of Heaven whose Gates they might open and shut at
> Pleasure, with the Power of Dispensation over all the Rules and Types
> of Morality, the Power of Licensing all sorts both of sins and Crimes,
> with the Power of Deposing Princes, and absolving all their subjects
> from their Allegiance, with the Power of Procuring or withholding
> the Rain of Heaven, and the Beams of the Sun, with the Power of
> Earthquakes, (Plagues,) Pestilence, Famine; nay with the Power of
> creating Blood Nay the Blood of God out of Wine, and Flesh the Flesh
> of God out of Bread. Thus was human Nature held for Ages, fast
> Bound in servitude, in a cruel, shameful, deplorable Bondage to him
> and his subordinate Tyrants who it was foretold in the Apocalypse,
> would exalt himself above all that is called God and that is wor-
> shipped.[53]

---

51. John Adams to Abigail Adams, October 9, 1774; reprinted in *Abigail and John.* I have
included this material because it is essential to an understanding of the mind and spirit of John
Adams and trust Catholic readers will not find it offensive. John Adams himself must be
judged in part according to the New England environment in which he was raised.

52. Ibid.

53. John Adams, Fragmentary Draft of a Dissertation on Canon and Feudal Law,
February 1765; reprinted in Adams, *Autobiography,* I:255–56.

Adams found the Catholic Church in France just as disgusting. While in France he attended Protestant services whenever possible; occasionally he attended Catholic services for social or political reasons or to understand the French nation better. When he did he was impressed by their beauty but appalled by what he considered to be superstition, paganism, and burden on the poor.[54] Adams's diplomatic duties conflicted with his Protestant and/or republican principles once when he was touring Spain:

> It was the day of the Feast of the King and We happened to be at the celebration of High Mass. We saw the Procession of the Bishop and of all the Canons, in rich habits of Silk, Velvet, Silver and gold. The Bishop as he turned the Corners of the Church spred out his hand to the People, in token of his Apostolical Benediction; and those, in token of their profound gratitude for the heavenly Blessing prostrated themselves on their Knees as he passed. Our Guide told Us We must do the same. But I contented myself with a Bow. The Eagle Eye of the Bishop did not fail to observe an Upright figure amidst the Crowd of prostrate Adorers: but no doubt perceiving in my Countenance and Air, but especially in my dress something that was not Spanish, he concluded I was some travelling Heretick and did not think it worth while to exert his Authority to bend my stiff Knees. His Eyes followed me so long that I thought I saw in his Countenance a reproof like this "You are not only a Heretick but you are not a Gentleman, for a Gentleman would have respected the Religion of the Country and its Usages so far as to have conformed externally to a Ceremony that cost so little."[55]

His blunt honesty was both an asset and a liability while he served as ambassador. The French respected Adams but were not as cordial to him as they were to Franklin and Jefferson; they sensed that Adams did not fully approve of them. But Adams was an effective ambassador: He was called on to travel to the Netherlands to arrange a treaty and commerce; and he worked with Franklin and Jefferson to negotiate treaties of friendship and commerce with twenty-three European and African powers. In 1785 he was elected by Congress to be U.S. Ambassador to England. On June 1, 1785, Adams went before King George III of England, at which time the king declared that while he had opposed American independence, now that it was an established fact he would be the first to recognize the United States as an independent power. He then commented

54. Ibid., IV:212.
55. Ibid., IV:222.

rather lightly to Adams, "There is an opinion among some people that you are not the most attached of all your countrymen to the manners of France." Adams replied, "That opinion, sir, is not mistaken; I must avow to Your Majesty I have no attachment but to my own country." The king answered, "An honest man will never have any other."[56]

Shortly before Adams's meeting with the king, his wife Abigail and daughter Nabby joined him. John Quincy returned to Massachusetts to begin studies at Harvard.

Adams found England more to his taste than France, though not up to the standards of America and certainly not of New England. The Adamses attended church and found services in England much more compatible than those in France, but Abigail commented on the "modern, flimsy discourse of the preacher" which would never have been tolerated in Braintree, Massachusetts.[57] In Adams's opinion, the nation that was the most natural ally of the United States was the Netherlands. He stated "the two nations resemble each other more than any other"[58] in religion, in forms of government, and in liberty of conscience.

Adams served as U.S. Minister to England until 1788. In 1787-1788 he published a three-volume work titled "A Defence of the Constitutions of Government of the United States of America," in which he explained his political convictions in great detail. At the same time, the United States was embroiled in a debate over ratification of the new Constitution. Adams, living in England, did not take a direct role in its writing or ratification, but his "Defence" was widely read in America and helped persuade the American people to support ratification. The "Defence" was written about constitutional government in general, not specifically in relation to the U.S. Constitution.[59] Adams had doubts about certain provisions of the Constitution, but for the most part he found it to be a well-balanced document and he supported its ratification.

At his own request, Adams was relieved of his position as U.S. Minister to England in February 1788. When he returned to Boston in June he was elected to Congress; but he never served in that capacity because in the spring of 1789 he was elected Vice-President of the United States.

Adams once described the Vice-Presidency as the most insignifi-

---

56. Smith, *John Adams*, II:629.
57. Abigail Adams; quoted by ibid., II:711.
58. Adams; quoted by ibid., I:494.
59. Chinard, *Honest John Adams*, pp. 189–90.

cant office ever devised by man. However, he served loyally and well, and on the whole he was pleased with George Washington as President. But Adams was skeptical of efforts to "deify" Washington after his death. He had a high regard for Washington as a person; shortly before the end of Washington's second term, Adams described a conversation in which the reserved Washington was "more frank and open about politics" than Adams had ever seen him. "I find his opinions and sentiments are more exactly like mine than I ever knew before," Adams wrote to Abigail.[60]

Washington refused to run for a third term in 1796, so the Federalists chose Adams to be his successor. Adams was elected but was disappointed that his Republican cousin, Governor Samuel Adams, opposed his election and tried unsuccessfully to be a pro-Jefferson elector from Massachusetts. But Samuel Adams hailed his cousin's election, congratulating John as "the first citizen of the United States—I may add of the world," and signing "your old and unvaried friend, S. Adams."[61]

Adams's term of office began amid general good will of all parties and factions. He retained his loyalty to God and the Christian religion. Several months before becoming President he wrote in his diary, "The Christian religion is, above all the Religions that ever prevailed or existed in ancient or modern Times, the Religion of Wisdom, Virtue, Equity, and Humanity, let the Blackguard Paine say what he will. It is Resignation to God, it is Goodness itself to Man."[62] He did not keep a diary as President, but as Vice-President his diary reveals regular church attendance and considerable thought about spiritual matters. Adams declared to Congress on November 23, 1797:

> The state of society has so long been disturbed, the sense of moral and religious obligations so much weakened, public faith and national honor have been so much impaired, respect to treaties has been so diminished, and the law of nations has lost so much of its force, while price, ambition, avarice, and violence, have been so long unrestrained, there remains no reasonable ground on which to raise an expectation, that a commerce, without protection of defence, will not be plundered.[63]

60. John Adams to Abigail Adams, March 25, 1796; quoted by Smith, *John Adams,* II:891.

61. Samuel Adams to John Adams, March 27, 1797; quoted in ibid., II:920.

62. Adams, *Diary;* III:233–34; July 26, 1796.

63. Adams, Message to Congress, November 23, 1797; quoted by Chinard, *Honest John Adams,* p. 269.

On March 6, 1799, Adams issued a proclamation establishing April 25 as "a day of solemn humiliation, fasting, and prayer" to be devoted "to the sacred duties of religion in public and private," to repentance, thanksgiving, and the prayer that the Lord would protect the United States "from unreasonable discontent, from disunion, faction, sedition, and insurrection; that He would preserve our country from the desolating sword" and spread peace and prosperity among the nations of the earth.[64]

A day of prayer and repentance was desperately needed. The general aura of good will at the onset of the Adams administration was soon replaced by resurfacing partisanship and factionalism. As a result, Adams's popularity suffered. Adams had been unsuccessful in trying to steer a middle course between the Federalists and the Republicans as Washington had done. As a Federalist he tried to appease the Republicans; he appeared for his inauguration in plain dress and kept the pomp and ceremony to a minimum, and in his inaugural address he assured the nation of his dedication to basic republican principles. The Republicans were reassured, but only for a short time; the Federalists became skeptical, and their skepticism remained.

The election of 1800 has been hailed as a victory of Republicanism over Federalism. In reality, the Federalists defeated themselves. The Federalist stalwarts, led by Hamilton, were dissatisfied with Adams and looked for alternatives. Earlier Hamilton had tried to persuade Washington to run against Adams, but Washington would have nothing to do with it, and he died in 1799. Hamilton then tried Charles Pinckney, Patrick Henry, and others, without success. Hamilton's maneuvering cost Adams so much support that the vote in the Electoral College was Jefferson 73, Burr 73, Adams 65, and Pinckney 63. Of these four, Adams and Pinckney were Federalists; Burr was a maverick, running as a nominal Republican but thought to have Federalist leanings; and Jefferson was a Republican. It was up to the House of Representatives to choose between the two top vote-getters, Jefferson and Burr. Hamilton was forced to choose between his two opponents: he regarded Jefferson as "an atheist in religion and a fanatic in politics,"[65] and he considered Burr totally unscrupulous and dangerous. Hamilton chose Jefferson, and Jefferson was then elected. Burr became vice-president.

64. John Adams, Presidential Proclamation, March 6, 1799; quoted in Smith *John Adams,* II:1004.

65. Alexander Hamilton, Letter to John Jay, May 7, 1800; quoted by Saul K. Padover, *The Mind of Alexander Hamilton* (New York: Harper, 1958), p. 444.

Adams's defeat left him feeling unappreciated by the country he loved and faithfully served. Abigail expressed concern that the nation would be governed by non-Christian men:

What is the difference of Character between a Prince of Wales, & a Burr? Have we any claim to the favour or protection of Providence, when we have against warning admonition and advise Chosen as our chief Majestrate a man who makes no pretentions to the belief of an all wise and supreme Governour of the World, ordering or directing or overruling the events which take place in it? I do not mean that he is an Atheist, for I do not think that he is—but he believes Religion only usefull as it may be made a political Engine, and that the outward forms are only, as I once heard him express himself—mere Mummery. In short, he is not a believer in the Christian system—The other [presumably Burr] if he is more of a believer, has more to answer for, because he has grosely offended against those doctrines by his practise.

Such are the Men whom we are like to have as our Rulers. Whether they are given us in wrath to punish us for our sins and transgressions, the Events will disclose—But if ever we saw a day of darkness, I fear this is one which will be visible untill kindled into flames.[66]

John and Abigail accepted their defeat as part of the plan of God: "There is nothing more to be said, but let the Eternal will be done."[67]

In March 1801, Adams left Washington and returned to Braintree (renamed Quincy), which supported him in the election. The next five years he worked on his *Autobiography*, not knowing that at age sixty-five he had a quarter-century to live. He pursued his farming interests, and corresponded with old friends—including Jefferson. Their strained relationship during his years in the presidency became a warm friendship through the intercession of their mutual Christian friend Dr. Benjamin Rush.

Adams remained a scholar. He had the most extensive library in America at the time, and one can learn a lot about a man from his library. He had the habit of writing extensive notes in the margins of his books; he almost carried on a dialogue with the writer. These candid comments provide many insights into his thinking.

He frequently read the works of authors who were often liberal in

66. Abigail Adams to Mary Cranch, February 7, 1801; reprinted in *New Letters of Abigail Adams 1788-1801*, ed. Stewart Mitchell (Boston: Houghton Mifflin, 1947), pp. 265–66.
67. Chinard, *Honest John Adams*, p. 308.

both their politics and religion. Adams's comments are generally quite critical and show him on the side of revealed religion in general and Christianity in particular. Sometimes Adams was quite caustic. In *Outlines of an Historical View of the Progress of the Human Mind,* Marquis de Condorcet wrote glowingly about man's ability to improve himself and his institutions by learning from the past. Adams wrote in the margin, "Fool! Fool!"[68] Later Condorcet spoke of "how much more pure, accurate, and profound are the principles upon which the constitution of France has been founded than those which directed the Americans. . . ." Adams wrote in the margin, "Pure! accurate! profound! indeed!"[69] Many of Adams's comments were more reflective. When Condorcet referred to the "immensity of ages" during which the human species has experienced modifications, Adams wrote "Immensity of ages. Eternity I suppose he means, for I presume he was no believer in creation."[70] Condorcet attacked organized religion, claiming that the priests have forgotten the truths behind their allegories and have become dupes of their own fables. Adams commented, "Just as you and yours have become the dupes of your own atheism and profligacy, your nonsensical notions of liberty, equality, and fraternity."[71] Condorcet, like most liberals of his age, praised the accomplishments of the Greeks; Adams responded, "As much as I love, esteem and admire the Greeks, I believe the Hebrews have done more to enlighten and civilize the world. Moses did more than all their legislators and philosophers."[72] Adams was quick to point out the double standard practiced by Condorcet and much of the liberal intellectual community of his time. When Condorcet complained that genius had been suppressed by religious superstition, Adams retorted, "But was there no genius among the Hebrews? None among the Christians, nor Mahometans? I understand you, Condorcet. It is atheistical genius alone that you would honor or tolerate."[73] And when Condorcet complained that religious liberty existed only for Christians everywhere except in France, Adams noted, "In France it exists not for Christians or anything else [since]

68. John Adams, handwritten comments on his copy of a book by the Marquis de Condorcet, *Outlines of an Historical View of the Progress of the Human Mind,* reprinted in Haraszti, *Adams and the Prophets,* p. 255.
69. Ibid., p. 256.
70. Ibid., pp. 241–42.
71. Ibid., p. 245.
72. Ibid., p. 246.
73. Ibid., p. 250

1798."[74] When Condorcet claimed that kings and priests have waged a continual war against truth, Adams replied, "Your philosophy, Condorcet, has waged a more cruel war against truth than was ever attempted by king or priest."[75] When Condorcet delineated "natural equality of mankind" as the foundation of all morality, Adams declared, "There is no such thing without a supposition of a God. There is no right or wrong in the universe without the supposition of a moral government and an intellectual and moral governor."[76]

Adams interacted in a similar manner with the works of Mary Wollstonecraft, a liberal apologist for the French Revolution. When Wollstonecraft declared that it is time to get rid of all notions drawn from "the wild traditions of original sin," Adams sensed her meaning and wrote, "i.e. we must get entirely clear of Christianity."[77] When Wollstonecraft loftily proclaimed that man is free today to follow any scientific pursuit, Adams pointed out that "it is religion and government that have effected this."[78] When Wollstonecraft spoke of national morality, Adams asked, "Whence is this morality to come? If the Christian religion and all the power of government has never produced it, what will? Yet this mad woman is for destroying the Christian religion."[79] Wollstonecraft spoke of improvement in morals over the ages, but Adams responded, "I know of no improvements in morals since the days of Jesus."[80] Wollstonecraft argued that improvement of the understanding will prevent excesses of passion; the realist Adams answered that "The understanding will only make rivalries more subtle and scientific, but the passions will never be prevented, they can only be balanced."[81] When Wollstonecraft praised David Hume, Adams said Hume was "a greater blockhead than he pronounced Mr. Locke to be," and added, "If ever there existed a wise fool, a learned idiot, a profound deep-thinking coxcomb, it was David Hume. As much worse than Voltaire and Rousseau as a sober decent libertine is worse than a rake."[82] In regard to Wollstone-

74. Ibid., p. 252.

75. Ibid., p. 246.

76. Ibid., pp. 251–52.

77. John Adams, handwritten notes on his copy of *Historical and Moral View of the Origin and Progress of the French Revolution*; reprinted in Haraszti, *Adams and the Prophets*, p. 187.

78. Ibid., p. 194.

79. Ibid., p. 198.

80. Ibid., p. 218.

81. Ibid., p. 229.

82. Ibid., p. 214.

craft's views of equality, Adams declared, "The only equality of man that is true was taught by Jesus: 'Do as you would be done by.' The same Jesus taught 'Render to Caesar the things that are Caesar's.'"[83] At the end of the book Adams may have decided he was too hard on the woman, so he wrote:

> This is a lady of masculine masterly understanding. Her style is nervous and clear, often elegant; though sometimes too verbose. With a little experience in public affairs and the reading and reflection which would result from it, she would have produced a history without the defects and blemishes pointed out with too much severity perhaps and too little gallantry in the notes.
>
> The improvement, the exaltation of the human character, the perfectibility of man, and the perfection of the human faculties are the divine objects which her enthusiasm beholds in beatific vision. Alass, how airy and baseless a fabric!
>
> Yet she will not admit of the only means that can accomplish any part of her ardent prophecies: forms of government, so mixed, combined and balanced, as to restrain the passions of all orders of men.[84]

Similar notes were found in Adams's copies of the works of Voltaire, Rousseau, d'Alembert, Priestley, Bolingbroke and others. John Adams was firmly on the side of revealed religion, organized Christianity, and divine principles of government.

While Adams strongly defended and supported orthodox Christianity, in his later years he does seem to question some basic Christian doctrines. These questions primarily centered around the Trinity and were most apparent in his letters to Jefferson, Rush, and Van der Kamp. He declared in an 1816 letter to F. A. Van der Kamp that "The Hebrew unity of Jehovah, the prohibition of all similitudes, appears to me the greatest wonder of antiquity."[85] An 1813 letter to Jefferson summarized his doubts but also demonstrated his faith:

> This revelation had made it certain that two and one make three, and that one is not three nor can three be one. We can never be so certain of any prophecy, or the fulfillment of any prophecy, or of any miracle, or the design of any miracle, as we are from the revelation

83. Ibid., p. 213.

84. Ibid., p. 187; insert between pages 188 and 189.

85. John Adams, letter to F. A. Van der Kamp. December 27, 1816; reprinted in Norman Cousins, "*In God We Trust*" (New York: Harper, 1958), p. 104.

of nature, that is, nature's God, that two and two are equal to four. . . .

Had you and I been forty days with Moses on Mount Sinai, and admitted to behold the divine Shechinah, and there told that one was three and three one, we might not have had courage to deny it, but we could not have believed it. . . .

God has infinite wisdom, goodness and power; he created the universe; his duration is eternal, a parte ante and a parte post. His presence is as extensive as space. What is space? An infinite spherical vacuum. He created this speck of dirt and the human species for his glory; and with the deliberate design of making nine-tenths of our species miserable for ever for his glory. This is the doctrine of Christian theologians, in general, ten to one. Now, my friend, can prophecies or miracles convince you or me that infinite benevolence, wisdom, and power, created, and preserves for a time, innumerable millions, to make them miserable forever, for his own glory? Wretch! What is his glory? Is he ambitious? Does he want promotion? Is he vain, tickled with adulation, exulting and triumphing in his power and the sweetness of his vengeance? Pardon me, my Maker, for these awful questions. My answer to them is always ready. I believe no such things. My adoration of the author of the universe is too profound and too sincere. The love of God and his creation—delight, joy, triumph, exultation in my own existence—though but an atom, a molecule organique in the universe—are my religion.

Howl, snarl, bite, ye Calvinistic, ye Athanasian divines, if you will; ye will say I am no Christian; I say ye are no Christians, and there the account is balanced. Yet I believe all the honest men among you are Christians, in my sense of the word.[86]

During this same period Adams wrote to F. A. Van der Kemp, "My religion is founded on the love of God and my neighbor; on the hope of pardon for my offences; upon contrition; upon the duty as well as the necessity of supporting with patience the inevitable evils of life; in the duty of doing no wrong, but all the good I can, to the creation, of which I am but an infinitesimal part."[87]

These comments only indicate that Adams questioned the doctrine of the Trinity and the belief that only those who accept Christianity shall have a place in heaven[88]—he did not renounce Christianity. He remained a strong friend of the Christian religion

86. Adams to Jefferson, September 14, 1813; reprinted in Wilstach, *Correspondence*, pp. 80–83.

87. Adams to F. A. Van der Kemp, July 13, 1815; reprinted in Cousins, *"In God We Trust,"* p. 104.

88. The author does not share Adams's doubts concerning the Trinity and the need for faith in Jesus Christ.

and considered himself a Christian despite these reservations. He told Jefferson in 1816, "Conclude not from all this that I have renounced the Christian religion, or that I agree with Dupuis in all his sentiments. Far from it. I see in every page something to recommend Christianity in its purity, and something to discredit its corruption."[89] He declared that Christianity:

> . . . will hold its ground in some degree as long as human nature shall have any thing moral or intellectual left in it. The Christian religion, as I understand it, is the brightness of the glory and the express portrait of the character of the eternal, self-existent, independent, benevolent, all powerful and all merciful creator, preserver, and father of the universe, the first good, first perfect, and first fair. It will last as long as the world.[90]

He also said Christianity was the product of divine revelation, not simply human reason: "Neither savage nor civilized man, without a revelation, could ever have discovered or invented it."[91]

Adams held a strong appreciation for Calvinism even though he could not agree with all of its doctrines. He wrote in 1820:

> I must be a very unnatural son to entertain any prejudices against the Calvinists, or Calvinism, according to your confession of faith; for my father and mother, my uncles and aunts, and all my predecessors, from our common ancestor, who landed in this country two hundred years ago, wanting five months, were of that persuasion. Indeed, *I have never known any better people than the Calvinists.* Neverthe-less, I must acknowledge that I cannot class myself under that denomination. My opinions, indeed, on religious subjects ought not to be of any consequence to any but myself. To develop them, and the reasons for them, would require a folio larger than Willard's Body of Divinity, and, after all, I might scatter darkness rather than light.[92] [emphasis added]

Adams was willing to accept the Calvinists as fellow Christians. He objected to the divisions that occurred among Christians; he was interested in study, speculation, and discussion about doctrinal matters but he abhorred bitter divisions over such matters. He

89. Adams to Jefferson, November 4, 1816; reprinted in Wilstach, *Correspondence*, p. 147.

90. Adams to Benjamin Rush, January 21, 1810; reprinted in Cousins, *"In God We Trust"*, p. 101.

91. Ibid.

92. Adams to Samuel Miller, July 8, 1820; reprinted in ibid., p. 111.

acknowledged that many of these matters remained unresolved in his mind. He wrote to Jefferson that "I have found so many difficulties that I am not astonished at your stopping where you are; and, so far from sentencing you to perdition, I hope soon to meet you in another country."[93] Later he wrote, "there is now, never will be, and never was, but one being who can understand the universe, and that it is not only vain but wicked for insects to pretend to comprehend it."[94] Adams was willing to accept all who named the name of Christ as his brethren: "Ask me not, then, whether I am a Catholic or Protestant, Calvinist or Arminian. As far as they are Christians, I wish to be a fellow-disciple with them all."[95]

Adams continued, a confirmed scholar, true lover of Christianity, American patriot, and honest man, into his declining years. In 1826, as America prepared to celebrate the fiftieth anniversary of the Fourth of July, the inhabitants of his hometown begged him to make a final speech; but at age ninety he refused. Finally they asked him to give them a toast they could present in his name. He answered, "I will give you, 'Independence Forever'!" When asked if he would add more, he replied "Not a word."[96]

That Fourth of July was his last. One of the strangest coincidences of history—or perhaps the working of the divine providence in which they both believed—was that Jefferson who wrote the Declaration of Independence and Adams who made the principal speech favoring passage of that Declaration, both died on the fiftieth anniversary of independence. Adams's last words on July 4, 1826, were, "Thomas Jefferson still survives"—unaware that Jefferson had died only about three hours before.[97]

The following points summarize Adams's religious and political convictions.

1. *A belief in revealed religion.* Adams believed that God revealed truth to man and also in God-given powers of human reason. He emphasized that no one could have developed the Christian religion by human reason alone; it had to have been revealed to men by God.[98] That was the orthodox Calvinist position as well as the general Christian position. Adams defended that position during his

---

93. Adams to Jefferson, July 18, 1813; reprinted in Wilstach, *Correspondence*, p. 70.

94. Adams to Jefferson, September 14, 1813; reprinted in ibid., p. 85.

95. Adams to Benjamin Rush, January 21, 1810; reprinted in Cousins, *"In God We Trust"*, p. 101.

96. Chinard, *Honest John Adams*, p. 345.

97. Ibid., p. 346.

98. Adams to Benjamin Rush, January 21, 1810; reprinted in Cousins, *"In God We Trust"*, p. 101.

conversations with the skeptic lawyer Putnam, as he argued "in favor of natural and revealed Religion, and a future State of Rewards and Punishments."[99] He held the same position later in life. He spoke of the Jews and the Old Testament in a letter to Van der Kemp in 1816:

> How could that nation [Israel] preserve its creed among the monstrous theologies of all the other nations of the earth? Revelation, you will say, and especial Providence; and I will not contradict you, for I cannot say with Dupuis that a revelation is impossible or improbable.
>
> Christianity, you will say, was a fresh revelation. I will not deny this. As I understand the Christian religion, it was, and is, a revelation.[100]

2. *The Bible as the revelation of God's truth.* Adams saw the Bible as the source of God's truth. He repeatedly spoke of the Old Testament and the New Testament as revelations from God. He believed that the Bible contained all the wisdom man needed to guide and order his life and that it comprised "the most perfect philosophy, the most perfect morality, and the most refined policy." The Bible was "the most republican book in the world," because it contained the commandments necessary to establish and maintain the moral fiber essential to republican society.[101]

Adams regretted that the original manuscripts of the Bible were not available. He suspected that church officials had as much to do with their destruction as enemies of the church.[102] Adams declared his belief that the Christian religion is a revelation, but then asks:

> . . . how has it happened that millions of fables, tales, legends, have been blended with both Jewish and Christian revelation that have made them the most bloody religion that ever existed? How has it happened that all the fine arts, architecture, painting, sculpture, statuary, music, poetry, and oratory, have been prostituted, from the creation of the world, to the sordid and detestable purposes of superstition and fraud?[103]

It is unclear whether he means that the Bible has been corrupted in

---

99. Adams, *Autobiography*, III:264–65.

100. Adams to Van der Kemp, December 27, 1816; reprinted in Cousins, *"In God We Trust"*, pp.104–5.

101. Adams to Benjamin Rush, September 1806; February 2, 1807; quoted and cited in Smith, *John Adams*, II:1078.

102. Adams to John Taylor, 1814; reprinted in Cousins, *"In God We Trust"*, pp. 105–11.

103. Adams to Van der Kemp, December 27, 1816; reprinted in ibid., pp. 104–5.

its present form from the purity of the original manuscripts, or that the church traditions (particularly Roman Catholicism, which he regarded as having many pagan aspects) had corrupted it.

Adams took the Bible literally despite his unanswered questions. He spoke of biblical figures such as Adam, Noah, Moses, and Elijah as actual persons. He spoke of the creation of the universe as if he accepted the literal six-day creation account of Genesis.

3. *A respect for Jesus Christ.* It is not clear what Adams thought of Jesus Christ. He probably accepted the trinitarian doctrine adhered to by orthodox Calvinism and Christianity when he was young and while he was in public life. But it appears he doubted, or at least questioned, the doctrine of the Trinity during his retirement years. He did consider Jesus to be more than a mere human being, if not part of the Trinity. Adams was acquainted with the works of Dr. Joseph Priestley, a controversial theologian of that time, who was a forerunner of the liberal and neo-orthodox theologians a century later. Adams insisted that Priestley was not as much a heretic as some believed: "We are to understand, no doubt, that he believed the resurrection of Jesus, some of his miracles, his inspiration; but in what degree? He did not believe in the inspiration of the writings that contain his history. Yet he believed in the Apocalyptic beast, and he believed as much as he pleased in the writings of Daniel and John."[104] Adams seemed to believe in the resurrection of Jesus and in some if not all of his miracles. This would indicate that he regarded Jesus as more than a man, if not fully God.

It is clear that John Adams had the highest respect and reverence for the person of Jesus Christ and for his Word. In Adams's writings he frequently quoted Jesus.

4. *An interest in Millennialism.* Many if not most of the New England Puritans held to post-millennialism, the belief that at some future date Jesus Christ and his followers would rule the world for a literal thousand-year period during which conditions on earth would be ideal. Whether Adams accepted post-millennialism is uncertain, but there are indications that he did. In Adams's diary entry June 5, 1771, he described a conversation with a Dr. William McKinstry in which Dr. McKinstry expressed belief in a literal millennium that was about to occur. According to Dr. McKinstry, the history of the world is to conform to the Jewish calendar. The world was created in six days, and on the seventh God rested. Therefore the history of the world will span six-thousand years,

---

104. Adams to Jefferson, July 18, 1813; reprinted in Wilstach, *Correspondence,* p. 68.

from creation around 4,000 B.C. to the dawn of the millennium around A.D. 2,000, at which time the thousand-year millennium will correspond to the Sabbath day of rest. Adams did not appear to accept this viewpoint, but he did record it.[105] Later in his life he echoed millennial themes:

> Can you give me any news of the millennium? Is it to commence soon enough for me to entertain a hope that I may live a thousand years longer? I want to study the Chaldean language, the Dialects, and all the books that are written in them. I want to read all the Christian Fathers and Ecclesiastical historians. I want to learn the Chinese language, and to study all the Asiatic researches.[106]

Abigail also occasionally expressed a millennial theme. Wishing that Europe could be at peace, Abigail added that perhaps "this is wishing for more than mankind are capable of attaining till the millennium or the thousand years in which we are told the just shall reign upon the earth."[107] It cannot be stated for fact that John or Abigail believed in a literal millennium, but the concept occurs in their writings enough to conclude that it was part of their thinking.

    5. *Faith in God.* Throughout Adams's life he maintained a constant faith in God as the supreme, omniscient, omnipotent, beneficient, loving and forgiving Creator and preserver of the universe and mankind. Near the end of his life Adams confessed to David Sewall, that "a kind Providence has preserved and supported me for eighty-five years and seven months, through many dangers and difficulties, though in great weakness, and I am not afraid to trust in its goodness to all eternity. I have a numerous posterity, to whom my continuance may be of some importance, and I am willing to await the order of the Supreme Power."[108]

    6. *A belief in natural law and natural rights.* Adams was a strong believer in natural law and natural rights as most of his contemporaries. He carefully studied Isaac Newton's works and believed the universe was governed by fixed, uniform laws of science, such as gravitation. But Adams's belief in natural law did not preclude him from believing in miracles, which the deists totally rejected. He wrote in his diary, "The great and almighty Author of nature, who at first established those rules which regulate the World, can as

    105. Adams, *Diary*, II:25.
    106. Adams to Van der Kemp, June 5, 1812; quoted in Smith, *John Adams*, II:1076.
    107. Abigail Adams, to Elizabeth Shaw, July 14, 1786; quoted in ibid., II:640.
    108. Adams to David Sewall, May 22, 1821; reprinted in Cousins, *"In God We Trust"*, pp. 112–13.

easily Suspend those Laws whenever his providence sees sufficient reason for such suspension. This can be no objection, then, to the miracles of J[esus] C[hrist]."[109]

Adams also believed in moral laws which should govern the affairs of men. He studied and believed the teachings of those who stressed natural law—John Locke, John Milton, Sir Edward Coke, and Sir William Blackstone. He credited Christianity for natural law: "One great Advantage of the Christian Religion is that it brings the great Principle of the Law of Nature and Nations, Love your Neighbor as yourself, and do to others as you would that others should to do you, to the Knowledge, Belief and Veneration of the whole People."[110] Adams stated that the "gallant Struggle in America, is founded in Principles so indisputable, in the moral Law, in the revealed Law of God, in the true Constitution of great Britain, and in the most apparent Welfare of the Nation as well as the People in America, that I must confess it rejoices my very Soul."[111]

He often used the Lockean phrase "life, liberty and property," when speaking about natural rights.[112]

7. *A belief in the sinfulness of human nature.* The underlying principle of John Adams's political philosophy is his pessimistic view of human nature. In his day there were those who believed in the essential goodness or perfectibility of man. Such thinking formed the basis for the French Revolution. Adams and the majority of Americans did not share this view. Adams was taught the Calvinistic doctrine of the total depravity of man. He insisted that man had not changed and could not change "since the Garden of Eden." Consequently "no such passion as a love of democracy, stronger than self-love, or superior to the love of private interest, ever did, or ever can prevail in the minds of the citizens in general," for "no love of equality, at least since Adam's fall, ever existed in human nature."[113] Surveying the wreckage of the French Revolution, he wrote to Jefferson, "Let me ask you very seriously, my friend, where are now in 1813 the perfection and perfectibility in human nature? Where is now the progress of the human mind? Where is the amelioration of society? Where the augmentation of human comforts? Where the diminution of human pains and miseries?"[114]

109. Adams, *Diary*, March 2, 1756, I:11.
110. Ibid., August 14, 1796, III:240–41.
111. Adams, letter to *Boston Gazette*, January 20, 1766; ibid., December 26, 1765, I:275–76.
112. Smith, *John Adams*, I:182, 416; Chinard, *Honest John Adams*, pp. 52, 174–75.
113. Adams; quoted in ibid., pp. 214–15.
114. Adams to Jefferson, July 15, 1813; quoted in Smith, *John Adams*, II:1112.

Smith notes that, "Adams was converting into secular political terms the Puritan concept of sin. Self-interest is the political or secular equivalent of original sin. Public spirit is sanctification."[115] A friend commented that Adams took his notions of sin from the Word of God. "Mr. Adams reads the Scriptures and there he finds that man is as stupid as the wild ass's colt. He believes what he reads and infers his necessary consequences from it, that is all. Mr. Adams is not to blame. He did not write the Scriptures. He only reads and believes."[116] Adams did not go as far as some Calvinists in the doctrine of total depravity. In 1817 he declared to Jefferson that, "there is no individual totally depraved. The most abandoned scoundrel that ever existed, never yet wholly extinguished his conscience, and, while conscience remains, there is some religion."[117] The God-given human conscience (Rom 2:14-15), when nourished by the Christian religion, produces a limited amount of virtue and public-spiritedness which enables society to function effectively. Adams conceded, toward the end of his life, that the world was somewhat better than when he was young: "Superstition, persecution, and bigotry are somewhat abated; governments are a little ameliorated; science and literature are greatly improved, and more widely spread."[118] This was due to the refinement of the Christian religion and republican institutions, not to any change in human nature. If these influences were eliminated, society could easily degenerate into an age of darkness.

Adams is sometimes viewed as a bitter old man, but his view of human nature made him more generous in assessing human faults, and more appreciative of human virtues. When Adams was asked how he could resume a friendship with Jefferson when Jefferson had fought him for the presidency, he answered:

> I do not believe that Mr. Jefferson ever hated me. On the contrary I believe that he always liked *me*, but he detested Hamilton and my whole administration. Then, he wished to be President of the United States, and I stood in his way. So he did everything he could to pull me down. But if I should quarrel with him for that, I might quarrel with every man I have had anything to do with in life. *This is human nature.* . . . I forgive all my enemies and hope they may find mercy

115. Ibid., I:234.
116. John Adams to Abigail Adams, December 7, 1792; quoted in ibid., II:832.
117. Adams to Jefferson, April 19, 1817; reprinted in Wilstach, *Correspondence*, pp. 157–58.
118. John Adams to David Sewall, May 22, 1821; reprinted in Cousins, "*In God We Trust*", p. 113.

in heaven. Mr. Jefferson and I have grown old and retired from public life. So we are upon our ancient terms of good will. [first emphasis original, second emphasis added][119]

Although Adams vehemently attacked the optimism of Condorcet and others on the perfectibility of human nature, Haraszti notes that "his idea that the world could go muddling along for the next three thousand years shows him, in spite of his forebodings, a far greater optimist than Condorcet ever was."[120]

8. *A distrust of power.* Adams greatly distrusted absolute power, whether in the hands of kings or popes, because he knew the sinfulness of man. This fear of power, which was consistent with his Calvinistic upbringing, made him an ardent champion of republican principles and a staunch defender of the American cause against British abuses.

9. *A distrust of democracy.* Adams distrusted absolute power in the hands of rulers, but he equally distrusted absolute power in the hands of the majority. Since rulers possess sinful natures, they can abuse power and oppress the people. But the masses also possess sinful natures, and can also misuse the power of majority rule and oppress minorities; furthermore, blinded by passion and self-interest, they can make poor decisions that result in national disaster. He made this point in a letter to Jefferson in 1815. "The fundamental article of my political creed is, that despotism, or unlimited sovereignty, or absolute power, is the same in a majority of a popular assembly, an aristocratical council, an oligarchical junto, and a single emperor. Equally arbitrary, cruel, bloody, and in every respect diabolical."[121] In response to the slogan of the French liberals that "vox populari est vox dei" ("The voice of the people is the voice of God"), Adams inquired, "If the majority is 51 and the minority 49, is it certainly the voice of God? If tomorrow one should change to 50 vs. 50, where is the voice of God? If two and the minority should become the majority, is the voice of God changed?"[122] In contrast to that notion Adams declared that vox populari est *non* vox dei; that the voice of the people was "sometimes the voice of Mahomet, of Caesar, of Catiline, the Pope, and the Devil."[123]

119. John Adams; quoted in Smith, *John Adams*, II:1113.

120. Haraszti, *Adams and the Prophets*, p. 258.

121. Adams to Jefferson, November 13, 1815; reprinted in Wilstach, *Correspondence*, pp. 117–18.

122. John Adams, handwritten note on his copy of Jean-Jacques Rousseau's *Discours sur l'inegalite* (Discourse on Inequality); quoted in Haraszti, *Adams and the Prophets*, p. 93.

123. John Adams; quoted by Chinard, *Honest John Adams*, p. 248.

Adams believed pure democracy—that is, absolute, unfettered majority rule—was therefore as dangerous as pure despotism, and would inevitably lead to the same result.

10. *Support for balanced, constitutional republican government.* In John Adams's view the most effective government for a fallen human race is balanced, constitutional republican government. Government should have certain, delegated powers, delineated in the Constitution. These powers should be separated between executive, legislative, and judicial branches, with the legislature consisting of more than one (preferably three) houses.

All men, rulers and commoners must be under the law, not above it. Adams's Calvinistic training, his experience in law practice, his defense of the British soldiers in the Boston Massacre, his work as a Congressman, his dealings with European governments, and his terms as Vice-President and President, convinced him that no man should be above the law, and that constitutions, laws, and procedures were designed to protect human freedom and promote the administration of justice. He summarized, "The very definition of a republic is 'an empire of laws, and not of men.' "[124]

Adams saw limited, constitutional republican government as the means of restraining the sinful nature of man.

11. *The need for virtue and morality.* Even the best of constitutional republics will fail in an immoral society. Adams emphasized again and again that people cannot live in a free society unless they have strong moral fiber; for that reason, he predicted, the French Revolution was doomed to failure because French immorality could not sustain a free nation. Speaking about America, he said, "Our constitution was made only for a moral and religious people. It is wholly inadequate for the government of any other."[125] People must be virtuous for republican government to succeed. Adams sincerely hoped America could sustain the necessary moral qualities to remain free:

> There must be a positive passion for the public good, the public interest, honor, power and glory, established in the minds of the people, or there can be no republican government, nor any real liberty; and this public passion must be superior to all private passions. Men must be ready, they must pride themselves, and be

124. John Adams, 1789; quoted in *War on Religious Freedom*, p. 1.
125. John Adams, *Thoughts on Government*; quoted in John R. Howe, Jr., *The Changing Political Thought of John Adams* (Princeton, New Jersey: Princeton University Press), p. 384.

happy to sacrifice their private pleasures, passions and interests, nay, their private friendships and dearest connections, when they stand in competition with the rights of society. [Adams notes that the people of few nations possess such qualities.] Our dear Americans perhaps have as much of it as any nation now existing, and New England perhaps has more than the rest of America. But I have seen such selfishness and littleness even in New England, that I sometimes tremble to think that, although we are engaged in the best cause that ever employed the human heart, yet the prospect for success is doubtful not for want of power or of wisdom but of virtue.[126]

These thoughts might appear contradictory. On the one hand Adams says an immoral society cannot sustain republican government. On the other hand he insists that all men are basically sinful and selfish. How, then, can any society maintain a republican government?

The answer is: through the influence of law and Christianity. Good laws and sound constitutions can to some degree restrain the sinful impulses of men, and Christianity can implant in men a better nature.

12. *Christianity must be the cornerstone of republican government.* Smith says that John Adams:

> . . . showed in many ways an extraordinary consistency throughout his life. In his fundamental convictions—the moral basis of life, the need for religion, the authority of a divine Being, the necessity of balance and refinement in government, his orthodox view of the nature of original sin, his veneration for the law, his belief in the civilized as opposed to the "natural" man—in all these he was remarkably steadfast. Insights achieved in his early twenties remained with him to his death almost three quarters of a century later, possibly wearing a different costume but nonetheless recognizable for that.[127]

This is particularly true of his view of the role of Christianity in society. At age twenty, Adams believed the nation should be governed by the Bible:

> Suppose a nation in some distant Region, should take the Bible for their only law Book, and every member should regulate his conduct by the precepts there exhibited. Every member would be obliged in Conscience to temperance and frugality and industry, to justice and

126. Ibid.
127. Smith, *John Adams*, I:273–74.

kindness and Charity towards his fellow men, and to Piety and Love, and reverence towards almighty God. In this Commonwealth, no man would impair his health by Gluttony, drunkenness, or Lust—no man would sacrifice his most precious time to cards, or any other trifling and mean amusement—no man would steal or lie or any way defraud his neighbour, but would live in peace and good will with all men—no man would blaspheme his maker or profane his worship, but a rational and manly, a sincere and unaffected Piety and devotion, would reign in all hearts. What a Eutopa, what a Paradise would this region be. Heard Thayer all day. He preach'd well.[128]

As he grew older, Adams realized that not all men would accept the Bible and live by its precepts. Adams saw the influence of the Christian religion as the only hope for improving human virtue and morality. He wrote to Benjamin Rush in 1811 that "religion and virtue are the only foundations, not only of republicanism and of all free government, but of social felicity under all governments and in all the combinations of human society."[129]

He believed this morality must have its roots in the Christian religion. He rhetorically asked Mary Wollstonecraft, "Whence is this morality to come? If the Christian religion and all the power of government has never produced it, what will?"[130] For, as he commented concerning the views of Condorcet, "There is no such thing [as morality] without a supposition of a God. There is no right or wrong in the universe without the supposition of a moral government and an intellectual and moral governor."[131]

On another occasion Adams wrote a description of Christianity:

No other Institution for Education, no kind of political Discipline, could diffuse this kind of necessary Information, so universally among all Ranks and Descriptions of Citizens. The Duties and Rights of the Man and the Citizen are thus taught from early Infancy to every Creature. The Sanctions of a future Life are thus added to the Observance of civil and political, as well as domestic and private Duties. Prudence, Justice, Temperance, and Fortitude, are thus taught to be the means and Conditions of future as well as present Happiness.[132]

128. Adams, *Diary*, February 22, 1756; I:9.
129. John Adams to Benjamin Rush, August 28, 1811; reprinted in Cousins, *"In God We Trust"*, pp. 101–2.
130. Adams; quoted in Haraszti, *Adams and the Prophets*, p. 198.
131. Ibid., pp. 251–52.
132. Adams, *Diary*, August 14, 1796; III:240–41.

In John Adams's view, the production of these virtues and the inculcation of them in the minds of the people is, "One great Advantage of the Christian Religion."[133]

Adams spoke of the Christian religion and "all the power of government" operating to produce morality and virtue; the two work together. Government can promote virtuous and moral behavior, even if it cannot produce virtuous intent, by restraining the sinful nature of man and curbing his excesses with the power of law. The Christian religion and the power of government combine to raise the virtue and morality of the people to a level at which they are sufficiently public-spirited and self-restrained that republican government can work. In this sense Adams was a visionary; he desired a more moral society along with a freer society. The Puritanism of old reasserted itself. As Smith says:

> Adams' Puritan ancestors had insisted that they were engaged in an effort to establish a new and purified kind of religious community founded on the teachings of the Bible and the precepts of John Calvin. Adams, in a similar spirit, insisted that he and his contemporaries were concerned with establishing a new and purified kind of political community, founded on the Christian religion and the precepts of John Locke and James Harrington among others.[134]

This obviously means Christianity and government are interrelated. While Adams was a believer in religious liberty and toleration, he would not have endorsed the modern notion of absolute separation of church and state. The church should inculcate public virtues, just as the state seeks to restrain vice and promote virtue. He wrote to Abigail, "My opinion of the duties of religion and morality comprehends a very extensive connection with society at large and the great interests of the public."[135] He declared that the clergy have a duty to preach on social and political issues as they draw their inspiration and principles from the Word of God:

> Massachusetts is then seized with a violent fit of anger at the clergy. It is curious to observe the conduct of the tories toward this sacred body. If a clergyman, of whatever character, preaches against the principles of the revolution, . . . the tories cry him up as an excellent man and a wonderful preacher . . .:
>
> But if a clergyman preaches Christianity, and tells the magistrates

---

133. Ibid., I:240.
134. Smith, *John Adams*, I:235.
135. John Adams to Abigail Adams, October 29, 1775; quoted in ibid., I:219.

that they were not distinguished from their brethren for their private emolument, but for the good of the people; that the people are bound in conscience to obey a good government, but are not bound to submit to one that aims at destroying all the ends of government,— oh sedition! treason!

The clergy in all ages and countries, and in this in particular, are disposed enough to be on the side of government as long as it is tolerable. If they have not been generally in the late administration on that side, it is a demonstration that the late administration has been universally odious. The clergy of this province are a virtuous, sensible, and learned set of men, and they do not take their sermons from newspapers, but the Bible; unless it be a few, who preach passive obedience. These are not generally curious enough to read Hobbes. It is the duty of the clergy to accommodate their discourses to the times, to preach against such sins as are most prevalent, and recommend such virtues as are most wanted. For example,—if exorbitant ambition and venality are predominant, ought they not to warn their hearers against those vices? If public spirit is much wanted, should they not inculcate this great virtue? If the rights and duties of Christian magistrates and subjects are disputed, should they not explain them, show their nature, ends, limitations, and restrictions, how much soever it may move the gall of Massachusettensis?[136]

This was the political creed of John Adams. He believed in liberty but recognized that only a virtuous people can live in a state of liberty. The Bible and experience taught him the fact of original sin. So he favored a limited, balanced constitutional republic which restrained sin, and the Christian religion which alone can take sin away.

John Adams's religious and political philosophy, which he believed and lived, is best summarized with two passages of Scripture. The first is (Prov. 14:34): "Righteousness exalteth a nation: but sin is a reproach to any people." The second is (2 Cor. 3:17): "Where the Spirit of the Lord *is,* there *is* liberty."

---

136. John Adams, "Novanglus: A History of the Dispute with America, from its Origin, in 1754, to the Present Time:" 1774; reprinted in Cousins, "*In God We Trust*", pp. 89–90.

16 Patrick Henry

"G ive me liberty or give me death!" Generations of school children remember Patrick Henry's stirring call to arms. Today he is perhaps the most underestimated man of his generation.

Patrick Henry is often dismissed as nothing more than a fiery orator of the 1700s. Henry's rival Jefferson conceded that Henry's talents as an orator were "great, indeed; such as I have never heard from any other man. He appeared to me to speak as Homer wrote."[1] On another occasion Jefferson called him "the greatest orator that ever lived."[2] John Randolph of Roanoke, another great orator of that time, said of Henry, "The united powers of painting and eloquence could, alone, give a faint idea of what he was . . . a Shakespeare and Garrick combined . . . when Henry was speaking one felt like whispering to his neighbor, 'Hush, don't stir, don't speak, don't breathe!' "[3]

---

1. Thomas Jefferson, *Autobiography* in Albert Ellery Bergh, ed., *The Writings of Thomas Jefferson*, 20 vols. (Washington, D. C.: The Thomas Jefferson Memorial Association, 1907); quoted in Andrew M. Allison, M. Richard Maxfield, K. DeLynn Cook, and W. Cleon Skousen, 2nd ed. *The Real Thomas Jefferson* (Washington, D. C.: National Center for Constitutional Studies, 1983), p. 472.

2. Thomas Jefferson, Letter to William Wirt; quoted by Norine Dickson Campbell, *Patrick Henry: Patriot and Statesman* (Old Greenwich, Connecticut: Devin-Adair, 1969, 1975), p. 63.

3. John Randolph; quoted by ibid., p. 66.

But Henry was more than the greatest orator of his generation. A great orator might be elected governor once through popular appeal, but to be reelected to five terms as governor of Virginia (at that time the largest state in the Union), indicates that he was also a capable governor. A President might feel compelled to offer a government post to a popular leader just to assuage public opinion, but it was unlikely that President Washington offered Patrick Henry the post of Secretary of State and then the post of Chief Justice of the Supreme Court, unless he had great respect for Henry. A fiery orator might make a stirring speech against ratification of the U.S. Constitution, but unless Henry possessed superior intellect it was unlikely that he could have held the field before the Virginia ratifying convention for twenty-three days, against such adversaries as James Madison, George Wythe, John Marshall, and Governor Edmund Randolph.

Patrick Henry was more than a dynamic orator; he was also a great intellect, statesman, and Christian.

A Great Intellect

Patrick Henry was born on May 29, 1736, in Studley, Virginia. His parents, Colonel John and Sarah Henry, came from prominent families of Scottish and English backgrounds. His mother's family were descendants from King Alfred the Great; his father's family traced its ancestry through the Norman invaders under William the Conqueror. There were many educators, orators, statesmen and preachers on both sides of his family. Dr. William Robertson, a first cousin once-removed, was a well-known Scottish preacher and scholar whose essay on "Chivalry" impressed Henry with the principles of honesty, generosity, courage, and loyalty. Madison's wife Dolley was a first cousin once-removed of Patrick Henry.

Henry's formal education consisted of a few years at an English common school where he learned reading, writing, and a little arithmetic.[4] His father took him out of school when he was about ten and taught him at home. Patrick Henry loved nature and enjoyed canoe trips, fishing, hunting, and rambling through the woodlands and hillsides. But Patrick also acquired a knowledge of Greek and Latin and of the classics as well as the Bible through his

4. George Morgan; cited by ibid., p. 10.

father's diligent efforts. Patrick seemed fond of mathematics and
history as Judge Spencer Roane relates:

> His genius was as far-soaring above those of ordinary men as is the
> first qualified land of Kentucky beyond the sandy barrens of Pea
> Ridge [a barren ridge in King and Queen].
> That he was acquainted with Ancient History and Mythology
> needs no further proof than the eloquent parallel used by him in his
> argument on the British Debt Case, between Rhadamanthus, Nero,
> and George III. I believe he was very fond of History, Magazines,
> good poetry or plays (says Shakespeare's) and I think he was a very
> good geographer. He was particularly well acquainted with geogra
> phy, rivers, soil, climate, etc. of America. His speeches show that he
> was well acquainted with English History. I think he had some
> acquaintance with Mathematics and Natural Philosophy.[5]

Patrick Henry decided to become a lawyer around 1760, at about
age twenty-four. Accounts vary as to how long he studied law,
ranging from six weeks to nine months; he told a friend he studied
one month, during which time he read Coke upon Littleton and the
Virginia laws. At first the examiners were reluctant to approve him,
claiming, as Jefferson wrote later, ". . . he was very ignorant of law,
but that they perceived him to be a young man of genius, and did
not doubt he would soon qualify himself."[6] Judge John Tyler relates
that one of Henry's bar examiners was:

> Mr. John Randolph, who was afterwards the king's attorney-general
> for the colony,—a gentleman of the most courtly elegance of person
> and manners, a polished wit, and a profound lawyer. At first, he was
> so much shocked by Mr. Henry's very ungainly figure and address,
> that he refused to examine him. Understanding, however, that he
> had already obtained two signatures, he entered with manifest
> reluctance on the business. A very short time was sufficient to satisfy
> him of the erroneous conclusion which he had drawn from the
> exterior of the candidate. With evident marks of increasing surprise
> (produced, no doubt, by the peculiar texture and strength of Mr.
> Henry's style, and the boldness and originality of his combinations),
> he continued the examination for several hours; interrogating the
> candidate, not on the principles of municipal law, in which he no
> doubt soon discovered his deficiency, but on the laws of nature and
> of nations, on the policy of the feudal system, and on general history,

---

5. Judge Spencer Roane, *Memorandum;* cited by ibid., p. 11.
6. Thomas Jefferson; quoted by Moses Coit Tyler, *Patrick Henry* (New York: Frederick
Ungar Publishing Company, 1898, 1966), p. 23.

which last he found to be his stronghold. During the very short portion of the examination which was devoted to the common law, Mr. Randolph dissented, or affected to dissent, from one of Mr. Henry's answers, and called upon him to assign the reasons of his opinion. This produced an argument, and Mr. Randolph now played off on him the same arts which he himself had so often practiced on his country customers; drawing him out by questions, endeavoring to puzzle him by subtleties, assailing him with declamation, and watching continually the defensive operations of his mind. After a considerable discussion, he said, "You defend your opinions well, sir; but now to the law and to the testimony." Hereupon he carried him to his office, and, opening the authorities, said to him: "Behold the force of natural reason! You have never seen these books, nor this principle of the law; yet you are right and I am wrong. And from the lesson which you have given me (you must excuse me for saying) I will never trust to appearances again. Mr. Henry, if your industry be only half equal to your genius, I augur that you will do well, and become an ornament and an honor to your profession.[7]

At that point, Patrick Henry began a promising legal career. Unfortunately, Henry's reputation as a lawyer suffered because of his earliest biographer, William Wirt. Wirt was kind to Henry for the most part in *Sketches of the Life and Character of Patrick Henry* (1817), but his account was prejudiced by an 1816 letter written to him by Henry's old adversary, Thomas Jefferson. By this time Jefferson was old and failing in memory. He conceded Henry's oratorical powers in the letter, but also claimed that Henry was poorly educated, did not converse with educated people, and was not particularly successful as a lawyer because:

> . . . he was too lazy. Whenever the courts were closed for the winter session, he would make up a party of poor hunters of his neighborhood, would go off with them to the piny woods of Fluvanna, and pass weeks in hunting deer, of which he was passionately fond, sleeping under a tent before a fire, wearing the same shirt the whole time, and covering all the dirt of his dress with a hunting-shirt. He never undertook to draw pleadings, if he could avoid it, or to manage that part of a cause, and very unwillingly engaged but as an assistant to speak in the cause. And the fee was an indispensable preliminary, observing to the applicant that he kept no accounts, never putting pen to paper, which was true.[8]

---

7. Ibid., pp. 24-25.
8. Thomas Jefferson, Letter to William Wirt; quoted by ibid., pp. 29-30.

Jefferson's recollection was marred by his age, his failing memory, and his enmity with Henry. For Henry *did* keep account books, and when they were discovered, they revealed that Henry was an industrious lawyer. He handled 1,185 lawsuits and prepared many legal papers out of court during his first three and one-half years of law practice. In contrast, during Jefferson's first four years of practice he handled only 504 cases.[9] Henry made a fortune in the practice of law while Jefferson died in debt.[10]

Patrick Henry's legal skills became prominent through a well-publicized case known as "The Parson's Cause." Several Anglican clergymen were suing some tobacco planters under a Virginia colony law that required a certain portion of tobacco revenues be paid for the support of the clergy. Henry agreed to defend the planters when their previous attorney declared the case hopeless and withdrew. He assailed the Anglican clergy without mercy, amid a packed courtroom filled with Anglican clergymen confident of victory, and "Dissenters" (Methodists, Baptists and Presbyterians) looking to Henry as their champion:

> We have heard a great deal about the benevolence and holy zeal of our reverend clergy, but how is this manifested? Do they manifest their zeal in the cause of religion and humanity by practicing the mild and benevolent precepts of the Gospel of Jesus? Do they feed the hungry and clothe the naked? Oh, no, gentlemen! Instead of feeding the hungry and clothing the naked, these rapacious harpies would, were their powers equal to their will, snatch from the hearth of their honest parishioner his last hoe-cake, from the widow and her orphan children their last milch cow! The last bed, nay, the last blanket from the lying-in woman![11]

Henry could not demand a verdict for the planters since the law was clearly on the side of the clergy. Instead, he asked the jury to bring forth a verdict for the clergy in the amount of one penny—which the jury did.

A Great Statesman

Henry's fame spread after the Parson's Cause and in 1765 he was elected to the Virginia House of Burgesses. Nine days after his election, the Burgesses were notified that the British Parliament had passed the Stamp Act, designed to raise revenues among the

9. Ibid., pp. 30-31.
10. Campbell, *Patrick Henry*, p. 25.
11. Henry; quoted by ibid., p. 35.

colonies on behalf of the Crown by requiring that all legal documents have a stamp affixed, the stamp being sold for a certain sum of money. Henry authorized seven resolutions against the Stamp Act, five of which passed the House. He gave a second memorable, stirring speech in the debate on these resolutions. "'Caesar had his Brutus, Charles the First his Cromwell, and George the Third'— 'Treason!' shouted Speaker Robinson, 'Treason, Treason!' exclaimed some of the older members. 'And George the Third,' he repeated, 'may profit by their example—if this be treason make the most of it.'"[12]

Later Henry wrote about the passage of the Stamp Act Resolves:

> This brought on the war which finally separated the two countries and gave independence to ours. Whether this will prove a blessing or a curse, will depend upon the use our people make of the blessings which a gracious God hath bestowed on us. If they are wise, they will be great and happy. If they are of a contrary character, they will be miserable. Righteousness alone can exalt them as a nation. Reader! Whoever thou art, remember this: and in thy sphere practice virtue thyself, and encourage it in others.[13]

Henry, an early advocate of independence, was elected as a delegate to the First Continental Congress in Philadelphia in 1774. Once again his eloquence and force of argument electrified the audience and stirred them to action. Silas Deane, a delegate from Connecticut, wrote:

> Mr. Henry . . . is the completest speaker I have ever heard. If his future speeches are equal to the small samples he has hitherto given us, they will be worth preserving; but in a letter I can give you no idea of the music of his voice, or the high wrought yet natural elegance of his style and manner. Col. Lee is said to be his rival in eloquence, and in Virginia and to the Southward they are styled the Demosthenes and Cicero of America. God grant they may not, like them, plead in vain for the liberties of their country! These last gentlemen are now in full life, perhaps near fifty, and have made the constitution of Great Britain and America their capital study ever since the late troubles between them have arisen.[14]

John Adams, another delegate, wrote to Thomas Jefferson, "In the Congress of 1774, there was not one member, except Patrick

---

12. Henry; quoted by ibid., p. 60.
13. Henry; quoted by ibid., p. 57.
14. Silas Deane; quoted by ibid., p. 111.

Henry, who appeared to me sensible of the precipice, or rather, the pinnacle on which he stood, and had candor and courage enough to acknowledge it."[15]

In 1775, as a delegate to the Second Virginia Convention held in St. John's Church to escape British surveillance, Henry delivered the "Give me liberty or give me death!" speech. Judge St. George Tucker, another delegate, described Henry's speech:

> Imagine to yourself this speech delivered with all the calm dignity of Cato of Utica; imagine to yourself the Roman Senate assembled in the capital when it was entered by the profane Gauls, who at first were awed by their presence as if they had entered an assembly of the gods. Imagine that you had heard that Cato addressing such a Senate. Imagine that you saw the handwriting on the wall of Belshazzar's palace. Imagine that you had heard a voice as from heaven uttering the words, "We must fight," as the doom of Fate, and you may have some idea of the speaker, the assembly to whom he addressed himself, and the auditory, of which I was one.[16]

Another spectator described the speech:

> When Patrick Henry pled, "Forbid it, Almighty God," his arms were extended aloft; his body was thrown back, his coat flung right and left. The tendons of his neck stood out white and rigid like whipcords. His brow was knit, every feature marked with the resolute purpose of his soul. . . . The sound of his voice was like that of a Spartan paean on the field of Plataea. . . . "Liberty" he spoke with an emphasis never given it before. His countenance was radiant; he stood erect and defiant; while the sound of his voice and the sublimity of his attitude made him appear a magnificent incarnation of Freedom, and expressed all that can be acquired or enjoyed by nations and individuals invincible and free.[17]

Henry was a delegate to the Second Continental Congress in 1775, but left when notified that he had been appointed Colonel of Virginia's First Regiment. He briefly served in the military, resigned in 1776 due to political intrigue, and was elected Governor of Virginia later the same year. As governor he served ably and was re-elected in 1777 and 1778. Between 1779 and 1784 he was leader of the Virginia General Assembly. He was greatly esteemed by the common people of Virginia as revealed by a 1780 incident; the

15. John Adams to Thomas Jefferson, November 12, 1813; quoted by ibid., p. 111.
16. Judge St. George Tucker; quoted by ibid., p. 127.
17. Ibid., p. 128.

British army marched toward Charlottesville with instructions to seize the legislators, who fled to Staunton when:

> It is said that as Patrick Henry, Benjamin Harrison, Judge Tyler, and Colonel Christian were hurrying along, they saw a little hut in the forest. An old woman was chopping wood by the door. The men were hungry, and stopped to ask her for food.
>
> "Who are you?" she asked.
>
> "We are members of the legislature," said Patrick Henry; "we have just been compelled to leave Charlottesville on account of the British."
>
> "Ride on, then, ye cowardly knaves!" she said in wrath. "Here are my husband and sons just gone to Charlottesville to fight for ye, and you running away with all your might. Clear out! Ye shall have nothing here."
>
> "But," replied Mr. Henry, "we were obliged to flee. It would not do for the legislature to be broken up by the enemy. Here is Mr. Benjamin Harrison; you don't think he would have fled had it not been necessary?"
>
> "I always thought a great deal of Mr. Harrison till now," answered the old woman, "but he'd no business to run from the enemy." And she started to shut the door in their faces.
>
> "Wait a moment, my good woman," cried Mr. Henry; "would you believe that Judge Tyler or Colonel Christian would take to flight if there were not good cause for so doing?"
>
> "No, indeed that I wouldn't."
>
> "But," he said, "Judge Tyler and Colonel Christian are here."
>
> "They are? Well, I would never have thought it. I didn't suppose they would ever run from the British; but since they have, they shall have nothing to eat in my house. You may ride along."
>
> Things were getting desperate. Then Judge Tyler stepped forward: "What would you say, my good woman, if I were to tell you that Patrick Henry fled with the rest of us?"
>
> "Patrick Henry!" she answered angrily, "I should tell you there wasn't a word of truth in it! Patrick Henry would never do such a cowardly thing."
>
> "But this is Patrick Henry," said Judge Tyler.
>
> The old woman was astonished; but she stammered and pulled at her apron string, and said: "Well, if that's Patrick Henry, it must be all right. Come in, and ye shall have the best I have in the house."[18]

Patrick Henry remained in public life after the War of Independence. He returned to the governorship in 1784, was re-elected to a

---

18. Burton, *The Story of Patrick Henry*; and William Wirt Henry, *Patrick Henry*; quoted by ibid., p. 288.

fifth term in 1785, and served in the House of Burgesses from 1787 to 1790.

Like many of his day, Henry saw the need to strengthen the federal government to correct the weaknesses of the Articles of Confederation.[19] However, largely because he opposed Congress's proposal to surrender navigation rights on the Mississippi River to Spain for twenty-five or thirty years, he refused to serve as a delegate to the Constitutional Convention of 1787.[20] This proposal, which limited the rights of the southern states, increased Henry's fear of centralized power.

When the Constitution was sent to the states for ratification, Henry was firm in his opposition. He fought the Constitution with both courage and eloquence, even though it was a battle he was almost certain to lose. Tyler writes:

> . . . within the convention itself, at the opening of the session, it was claimed by the friends of the new government that they then outnumbered their opponents by at least fifty votes. Their great champion in debate was James Madison, who was powerfully assisted, first or last, by Edmund Pendleton, John Marshall, George Nicholas, Francis Corbin, George Wythe, James Innes, General Henry Lee, and especially by that same Governor Randolph who, after denouncing the Constitution for "features so odious" that he could not "agree to it," had finally swung completely around to its support.
>
> Against all this array of genius, learning, character, logical acumen, and eloquence, Patrick Henry held the field as protagonist for twenty-three days,—his chief lieutenants in the fight being Mason, Grayson, and John Dawson, with occasional help from Harrison, Monroe, and Tyler. Upon him alone fell the brunt of the battle. Out of the twenty-three days of that splendid tourney there were but five days in which he did not take the floor. . . . in the aggregate, his speeches constitute nearly one quarter of the entire book,—a book of six hundred and sixty-three pages.
>
> Any one who has fallen under the impression, so industriously propagated by the ingenious enmity of Jefferson's old age, that Patrick Henry was a man of but meagre information and of extremely slender intellectual resources, ignorant especially of law, of political science, and of history, totally lacking in logical power and in precision of statement, with nothing to offset these deficiencies excepting a strange gift of overpowering, dithyrambic eloquence, will find it hard, as he turns over the leaves on which are recorded the

19. Ibid., pp. 315–16.
20. Ibid., pp. 316–18.

debates of the Virginia convention, to understand just how such a person could have made the speeches which are there attributed to Patrick Henry, or how a mere rhapsodist could have thus held his ground, in close hand-to-hand combat, for twenty-three days, against such antagonists, on all the difficult subjects of law, political science, and history involved in the Constitution of the United States,—while showing at the same time every quality of good generalship as a tactician and as a party leader. "There has been, I am aware," says an eminent historian of the Constitution, "a modern scepticism of Patrick Henry's abilities; but I cannot share it. . . . The manner in which he carried on the opposition to the Constitution in the convention of Virginia, for nearly a whole month, shows that he possessed other powers besides those of great natural eloquence."[21]

Henry argued that the new Constitution created a central government that was too powerful and unchecked; for example, there was no limit on the number of terms a person could be elected President, and a President could easily make himself king with the army at his disposal. Furthermore, the Constitution contained no bill of rights by which individual liberties could be safeguarded. In some ways Henry possessed greater foresight than his opponents—given the expanded and expanding scope of federal power, the mushrooming growth of the executive branch replete with its multiplying agencies which had little accountability to the public, and a virtually unchecked federal judiciary.

But the Constitution passed 87 to 79—far short of the fifty-vote majority its proponents had boasted at the start of the convention. But Henry did succeed in persuading the delegates to approve resolutions calling for amendments to the Constitution in the form of a bill of rights. Henry also advised those of his supporters who threatened violence if the Constitution was ratified, to peaceably submit to the new Constitution, and to work for passage of amendments which would safeguard personal liberty.

A short time later Henry returned to his family, his farm, and the practice of law, having seriously jeopardized his own finances by his unpaid public service. He declined appointments to serve on the U.S. Senate, as Secretary of State, as Chief Justice of the Supreme Court, and also to serve for a sixth term as governor of Virginia. He finally agreed to allow himself to be elected to the Virginia General Assembly; but he died on June 6 before he could take office.

21. Tyler, *Patrick Henry*, 320–22.

Henry's public life, character, and stature were summarized by George Mason, a leading delegate to the Constitutional Convention:

> He is by far the most powerful speaker I have ever heard. Every word he says not only engages, but commands the attention, and your passions are no longer your own when he addresses them. But his eloquence is the smallest part of his merit. He is, in my opinion, the first man upon this continent, as well in abilities as public virtues; and had he lived in Rome about the time of the first Punic war, when the Roman people had arrived at their meridian glory, and their virtue not tarnished, Mr. Henry's talents must have put him at the head of that glorious commonwealth.[22]

A Great Christian

The most important aspect of Patrick Henry's life was its spiritual dimension. Henry's sometime rival, John Randolph of Roanoke, said of him, "Patrick Henry was not less admirable as a man than as an orator, for his religious convictions were even profounder than his political, and he was irreproachably faithful, besides, to every obligation of civic, social, and domestic life."[23] *Encyclopedia Britannica,*[24] *Encyclopedia Americana,*[25] *World Book,*[26] and *Collier's Encyclopedia*[27] fail to mention Henry's religious convictions, except (in some) in brief references to the "Parson's cause" in which Henry is wrongly portrayed as an enemy of the church—actually Henry was an Anglican and took the case out of opposition to the worldliness and corruption of the clergy and in sympathy for the rights of Dissenters.

Henry's religious beliefs were also misrepresented in his own day. Late in life he wrote to his daughter:

> Amongst other strange things said of me, I hear it is said by the deists that I am one of the number; and indeed, that some good people think I am no Christian. This thought gives me much more pain than the appellation of Tory; because I think religion of infinitely higher importance than politics; and I find much cause to reproach myself that I have lived so long, and have given no decided and public proofs

22. George Mason, Letter to Mr. Cockburn, dated May 26, 1774; quoted by ibid., pp. 421–22.
23. John Randolph: quoted by ibid., p. 66.
24. *Encyclopedia Britannica: Macropaedia—Knowledge in Depth,* s.v. "Henry, Patrick."
25. *Encyclopedia Americana,* s.v. "Henry, Patrick."
26. *World Book Encyclopedia.*
27. *Collier's Encyclopedia,* s.v. "Henry, Patrick."

of my being a Christian. But, indeed, my dear child, this is a character which I prize far above all this world has, or can boast.[28]

Patrick Henry gave consistent evidence of his Christian character and convictions throughout his life. His faith can be traced back to his early childhood. In his immediate family he was exposed to two rich religious traditions. His father was a devout Anglican and a vestryman of St. Paul's Parish, a man of "irreproachable integrity and exemplary piety, and won the full confidence of the community in which he lived."[29] His uncle, Rev. Patrick Henry, served as rector of St. Paul's Parish for forty years,[30] and assisted Colonel Henry in young Patrick's education. Henry once related that he was instructed by his uncle "not only in the catechism but in the Greek and Latin classics," and that Rev. Henry taught him these maxims of conduct, "To be true and just in all my dealings. To bear no malice nor hatred in my heart. To keep my hands from picking and stealing. Not to covet other men's goods; but to learn and labor truly to get my own living, and to do my duty in that state of life unto which it shall please God to call me."[31] Henry's mother was an equal influence. Sarah Henry was a Scottish Presbyterian, known in that day as Dissenters. Her son-in-law, Colonel Samuel Meredith, wrote upon her death, "Never have I known a Christian character equal to hers."[32] Henry acquired his father's love of the church, his mother's zeal and Calvinist doctrine, and the piety and character of both. Patrick attended services with his mother and heard the Dissenting ministers at Morris' reading house and Hanover Church, later known as Pole Green Presbyterian Church. For eleven years he heard the preaching of Samuel Davies, a follower of John Knox, who was a strong advocate of civil rights and liberties and preached Calvinist doctrine. Henry's mother would ask her son to repeat the sermon text and summarize Rev. Davies' sermon on the way home from church meetings. Henry's grandson wrote:

> She could have done her son no greater service. Young Patrick from the first showed a high appreciation of this preacher. His sympathetic genius was not only aroused by this preacher, who he ever declared was the greatest orator he ever heard, but he learned from him that

28. Patrick Henry, Letter to daughter Betsy, August 20, 1796; quoted by William Wirt, *Sketches of the Life and Character of Patrick Henry*, Rev. ed. (New York: M'Elrath and Sons, 1835), pp. 402–3.

29. Ibid., p. 7.

30. Ibid., p. 9.

31. Henry; quoted by Tyler, *Patrick Henry*, p. 15.

32. Colonel Samuel Meredith, Letter to Patrick Henry, November 22, 1784; quoted by ibid., p. 299.

robust system of theology which is known as Calvinsim, and which has furnished to the world so many of her greatest characters. . . .[33]

When Patrick was twelve, Rev. Davies delivered a sermon titled "The Curse of Cowardice," which influenced the rest of Henry's life. Campbell concludes, "It was, no doubt, the eloquent Samuel Davies who helped to shape the thinking and oratory of Patrick Henry."[34]

Henry's religious beliefs formed the basis of his political beliefs. His strong faith in God gave him respect for the natural rights of man, for he believed those rights to be God-given. His fear of concentrated, centralized government power was based on his Calvinist recognition of the sinful nature of man. He declared his opposition to the Constitution at the Virginia ratifying convention:

> Where are your checks in this government? Your strongholds will be in the hands of your enemies. It is on a supposition that your American governors shall be honest, that all the good qualities of this government are founded; but its defective and imperfect construction puts it in their power to perpetrate the worst of mischiefs, should they be bad men. And, sir, would not all the world, from the eastern to the western hemispheres, blame our distracted folly in resting our rights upon the contingency of our rulers being good or bad? Show me that age and country where the rights and liberties of the people were placed on the sole chance of their rulers being good men, without a consequent loss of liberty. . . .[35]

Henry's religious beliefs, coupled with his early exposure to religious Dissenters, led him to champion religious liberty. The Anglican Church was the established church in Virginia and most of the southern colonies; everyone was required to pay taxes to support it and, in some areas, attendance was compulsory. Dissenters were required to register their meeting houses, and only a limited number were permitted. Dissenting ministers had to be licensed, and in some instances they were not allowed to preach or conduct weddings unless they agreed to accept Anglican ordination.[36] Henry was an Anglican, but he:

> . . . had no patience with the favored position of the Anglican

33. William Wirt Henry; quoted by Campbell, *Patrick Henry*, p. 18.
34. Ibid., p. 18.
35. Patrick Henry, Virginia Ratifying Convention Debates; quoted by Tyler, *Patrick Henry*, p. 328.
36. Chandler and Thamse; cited by Campbell, *Patrick Henry*, p. 17.

Church. . . . Henry traveled many weary miles, riding from courthouse to courthouse, through rain and snow, denouncing all such
practices of the established church. "He often listened to the
Dissenters, while they were waging their steady and finally effectual
war against the burthenes of the established church and from a
repetition of his sympathy with the history of their sufferings, he
unlocked the human heart, and transferred into civil discussions
many of the bold licenses which prevailed in the religious.[37]

In *Baptists in Virginia*, Semple writes of Henry's efforts to defend
the Baptists against persecution, particularly in Judge Pendleton's
court in Caroline County:

> . . . they were so fortunate as to interest in their behalf the
> celebrated Patrick Henry; being always a friend of liberty, he only
> needed to be informed of their oppression; without hesitation he
> stepped forward to their relief. From that time until the day of their
> complete emancipation from the shackles of tyranny, the Baptists
> found in Patrick Henry an unwavering friend. May his name descend
> to posterity with unsullied honor![38]

One Baptist minister, Rev. John Weatherford, was jailed for five
months in Chesterfield County for the "crime" of creating a
disturbance by preaching. Henry obtained an order for his release;
but the authorities refused to release him until he paid the costs of
his previous imprisonment. The minister was finally released when
an anonymous donor paid the fees for him. Twenty years later Rev.
Weatherford learned that Patrick Henry had paid his jail fees as well
as represented him.[39]

Henry took a leading role in the preparation and passage of the
Virginia Declaration of Rights in 1776. He prepared the sections
which called for the free, unfettered exercise of religion.[40] In 1784
Henry supported a "Bill Establishing a Provision for Teachers of the
Christian Religion," with the understanding that it would apply
equally to all Christian religions, because "the general diffusion of
Christian knowledge hath a natural tendency to correct the morals
of men, restrain their vices, and preserve the peace of society. . . ."[41] This brought him into conflict with James Madison, who
wrote the "Memorial and Remonstrance against Religious Assess-

---

37. Henry; quoted by ibid., pp. 100–1.
38. Semple; quoted by ibid., p. 101.
39. Henry; cited by ibid., p. 102.
40. Ibid., pp. 228–32.
41. Leo Pfeffer, *Church, State and Freedom* (Boston: Beacon Press, 1953), pp. 97–98.

ments" in opposition to this proposal. The bill had to pass the legislature three times in order to become law. Henry narrowly defeated Madison twice, but Madison delayed the third reading until 1785. In the meantime Henry was elected governor, and Madison was able to defeat the bill on its third reading with Henry out of the legislature.[42] Although he had served as a Colonel in the Continental Army, Henry also worked to secure exemption from military service for Quakers.

Henry's Christian conscience was troubled by the slave trade. He could not run his plantations without slaves, but also saw the problems associated with releasing slaves in a slave economy. He kept his slaves, but his agony over the problem is reflected in a 1773 letter to Robert Pleasants:

> I take this opportunity to acknowledge the receit of Anthony Benezet's Book against the slave trade. I thank you for it. It is not a little surprising that the professors of Christianity, whose chief excellence consists in softening the human heart, and in cherishing and improving its finer feelings, should encourage a practice so totally repugnant to the first impressions of right and wrong. . . . Is it not amazing, that at a time when the rights of humanity are defined and understood with precision in a country above all others fond of liberty, that in such an age and in such a country, we find men professing a religion the most humane, mild, meek, gentle and generous, adopting a Principle as repugnant to humanity, as it is inconsistent with the Bible and destructive to liberty?
>
> . . . Would any one believe that I am master of slaves of my own purchase? I am drawn along by the general inconvenience of living without them. I will not, I cannot justify it. However culpable my conduct, I will so far pay my devoir to virtue, as to own the excellence and rectitude of her precepts and to lament my want of conformity to them.
>
> I believe a time will come when an opportunity will be offered to abolish this lamentable evil. . . . If we cannot reduce this wished-for reformation to practice, let us treat the unhappy victims with lenity, it is the furthest advance we can make toward justice. It is a debt we owe to the purity of our Religion to show that it is at variance with that law which warrants slavery.
>
> I know not when to stop. I would say many things on this subject, a serious review of which gives gloomy perspective to future times.[43]

---

42. Ibid.
43. Henry; quoted by Campbell, *Patrick Henry*, pp. 99–100.

Henry also called for humane treatment of the American Indians and stressed the need to bring them to Jesus Christ, even advocating intermarriage as a means toward that end.[44] Patrick Henry's belief in the God-given rights of free men led him to feel that neither slaves nor the economy should be restricted. "Fetter not commerce, sir. Let her be as free as air; she will range the whole creation, and return on the wings of the four winds of heaven, to bless the land with plenty."[45]

God-given liberty was the touchstone of Patrick Henry's philosophy. Liberty was the condition in which God created man; liberty is the condition to which God has called man; liberty is the condition to which the God-given rights of man entitle him; liberty is the condition in which man is best able to respond to God and serve him. Tyranny, the great enemy of liberty, has its roots in human sin and evil. Throughout history Calvinists have been champions of human liberty; believing in the sovereignty of God, they reject the tyranny of man. Henry's Calvinist beliefs guided his political career. One factor which led Henry to detest the French Revolution was its anti-Christian character:

> As regards his religious faith, Patrick Henry, while never ostentatious of it, was always ready to avow it, and to defend it. The French alliance during our Revolution, and our close intercourse with France immediately afterward, hastened among us the introduction of certain French writers who were assailants of Christianity, and who soon set up among the younger and perhaps brighter men of the country the fashion of casting off, as parts of an outworn and pitiful superstition, the religious ideas of their childhood, and even the morality which had found its strongest sanctions in those ideas. Upon all this, Patrick Henry looked with grief and alarm. . . . he determined to confront it, if possible, with an equal diligence; and he then deliberately made himself, while still a Virginia lawyer and politician, a missionary also,—a missionary on behalf of rational and enlightened Christian faith. Thus during his second term as governor he caused to be printed, on his own account, an edition of Soame Jenyn's "View of the Internal Evidence of Christianity;" likewise, an edition of Butler's "Analogy;" and thenceforward, assailed as they were by the fashionable scepticism, this illustrious colporteur was active in the defense of Christianity, not only by his own sublime and persuasive arguments, but by the distribution, as the fit occasion offered, of one or the other of these two books.[46]

44. Tyler, *Patrick Henry*, p. 293.
45. Ibid., p. 293.
46. Ibid., pp. 393–94.

Henry was so disturbed by Thomas Paine's "Age of Reason," that he wrote an elaborate defense of Christianity which he directed his wife to destroy because he was unsatisfied with his rebuttals. However, some who saw it described it as "the most eloquent and unanswerable argument in defense of the Bible which was ever written."[47]

Christianity was closely interwoven in Henry's personal life. Throughout his life he was extremely close to his family, even though the demands of public life often forced him to be away. His grandson, Patrick Henry Fontaine, wrote that he was "very abstemious in his diet, and used no wine or alcoholic stimulants." Disturbed by the rise of drunkenness after the war, Henry tried to introduce into this country a low-alcohol form of beer from Scotland and as an example he always served it while he was governor.[48]

Fontaine related that his grandfather was a confirmed Episcopalian [Anglican], "baptized and made a member of it early in life," and that he "lived and died an exemplary member of it." Fontaine also said that Patrick Henry regularly spent "one hour every day . . . in private devotion. His hour of prayer was the close of the day, including sunset . . . and during that sacred hour, none of his family intruded upon his privacy."[49] He studied the Bible at length, and read sermon notes "every Sunday evening to his family; after which they all joined in sacred music while he accompanied them on the violin."[50] His widow related that Patrick Henry received "the communion as often as an opportunity was offered, and on such occasions always fasted until after he had communicated, and spent the day in the greatest retirement. This he did both while governor and afterward."[51] Roger Atkinson described Henry as "moderate and mild, and in religious matters a saint; but the very devil in politics; a son of thunder. He will shake the Senate."[52] William Wirt Henry said that Patrick Henry "looked to the restraining and elevating principles of Christianity as the hope of his

47. Ibid., pp. 394–95. Tyler cites a manuscript by Henry's grandson, Patrick Henry Fontaine, one by Henry's grandson William Wirt Henry, and Meade, *Old Churches*, etc. ii. 12.

48. Patrick Henry Fontaine, Manuscript; quoted by Tyler, *Patrick Henry*, p. 386.

49. Patrick Henry Fontaine, Manuscript; quoted by ibid., pp. 392-93.

50. James W. Alexander, *The Life of Archibald Alexander* (New York: 1854), p. 193; quoted by ibid., p. 391.

51. William Meade, *Old Churches, Ministers and Families of Virginia* (Philadelphia: 1872), II:12; quoted by ibid., p. 392.

52. Roger Atkinson, Letter quoted by Meade; quoted by ibid., pp. 102-3.

country's institutions."[53] In Fontaine's words, he gave himself to "earnest efforts to establish true Christianity in our country."[54]

Henry freely shared his Christian faith with his family. In 1786, he wrote his sister Ann on her husband Colonel Christian's death:

> I am at a loss how to address you my dearest sister. Would to God I could say something to give relief to the dearest of women and sisters. . . . This is one of the trying scenes in which the Christian is eminently superior to all others, and finds a refuge that no misfortune can take away. To this refuge let my dearest sister fly with humble resignation. I think I can see some traces of a kind Providence to you and the children in giving you a good son-in-law, so necessary at this time to take charge of your affairs. . . . For indeed, my dearest sister, you never knew how much I loved you and your husband. My heart is full. Perhaps I may never see you in this world. O may we meet in heaven, to which the merits of Jesus will carry those who love and serve him. Heaven will, I trust, give you its choicest comfort and preserve your family. Such is the prayer of him who thinks it his honor and pride to be
>
> Your Affectionate Brother,
> Patrick Henry[55]

Henry's health deteriorated in 1799. At George Washington's insistence he consented to stand for election to the Virginia legislature. He was so weak that he was unable to go to the polls on election day, but he was elected by a huge majority. Two weeks later he learned that the U.S. Senate had asked him to serve as U.S. Minister to France; from his sickbed he wrote to President Adams declining the appointment. He was aware that he was likely to die, and he declared to his family, "Oh, how wretched should I be at this moment, if I had not made my peace with God!"[56]

He died on June 6, 1799, at the age sixty-three of an intestinal ailment known as intussusception, surrounded by his loving family. At no time was Henry's faith more apparent than the hour of his death. Fontaine was present and gave an eloquent account of his last minutes.

> On June 6, all other remedies having failed, Dr. Cabell proceeded to administer to him a dose of liquid mercury. Taking the vial in his hand, and looking at it for a moment, the dying man said: "I

53. Henry; quoted by Campbell, *Patrick Henry*, p. 415.
54. Fontaine, Manuscript; quoted by Tyler, *Patrick Henry*, p. 415.
55. Henry; quoted by Campbell, *Patrick Henry*, pp. 271–72.
56. Henry; quoted by ibid., p. 417.

suppose, doctor, this is your last resort." The doctor replied: "I am sorry to say, governor, that it is. Acute inflammation of the intestines has already taken place; and unless it is removed mortification will ensue, if it has not already commenced, which I fear." "What will be the effect of this medicine?" said the old man. "It will give you immediate relief, or—" the kindhearted doctor could not finish the sentence. His patient took up the word: "You mean, doctor, that it will give relief or prove fatal immediately?"

The doctor answered: "You can only live a very short time without it, and it may possibly relieve you." Then Patrick Henry said, "Excuse me, doctor, for a few minutes;" and drawing over his eyes a silken cap which he usually wore, and still holding the vial in his hand, he prayed, in clear words, a simple child-like prayer for his family, for his country, and for his own soul then in the presence of death. Afterward, in perfect calmness, he swallowed the medicine. Meanwhile Dr. Cabell, who greatly loved him, went out upon the lawn, and in his grief threw himself down upon the earth under one of the trees weeping bitterly. Soon, when he had sufficiently mastered himself, the doctor came back to his patient, whom he found calmly watching the congealing of the blood under his finger-nails and speaking words of love and peace to his family, who were weeping around his chair. Among other things, he told them that he was thankful for that goodness of God, which having blessed him all his life, was then permitting him to die without any pain. Finally, fixing his eyes with much tenderness on his dear friend, Dr. Cabell, with whom he had formerly held many arguments respecting the Christian religion, he asked the doctor to observe how great a reality and benefit that religion was to a man about to die. And after Patrick Henry had spoken to his beloved physician those few words in praise of something which, having never failed him in all his life before, did not then fail him in his very last need of it, he continued to breathe very softly for some moments; after which they who were looking upon him, saw that his life had departed.[57]

Henry's last will and testament, penned in his own hand, contained one final affirmation of faith, "This is all the inheritance I can give to my dear family. The religion of Christ can give them one which will make them rich indeed."[58]

---

57. Patrick Henry Fontaine, Manuscript; quoted by Tyler, *Patrick Henry*, pp. 421–23. Campbell, *Patrick Henry*, pp. 417–18.

58. Certified copy of Last Will and Testament of Patrick Henry; quoted by Tyler, *Patrick Henry*, p. 395.

17 Roger Sherman

R oger Sherman has a distinct place among America's founding fathers—he is the only one who signed all four major documents which formed the foundation for American government: the 1774 Articles of Association, the 1776 Declaration of Independence, the 1777 Articles of Confederation, and the 1787 U.S. Constitution.

Roger Sherman, along with Thomas Jefferson, John Adams, Robert Livingston, and Benjamin Franklin, served on the congressional committee that drafted the Declaration of Independence. Sherman also served on the committee that drafted the Articles of Confederation. At the Constitutional Convention Roger Sherman proposed the Great Compromise which established that one house of Congress was to be chosen by the people proportionate to population while the other house was to be chosen by the state legislatures with each state having an equal vote. Lewis Henry Boutrell says that by laying the groundwork for resolving this issue, "Roger Sherman will ever be conspicuous as the statesman to whose wise and conciliatory spirit it was largely due that the Federal Convention was not held in vain."[1]

At age sixty-six Roger Sherman was the second oldest man at the Convention; only Benjamin Franklin was older. He brought to the

1. Lewis Henry Boutell, "Roger Sherman in the Federal Convention," *Annual Report of the American Historical Association for the Year 1893* (Washington, D.C.: Government Printing Office, 1894), pp. 231, 247.

Convention a broad range of experience, native intellect, and good common sense. Sherman had risen from poverty to become a shoemaker, surveyer, lawyer, justice of the peace, judge, shopkeeper, member of the Connecticut General Assembly, member of the Governor's Council, and Congressman.

John Adams described Sherman as "an old Puritan, as honest as an angel and as firm in the cause of American independence as Mount Atlas."[2] Adams added, "Destitute of all literary and scientific education, but such as he acquired by his own exertions, he was one of the most sensible men in the world. The clearest head and steadiest heart."[3] Patrick Henry described him as, along with George Mason, the greatest statesman he ever knew, and said of Congress, "the first men in that body were Washington, Richard Henry Lee, and Roger Sherman."[4] Historian Forrest Morgan says Sherman "was noted and esteemed for his calmness of nature and evenness of disposition. His rationality was his distinguishing trait: common-sense in him rose almost to genius."[5] His plain clothes and close-cropped hair amid a society of polished wigs and elegant dress made him stand out in Congress and at the Convention. A South Carolina delegate to the Convention noted Sherman's uniqueness and described him as "awkward" and possessed of "that strange New England cant which runs through his public as well as his private speaking" and makes "everything that is connected with him grotesque and laughable." However, he said, Sherman:

> deserves infinite praise,—no man has a better Heart or a clearer Head. . . . I am told he sits on the Bench in Connecticut, and is very correct in the discharge of his Judicial functions. In the early part of his life he was a Shoe-maker,—but, despising the lowness of his condition, he turned Almanack maker, and so progressed upwards to a Judge. He has been several years a Member of Congress, and discharged the duties of his Office with honor and credit to himself, and advantage to the State he represented.[6]

2. John Adams; quoted by Dr. M. E. Bradford, *A Worthy Company: Brief Lives of the Framers of the United States Constitution* (Marlborough, New Hampshire: Plymouth Rock Foundation, 1982), p. 22.

3. John Adams to John Sanderson, November 19, 1822; quoted by Christopher Collier, *Roger Sherman's Connecticut* (Middletown, Connecticut: Wesleyan University Press, 1971), p. 283.

4. Patrick Henry; quoted by Collier, *Roger Sherman's Connecticut*, p. 193.

5. Forrest Morgan, *Connecticut as Colony and as State* (Hartford: Publishing Society of Connecticut, 1904), II:201.

6. Pierce Butler or William Pierce; quoted by Roger Sherman Boardman, *Roger Sherman: Signer and Statesman* (New York: Da Capo Press, 1971), pp. 231–32.

Sherman delivered 138 speeches at the Constitutional Convention; only Gouverneur Morris, James Wilson, and James Madison spoke more often. Rufus W. Griswold wrote:

> He is no orator, and yet not a speaker in the convention is more effective; the basis of his power is found, first, in the thorough conviction of his *integrity*; his countrymen are satisfied that he is a *good man*, a real patriot, with no little or sinister or personal ends in view; next, he addresses the reason, with arguments, logically arrayed, so clear, so plain, so forcible, that, as they have convinced him, they carry conviction to others who are dispassionate.[7] [emphasis original]

To understand the real Roger Sherman it is necessary to examine his Calvinist spirit. Roger Sherman Boardman wrote, ". . . the Puritan traditions of the earlier day were born in him, and an upright and somewhat unimaginative Puritan we find him throughout. Not that he exhibited the narrow, illiberal, sour aspect we ascribe (with scant justice) to this name. Sherman was open-minded and forward-looking. But the stern sense of duty, the 'New England Conscience,' was ever his guiding star."[8]

Roger Sherman was born in New Milford on April 19, 1721, to William and Mehetabel Sherman, the third of seven children. Two of his brothers became ministers of the gospel. His parents regularly attended the Congregational Church, though they were not members. The Sabbath was faithfully observed in the Sherman home.[9] Roger learned to read using the Bible, some of Cotton Mather's works, and the Westminster Catechism. He probably attended the community schoolhouse which used the Christian-oriented textbook the *New England Primer*.[10]

The First Great Awakening swept through the nation when Roger Sherman was a young man. Some of the revival's effects wore off with time, but others remained. Connecticut returned to the faith of its founders. Theology and politics became divided between "Old Lights" and "New Lights." Generally, Old Lights opposed the Awakening as too emotional and unstable, with excessive emphasis on conversion and not enough on long-term consistent Christian living. New Lights favored the Awakening and believed the conver-

7. Rufus W. Griswold, *The Republican Court* (Appleton, 1855), p. 51; quoted by Boardman, *Roger Sherman*, p. 232.

8. Ibid., p. 64.

9. Ibid., pp. 7, 8, 16; Collier, *Roger Sherman's Connecticut*, p. 43.

10. Boardman, *Roger Sherman*, pp. 16–19.

sion experience it stressed was necessary for salvation. Some characterize the Old Lights as conservative and the New Lights as radical, but both were conservative in believing in the Bible as the Word of God and in the need for orthodox Christian theology.

Roger Sherman favored the Old Lights at first, believing that the "threatenings of divine law against impenitent sinners . . . are [as important] as the promises of the Gospel."[11] But he gradually moved toward the New Light position. When he moved to New Haven, Connecticut, in 1761, he joined the White Haven Church which was associated with the New Lights.[12] The church he belonged to in New Milford supported the Old Light position.

Sherman was an active and faithful worker in both churches. He served as clerk, deacon, and member of the school committee for the New Milford church—several of his children were baptized there.[13] He served as moderator of the annual meeting, chairman of the committee on pulpit supply, and in other capacities at the White Haven church. Rev. Jonathan Edwards, Jr., son of the famous theologian Jonathan Edwards, became pastor of White Haven Church in 1769 and remained there until after Sherman's death. Dr. Edwards referred to Sherman as his "great and good friend," and said concerning Sherman's theology, "He could with reputation to himself and improvement to others converse on the most important subjects of theology. I confess myself to have been often entertained, and in the general course of my long and intimate acquaintance with him to have been much improved by his observations on the principal subjects of doctrinal and practical divinity."[14] Sherman was Edwards's strongest supporter when Edwards faced opposition from the congregation over his insistence that a personal profession of faith and a convincing statement of personal regeneration was necessary before baptism. When Edwards accused a New Haven councilman of believing in universal salvation, Sherman backed Edwards, arguing that universalism is "very erroneous and if believed will tend to relax the restraints on vice arising from the threatenings of the divine law against impenitent sinners . . . I think we are as much bound to believe the threatenings as the promises of the gospel."[15]

In 1789 Sherman wrote a sermon titled "A Short Sermon on the

11. Roger Sherman; quoted by Bradford, *A Worthy Company*, p. 29.
12. Boardman, *Roger Sherman*, pp. 71–73.
13. Collier, *Roger Sherman's Connecticut*, p. 35.
14. Jonathan Edwards, "God a Refuge and Help"; quoted by ibid., p. 328.
15. Roger Sherman to David Austin, March 1, 1790; quoted by ibid., p. 327.

Duty of Self-Examination Preparatory to Receiving the Lord's Supper." Declaring that "Self-examination previous to an approach to the holy supper of the Lord is a necessary, tho' I fear too much neglected duty," he listed five points on which the believer should examine himself: his "knowledge of the Gospel scheme of salvation," his repentance, his faith in Jesus Christ, his love to God and man, and his obedience to the commands of God. He urged Christians to confess their sins and renew their surrender to Christ, "admiring and thankfully acknowledging the riches of redeeming love, and earnestly imploring that divine assistance which may enable us to live no more to ourselves, but to him who loved us and gave himself to die for us."[16]

Sherman was closely associated with Yale College. He contributed generously to the support of the college chapel, served as the college treasurer, and fought to maintain clergy control over the college, believing that such control was necessary to maintain the Christian character of the institution. Sherman's daughter Martha married Rev. Jeremiah Day, who served as President of Yale from 1817 to 1846. Rev. Timothy Dwight, also a president of Yale, described Sherman as "profoundly versed in theology" and declared that "he held firmly the doctrines of the Reformation."[17] Boardman notes that a copy of the 1788 creed of White Haven Church exists in Sherman's handwriting. It contains the basic doctrines of the Reformation, including the Trinity, the Scriptures as a revelation from God, original sin, eternal punishment for unrepentant sinners, foreordination, salvation for all "willing to accept the gospel offer," the perseverance of the saints, the sacraments as an aid to growth in grace, the resurrection of the dead, the final judgment, and a visible church consisting only of those who profess their faith in Christ (a New Light doctrine).[18]

Sherman did not look for debate about religious issues, but he did not hesitate to speak up for what he believed to be the truth, even if it meant disagreeing with a clergyman. He took a firm stand against Hopkinsianism, the theological system of Rev. Samuel Hopkins of the Congregational Church in Newport, Rhode Island. Hopkins insisted that self-love was the source of moral evil, and therefore one should even be willing to give up his eternal salvation

16. Roger Sherman, "A Short Sermon on the Duty of Self Examination Preparatory to Receiving the Lord's Supper," 1789; quoted by ibid., p. 320.

17. Timothy Dwight, *Statistical Account of the City of New Haven* (New Haven, Connecticut: Connecticut Academy of Arts and Sciences, 1811); quoted by Boardman, *Roger Sherman*, pp. 318–19.

18. Ibid., p. 319.

and suffer eternal damnation for the glory of God. Sherman wrote to Hopkins from New York while Congress was in session. He recognized that there was an evil side to self-love but emphasized God's sovereign grace: "That a God of infinite Goodness can (through the atonement) have mercy on whom he will, consistent with the honor of his Law and Government and of all his perfections, is a much better ground of hope than the denial of self-love."[19] Hopkins apparently based his doctrine on Paul's words: "For I could wish that myself were accursed from Christ for my brethren" (Rom 9:3). Sherman responded:

> St. Paul's wish, Rom. 9,3, taken literally I think can't be vindicated. 1. Because it would have been opposite to the revealed will of God concerning him, he being a true Saint, could not be accursed from Christ. 2. It could have been of no use to his brethren—His [Paul's] damnation could not atone for their sins; and there was a sufficient atonement made by Jesus Christ. . . .

Sherman urged Hopkins to reconsider this doctrine because of the bad effects it could have on his hearers, stating that it could "give uneasiness to pious minds;" it could cause "Pious-orthodox Christians who think it an Error [to become] prejudiced against the books that contain it, however orthodox and useful in other respects;" and "It will give the enemies of truth occasion to speak reproachfully of the authors of such books, and prejudice the minds of people against them, and so obstruct their usefulness."[20]

The concept of self-love found its way into much of Roger Sherman's thinking. Self-love is not bad in itself, he thought. God planted it in man's heart for man's preservation. The fall of man perverted self-love, into an instrument for greed and exploitation. In 1778 Sherman wrote, "When we see self-love, the first principle planted in the human breast by the all-wise Creator for our benefit and preservation, through misapplication and corruption, applied to our destruction, we feel the necessity of correcting so pernicious an error and directing the operation of it in such a manner as that our self and social love may be the same."[21] This concept of enlightened self-interest formed much of the basis for the thinking behind the Constitution.

19. Ibid.
20. Roger Sherman to Samuel Hopkins, August 2, 1790, October 1790; quoted by ibid., pp. 314–18.
21. Roger Sherman, 1778; quoted by Collier, *Roger Sherman's Connecticut*, p. 177.

Roger Sherman shared his religious faith with his family. On May 30, 1770, he wrote to his wife Rebecca:

> This is your birthday. Mine was the 30th of last month. May we so number our days as to apply our Hearts to wisdom: that is, true Religion. Psalm 90:12. ["So teach us to number our days, that we may get us a heart of wisdom."]
> I remain affectionately yours,
>   Roger Sherman[22]

Sherman was also concerned that his children know and love the Word of God. He would buy a new Bible at the opening of each session in Congress, use it daily in his private devotions throughout the session, and when the session adjourned he would present it to one of his children upon his return to New Haven.[23]

Sherman's son William died at age 37. Sherman's daughter Elizabeth wrote to assure her father that before William died, he "expressed penitence for sins and his belief of a necessity of the atonement by Christ. . . ."[24] Sherman was in Congress in New York at the time and wrote to his wife, "It is my earnest Prayer that this Providence may be Suitably regarded by me and all the family—and especially the surviving children, of our family and his [William's] child—that may be excited to be always in an actual readiness for death." Even though the grandchildren were baptized, Sherman said, for those who have come of age, "it is indispensably necessary for them to give their cordial consent to the covenant of grace and that it is their duty to make a public profession of Religion and attend all the ordinances of the Gospel. . . ."[25]

Roger Sherman always loved and cared about his church. When he was in Congress in New York, he heard that Rev. Edwards had aroused considerable opposition at the White Haven Church by insisting on personal regeneration. Sherman was concerned and wrote to fellow congregation member Simeon Baldwin:

> . . . I wish to be informed whether there is any new difficulty arisen, and how the members stand affected to Dr. Edwards. . . . I hope all the well wishers to pure religion will use their influence to preserve Peace, and avoid calling Society meetings unnecessarily, as I think it

22. Roger Sherman to Rebecca Sherman, May 30, 1770; quoted by Boardman, *Roger Sherman*, p. 109.

23. Ibid., p. 322.

24. Elizabeth Sherman to Roger Sherman, 1789; quoted by ibid., pp. 324–25.

25. Roger Sherman to Rebecca Sherman, June 29, 1789; quoted by Collier, *Roger Sherman's Connecticut*, p. 321.

would only promote dissention. Our Savior says "Wo to the world because of offences; but wo to that man by whom the offence cometh." I am willing that anything I have written should be made known if it will do any good, not only to the friendly but to the disaffected if there be any such—I feel well affected to all the members, and wish to have cordial harmony restored. Perhaps there is nothing more pleasing to the adversary of mankind than discord among Christian brethren.[26]

Sherman believed the Scriptures should be applied to current problems. When faced with the divorce of one of his children, he wrote to President Witherspoon at the College of New Jersey asking about scriptural justification for divorce. Rev. Benjamin Trumbull had written that fornication was the only basis for divorce, but Sherman suggested to Witherspoon that willful desertion set forth by Paul in I Corinthians 7:15, may also be grounds for divorce. Sherman mentioned that Connecticut law allowed for divorce in such circumstances. Witherspoon wrote back, agreeing that willful desertion was a valid ground for divorce.[27]

Sherman believed the law of God applied to American society. While in Congress, he objected to a War Committee report which recommended 500 lashes as a punishment to be imposed by courts-martial. Sherman successfully argued that Deuteronomy 25:3 limits the number of lashes to forty: "Forty stripes he may give him, and not exceed: lest, if he should exceed, and beat him above these with many stripes, then thy brother should seem vile unto thee."[28] In revising the laws of Connecticut, Sherman included a declaration of rights holding that life, property, wife, or children could not be taken away except under the laws of the state or "by some clear plain rule warranted by the word of God"; however, the lower house of the legislature, perhaps recognizing difficulties in referring to the Bible generally without enacting specific provisions of it into law, substituted "unless clearly warranted by the Laws of this State."[29]

Roger Sherman was not a strict separationist in church-state relations. Boardman says, "his faith in the new republic was largely because he felt it was founded on Christianity as he understood

26. Roger Sherman to Simeon Baldwin, February 4, 1790; quoted by Boardman, *Roger Sherman*, p. 322.

27. Roger Sherman to John Witherspoon, July, 1788; John Witherspoon to Roger Sherman, July 25, 1788; cited by ibid., p. 318.

28. Collier, *Roger Sherman's Connecticut*, p. 185.

29. Ibid., p. 196.

it."[30] In 1776, when serving on a congressional committee which wrote instructions for an embassy going to Canada, Sherman included an order that the delegation was "further to declare that we hold sacred the rights of conscience, and may promise to the whole people, solemnly in our name, the free and undisturbed exercise of their religion," but added that all civil rights and the right to hold office were to be extended to persons of any *Christian* denomination.[31] As a judge in New Milford in 1758, Sherman adjudged a defendant guilty of failing to "attend the publick worship of God in any congregation allowed by law in sd New Milford or elsewhere, neither hath he attended the public worship of God in any lawful congregation at any time on ye Lord's day for one month next before sd 29th of January, but did willingly and obstinately, without any lawful or reasonable cause or excuse forbaire and neglect to do the same. . . .", and fined this "criminal" for the offense.[32]

Sherman, a staunch Congregationalist, wrote a letter objecting to Parliament's proposal to appoint an Episcopal bishop over the United States, but added that if such a bishop were "divested of the power annexed to that office by the common law of England," so that he would have no power over the civil or religious interests of other denominations, "then we shall be more easy about this."[33] He noted with pleasure following the surrender of Cornwallis at Yorktown, "The dispatches from General Washington were received yesterday morning, and at two o'clock in the afternoon Congress went in a body to the Lutheran Church where Divine service, suitable to the occasion, was performed by the Rev. Mr. Duffield, one of the chaplains of Congress."[34]

Sherman was an advocate of states' rights at the Constitutional Convention. He believed the masses had insufficient information to make congressional choices, and favored choosing both houses of Congress by state legislatures. However, it was Sherman who suggested the compromise idea of one lower house based on population and elected by the people, and one upper house chosen by the legislatures in which each state has an equal vote. Sherman originally made that suggestion in 1777, when Congress was deliberating on the Articles of Confederation. At that time he said,

30. Boardman, *Roger Sherman*, p. 319.
31. Collier, *Roger Sherman's Connecticut*, p. 129.
32. Boardman, *Roger Sherman*, pp. 56–57.
33. Roger Sherman, 1768; quoted by ibid., pp. 104–5.
34. Roger Sherman and Richard Law, October 25, 1781, to Gov. Trumbull; quoted by ibid., p. 196.

"The vote should be taken two ways; call the Colonies, and call the individuals, and have a majority of both."[35] Thus was the Great Compromise born.

Sherman's fear of concentrated power in the hands of an executive led him to oppose excessive independence for the President. Sherman believed the President should be chosen by Congress and subject to removal by Congress at will; in this way the President's power could be checked. He saw the President as primarily an executive doing the bidding of Congress, rather than as a branch of government equal to Congress. Sherman also opposed the issuance of paper money. He amended the provision that would have given the President complete control over the militia to read that the President commands "the Militia of the several States, when called into the actual service of the U.S.," authored the provision that made congressmen inelligible for appointment to offices for which they had voted to increase the salaries while in office, changed the provision that undecided elections should go to the Senate so that such elections would be decided by the House of Representatives, and authored the basic provision for amending the Constitution. At first Sherman opposed the Bill of Rights because he considered the protection of rights to be a matter of state rather than federal sovereignty; however, he decided in the deliberations that "they will probably be harmless and Satisfactory to those who are Fond of Bill of rights."[36] Sherman seconded Franklin's motion for daily prayer at the Convention; and when the First Amendment was adopted, Sherman argued successfully in favor of a national day of prayer.

Sherman's health began to decline after he served several terms in the new Congress. He died on July 23, 1793. Rev. Jonathan Edwards, Jr., the pastor Sherman loved and supported for many years, preached his eulogy. Edwards spoke of Sherman's theological knowledge and dedication to Christianity, but added:

His proper line was politics. For usefulness and excellence in this line, he was qualified not only by his acute discernment and sound judgment, but especially by his knowledge of human nature. He had a happy talent of judging what was feasible and what was not feasible, or what men would bear, and what they would not bear in government. And he had a rare talent of prudence, or of timing and adapting his measures to the attainment of this end.[37]

35. John Adams; quoted by Collier, *Roger Sherman's Connecticut*, p. 157.
36. Roger Sherman; quoted by ibid., p. 298.
37. Rev. Jonathan Edwards, Jr.; quoted by ibid., p. 332.

As Collier says, to the Puritan mind morality and politics are simply two different aspects of life.[38] God had called Roger Sherman into politics, and throughout his life he was faithful to that calling.

Ezra Stiles summarized Roger Sherman's life well: He had "that Dignity which arises from doing every Thing perfectly right. He was an extraordinary Man—a venerable uncorrupted Patriot."[39]

38. Ibid., p. 12.
39. Ezra Stiles; quoted by ibid., p. 332.

18 Charles Cotesworth Pinckney

A discussion of the founding fathers would be incomplete without a representative of the southern colonies: North Carolina, South Carolina, and Georgia. Charles Cotesworth Pinckney was the leading southern statesman.

Pinckney was a General in the Continental Army; he was also a prisoner of war of the British. As chairman of the committee for the South Carolina Constitution he gained experience drawing up constitutions. At the Convention Pinckney proposed the committee which later suggested the great compromise of a two-house legislature. He was the main speaker for the Constitution at the South Carolina ratifying convention. Pinckney was named U.S. Minister to France under the Washington administration; but at first the French Revolutionary government refused to receive him. They later accepted him, along with Elbridge Gerry and John Marshall. Pinckney issued the famous reply, "No, no, not a sixpence!" when the French pressed him for a loan or gift from the United States in return for France's agreement to refrain from forcibly capturing American ships. Pinckney's sentiments leaned toward the Republicans initially, but his viewpoint gradually changed and he served as the Federalist candidate for President in 1804 and 1808. He also received votes for President in 1800.

"The Pinckneys, like many other South Carolina revolutionary leaders, were of aristocratic birth and politics, closely connected with England by ties of blood, education and business relations. This renders all the more remarkable their attitude in the American Revolution, for which they made great sacrifices."[1]

Charles Cotesworth Pinckney was born in Charleston, South Carolina, on February 14, 1745. His father, also Charles Pinckney, was a respected lawyer, legislator, judge, and a "devout Anglican known for his generous gifts of time and money to the church."[2] He supported the toleration for dissenters of other religions, and contributed to the building of a schoolhouse where blacks were taught reading and religion.[3] Charles Cotesworth's mother, Eliza, was also a devout Christian.

Zahniser describes the Pinckney family as "devout Christians and regular attendants at divine worship," and further summarizes their religious training:

> The children were required at an early age to listen for the sermon text and to find it in the Bible as soon as they returned home from service. They were also expected to memorize the collect for the day, a task that seemed truly formidable to them. This early religious training had a profound impact on the Pinckney children, perhaps more on Charles Cotesworth than on his brother and sister. In later life his piety never seemed labored but arose spontaneously from a mind and heart trained from childhood to love Christ and the church.[4]

The Pinckneys also provided for the academic training of their children. Charles Pinckney built a set of toys to teach his son the alphabet; Charles Cotesworth learned to recognize letters before he could pronounce them. He could spell before he was two years old. Charles took his family to England from 1753-1758 to give them the best education possible. When Charles Cotesworth was thirteen years old his parents and sister returned to Charleston, leaving him and his brother Thomas at school in England. On July 12 of that same year (1758), his father died of a fever. His mother wrote to him and Thomas:

> He has set you a great and good example, may the Lord enable you both to follow it, and may God almighty fulfill all your pius father's prayers upon both of your heads; they were almost incessant for blessings both spiritual and temporal upon you both. . . . His affec-

---

1. *Encyclopedia Britannica*, s.v. "Pinckney, Charles."
2. Marvin R. Zahniser, *Charles Cotesworth Pinckney: Founding Father* (Chapel Hill, North Carolina: University of North Carolina Press, 1967), p. 4.
3. Ibid., p. 5.
4. Ibid., p. 9.

tion for you was as great as ever was upon Earth, and you were good children and deserved it; he thought you so, he blessed and thanked God for you and had most comfortable hopes of you— . . . God Almighty bless guide and protect you, make you his own children, and worth such a father as yours was. . . .[5]

Charles Pinckney spoke of his son in his last will and testament:

And to the end that my beloved son Charles Cotesworth may the better be enabled to become the head of his family, and prove not only of service and advantage to his country, but also an honour to his stock and kindred, my order and direction is that my said son be virtuously, religiously and liberally brought up so . . . that he will employ all his future abilities in the service of God and his country, in the cause of virtuous liberty, as well religious as civil, and in support of private right and justice between man and man.[6]

Eliza Pinckney urged her son to follow the Christian way. She wrote, "you must know the welfair of a whole family depends in a great measure on the progress you make in morral Virtue, Religion and Learning." She encouraged him to guard against "those Errors into which you are most easily led by propensity. What I most fear for you is heat of temper. . . ."[7]

Charles Cotesworth attended high school at Westminster in England. There he faced a tough regimen of classes from eight to nine hours every day, with Thursday and Saturday afternoons off, but Bible lessons to be prepared even on Saturday afternoons. His two strongest areas were classical literature and religion. He read such classics as Phaedrus, Martial, Ovid, Homer, and Virgil, studied Latin, Greek, and Hebrew, and translated some of the Psalms. He once commented, apparently in reference to 1 Peter 3:15, that one could not go through Westminster "without being a fair Latin and Greek scholar and being able to assign a reason for the faith that is in you."[8]

After high school, Charles Cotesworth enrolled in Christ Church, part of Oxford University, to study law under the teaching of Sir William Blackstone, the British jurist who systematized the common law of England. As noted earlier, Blackstone was an orthodox Christian who believed natural law was dictated by God Himself.

---

5. Eliza Pinckney, "To my dear Children, Charles and Thomas Pinckney," August, 1758; quoted by ibid., p. 11.
6. Charles Pinckney, Last Will and Testament, 1752; quoted by ibid., p. 3.
7. Eliza Pinckney to Charles Cotesworth Pinckney, April, 1758; quoted by ibid., p. 11.
8. Pinckney, Letter to unknown correspondent, September, 1819; quoted by ibid., p. 13.

Zahniser says, "Pinckney attended the lectures and diligently jotted down four volumes of notes. Blackstone had gained another disciple."[9]

Pinckney continued to study at Oxford after graduation in 1764. For several years, he read widely, attended sessions of Parliament, viewed courtroom trials, etc. He was so conscientious in his studies that his mother, blaming herself for having encouraged such diligent study, urged him to guard his health: "Should I by my over solicitude for your passing thro' life with every advantage, be a means of injuring your consititution, how shall I answer to myself, the hurting of a child so truly dear to me, and deservedly so; who has lived to near twenty-three years of age without once offending me."[10]

Pinckney took a break from his studies at Oxford and toured the Continent, then attended the Royal Military Academy at Caen, France, to study military science—training that proved valuable during the War of Independence. In January 1769 he was admitted to the bar and returned to South Carolina. In December of the same year his career of public service began when he was elected to the South Carolina Commons House of Assembly.

Pinckney identified himself as an American patriot despite his sixteen years in England. When captured during the War of Independence, the British made a futile attempt to win him over to their cause by capitalizing on his English background but Pinckney stated his position: "If I had a vein which did not beat with the love of my country, I myself would open it. If I had a drop of blood that could flow dishonourably, I myself would let it out!"[11]

Besides being a patriot, Pinckney was known as a "sterling Christian."[12] He served for many years as a church vestryman and spent two years as a church warden.[13] He adamantly opposed shortening the Episcopal communion. He believed in the "absolute values of the Christian religion,"[14] and "Throughout his lifetime Pinckney adhered to the practices of the Episcopal Church whose ritual and order suited his temperament well. And as he grew older, he clung increasingly to the ancient practices, to the service and the

9. Ibid., p. 17.

10. Eliza Pinckney to Charles Cotesworth Pinckney, ca. 1767; quoted by ibid., p. 18.

11. Charles Cotesworth Pinckney; quoted by Catherine Dunker Bowen, *Miracle at Philadelphia: The Story of the Constitutional Convention, May to September 1787* (Boston: Little, Brown & Co., 1966), p. 76.

12. Zahniser, *Founding Father*, p. 27.

13. Ibid., p. 30.

14. Ibid., p. 270.

customs exactly as he had known them from his earliest days."[15]
He opposed efforts to shorten the liturgy, insisting that it was not
too long "for those who carry a devout mind to the Church. . . .[16]
He numbered himself among those who "dread innovation in the
service of our Church, and I would much rather hear the sermon
confined to 20 or 30 minutes than any part of our Liturgy be
destroyed."[17]

Although Pinckney was an Anglican, he respected ministers of
other Christian religions and frequently invited them into his home.
His father's last will and testament specified that ten guineas be
charged against his Charleston mansion each year so a minister
could be engaged each May and October to preach a sermon on the
"Greatness and Goodness of God." Every year the Pinckney family
or a minister friend chose the guest preacher, and on the day of the
sermon the town clergymen were invited to the Pinckneys' home
for dinner.[18]

Pinckney developed a close friendship with Rev. Richard Furman, a Baptist minister. He wrote to Rev. Furman around 1790,
"Religion is always venerable, always necessary; and when she is
delineated with the beauty and eloquence she was today in the
[Baptist] church, we are enraptured with her portrait and sensibly
feel that all her ways are ways of pleasantness and all her paths are
paths of peace."[19] Rev. Furman wrote to Pinckney more than three
decades later:

> God has been pleased, dear General to give you Length of Days, with
> the Power and Disposition to do good. The Voice of the Community
> declares, that Respectability and Worth are connected in your
> Character. This is grateful to your Friends. May you continue to live
> as long as Life, on Earth, is desirable; To be the Supporter of pious
> and Benevolent Institutions; to exhibit the Excellences of the Chris-
> tian . . . Character in Acts of private Beneficiance, publick Liberality
> and all that is aminble and Praiseworthy, and at last obtain Glory in
> the Heavens. . . .[20]

Zahniser notes that "Religion was a constant comfort to the old
general in his later years, as were the good opinions and compan-

---

15. Ibid., p. 271.
16. Pinckney to Rev. Christopher Gadsden, August 15, 1816; quoted by ibid., p. 271.
17. Ibid.
18. Ibid., pp. 270–71, 274.
19. Pinckney to Rev. Richard Furman, ca. 1790; quoted by ibid., p. 270.
20. Rev. Richard Furman to Pinckney, October 16, 1823; quoted in ibid., p. 275.

ionship of his many friends."[21] Particularly he valued the friendship of Rev. Furman. "As time passed, the staunch Episcopalian and the fervent Baptist drew close in spirit."[22]

Pinckney manifested his Christian faith both in character and good works. In speaking about Pinckney to Washington, Thomas Lynch, Jr., said, "No man living had a higher spirit, a nicer sense of Honour or a more incorruptible Heart than he has."[23] Even as a youth Pinckney was known for his incorruptibility. In a school dispute at Westminster which involved contradictory evidence, the headmaster turned to Pinckney and said, "I know the strictness of your principles, and your attachment to *truth*. Speak, Pinckney. My decision shall be guided by your sentiment."[24]

He was also known for his kindness. In 1779, when British forces destroyed his brother Thomas' plantation and seriously damaged his mother's home, Charles Cotesworth Pinckney offered to divide his own estate three ways. The same spirit led him to oppose confiscation of British loyalists' property after the war.[25] In retirement he served as: president-general of the Society of the Cincinnati (a war veterans' organization,) as president of the Charleston Library Society, and as a leader in the Agricultural Society, where he experimented in botany and chemistry and became a student of medicine and medical practices.[26]

Pinckney helped establish the Bible Society of Charleston in 1810, "an action revealing that evangelical radical currents had reached South Carolina."[27] Under his leadership the Society became part of the American Bible Society in 1817; as a result, Pinckney was elected to be one of twenty national vice-presidents. For health reasons he was forced to withdraw from most public activities late in life, but he continued to serve the Charleston Bible Society; meetings of the Society were usually held in his home.[28] Rev. Christopher Gadsen says that he "continued to discharge to the close of life the duties of his office" as head of the Charleston Bible Society.[29]

21. Ibid., p. 275.
22. Ibid.
23. Thomas Lynch, Jr., to George Washington, ca. 1777; quoted by ibid., pp. 51–52.
24. Ibid., pp. 12–13.
25. Ibid., p. 72.
26. Ibid., pp. 264–70.
27. Ibid., p. 272.
28. Ibid., p. 272.
29. Rev. Christopher Gadsden, "Sermon on the Decease of Pinckney," quoted by ibid., p. 272.

His work with the Bible Society brought him into controversy, for the Society was determined to evangelize black slaves. Some South Carolinians were concerned that such efforts would lead to unrest and dissatisfaction among slaves. In 1822 a free black man named Denmark Vesey used biblical texts to stir up blacks to support his cause. He raised a secret army which had weapons hidden in strategic locations with plans to massacre the white community in Charleston. As a result, many whites wanted to stop the distribution of Bibles to slaves but Pinckney supported their evangelization.

Unlike many of his colleagues at the Constitutional Convention, Pinckney did not oppose black slavery. He justified it as part of God's order. But he was determined that blacks should have a right to hear the gospel. To appease the slaveholders, the Charleston Bible Society went on record that it had "no doubts concerning the moral and Religious Right of holding Slaves, lawfully obtained, when they are treated with justice and humanity."[30] They hoped for a society of slaves that were Christianized and willing to accept Paul's exhortation that slaves obey their masters (Ti. 2:9). Zahniser says, "The dilemma facing a slaveowner and a Christian was cruel indeed. Rather than being condemned for his acceptance of the institution of slavery, Pinckney may be commended for his determination to let nothing stand in the way of Christianizing the slaves, not even the possibility of Charleston's destruction by gospel-inspired Negroes."[31]

Charles Cotesworth Pinckney went to the Contitutional Convention well-grounded in Christian doctrine, well-educated in law, and experienced in government and military science. He was skeptical of government power like many of his fellow southerners, and generally believed that "the great art of government is not to govern too much."[32] He believed Congress should assume power over foreign trade, and wanted the federal government to assume state war debts. But he wanted no interference with interstate commerce or the slave trade, declaring that even if he could support such a power, South Carolina would never ratify the Constitution under such conditions. Unlike his cousin Charles, who defended slavery as an institution which, like marriage, should be "sacredly pre-

30. Charleston Bible Society Papers, South Carolina Historical Society; quoted by ibid., p. 273.

31. Ibid., p. 274.

32. Pinckney to General [Pickens?], March 31, 1790; quoted by ibid., p. 88.

served,"[33] Charles Cotesworth Pinckney was content to declare that "even if he and his colleagues were to sign the Constitution and use their personal influence, it would be of no avail towards obtaining the assent of their constituents. South Carolina and Georgia cannot do without slaves."[34]

The fact that the Convention had departed from its original purpose of revising the Articles of Confederation disturbed Pinckney; he questioned whether the Convention had authority to do more than that. He finally resolved the dilemma by resorting to social contract theory: "The Confederation was a compact. It was so; but it was a compact that had been repeatedly broken by every state in the Union; and all the writers on the laws of nations agree that, when the parties to treaty violate it, it is no longer binding." Since the Articles of Confederation had been repeatedly broken, it was no longer a binding document, and it was the right and duty of the citizens to formulate a new government.[35]

Pinckney stood for balance between federal and state authority, and for government by the wise and virtuous. He distrusted democracy just as he distrusted government power. He opposed popular election of congressmen, believed senators should hold office for four years instead of six, and believed legislators should receive no compensation for their services so that money-hungry individuals would not seek the office. He wanted the Senate to ratify treaties, and proposed the establishment of the committee that worked out the Great Compromise in which one house of Congress is based on population and the other by states. He worked diligently for ratification of the Constitution. Dr. M. E. Bradford declares that "Without Charles Cotesworth Pinckney, no Constitution could have been agreed upon in Philadelphia or approved in the Lower South."[36]

Charles Cotesworth Pinckney was considered the Federalist candidate for both President and Vice-President in 1800, and for President in 1804 and 1808. But his political philosophy contained both Federalist and Republican ideas. His opposition to centralized government was more consistent with republicanism. But his belief in government by an aristocracy of the wise and virtuous—meaning

33. Charles Pinckney; quoted by M. E. Bradford, *A Worthy Company* (Marlborough, New Hampshire: Plymouth Rock Foundation, 1982), p. 213. Charles Pinckney also suggested that South Carolina, if left alone, might do away with slavery on their own.

34. Charles Cotesworth Pinckney; cited by W. Cleon Skousen, *The Making of America* (Washington, D.C.: National Center for Constitutional Studies, 1985), p. 470.

35. Charles Cotesworth Pinckney; quoted by ibid., p. 124.

36. Bradford, *A Worthy Company*, p. 206.

the well-educated, highly religious, and moral aristocratic families like his own—was closer to Hamilton's thinking than Jefferson's. Pinckney was somewhere between the two. He was an aristocratic supporter of limited government, guided by Christian principles, opposing both the tyranny of big government and the tyranny of mob power.

Pinckney gradually moved toward Federalism during the 1790s. Several factors influenced this move. First, Alexander Hamilton may have convinced him that while government should be limited, it cannot be as limited as Pinckney envisioned.

A second influence was the French Revolution. At first Pinckney saw the Revolution as necessary to bring about Republican principles in France, but as the horrors of the Revolution became apparent his opinion gradually changed. The shameful treatment Pinckney received during his brief ambassadorship in France undoubtedly soured him further, as did the French practice of seizing American ships and impressing American sailors into French service.

The combination of these factors led the aging general to conclude that America must be prepared for war with France. He was convinced that the Republicans under Jefferson were neglecting the nation's defense.

Finally, he was concerned that America was sinking into factionalism and partisanship, and rightly or wrongly he blamed Jefferson and the Republicans for this more than the Federalists.[37]

Charles Cotesworth Pinckney's last public appearance was at a meeting of the Charleston Bible Society; he was so feeble he had to be supported as he went to the chair. Two months later, on August 16, 1825, he died at the age of eighty. He was buried in the churchyard of the St. Michael's Church he loved and served. A plaque on the wall of the church offers him this eulogy:

TO THE MEMORY OF
GENERAL CHARLES COTESWORTH PINCKNEY
ONE OF THE FOUNDERS OF
THE AMERICAN REPUBLIC.

IN WAR
HE WAS THE COMPANION IN ARMS
AND THE FRIEND OF WASHINGTON.

IN PEACE
HE ENJOYED HIS UNCHANGING CONFIDENCE

37. Zahnizer, *Founding Father*, pp. 196–260.

AND MAINTAINED WITH ENLIGHTENED ZEAL
THE PRINCIPLES OF HIS ADMINISTRATION
AND OF THE CONSTITUTION.

AS A STATESMAN
HE BEQUEATHED TO HIS COUNTRY THE SENTIMENT,
MILLIONS FOR DEFENCE
NOT A CENT FOR TRIBUTE.

AS A LAWYER,
HIS LEARNING WAS VARIOUS AND PROFOUND
HIS PRINCIPLES PURE HIS PRACTICE LIBERAL.

WITH ALL THE ACCOMPLISHMENTS
OF THE GENTLEMAN
HE COMBINED THE VIRTUES OF THE PATRIOT
AND THE PIETY OF THE CHRISTIAN.

HIS NAME
IS RECORDED IN THE HISTORY OF HIS COUNTRY
INSCRIBED ON THE CHARTER OF HER LIBERTIES,
AND CHERISHED IN THE AFFECTIONS OF HER CITIZENS.[38]

---

38. Inscription, St. Michael's Church, Charleston, South Carolina; quoted by ibid., p. 281.

19 And in Summary . . .

W hat can be concluded about the religious beliefs of the thirteen founding fathers?

Eight of these thirteen men—John Witherspoon, Alexander Hamilton, John Jay, Samuel Adams, Patrick Henry, Roger Sherman, Charles Cotesworth Pinckney, and probably George Washington—were Christians. It is likely Gouverneur Morris was also a Christian. John Adams, a strong Congregationalist/Puritan in his early years, liberalized his beliefs in the 1800s but could still be considered a Christian. James Madison is an enigma; he was an orthodox Christian in his early years but in later years he was silent about his religious beliefs. Ben Franklin was a deist in his early years but moved toward faith in a God who answers prayer and guides human history, though he still had doubts about the divinity of Christ. Thomas Jefferson could probably be classified as a deist in his early years, but in later years moved toward Unitarianism; unlike the deists he recognized a God who answers prayer and intervenes in human affairs. He called himself a Christian, using a liberal definition of the word, but did not consider Jesus Christ to be the Second Person of the Trinity.

How do their political and religious beliefs relate? Some think the Republicans and Antifederalists, influenced by free-thinkers and rationalists, were less likely to be Christians than the Federalists. However, there were Christians in both groups. It is difficult for twentieth-century conservatives to identify strictly with either position.

If Washington, Hamilton, Jay, Morris, John Adams, and Pinckney are broadly categorized as Federalists; and Witherspoon, Madison, Samuel Adams, Franklin, Jefferson, Sherman, and Henry are classified as Republicans, the following chart can be drawn:

	Strongly Christian	Probably Christian	Probably Not Christian
Federalist			
George Washington	x		
Alexander Hamilton	x		
John Jay	x		
Gouverneur Morris		x	
John Adams		x	
Charles C. Pinckney	x		
Republican			
John Witherspoon	x		
James Madison		x	
Samuel Adams	x		
Benjamin Franklin			x
Thomas Jefferson			x
Patrick Henry	x		
Roger Sherman	x		

Four of the six Federalists were Christian and two were probably Christians. Four of the seven Republicans were Christian, one was probably Christian, and two were probably not Christian.

While Christians predominated in both groups, they came to differing conclusions concerning government matters. Their basic world view was the same; but they differed in opinion as to how to apply that world view in establishing America's political system.

The founding fathers (with the partial exception of Thomas Jefferson, who was not at the Convention), held a low view of human nature; they agreed with the biblical view of the sinful nature of man. But this view of human nature led them to different political applications. Alexander Hamilton and Gouverneur Morris distrusted the sinful nature of the masses and believed a strong central government was necessary to keep the masses in check. Patrick Henry and Samuel Adams distrusted the sinful nature of rulers and feared that a strong central government would become tyrannical. Rev. Witherspoon, through his student James Madison, suggested the solution that was finally adopted: Prevent any one individual or group from becoming too powerful by separating power into legislative, executive, and judicial branches, with each checking and balancing the others.

The following conclusions emerge about the religious beliefs of the founding fathers:

1. Each of them professed and exhibited a deep faith in God. They believed not only in a God of creation, but also in a God who is active in human history. Franklin and Jefferson came to that belief later in life; the other eleven held that belief throughout their lives.

2. At least eight and probably eleven believed Jesus Christ is the Son of God. One of these eleven, John Adams, questioned whether Jesus Christ was the Second Person of the Trinity, but he affirmed a belief in Jesus' resurrection and apparently believed Jesus was more than a man. Madison believed in the Trinity early in life, but his later views are enigmatic because of his silence. It appears Morris accepted Jesus as God, but he said so little on the subject it is difficult to say for certain. Franklin had great respect for Jesus but had "some doubts" concerning his divinity; Jefferson also respected the teachings and example of Jesus but did not believe he was divine.

3. The founding fathers were students of the Bible. They quoted it authoritatively and made frequent allusions to Scripture in their writings and speeches. All of them except Thomas Jefferson indicated that they considered Scripture to be revelation from God. John Adams believed Scripture to be God's revelation, but he suspected that certain passages of Scripture were not part of the original text. Jefferson preceded both Albert Schweitzer's "quest for the historical Jesus" and Rudolf Bultmann's "demythologization," by issuing his own version of the Bible in which some passages including the miracles were omitted. The rest of these men appeared to have held an orthodox view of Scripture as God's authoritative revelation to man. They respected the Scriptures and studied the Bible extensively. John Jay and Charles Cotesworth Pinckney were leaders in the American Bible Society.

4. All of the founding fathers except Jefferson concurred with the Bible that man is basically sinful and self-centered; they did recognize that man is capable of certain civic virtue (Rom. 2:14-15). Jefferson had more faith in the goodness of man than the other founding fathers did. But Jefferson recognized that man has a sinful side; he did not share the beliefs of the French philosophes in human perfectability. Franklin did not adhere to the Calvinist view of total depravity, but he had a lower view of human nature than Jefferson.

   In this respect and others, Jefferson (and to a lesser extent Franklin) stand out from the other founding fathers. The world view of the others was strongly Christian even if several questioned certain Christian doctrines. The other eleven were spiritual descendents of John Calvin; only Jefferson, and to some extent Franklin, were children of the Enlightenment. And yet, modern thinkers are likely to cite Jefferson above all the others as representing the spirit of that age.

5. All thirteen of the founding fathers had great respect for organized religion, particularly for Christianity. Several were not church members, but, including Jefferson and Franklin, they attended church and contributed to churches. Some contributed to several different denominations. Most believed in Christian unity and rose above the narrow denominationalism of that time.

Thomas Jefferson disagreed with the Calvinist leaders of New England, but respected Christianity in general. Ben Franklin held bitter feelings toward his Calvinist upbringing early in life, but reversed these feelings later in life and wanted his grandson brought up as a Presbyterian.

Most of these founding fathers sincerely believed the tenets of orthodox Christianity. The few who had reservations about certain doctrines recognized the positive influence the Christian religion had on society. They all agreed that, in Washington's words, "national morality (cannot) prevail in exclusion of religious principle." They realized that the only way a free society can exist is among a highly religious and moral people.

The founding fathers who did not choose to be Christians expressed gratitude for Christianity's influence within their nation. If the founding fathers were to see the hostile contempt with which modern thinkers treat Christianity, I believe they would consider it strange, offensive, and self-destructive.

PART 3

The Constitution Then and Now

20 The Constitution Is Born

T he previous chapters have examined the delegates to the Constitutional Convention in great detail: their backgrounds, education, character, writings, and religious and political convictions. What happened when these men gathered at Independence Hall?

On June 28, 1787, Independence Hall was in a state of discord. The delegates seemed ready to give up and go home when Ben Franklin, the oldest delegate to the Convention, rose and pointed to the limits of human wisdom and the need for divine wisdom, declaring his belief that "God governs in the affairs of men." Franklin then moved that the Philadelphia clergy be requested to officiate in daily prayers at the Convention. Roger Sherman, the Connecticut Puritan, immediately seconded Franklin's motion.

But the motion never came to a vote. Alexander Hamilton and others suggested that such a motion would have been appropriate at the beginning of the Convention, but at this point would "lead the public to believe that the embarrassments and dissensions within the Convention, had suggested this measure."[1] (The delegates had resolved to conduct their deliberations in total secrecy.)

Franklin, Sherman, and others replied that "the past omission of a duty could not justify a further omission—that the rejection of

1. James Madison, *Notes of Debates in the Federal Convention* (Athens: Ohio University Press, 1787, 1840, 1966, 1985), p. 210.

such a proposition would expose the Convention to more unpleas-
ant animadversions than the adoption of it: and that the alarm out
of doors that might be excited for the state of things within, would
at least be as likely to do good as ill."[2]

Hugh Williamson of North Carolina pointed out that the Convention had no funds with which to pay a preacher. As an alternative,
Edmund Randolph of Virginia moved that a clergyman be asked to
preach a sermon to the Convention the following Wednesday, July
4, which was seconded by Franklin. But the Convention adjourned
that day without voting on either motion.[3]

However, Ben Franklin's motion reminded the delegates that
they could not rely on the "imperfection of the Human Understanding," and that instead they must find understanding by "humbly
applying to the Father of lights." Although the delegates chose not
to have official prayers and sermons, many of them prayed regularly
for the success of the Convention. Boardman says, "There can be
little doubt that Sherman and many another delegate made the
issues of the Convention the object of frequent and earnest
prayer."[4]

A spirit of harmony did eventually return to the Convention. The
delegates reached general agreement on most issues, and compromised elsewhere.

The issue that troubled the Convention the most was voting in
Congress. Probably no issue threatened to break up the Convention
as much as this one. The smaller states insisted that each state
should have the same number of votes; otherwise the larger states
would dominate the smaller. The larger states argued that voting
should be proportional to population; otherwise citizens of the
smaller states would have a greater voice than citizens of larger
states.

The solution was obvious to Roger Sherman: Give each state an
equal vote in the Senate, and apportion the House of Representatives according to population. Sherman suggested the idea as early
as June 11; in fact, he made the same proposal before the
Continental Congress in 1777. It finally passed 5-4 on July 16, when
Connecticut, New Jersey, Delaware, Maryland, and North Carolina
voted yes; and Pennsylvania, Virginia, South Carolina and Georgia
voted no; Massachusetts remained divided. This became the Great

---

2. Ibid.
3. Ibid., p. 211.
4. Roger Sherman Boardman, *Roger Sherman: Signer and Statesman* (New York: Da
Capo Press, 1971), p. 248.

Compromise, also known as the Connecticut Compromise and the Sherman Compromise.[5]

The Great Compromise solved the problem of voting in the two houses of Congress, but another matter needed to be settled—in apportioning delegates to the various states on the basis of population, should slaves be counted as people? The south insisted that they should be counted; that way the southern states would have more votes in the House. But that presented another problem for the South, because direct taxes were to be apportioned according to population. The southern delegates insisted that slaves not be counted as people for purposes of taxation. Elbridge Gerry of Massachusetts commented sarcastically that since "blacks are property, and are used to the southward as cattle and horses to the northward,"[6] then cattle and horses should count as people for representation in the North!

James Wilson of Pennsylvania suggested that they revert to the "three-fifths rule" of the Confederation Congress of 1783, whereby the representation would be in proportion to the "whole number of white and other free citizens and three-fifths of all other persons except Indians not paying taxes. . . ."[7] This compromise was adopted to solve the problem of representation and taxation. In a further compromise on the slavery issue it was agreed that Congress could not prohibit the importation of slaves for twenty years, until 1808.

5. Madison, *Notes*, pp. 98–103; 297–98; cf. Catherine Drinker Bowen, *Miracle at Philadelphia* (Boston: Little, Brown & Co., 1966), pp. 92–95, 185–86. A comment about sources of information about the convention would be appropriate. There are no day-to-day newspaper accounts of the Convention's progress. The delegates chose Major William Jackson to be the convention secretary, and his notes were published in 1819. But they are sketchy compared to the detailed daily notes kept by James Madison. Madison's *Notes of Debates in the Federal Convention of 1787* were published in 1840 and comprise the best contemporary source of information; but they do reflect his perspective, and as an active delegate himself he cannot be expected to have recorded everything. Others took notes from time to time, including Luther Martin, Robert Yates, William Pierce, Rufus King, William Patterson, Alexander Hamilton, James McHenry, and John Lansing. Others made comments after the Convention that gave insights as to what happened. To get a full picture of what happened at the Convention, it is necessary to combine Madison's notes with those of other observers. The most scholarly and thorough attempt to combine these accounts are *The Records of the Federal Convention of 1787* by Max Farrand, (New Haven, Connecticut: Yale University Press, 1966). It is lengthy (four volumes) and currently undergoing revision. I also recommend Catherine Drinker Bowen's *Miracle at Philadelphia: The Story of the Constitutional Convention May to September 1787* (Boston: Little, Brown & Co., 1966, 1987). This narrative takes the various sources into account. A good discussion of the Constitution and its history is found in W. Cleon Skousen's *The Making of America: The Substance and Meaning of the Constitution* (Washington, D.C.: National Center for Constitutional Studies, 1985).

6. Ibid., p. 192.

7. Ibid., p. 206.

On July 26, with most of the important issues resolved, the convention chose a Committee on Detail consisting of John Rutledge of South Carolina, Edmund Randolph of Virginia, Nathaniel Gorham of Massachusetts, Oliver Ellsworth of Connecticut, and James Wilson of Pennsylvania, to prepare a constitution and present it when the Convention reconvened August 6.

From August 6 to September 8 the delegates refined the constitution presented by the Committee on Detail. On September 8, when those details were worked out, a Committee on Style was appointed to re-write the constitution in final form. William Samuel Johnson of Connecticut, Alexander Hamilton of New York, Gouverneur Morris of Pennsylvania, James Madison of Virginia, and Rufus King of Massachusetts were appointed to that committee. Most of the actual rewriting was done by Gouverneur Morris. The Constitution was presented on September 12, and with a few changes (such as a change in the number of votes required to override a presidential veto from ¾ to ⅔), the Constitution was adopted in final form on September 15.

On Monday, September 17, the delegates gathered to sign the Constitution. Franklin presented a written speech, which James Wilson read; in it he urged all delegates to sign the Constitution, declaring that while he did not agree with every detail, on the whole he thought it was in the best interest of the nation. He declared that:

> When you assemble a number of men to have the advantage of their joint wisdom you inevitably assemble with those men, all their prejudices, their passions, their errors of opinion, their local interest, and their selfish views. From such an assembly can a perfect production be expected? It therefore astonishes me, Sir, to find this system approaching so near to perfection as it does; and I think it will astonish our enemies, who are waiting with confidence to hear that our councils are confounded like those of the Builders of Babel; and that our States are on the point of separation, only to meet hereafter for the purpose of cutting one another's throats. Thus I consent, Sir, to this Constitution because I expect no better, and because I am not sure, that it is not the best. The opinions I have had of its errors, I sacrifice to the public good.[8]

The Struggle over Ratification

Not everyone agreed with Franklin. The Constitution was adopted unanimously in the sense that a majority of each state

---

8. Benjamin Franklin, Remarks to Convention, September 17, 1787; quoted in Madison, *Notes*, pp. 653–54.

present and voting supported it; but several individual delegates did not. Three delegates refused to sign the Constitution: Elbridge Gerry of Massachusetts, George Mason of Virginia, and Edmund Randolph of Virginia. Randolph later changed his mind and supported the Constitution in the Virginia Ratifying Convention; but Luther Martin of Maryland who signed the Constitution later joined the opposition.

The Convention delegates sent the Constitution to the Continental Congress, which approved it after eight days of hearings and sent it to the states for ratification. Then the battle began!

Modern historians, conditioned to believe that strong centralized power is essential to good government, have often made light of the Antifederalists, those who opposed the Constitution. But they too were Americans who loved their country and had fought and sacrificed for it. They were just as sincere in their opposition to the Constitution as the Federalists were in its support. Among the Antifederalists were some of America's leading patriots: Patrick Henry, George Mason, Richard Henry Lee, Elbridge Gerry, Luther Martin, George Clinton, Robert Yates, John Lansing, and Melancton Smith.

Some of the Antifederalists identified themselves with the old defenders of the Roman Republic and signed themselves "Brutus," "Cato," and "Agrippa," while Federalists responded with pseudonyms such as "Publius" (used by Hamilton, Jay, and Madison in *The Federalist Papers*) and "Caesar." It is difficult to know which side represented the majority of the American people.

The Antifederalists had some legitimate objections, and in some ways may have been more farsighted than the Federalists. The Antifederalists' chief objection was the lack of a bill of rights. The Convention had two reasons for not including a bill of rights. First, they believed that the Constitution gave the federal government only certain carefully delegated powers, and the federal government would have no powers other than those delegated. There was no reason to mention the right of free speech in the Constitution, because the Constitution gave the federal government no jurisdiction over speech.

Second, as Hamilton noted, the enumeration of certain rights could be dangerous. It would be impossible to make a comprehensive list of individual rights. The danger existed that if certain rights were enumerated, a future Congress might contend that since certain rights were named and protected, other rights not named were forfeited.

But many Americans—even men like Jefferson who supported

the Constitution—insisted on a bill of rights. To satisfy such concerns, the Federalist forces promised that they would work for a bill of rights as soon as the Constitution was ratified. That promise was kept. The first eight amendments guaranteed specific rights held by the people. The Ninth Amendment was included to guard against Hamilton's concern that other rights would be deemed forfeited, and also protects the rights Americans enjoyed at common law: "The enumeration in the Constitution of certain rights shall not be construed to deny or disparage others retained by the people."

The Bill of Rights became law due to the concerns of the Antifederalists. For this reason they must be included with the Federalists as architects of the American system of government. George Washington wrote of the Antifederalists:

> Upon the whole, I doubt whether the opposition to the Constitution will not ultimately be productive of more good than evil; it has called forth, in its defence, abilities which would not perhaps have been otherwise exerted that have thrown new light upon the science of Government, they have given the rights of man a full and fair discussion, and explained them in so clear and forcible a manner, as cannot fail to make a lasting impression.[9]

The Antifederalists recognized that changes were needed. They argued that the Articles of Confederation should have been amended rather than replaced. They pointed out, with some justification, that the original purpose of the Convention was to suggest amendments to the Articles of Confederation. The Convention had no lawful authority for going beyond its intended purpose.[10]

Both sides cited Montesquieu. Federalists noted his concept of separation of powers and claimed they had written that concept into the Constitution. Antifederalists noted that Montesquieu said a republic would succeed only in a small nation, that a large nation would gravitate toward empire. The Antifederalists wanted a loose confederation in which most power rested with the states and local

9. George Washington; quoted by Bowen, *Miracle at Philadelphia*, p. 305.
10. Herbert J. Storing, *What the Anti-Federalists Were For: The Political Thought of the Opponents of the Constitution* (Chicago: University of Chicago Press, 1981), pp. 7–8. Charles Cotesworth Pinckney and Elbridge Gerry raised similar concerns at the convention (Madison, *Notes*, pp. 35–36), but the general consensus of the delegates seemed to be that the Convention had authority to propose whatever it chose, and it was up to Congress and the states to accept or reject their proposals.

governments. In this way they believed a republican government could work.

The Antifederalists also argued that Congress did not have enough representatives; each congressman had such a large district that he could not be responsible to his constituents or know their needs. In addition, Patrick Henry pointed out that the Constitution simply said Congress *may* (not must) readjust the number of representatives as the population increases.[11] As a result, congressmen would be unresponsive to the popular will and subject to control by the upper classes.

The Antifederalists objected that the federal government had too much power under the proposed Constitution. Henry said the federal government has the power to tax and raise armies; and the presidency is such a powerful institution that it "squints toward monarchy."[12] In Henry's words, Congress has "the sword in one hand, and the purse in the other. Shall we be safe without either?"[13]

Many Antifederalists raised the specter of judicial review. They expressed concern that the Supreme Court of the United States may possess the power to strike laws of Congress as unconstitutional.

The Antifederalists expressed a legitimate concern that the Constitution opened the door for usurpation of federal power, and that the only barrier to despotism was the alleged goodness of the rulers. At one point Henry thundered:

> Where are your checks in this Government? Your strong holds will be in the hands of your enemies: it is on a supposition that our American governors shall be honest, that all the good qualities of this government are founded: But its defective, and imperfect construction, puts it in their power to perpetrate the worst of mischiefs, should they be bad men: And, Sir, would not all the world, from the Eastern to the Western hemisphere, blame our distracted folly in resting our rights upon the contingency of our rulers being good or bad. Shew me that age and country where the rights and liberties of the people were placed on the sole chance of their rulers being good men, without a consequent loss of liberty?[14]

Nevertheless, the Antifederalists were less organized than their

11. Patrick Henry, Speech before Virginia Ratifying Convention 5 June 1788; reprinted in Storing, *The Anti-Federalist*, p. 300.

12. Henry; quoted in ibid., p. 310.

13. Henry, Remarks to Virginia Ratifying Convention, 9 June 1788; reprinted in ibid., p. 322.

14. Henry, Remarks to Virginia Ratifying Convention, 5 June 1788; reprinted in ibid., pp. 310-11.

opponents. Time and again, the Federalist forces managed to claim victory out of what was almost certain defeat. Delaware unanimously ratified the Constitution on December 6, 1787; on December 12 Pennsylvania followed with a 46-23 vote. On December 18 New Jersey ratified unanimously, and Georgia ratified unanimously on January 2, 1788. On January 9 Connecticut ratified with a vote of 128-40, largely due to respect for Roger Sherman.

Massachusetts' ratification was in doubt. But Samuel Adams, an opponent, changed his mind and supported the Constitution toward the end of the convention debates, and Governor John Hancock left his sickbed to join the Convention and announced his support. On February 7 Massachusetts ratified 187 to 168.

By a vote of 63-11, Maryland ratified April 26, followed by South Carolina on May 23 by a 149-73 vote. New Hampshire completed the necessary nine states for ratification by approving the Constitution 57-46 on June 21.

Patrick Henry, Richard Henry Lee, and George Mason were pitted against James Madison, George Wythe, and John Marshall in Virginia's battle for ratification. The Federalist cause received unexpected support when Governor Edmund Randolph, one of three delegates who earlier refused to sign the Constitution, announced his support for ratification. Despite the oratory of Henry, Virginia ratified on June 26 by a vote of 87-79; at the same time it approved, at Henry's insistence, a Declaration of Rights which became part of the basis for the Bill of Rights. The Federalists celebrated, believing Virginia had the honor of being the ninth state to ratify—unaware that New Hampshire had taken that honor only five days before.

New York was the next battleground. There the Antifederalists were in the majority, but they were disheartened by the fact that ten states had already ratified. Under Hamilton's brilliant leadership aided by John Jay and James Duane, the Federalists won an unexpected 30-27 victory on July 26.

North Carolina did not ratify at its first convention, but a year later on November 21, 1789, it ratified by a vote of 194-77. Rhode Island was the last original state to ratify. It did not send delegates to the Convention but ratified on May 29, 1790, by a vote of 34-32.[15]

15. It is interesting to note the role played by the clergy in the ratification of the Constitution. Forty-four clergymen from various denominations served as delegates to the ratifying conventions of eight states. Clearly, the clergy took an active role in politics at the time this nation was founded. The table below notes how the clergymen of each state voted:

Despite its imperfections the Constitution has served the United States remarkably well for 200 years. The fledging republic of 1787 is currently one of the oldest republics in the world and one of the longest-lived republics in history due largely to the principles encased in the Constitution. History reveals that periods of freedom are rare and short-lived; they tend to collapse or evolve into dictatorships, either by foreign conquest or internal decay.

As we shall see in the next chapter, the reason the American republic these men founded has lasted so long and flourished so well is that it is founded on the timeless principles found in the Word of God.

	Clergy Delegates Voting *YES*	Clergy Delegates Voting *NO*
Massachusetts	14	4
Connecticut	3	0
New Hampshire	4	1
Pennsylvania	2	1
New Jersey	4	0
South Carolina	2	0
Virginia	1	1
North Carolina	2	5
Total	32	12*

*Delaware, Georgia, Maryland, New York and Rhode Island are not mentioned in this survey. It is not clear whether this is because they were not studied, or because no clergymen served as delegates to their conventions, or because inadequate information was available.

While this table indicates that the majority of the clergy were in favor of the Constitution, it must be remembered that the states represented supported ratification. In these states the vote among the clergy closely resembles that of the delegates as a whole, except for Massachusetts where the clergy were more in favor of the Constitution and North Carolina where the clergy were opposed.

The next table shows the vote of clergy/delegates according to denomination:

	Clergy Delegates Voting YES	Clergy Delegates Voting NO
Baptist	5	8
Congregationalist	16	1
Cong.-Unitarian	3	0
Episcopal	1	1
Lutheran	1	0
Moravian	0	1
Presbyterian	5	1
Reformed Dutch	1	0

(These figures were compiled from a study by James Hutchinson Smylie, "American Clergymen and the Constitution of the United States of America." Th.D. dissertation, Princeton Theological Seminary, Princeton, New Jersey, 1954.)

It is difficult to understand why Baptist clergymen were opposed to the Constitution. Possible reasons might include their basic independence, policy of local church autonomy rather than strong central organization, and their main settlements in Rhode Island which opposed the Constitution for a long time. Baptist concern about religious freedom, coupled with the lack of a bill of rights, may have been another factor.

21 Biblical Principles Found in the Declaration and the Constitution

D o the Declaration of Independence and the Constitution contain principles which are in keeping with those found in the Bible? Apparently the United States Congress thinks so. On October 4, 1982, Congress passed Public Law 97-280, declaring 1983 the "Year of the Bible." The President signed the bill into law. The opening sentences of the bill are:

> Whereas *Biblical teachings inspired concepts of civil government that are contained in our Declaration of Independence and the Constitution of the United States*;
> Whereas this Nation now faces great challenges that will test this Nation as it has never been tested before; and
> Whereas that renewing our knowledge of and faith in God through Holy Scripture can strengthen us as a nation and a people . . . (emphasis added)

Congress did not specify which concepts of civil government the Bible inspired. However, several are apparent and this chapter will identify them. First, four basic misconceptions must be clarified:

Misconception 1: Economic Interpretation

It is argued that the authors of the Declaration were not concerned about God-given laws and rights. Instead, they were men of property, concerned that their commercial interests were being threatened by England. Individuals making this argument cite the economic grievances against England listed in the Declaration: cutting off trade, and imposing taxes without consent.

The founders of this nation were concerned about property rights. They harbored no ascetic notions that property was evil or unscriptural. They believed, with Locke, that the right to own and use property was a God-given human right. The notion of modern liberals that "property rights" are somehow distinct from "human rights" would have seemed very strange to the founders who believed the God-given right to own and use property was just as much a "human right" as any other. And they would have deplored the tendency of recent courts to denigrate property rights to a status lower than other rights.

Property rights were not their only concern. The grievances listed in the Declaration include: dissolving legislatures, obstructing justice, quartering troops, depriving people of the right to trial by jury, ending colonial charters, invalidating colonial laws, and impressing American sailors into British service.

When the signers of the Declaration pledged their "lives, fortunes and sacred honor," they knew the penalty they faced. The penalty for treason was being hanged until unconscious, then further tortured and dismembered so no remains were left for burial.

Many signers of the Declaration suffered severely for their convictions. Five were captured by the British and tortured before they died. Twelve had their homes ransacked and burned. Two lost their sons in the war, another had two sons captured. Nine either died from war wounds or from hardships suffered in the war. Carter Braxton of Virginia, a wealthy planter and trader, watched his ships being destroyed by the British navy. He died impoverished. Thomas McKean had to keep himself and his family in hiding, and lost all his possessions. The British destroyed the property of Francis Lewis and jailed his wife; she died a few months later. John Hart was driven from his wife's bedside as she was dying; their thirteen children were forced to flee for their lives. His home and mill were destroyed, and he never saw his children again. For more than a year he lived in forests and caves, and a few weeks after he returned, he died from exhaustion and a broken heart. John Hancock, the wealthiest man in America, ordered an attack on occupied Boston knowing much of his own commercial property would be burned in the process.

Charles Beard charges the framers of the Constitution with being primarily concerned about personal gain in *An Economic Interpre-*

tation of the Constitution of the United States.[1] Beard's book, first published in 1913, was one of two books mentioned in *New Republic* which have done most to change American ways of thinking.[2] Prior to the publication of Beard's book, the Constitution was generally represented as the product of Anglo-American political genius, perhaps with God's help. Beard advanced the thesis that the Constitution was primarily the product of economic determinism, wealthy land speculators and investors in securities seeking to safeguard their economic interests through a strong central government. Throughout the twentieth century many or most historians have simply assumed the truth of Beard's thesis.

In one sense Beard is right. The founding fathers were anti-democratic. They feared and distrusted absolute and unchecked majority rule, and placed safeguards against majority rule into the Constitution. They believed the franchise should be limited to those who were qualified to vote intelligently and who had an economic stake in government affairs; so they frequently imposed property requirements for voters at the state level. And they did believe property rights were important.

Beard's thesis is flawed in many respects. First, the fact that some delegates to the Convention gained economically from a strong Constitution, does not mean they placed their own economic interests ahead of what they believed to be best for the nation. Practically *all* Americans stood to gain economically as well as in a variety of other ways from a stable government. If investors in securities and land speculators stood to gain from the Constitution, why would land speculators like Patrick Henry work against their own economic interest and oppose the Constitution?

Second, Beard's analysis is based on inadequate and sometimes misleading data. Frequently he acknowledges that proper data was unavailable, and then assumes the facts were such as would suit his thesis. Sometimes he simply failed to go after the proper data, as when he says "The materials bearing on the ratification of the Constitution in South Carolina which are available to the northern student are relatively scanty," and proceeds to say, "Nevertheless, . . . it may easily be imagined. . . ." Professor Brown of Michigan State University pointed out in his critique of Beard's thesis that Beard's figures for the amount of personal property holdings

1. Charles A. Beard, *An Economic Interpretation of the Constitution of the United States* (New York: MacMillan, 1913, 1960).

2. "Books That Changed Our Minds," *New Republic,* 1938; cited by Robert E. Brown, *Charles Beard and the Constitution: A Critical Analysis of "An Economic Interpretation of the Constitution"* (Princeton: Princeton University Press, 1956), p. 15.

(securities, etc.) of the framers of the Constitution is based on figures from 1792-1804, not from 1787 when the Constitution was written. During this latter period the value of securities had greatly increased due to Hamilton's program of assuming state debts and funding the national debt.[3]

Professor Brown points out, using Beard's figures, the actual proportion of property in real estate as against that in personalty (personal property) was 96.7 percent realty, 3.3 percent personalty. Brown asks why these agricultural, real estate-dominated legislatures would choose self-interested securities investors for their delegates to the Constitutional Convention.[4]

Furthermore, Beard's thesis ignores the inherent conflict between land speculators and investors in securities. For example, delegate Nathaniel Gorham of Massachusetts and Oliver Phelps contracted in 1788 to buy a million dollars' worth of western land to be paid for in Massachusetts securities. "When the securities rose in value, as according to Beard these men knew they would, Gorham, Phelps, Robert Morris, and others of the 'Fathers' lost a great deal of money."[5]

Finally, Beard's thesis fails to account for the regional differences in ratification. For example, he argues that in Connecticut as in most states the urban commercial centers supported the Constitution while the rural areas opposed it. However, New Hampshire which was almost entirely agricultural at the time, supported ratification. In fact, the three states which *unanimously* ratified the Constitution—Delaware, New Jersey, and Georgia—were *agricultural*.[6]

Beard's thesis is flawed in many ways. The founding fathers were concerned about economics, but that was not their primary concern.

Misconception 2: The Slavery Issue

Some critics have argued that the founders of this nation could not have been Christians because they owned slaves or countenanced slavery. The following points can be made in response:

First, in every age, Christians have had certain "blind spots," areas of unconscious sin in their lives that exist because of their lack of knowledge or misunderstanding of the gospel. Christians several

3. Brown, *Charles Beard*, p. 48.
4. Ibid., pp. 50, 60–61.
5. Ibid., p. 58.
6. Ibid., pp. 171–73, 179.

centuries ago could live alongside slavery because it was their blindspot. Some justified the institution with Old Testament references to slavery and New Testament admonitions such as "Servants, be obedient to them that are your masters" (Eph. 6:5).

Second, there were many Christians in that day who strongly opposed slavery. John Jay, Alexander Hamilton, John Adams, and others expressed their abhorrence for the institution. The abolitionist movement in the 1800s was generally led by church people.

Third, many Christians opposed slavery even though they owned slaves. Except for delegates from Georgia and the Carolinas, very few defended the institution. One might ask why they didn't free their slaves if they were really sincere; the answer is that in many cases they couldn't. In many instances the slaveholders had no power to free their slaves; they were mortgaged to creditors. Others were unable to run their plantations without slaves. It might be very difficult for a freed slave to make a living in that economy; under such circumstances setting slaves free was both inhumane and irresponsible. James Madison declared that "the whole Bible is against slavery";[7] yet he owned over 100 slaves. Thomas Jefferson opposed slavery but did not free his slaves until his death. Patrick Henry acknowledged that slavery was un-Christian yet asked, "Would any one believe that I am master of slaves of my own purchase?"[8] He felt that society had placed him in a moral dilemma in which the only Christian response was to keep his slaves and treat them with kindness.

Finally, many people at that time believed that the changing economic conditions were rendering slavery obsolete, and that if left alone the institution would disappear within twenty years.

These considerations do not justify slavery; they are not intended to. They help in understanding how the institution could have existed in a society of Christians.

Misconception 3: The Constitution Doesn't Mention God

How can the Constitution be considered a Christian document when it doesn't mention the Lord Jesus Christ (except for the closing reference to the "Year of Our Lord, 1787"), doesn't refer to the Bible, and doesn't even mention God?

7. Adrienne Koch, *Madison's Advice to My Country* (Princeton: Princeton University Press, 1966), p. 135.

8. Norine Dickson Campbell, *Patrick Henry: Patriot and Statesman* (Old Greenwich, Conn.: Devin-Adaire, 1969, 1975), pp. 99–100.

The Constitution does not mention God the Father or his Son Jesus Christ any other place. There was a valid reason for this. The delegates came from twelve different states (Rhode Island didn't send delegates), most had their own state churches. There was general agreement that the federal government would not establish any one of those state churches as the new federal church thereby creating resentment among the others, or interfere with any of the state establishments. A religious reference could have created divisions.

The Declaration of Independence does contain references to God. The first paragraph refers to "the Laws of Nature and of Nature's God." The second paragraph declares that "all men are created equal, that they are endowed by their Creator with certain unalienable Rights, that among these are Life, Liberty and the pursuit of Happiness." The final paragraph contains the words "a firm reliance on the Protection of Divine Providence." There is no indication that any delegate objected to any of these references.

Misconception 4: The Role of the Declaration of Independence

The role of the Declaration of Independence in American law is often misconstrued. Some believe the Declaration is simply a statement of ideas that has no legal force whatsoever today. Nothing could be further from the truth. The Declaration has been repeatedly cited by the U.S. Supreme Court as part of the fundamental law of the United States of America.[9]

The *United States Code Annotated* includes the Declaration of Independence under the heading "The Organic Laws of the United States of America" along with the Articles of Confederation, the Constitution, and the Northwest Ordinance. Enabling acts frequently require states to adhere to the principles of the Declaration; in the Enabling Act of June 16, 1906, Congress authorized Oklahoma Territory to take steps to become a state. Section 3 provides that the Oklahoma Constitution "shall not be repugnant to the

9. See *Gulf, C&S.F.Ry v. Ellis*, 165 U.S. 150 (1897); *Butchers' Union Slaughter-House & Live-Stock Landing Co. v. Crescent City Live-Stock Co.*, 111 U.S. 746 (1884); *Northern Pipeland Co. v. Marathon Pipe Line*, 73 L.Ed.2d 598, 608 (1982); *United States. v. Will*, 449 U.S. 200 (1980); *Dames & Moore v. Regan*, 453 U.S. 654 (1981); *Youngstown Sheet & Tube v. Sawyer*, 343 U.S. 579 (1952); *Nevada v. Hall*, 440 U.S. 410, 415 1979); *Parklane Hosiery Company v. Shore*, 439 U.s. 322, 340 (1979); *Faretta v. California*, 422 U.S. 806, 829 (1975); *South Carolina v. Katzenbach*, 383 U.S. 301, 359 (1966); see 16 *American Jurisprudence* 2d, Constitutional Review Section 14, p. 327.

Constitution of the United States and the principles of the Declaration of Independence."[10]

Others look at the Declaration as superior to the Constitution in its moral tone. In this view, the Declaration is a high-toned statement of the rights of man, written by "liberated" thinkers like Jefferson and influenced by the progressive thinking of the 1770s. It speaks of equality, the rights of life, liberty, and the pursuit of happiness, and the right to alter or abolish those governments which are destructive of those ends. But the reactionaries took over between 1776 and 1787, and the Constitution which emerged out of the Philadelphia Convention was a conservative document designed to protect the wealthy classes and keep the masses under control.

Actually it was the other way around, as Martin Diamond ably points out. The Declaration is a statement of the basic American values or principles: equality, God-given rights. The Constitution is the means by which these rights are to be secured: a federal republic consisting of a federal government and state governments, with certain powers delegated to the federal government and others reserved for the states, with those powers separated into legislative, executive, and judicial branches. The Declaration is the foundation; the Constitution is the structure built on that foundation.[11]

To understand Diamond's point, it needs to be understood that liberty was the basic goal of the framers of the Constitution; democracy, used in the general sense, was the means of achieving liberty. In Diamond's words:

> For the founding generation it was liberty that was the comprehensive good, the end against which political things had to be measured; and democracy was only a form of government which, like any other form of government, had to prove itself adequately instrumental to the securing of liberty.[12]

The Constitution goes beyond the Declaration. It not only embraces liberty (see the Preamble, "secure the blessings of liberty"); it also looks to representative government as the means of securing it. The Declaration does not do that. It speaks of "consent of the governed," but it uses that term in a limited sense. At that time the term meant that people agreed to set up a government, not that they

---

10. My thanks to Michael Schmidt, my research assistant (1983–84), now a North Carolina attorney, for bringing this information to light.

11. Martin Diamond, "The Declaration and the Constitution: Liberty, Democracy, and the Founders," *The Public Interest*, No. 41, Fall 1975, pp. 39–55, at 46ff.

12. Ibid., p. 47.

elected their particular rulers or consented to each act of government.[13]

The Declaration did not specify a form of government. Monarchies were not necessarily evil systems according to the Declaration (though some of the signers did think so). As Diamond says, "the Declaration holds George III 'unfit to be the ruler of a free people' not because he was a king, but because he was a *tyrannical* king."[14]

The Constitution eliminated monarchy so far as the United States was concerned, and set up a republican form of government. A major purpose of this republican form of government was to "secure the blessings of liberty" set forth in the Declaration.

The Constitution is built on the Declaration of Independence, and the Declaration finds practical expression in the Constitution. Neither can be fully understood without the other.

Biblical Principles Found in Both Documents

Several biblical principles can be found when examining the Declaration and Constitution together:

The Providence of God

The last sentence of the Declaration of Independence contains the words "a firm reliance on the protection of divine Providence." The founding fathers not only believed in God, but also recognized his ruling hand in human activity.

"Providence" is thought by some to be a deistic term for an impersonal God. But the meaning goes beyond that. Samuel Johnson's 1755 *Dictionary of the English Language* indicates:

> **Providence**—(Providentia, Latin). 1. Foresight; timely care . . . Sidney. 2. The care of God over created beings; divine superintendence—Raleigh.[15]

Noah Webster's 1828 *American Dictionary of the English Language* offers a similar definition:

> In *theology*, the care and superintendence which God exercises over his creatures. He that acknowledges a creation and denies a

13. Ibid., p. 49.
14. Ibid., p. 50 (emphasis original).
15. Samuel Johnson, *Dictionary of the English Language* (1775); quoted by William McAulay Hosmer, "Of Divine Providence in Our Declaration of Independence," (Hosmer Enterprises, P.O. Box 846, San Carlos, California, 1980), pp. 14–15.

providence, involves himself in a palpable contradiction; for the same power which caused a thing to exist is necessary to continue its existence. Some persons admit a *general providence,* but deny a *particular providence,* not considering that a *general providence* consists of *particulars.* A belief in divine *providence,* is a source of great consolation to good men. By *divine providence* is often understood God himself.[16]

"Providence" means more than a deistic God who creates and does nothing else. It involves a God, who, as Franklin said, "governs in the affairs of men."[17]

The Law of God

All the founding fathers believed in "the Laws of Nature and of Nature's God." This phrase from the Declaration, which both Blackstone and Locke used previously, reflects the universal belief in some form of higher law to which man's law should conform and by which man's law will be judged.

This was not a Hobbesian concept of natural law—doing that which comes naturally, such as self-preservation. It was a higher law that carried with it a moral imperative; for example, the "Laws of Nature and of Nature's God" entitled the colonists to assume their place as an independent nation.

The right to resist unlawful authority, as set forth in the part of the Declaration which says "That whenever any Form of Government becomes destructive of these ends, it is the Right of the People to alter or to abolish it," identifies a higher law of God to which man's laws must conform. Unless a person recognizes some form of supreme law by which man's laws must be judged, there is no basis for believing in any form of disobedience, or that any human law or act of government is unjust.

This higher law of God is revealed to men in Scripture, in nature, and in the human conscience. Romans 2:14-15:

> For when the Gentiles, which have not the law, do by nature the things contained in the law, these, having not the law, are a law unto themselves: Which shew the work of the law written in their hearts, their conscience also bearing witness, and their thoughts the mean while accusing or else excusing one another.

A basis for the law of nature in God's revelation of his glory

---

16. *American Dictionary of the English Language* (1828; reprinted 1980, San Francisco, Foundation for American Christian Education), s.v. "Providence."

17. Benjamin Franklin, June 28, 1787; quoted by Smyth, *Writings,* IX:600–1.

through nature might also be found in Psalm 119, and in the animals' innate love for order as expressed in Proverbs 30:24-28.

The Law of Nations

Article I, Section 8, Clause 10, of the Constitution authorizes Congress "To define and punish Piracies and Felonies committed on the high Seas, and Offences against the Law of Nations."

The founding fathers borrowed the phrase and concept "Law of Nations" from such thinkers as Grotius, Pufendorf, and Vattel. They developed the concept of "Law of Nations" as an extension of natural, God-given law. The fact a law exists which supersedes the legislative enactments of various nations, implies a power and authority higher than man.

The United States established war tribunals to bring foreign officials to trial for atrocities committed in violation of the Law of Nations or international law, based on this clause of the Constitution. The fact that such officials could be held to a higher standard of conduct and that simple "obedience to orders" was not considered an absolute defense to charges of violating international law, indicates further recognition that the laws of man are subject to the law of God.[18]

The Equality of Man

Scripture states that "God is no respecter of persons" (Acts 10:34) and that in Christ "there is neither Jew nor Greek" (Gal. 3:28). The Old Testament provides for equal justice under law. The judges were commanded not to take bribes or show partiality to the rich; likewise the judge must not "countenance a poor man in his cause" (Exod. 23:6).

The Declaration of Independence also declares as a "self-evident truth" that "all men are created equal." The Constitution reinforces this concept by guaranteeing that "No Title of Nobility shall be granted by the United States" (Article I, Section 9, Paragraph 8), and the Fourteenth Amendment forbids the states from denying to any person within their jurisdiction the "equal protection of the law."

Martin Diamond offers an explanation of the meaning of the term "created equal":

18. See *Application of Yamashita*, Philippine Islands, 1946, 327 U.S. 1, 66 Sup. Ct. 340, 90 L.Ed. 499.

The social contract theory upon which the Declaration is based teaches not equality as such but equal political liberty. The reasoning of the Declaration is as follows. Each man is equally born into the state of nature in a condition of absolute independence of every other man. That equal independence of each from all, as John Locke put it, forms a "Title to perfect Freedom" for every man. It is this equal perfect freedom, which men leave behind them when they quit the state of nature, from which they derive their equal "unalienable rights" in civil society. The equality of the Declaration, then, consists entirely in the equal entitlement of all to the rights which comprise political liberty, and nothing more. Thus Lincoln wisely interpreted the Declaration: "The authors of that notable instrument . . . did not intend to declare all men equal in all respects. They did not mean to say all were equal in color, size, intellect, moral developments, or social capacity. They defined with tolerable distinctness, in what rights they did consider all men created equal—equal in 'certain unalienable rights, among which are life, liberty, and the pursuit of happiness.' "[19]

The founding fathers never intended that everyone should be equal in ability, wealth, or achievement. They opposed radical utopian schemes of leveling income and establishing socialist or communist societies. They recognized that the person who works harder or has more ability or training or responsibility is entitled to more material rewards for his work. In that sense, they acknowledged that it is as great an injustice to treat unequals equally, as to treat equals unequally. They realized that such levelling concepts would limit human freedom—for in a sense free men are not equal, and equal men are not free.

But they did believe that all men are entitled to equal rights under the law, even if they didn't fully realize the implications of that doctrine as it applied to certain citizens.

The framers of the Constitution had a firm basis for believing in equality for they believed in a Creator: "All men are *created* equal." If one accepts the evolutionary humanist model, what is to prevent one from concluding that some men, or some races, have evolved to a point of superiority over others? Lest that notion sound far-fetched, let us remember that the Nazis believed exactly that. This is not to suggest that evolutionists do not believe in equality, only that they lack a firm basis for believing in equality.

God-Given Human Rights

All the founding fathers believed that God had given men certain rights, and that the "Laws of Nature and of Nature's God" required

19. Diamond, "The Declaration and the Constitution," p. 49.

respect for those rights. Natural rights were part of natural law; God-given rights were part of God's law.

John Locke summarized the God-given rights as "life, liberty, and property." This phrase is found in the Fifth and Fourteenth Amendments to the Constitution; in the Declaration of Independence Jefferson expanded "property" to "pursuit of happiness." but the meaning was clear: "All men are endowed by their Creator with certain unalienable rights, that among these are Life, Liberty, and the pursuit of Happiness." "Pursuit of Happiness" did not mean the seeking of hedonistic pleasure. That concept came from Vattel, and as Forrest McDonald says:

> The second object of good government, "to procure the true happiness of the Nation," bore no relation to the selfish concept of "doing one's own thing" that unthinking moderns might regard as the meaning of the phrase "pursuit of happiness" in the Declaration of Independence. Indeed, it was the antithesis of such a concept. On the part of the state, it entailed rigorous instruction of the people in good citizenship and the arts and sciences, both practical and "polite," and the cultivation of religious piety within the limits of the right to liberty of conscience. On the part of the individual, it entailed love of country and rigorous attention to the duty of making oneself as virtuous, moral and useful a member of society as possible. The matter provided "an infallible criterion, by which the nation may judge of the intentions of those who govern it. If they endeavor to render the great and the common people virtuous, their views are pure and upright; and you may rest assured that they solely aim at the great end of government, the happiness and glory of the nation." On the other hand, if they corrupted the morals of the common people with permissiveness, thus spreading "a taste for luxury, effeminacy, a rage for licentious pleasures . . . beware, citizens! beware of those corruptors! they only aim at purchasing slaves in order to exercise over them an arbitrary sway." (Vattel, *Law of Nations*; Book I, Chapter 11, paragraphs 110-24, pp. 47-55).[20]

Human rights are found in both the Declaration of Independence and the Constitution. Article I, Section 9, protects human rights by prohibiting Congress from doing certain things. It protects the right to petition for writ of habeas corpus and the right not to be prosecuted ex post facto.

The founding fathers did not intend to limit human rights to those examples alone. They recognized that man had certain rights under common law, and they expected the courts to fully protect those

20. Forrest McDonald, *Alexander Hamilton* (New York: W. W. Norton & Co., 1979), pp. 53–57.

rights. As soon as the Constitution was ratified they gave those rights explicit protection in the Bill of Rights.

Human rights find their basis in the Bible. The Scripture's recurring theme is that man is created in the image of God (Gen. 1:26-27; 9:6). God's image entails human dignity. Certain human rights come with that dignity.

God also confers certain positive rights through the negative commands of Scripture. The commandment, "Thou shalt not kill" (Exod 20:13), confers a right to life. The command not to kidnap or enslave confers a right to liberty (Exod. 21:16; Deut. 24:7). The command, "Thou shalt not steal" (Exod 20:15) confers a right to property. The three rights of life, liberty, and property mentioned by Locke come from the Bible.

According to the Declaration, rights are "endowed by their Creator." There is no real basis for believing in human rights, unless one also believes in a creator God. Jefferson's words, engraved on the Jefferson Memorial in Washington, D.C., say it well, "God who gave us life, gave us liberty at the same time. Can the liberties of a nation be secure when we have removed their only sure basis, a conviction in the minds of the people that those liberties are the gift of God?"

Governments Secure Rights

The Declaration continues: "That to secure these rights, Governments are instituted among Men." The Preamble of the Constitution declares that one of its purposes is to "secure the Blessings of Liberty to ourselves and our Posterity."

The founding fathers recognized that governments do not grant rights, nor do they have legitimate authority to take rights away. Rights are God-given, and for that reason they are "unalienable." Governments merely "secure," or make it possible for men to enjoy, the rights that God has given.

Government by Consent of the Governed

To secure these rights, the Declaration also states, "Governments are instituted among Men, deriving their just powers from the consent of the governed." And the Constitution begins, "We the People of the United States, in Order to form a more perfect Union. . . ."

What does the Declaration mean by "consent of the governed"? Martin Diamond explains what "consent of the governed" implied in the 1700s:

Now "to secure these rights," men quit the insecure state of nature and "Governments are instituted among men, deriving their just powers from the consent of the governed." Here we have the unambiguous meaning of the other phrase in the Declaration that is now so typically misunderstood. It has been transformed to mean rule by the consent of majorities, that is, consent according to the procedures of the democratic form of government. But the Declaration does not say that consent is the means by which the government is to operate; it says that consent is necessary only to institute or establish the government. It does not prescribe that the people establish a democratic form of government which operates by means of their consent. Instead, the Declaration says that they may organize government on "such principles" as they choose, and that they may choose "any form of government" they deem appropriate to secure their rights. (In this, the Declaration was again simply following Locke, who taught that when men consent "to joyn into and make one society," they "might set up what form of Government they thought fit.") And by "any form of government," the Declaration emphatically includes—as any literate 18th-century reader would have understood—not only the democratic form of government, but also a mixed form, and the aristocratic and monarchic forms as well. . . .

Thus the Declaration, accurately speaking, is neutral on the question of forms of government; any form is legitimate, provided it secures equal freedom and is instituted by popular consent. But as to how to secure that freedom the Declaration, in its famous passage on the principles of government, is silent.[21]

The Constitution builds on the foundation laid by the Declaration. It adopts the principles of the Declaration and builds a structured form of government. That form is a constitutional republic not a democracy. The Constitution guarantees a "Republican Form of Government" (Article IV, Section 4) to every state in the Union. There is a difference between a democracy and a republic.

The concept of "consent of the governed" has its roots in John Locke's social compact, which is in turn rooted in the Calvinist concept of the covenant, by which men, in the presence of God, join themselves together into a body politic. And correctly understood, the concept is biblical. Scripture teaches that God usually ordains government through people (Rom. 13; Dan. 2; 1 Peter 3). The Israelite monarchy was established by popular demand. The men of Israel wanted a king, and God gave them one even though it was not his perfect will (1 Sam. 8; Deut. 17:14-20). Throughout the Old

21. Diamond, "The Declaration and the Constitution," p. 50.

Testament people chose kings to rule over Israel: "The men of Israel said to Gideon, Rule thou over us." (Judg. 8:22) "The men of Shechem . . . made Ahimelech king" (Judg. 9:6) "Hushai said unto Absalom, Nay; but whom the Lord, and this people, and all the men of Israel choose, his will I be, and with him will I abide" (2 Sam. 16:18). "The people . . . took Azariah . . . and made him king" (2 Kings 14:21). God spoke through Moses to "all Israel" (Deut. 5:1) and later God directed the Israelites to choose judges: "Judges and officers shalt thou (speaking to 'all Israel') make thee (again, 'all Israel') in all thy gates, which the Lord thy God giveth thee, throughout thy tribes; and they shall judge the people with just judgment" (Deut. 16:18). These passages indicate that the Jewish kings and judges governed with the consent of the governed, and that the Israelites had some voice in the selection of their leaders.

The Sinful Nature of Man

Any theory of government must be based on a realistic view of human nature. Utopian philosophies such as socialism or communism are based on beliefs in human perfection or human perfectability. The biblical view that man is a sinner, capable of some civic virtue but basically self-centered and self-seeking, gravitates toward a different form of government.

The founding fathers' view of human nature was the same as the Bible's view: "All have sinned, and come short of the glory of God" (Rom. 3:23).

Their task was to shape a government that was consistent with this view of man. Madison explained in *The Federalist No. 51:*

> But what is government itself but the greatest of all reflections on human nature? If men were angels, no government would be necessary. If angels were to govern men, neither external nor internal controls on government would be necessary. In framing a government which is to be administered by men over men, the great difficulty lies in this: You must first enable the government to control the governed; and in the next place, oblige it to control itself.

Government will be unable to restrain the sinful acts of men unless it has sufficient power to govern effectively. The Articles of Confederation had given the framers of the Constitution experience with government that lacked sufficient power to control the governed. The result was chaos.

They realized that rulers also have sinful natures. If rulers are given too much power, they will use it to advance themselves and oppress their subjects. "All power tends to corrupt," Lord Acton said; "Absolute power corrupts absolutely."[22]

The basic question political scientists wrestle with is how to establish a balance of power: giving government enough power to restrain the sinful tendencies of the masses, but at the same time restricting the power of government so it does not become oppressive.

The solution is not found in majority rule. Majorities can take power and use power to oppress minorities. It matters little to the oppressed minority whether rights were violated by the whim of one prince or by the majority vote of Congress. The French observer Alexis de Tocqueville explained:

> I seek to trace the novel features under which despotism may appear in the world. The first thing that strikes the observation is an innumerable multitude of men all equal and alike, incessantly endeavouring to procure the petty and paltry pleasures with which they glut their lives. . . .
>
> Above this race of men stands an immense and tutelary power, which takes upon itself alone to secure their gratifications, and to watch over their fate. That power is absolute, minute, regular, provident, and mild. It would be like the authority of a parent, if, like that authority, its object was to prepare men for manhood; but it seeks on the contrary to keep them in perpetual childhood: it is well content that the people should rejoice, provided they think of nothing but rejoicing. For their happiness such a government willingly labours, but it chooses to be the sole agent and only arbiter of that happiness: it provides for their security, foresees and supplies their necessities, facilitates their pleasures, manages their principal concerns, directs their industry, regulates the descent of property, and subdivides their inheritances—what remains, but to spare them all the care of thinking and all the trouble of living
>
> Thus it every day renders the exercize of the free agency of man less useful and less frequent; it circumscribes the will within a narrower range, and gradually robs a man of all the uses of himself. The principal of equality has prepared men for these things: it has predisposed men to endure them, and often times to look on them as benefits.
>
> After having thus successively taken each member of the community in its powerful grasp, and fashioned them at will, the supreme power then extends its arm over the whole community. It covers the surface of society with a network of small complicated rules, minute and uniform, through which the most original minds and the most energetic characters cannot penetrate, to rise above the crowd. The

22. John Emerick Edward Dalberg Acton; quoted in *World Book Encyclopedia*, 1985, s.v. "Acton, Lord."

will of man is not shattered, but softened, bent, and guided: men are seldom forced by it to act, but they are constantly restrained from acting: such a power does not destroy, but it prevents existence; it does not tyrannize, but it compresses, enervates, extinguishes, and stupefies a people, till each nation is reduced to nothing better than a flock of timid and industrious animals, of which government is the shepherd.

I have always thought that servitude of the regular, quiet, and gentle kind which I have just described, might be combined more easily than is commonly believed with some of the outward forms of freedom; and that it might even establish itself under the wing of the sovereignty of the people.

Our contemporaries are constantly excited by two conflicting passions; they want to be led, and they wish to remain free: as they cannot destroy either one or the other of these contrary propensities, they strive to satisfy them both at once. They devise a sole, tutelary, and all-powerful form of government, but elected by the people. They combine the principle of centralization and that of popular sovereignty; this gives them a respite: they console themselves for being in tutelage by the reflection that they have chosen their own guardians. Every man allows himself to be put in leading-strings, because he sees that it is not a person or a class of persons, but the people at large that holds the end of his chain.[23]

The founding fathers disliked the term *democracy* because in their view it invariably resulted in mobocracy and the abuse of individual rights. They favored a constitutional republic, though they sometimes used the word *democracy* interchangeably with the word *republic*.

A republic and democracy differ in several respects:

First, a republic is government by representatives, whereas democracy is direct majority rule. This is more than a mechanical difference. In a republic the representative is to think *for* his constituents rather than *with* them. They elect him because they respect him and his judgment, not because he will be their rubber stamp. If his values differ from theirs they will choose someone else; but he is elected as their representative to vote as he thinks right.

Second, a republic places restrictions on majority rule. In the U.S. this happens in many ways: through a Congress consisting of

23. Alexis de Tocqueville, *On Democracy, Revolution, and Society: Selected Writings,* ed. John Stone and Stephen Mennell (Chicago: University of Chicago Press, 1980), pp. 375–76.

two houses, both of which must pass a bill before it becomes law; through a President who can veto legislation; through a court that can rule on the constitutionality of laws.

Third, a republic respects individual rights. The Constitution guarantees individual rights whether or not the majority agrees. If Congress were to pass a law restricting First Amendment rights to freedom of speech, or freedom of religion, that law would be unconstitutional; if the Supreme Court is doing its job properly, it will strike down the law as unconstitutional even if 90 percent of the public supports it.

And fourth, as John Adams said, "The very definition of a republic is 'an empire of laws and not of men.'"[24] Law is above men: above the subjects, above the rulers, even above the majority. The founding fathers tried to create a republic in which power was widely distributed making it impossible for any one individual or group of individuals to become too powerful—even a majority. Their goal was to *separate* the powers of government into legislative, executive, and judicial branches. They also added a unique feature of *checks and balances* by which each branch prevents the other branches from becoming too powerful. For example, the President can veto acts of Congress; but Congress can override his veto by a two-thirds vote of each house. The Supreme Court can declare acts of Congress unconstitutional, but the President appoints the court, subject to the advice and consent of the Senate. In this way interest checks interest. Each branch of government, jealous of its own power, seeks to limit the power of the other branches.

Given the biblical view of the sinful nature of man, this form of government is a realistic way of establishing and apportioning government power. It is not the *only* form of government that is consistent with the biblical view of man.

Limited, Delegated Powers

The founding fathers intended to limit the authority of rulers to the powers delegated in the Constitution.

This also relates to Locke's principle of social compact and the Calvinist concept of covenant. The people delegate certain powers to government; government has no powers other than those delegated. The phrase in the Declaration, "deriving their just powers

24. John Adams, "Thoughts on Government;" quoted in John R. Howe, Jr., *The Changing Political Thought of John Adams* (Princeton: Princeton University Press, 1966), p. 91.

from the consent of the governed" establishes this point. If the governed did not consent to give a certain power to the government through the Constitution, then the government does not have that power.

The framers of the Constitution thought that point was clear, but restated it in the Tenth Amendment: "The powers not delegated to the United States by the Constitution, nor prohibited by it to the states, are reserved to the States respectively, or to the people."

The Tenth Amendment has been called a "dead letter" and an "exercise in redundancy." In a sense it is, for it states what the founding fathers thought anyone would know to be true. But its principle is the cornerstone of limited government: except for a few powers over foreign affairs that pass inherently with national sovereignty, the federal government has no powers other than those which the people have delegated to it, expressed or implied, in the Constitution. If this limitation is ignored, a basic barrier to tyranny is removed.

The history of Israel is filled with political struggles between freedom-loving people and power-hungry kings. It is debatable whether a monarchy was ever God's perfect will for his people (see 1 Sam. 8), but he clearly intended for it to be limited in power. (Deut. 17:14-20). The confrontation between Solomon's son, Rehoboam, and the elders of Judah (1 Kings 12:6-19) is but one example of an ongoing struggle between ruler and the ruled.

Rights of Criminal Defendants

The founding fathers knew that punishment is necessary to deter crime. But they also recognized that an orderly process of justice is necessary to distinguish between the guilty and innocent. And in a free society which values human dignity, a defendant is presumed innocent until proven guilty.

For this reason the Constitution provides numerous protections for the rights of accused persons: protection against unreasonable searches and seizures, grand jury indictment in serious cases, privilege against self-incrimination, speedy and public trial, the right to be informed of the charges against oneself and to confront and cross-examine witnesses, to have assistance of counsel, the right to subpoena witnesses, and protection against excessive bail and cruel and unusual punishment.

In giving rights to the accused, the Jewish system of justice was one of the most advanced in the world. Israel had an orderly, multi-tier system of justice, with Moses as the Supreme Court (Exod. 18:13–16; Deut. 1:16–17; 19:15–21). Judges were commanded to be honest, to refuse bribes, and not to show favoritism (Exod. 23:1–8). A person was presumed innocent unless at least two witnesses testified against him (Deut. 17:6), and the penalty for perjury was severe (Deut. 19:16–21). Extrabiblical Jewish law went further than our current legal system in protecting the rights of the accused. The reason was the emphasis on man being created in the image of God, and that human life and dignity were to be greatly valued.

Property Rights

The Constitution places great value on property rights; for example, "life, liberty and property" in the Fifth and Fourteenth Amendments and the further guarantee of the Fifth Amendment that "nor shall private property be taken for public use without just compensation."

The Bible also values property rights; Much of the Mosaic law deals with property. Realty was held by families rather than individuals due to the unique relation of Israel to its land through the Mosaic and Abrahamic covenants, but other types of property were individually owned.[25] The commands, "Thou shalt not steal" and "Thou shalt not covet" (Exod. 20:15, 17) clearly imply property rights.

The Sanctity of Contract

The right to make contracts, expect others to obey them, and to expect the courts to enforce them if necessary is closely related to property rights. The Bible upholds the sacredness of an oath: "Lord, who shall abide in thy tabernacle? who shall dwell in thy holy hill? . . . He that sweareth to his own hurt, and changeth not" (Ps. 15:1, 4).

The Constitution forbids the states from enacting any "Law impairing the Obligation of Contracts." (Article I, Section 10, Paragraph (1)).

The courts have not interpreted this provision of the Constitution as literally as it was intended. Even Beard notes that the framers of the Constitution intended the contract clause to have a stricter meaning than has been interpreted—which is why early justices—men like John Marshall and Joseph Story—who knew the authors

---

25. John Eidsmoe, *God and Caesar: Christian Faith and Political Action* (Westchester, Illinois: Crossway, 1984), pp. 91–114.

dissented from decisions which accepted a relaxed interpretation of the contract clause.[26]

Two Witnesses

Scripture declares that, "At the mouth of two witnesses or three witnesses, shall he that is worthy of death be put to death; but at the mouth of one witness he shall not be put to death" (Deut. 17:6; cf. 19:15; Num. 35:30).

It is possible for a prosecuting witness to lie or be sincerely mistaken. It is less likely for two witnesses to lie or be mistaken. The scriptural injunction protects the accused from a false accusation. The Jews interpreted the passage to mean that the two witnesses must agree on every detail (Mark 14:55-59).

The Constitution provides a similar protection in Article III, Section 3, Paragraph (1): "No Person shall be convicted of Treason unless on the Testimony of two Witnesses to the same overt Act, or on Confession in open Court." Closely related is the protection against self-incrimination embodied in the Fifth Amendment. Jewish law not only did not require a person to incriminate himself; it also did not *allow* him to do so because self-incrimination was to participate in one's own destruction which was suicide. The Jewish Sanhedrin violated this prohibition in Jesus' trial (John 18:19–21).

Corruption of Blood

Scripture declares that the criminal, not his family, may be punished for his crime: "The fathers shall not be put to death for the children, neither shall the children be put to death for the fathers: every man shall be put to death for his own sin" (Deut. 24:16).

This principle is adopted in Article III, Section 3, Paragraph (2) of the Constitution: ". . . no Attainder of Treason shall work Corruption of blood, or Forfeiture except during the Life of the Person attained." If a parent was convicted of treason, this did not affect the civil rights of his children. This is unlike the practice in many pagan nations of executing the convicted criminal and also his entire family (see Dan. 6:24).

Sundays Excepted

The Bible commands:

(8) Remember the sabbath day, to keep it holy.
(9) Six days shalt thou labour, and do all thy work:

---

26. Beard, *Economic Interpretation*, pp. 179–83.

(10) But the seventh day is the sabbath of the Lord thy God: in it thou shalt not do any work (Exod. 20:8-10).

Article I, Section 7, Paragraph (2) of the Constitution sets forth the President's veto power, and declares that "If any bill shall not be returned by the President within ten days (*Sundays excepted*) after it shall have been presented to him, the Same shall be a Law, in like Manner as if he had signed it. . . ."

Christians take at least three positions on Sabbath observance: (1) Saturday is the Sabbath; (2) Sunday is the Christian Sabbath; (3) the command to honor the Sabbath is no longer applicable in this dispensation. Suffice it to say that most Christians in eighteenth-century America believed Sunday to be the Sabbath, and they believed they were to honor it by not working. This clause of the Constitution accommodates that belief and practice.

Separation of Church and State

Old Testament Israel is often thought to have been a theocracy. In one sense it was—and so is the United States in that same sense. For theocracy comes from two Greek words, "theos" for God, and "kratos" for ruler—meaning God is the ruler of the nation.

Israel was a theocracy recognizing God as its supreme ruler: all authority was derived from him. But government functions were separated from religious functions; the kings came from the tribe of Judah while the priests came from the tribe of Levi. King Saul was severely punished when he tried to usurp the function of the priesthood by offering sacrifices himself—his line was cut off from the kingship of Israel forever (1 Sam. 13). When King Uzziah tried to burn incense on the holy altar, God smote him with leprosy, and he remained a leper the rest of his life (2 Chron. 26:16-21). God seems to be telling the civil rulers in these passages, keep your hands off the church. In the New Testament Christ said, "Render therefore unto Caesar the things which are Caesar's, and unto God the things that are God's" (Luke 20:25). Christ also recognized two kingdoms, the church and the state. But each derives its authority from God.

America is also a nation of two kingdoms, the church and the state. But the country claims to be "one nation under God." The church and the state have separate spheres of authority, but both derive authority from God. In that sense America, like Israel, is a theocracy.

The two-kingdom concept is recognized in the First Amendment to the Constitution: "Congress shall make no law respecting an establishment of religion, or prohibiting the free exercise thereof. . . ."

In *The Christian Legal Advisor*[27] over three hundred pages were devoted to a detailed discussion of the background, framing, and meaning of the First Amendment and its application to specific contemporary problems. The First Amendment, when properly understood, is an admirable embodiment of the two-kingdom concept and is consistent with the Bible. In recent years the courts have frequently misinterpreted the First Amendment and required government to maintain a hostile indifference toward Christianity and religion in general. The result has been the elevation of the establishment clause at the expense of the free exercise clause, and an establishment of Secular Humanism. This is a far cry from what the framers of the Constitution intended. Joseph Story, a Unitarian, Harvard law professor and Supreme Court justice, in his 1833 *Commentaries on the Constitution* wrote:

> Probably at the time of the adoption of the Constitution, and of the amendment to it now under consideration, the general, if not the universal sentiment was, that Christianity ought to receive encouragement from the state, so far as was not incompatible with the private rights of conscience and the freedom of religious worship. An attempt to level all religions, and to make it a matter of state policy to hold all in utter indifference, would have created universal disapprobation, if not universal indignation.[28]

The Declaration of Independence and the Constitution of the United States are consistent with the principles found in the Bible, and for that reason these documents have served America well for two hundred years. Now the Constitution and Declaration of Independence enter their third century. Where does the United States go from here?

---

27. John Eidsmoe, *The Christian Legal Advisor* (Grand Rapids: Baker, 1984, 1987).

28. Joseph Story, *Commentaries on the Constitution of the United States* (Boston, 1833), II:593; quoted in Robert L. Cord, *Separation of Church and State: Historical Fact and Current Fiction* (New York: Lambeth Press, 1982), p. 13.

22

Into the Third Century: Where Does the United States Go From Here?

The United States enters a third century of constitutional history in 1987. After two hundred years the country remains, for the most part, a free society because it has stayed within the shadow of the Constitution. Will the republic the founding fathers created continue? Will the United States be a free society in 2087?

A Christian renewal seems to be blossoming today. The resurgence of patriotism along with the movement back to traditional values are signs of hope that a free society will continue.

But several dangers exist, which if left unchecked, could destroy the foundation of the republic.

Ignorance

Recent studies indicate that increasing numbers of Americans consider religion important, attend church, and claim to be "born again," but many are ignorant about the Bible. Without a solid knowledge of the foundational document of Christianity, Christian renewal will be shallow and short-lived.

The Declaration of Independence and the Constitution are the foundational documents of the United States. If citizens do not understand the principles of these fundamental documents the nation is vulnerable to the subversion of its republican principles.

When the Declaration and Constitution were originally written, they were printed in newspapers and eagerly read and discussed in homes, churches, halls, and open air meetings across the nation. As a result, Americans were familiar with the principles of republican government. The French observer Alexis de Tocqueville noted this during his travels in America in the 1830s. He remarked about American ignorance of European affairs, but added:

> But if you question (the average American) respecting his own country, the cloud that dimmed his intelligence will immediately disperse; his language will become as clear and precise as his thoughts. He will inform you what his rights are and by what means he exercises them; he will be able to point out customs which obtain in the political world. You will find that he is well acquainted with the rules of the administration, and that he is familiar with the mechanism of the laws. The citizen of the United States does not acquire his practical science and his positive notions from books; the instructions he has acquired may have prepared him for receiving those ideas, but it did not furnish them. The American learns to know the laws by participating in the act of legislation; and he takes a lesson in the forms of government from governing. The great work of society is ever going on before his eyes and, as it were, under his hands.[1]

Unfortunately, Americans today lack understanding about the nation's legal and constitutional system. They also lack appreciation for the underlying principles of the Declaration and the Constitution. Few schools or colleges have curricula which explain the philosophies of Montesquieu, Blackstone, Locke, Jonathan Edwards, Samuel Rutherford, or John Milton in relation to these principles.

According to a federally funded study called the National Assessment of Educational Progress, today's young people do not understand the most elementary principles of American government. This study revealed that only 42% of 13-year-olds and 74% of 17-year-olds could give an acceptable answer to the question, "What is democracy?"—this was a drop of 12% from a 1970 study. Although 1976 was an election year, only 36% of 17-year-olds and less than 20% of 13-year-olds understood how presidential candidates are nominated—this was a decline of 14% from 1970. Another report concluded that only 11% could describe how the President is chosen.[2]

---

1. Alexis de Tocqueville, *Democracy in America*, 1835; reprinted by Vintage Books, New York, 1945, I:329-30.
2. Martha Angle and Robert Walters, "Education Decline Continues," *Pittsburgh Press*, February 4, 1978.

A recent study conducted by the Hearst Corporation and released by the U. S. Bicentennial Commission revealed similar ignorance about the Constitution on the part of American adults. This study, consisting of telephone interviews with 1,004 American adults during the fall of 1986, revealed that 46% do not know that the purpose of the Constitution was to create a federal government and define its powers; 26% believe the purpose of the Constitution was to declare independence from England. While 76% understood, basically, how the Constitution is amended, only 34% know even approximately, how many amendments have been approved to date (26). Only 41% correctly identified the Bill of Rights as the first ten amendments to the Constitution; 27% think the Bill of Rights is the preamble to the Constitution.[3]

Americans need to promote greater understanding of the Constitution and the principles behind it. There are good materials available. (See the listing at the end of this chapter.) These and other materials can help familiarize citizens of all ages with the Constitution.

Immorality

John Adams declared, "Our constitution was made only for a moral and religious people. It is wholly inadequate for the government of any other."[4]

Americans in 1787 had sinful natures, but due to the influence of religion and tradition in that day, the outward expression of sin was greatly restrained. Oaths were considered sacred, and a man's word was his bond. Crime rates were lower, and sexual immorality was not as widespread as today.

Can the Constitution work in twentieth-century America—with soaring crime rates, rampant disregard for law, tax evasion, unreliable promises, common place infidelity and immorality, with divorce and abortion as easy solutions?

Gouverneur Morris insisted that the U. S. Constitution would not work in France because of the low moral character of the French people. He noted the French disrespect for religion, love of violence, breaking of promises, and sexual immorality. Morris accurately predicted the result of their behavior: revolution, anarchy, chaos,

---

3. Hearst Corporation Survey, "We the People," Official Newsletter of the Commission on the Bicentennial of the United States Constitution, March, 1987.

4. John Adams, 1789; quoted in *War on Religious Freedom* (Virginia Beach, Virginia: Freedom Council, 1984), p. 1.

terror, and ultimate despotism. What distinguishes twentieth-century America from eighteenth-century France?

In *Sex and Culture*, J. D. Unwin presents the results of his study of eighty past and present civilizations. He concluded that those nations which practiced sexual licentiousness either fell from greatness or never became great at all. He suggested the reason was that a certain sexual energy must be harnessed for a nation to achieve greatness, and if it is allowed to dissipate national decay and destruction will result. He found that the great and lasting civilizations restrict sex to monogamous marriage.[5]

America needs to return to the traditional, Bible-based moral standards the founding fathers believed in if our free society is to continue. If people cannot voluntarily restrain their sinful impulses through moral self-discipline it may be necessary for the government to supply that restraint.

The constitutional republic can be secure only when there is renewed respect for law and order, and for those who are responsible for keeping the peace; when the sacredness of all written or spoken contractual obligations is recognized; when parents and schools again teach sexual abstinence prior to marriage as the primary solution to problems such as unwanted pregnancy and sexually transmitted disease; when the right to life is preserved for all, including the unborn; when religion regains respect as the central source of all true morality.

A New Constitutional Convention?

The Constitution provides two procedures for its amendment (Article V):

> The Congress, whenever two-thirds of both Houses shall deem it necessary, shall propose Amendments to this Constitution, or, on the Application of the Legislatures of two-thirds of the several States, shall call a Convention for proposing Amendments, which, in either Case, shall be valid to all Intents and Purposes, as Part of this Constitution, when ratified by the Legislatures of three-fourths of the several States, or by Conventions in three-fourths thereof, as the one or the other Mode of Ratification may be proposed by the Congress. . . .

---

5. J. D. Unwin, *Sex and Culture* (Oxford: Oxford University Press, 1934), pp. vii, 23, 340, 414, 431, 618, 619. Cited by O. R. Johnston, *Who Needs the Family?* (Downers Grove, Illinois: InterVarsity Press, 1979), pp. 43-44.

The first procedure enables passage of an amendment by two-thirds of each house of Congress followed by ratification by three-fourths of the states. This process has been used successfully twenty-six times.

The second permits a constitutional convention called by two-thirds of the states, followed by ratification by three-fourths of the states. This method has never been used but may be used soon.

Thirty-two of the necessary thirty-four states have called for a constitutional convention; most have done so to request a balanced budget amendment; several have called for a convention to consider other amendments. No one knows what would happen if such a convention took place.

The Constitution provides no specific procedures to be followed at a convention. No one knows how soon must it take place, how delegates will be apportioned and selected, or what rules the convention will follow. Presumably Congress will make some rules for the convention, but it is by no means clear that the convention will be bound to follow those rules.

The type of amendments such a convention would consider is also unknown. If thirty-four states call for a convention for the purpose of considering a balanced budget amendment, is the convention limited to considering only that amendment? Or could it also consider a right-to-life amendment or school prayer amendment?

If thirty states call for a convention to consider a balanced budget amendment, and four call for a convention to consider a right-to-life amendment, will they combine to constitute the necessary thirty-four states? May the convention consider both amendments?

Could these convention delegates decide to create an entirely new constitution? *No one knows.* Legal scholars have come to opposite conclusions. The only precedent is the Great Convention of 1787 which was called to suggest a few revisions to the Articles of Confederation, and ended up writing and then ratifying a new Constitution. Those who believe in a one-world government have a model constitution ready to submit if this convention takes place. This model constitution would reduce American sovereignty and essentially make the nation a vassal-state under the proposed world government.

Proponents of a convention point to a safeguard: The present Constitution says the changes shall be effective only if approved by three-fourths of the states, acting in conventions of their respective legislatures as Congress shall direct. This may provide some protection; but what if the proposed constitution provides a different means of ratification?

The point is that a new constitutional convention could endanger the free republican system. Several proposed amendments are worthy of consideration, but they should not be pursued by means which could jeopardize the entire constitutional structure. Contacting senators with suggestions for an amendment which would clarify and restrict the scope of and procedure for a constitutional convention may help to protect the republic's future.

Erosion of the Separation of Powers

The founding fathers established a system in which the powers of government were either to be equally separated between legislative, executive, and judicial branches, or that the legislature would be supreme. A reading of Montesquieu might indicate the former view; a reading of Blackstone, the latter.

Today the separation of powers is eroding. The judiciary and executive branches are usurping more powers at the expense of the legislative branch which is designed to best express the will of the people.

Growing Judicial Power

In the celebrated *Marbury v. Madison* case in 1803, the U. S. Supreme Court ruled that the judiciary has the power to strike down acts of Congress which violate the Constitution. Chief Justice Marshall reasoned that this power is implied from the fact that the Supreme Court has power over all cases arising under the Constitution and laws of the United States (Article III, Section 2, Paragraph 1), and that the Constitution and laws of the United States are the "supreme law of the land" (Article VI, Section 2). If the Constitution and a statute come into conflict, the Court has power to interpret them and decide between the two.

Some conservatives oppose judicial review per se. However, it appears most of the founders anticipated and approved the concept of judicial review. Hamilton clearly did so in the *Federalist Papers,* and some of the other founding fathers did so in their remarks at the Convention.[6]

---

6. *Federalist* No. 16, 78, 81; James Madison, *Notes of Debates in the Federal Convention* (Athens, Ohio: Ohio University Press, 1787, 1840, 1966, 1985), pp. 336-37 (James Wilson); 463 (Gouverneur Morris); 539 (James Madison). On p. 61, Elbridge Gerry notes that all state courts had all at times set aside laws as unconstitutional, and that this had met with general approval. On p. 462, John Mercer expresses his disapproval of judicial review.

Judicial review is necessary to protect individual rights from the tyranny of the majority. It is an integral part of the constitutional republican system of government.

Gouverneur Morris' belief in judicial independence has merit. A person is unlikely to get a fair and impartial trial from a judge worried about reelection or reappointment—especially in an unpopular or controversial case. However, judges with life tenure occasionally get the idea that they are only accountable to themselves, not to God as Morris suggested. For this reason, the "Missouri Plan," which allows the governor to appoint judges following a screening process, and permits the people to vote every several years to determine whether the judge shall be retained has some value.

But courts today go beyond judicial review and engage in judicial policy-making. In doing so they usurp the functions that belong to the legislative and the executive branches. It is proper for the courts to strike down segregated school systems as violating the "equal protection" clause of the Fourteenth Amendment if the facts so indicate. But when they impose restrictions, such as busing, on a local school system, they have gone beyond judicial review and are practicing judicial policymaking. Nor is it improper for courts to declare unsafe and unfair prison conditions to be unconstitutional violations of the due process clause or the cruel and unusual punishment clause, provided they have good factual and legal grounds for doing so. But when the courts draft complex rules and timetables for prison officials, they have gone far beyond the role the founders envisioned.

And the worst offense, in my opinion, is when daydreamers in judicial robes create previously unheard of "fundamental rights" out of thin air—such as the "right" to an abortion!

Since federal judges and many state judges are not elected by the people, they are less responsive to the popular will than is the legislature. A judicial position can be a real "ego trip." Judges need to practice humility and exercise judicial restraint. These qualities should be expected of judges. Citizens should ask elected officials to appoint judges who believe in judicial restraint.

Growth of Executive Power

The primary role of the executive as envisioned by the founding fathers, was to carry out or execute the policies set forth by Congress. But since that time the executive branch has usurped many powers that the founding fathers gave to the legislature and the judiciary.

One major danger is the use of "executive orders." When the President promulgates such orders, he is in effect making laws that should be made by the legislature.

The "line-item veto," which would allow the President to veto certain portions of bills passed by Congress without vetoing the entire bill, has the support of many conservatives as a means of cutting expenditures. But it also endangers the constitutional concept of separation of powers, because it increases the President's veto power beyond what the founding fathers intended. We must be careful not to use bad means to achieve a good result. I heartily support efforts to slash expenditures, but not by means which could endanger constitutional structure.

The growth of "administrative law" is even more dangerous. Administrative agencies, appointed rather than elected and in some cases not even subject to removal or scrutiny by the President, announce rules and regulations and enforce them as though they had the force of law. By doing this they usurp the function of the legislature. Administrative tribunals, quasi-judicial "courts" functioning under the auspices of the Social Security Administration, the International Revenue Service, the Occupational Health and Safety Administration and others, conduct "hearings" (read: trials) and impose "civil penalties" (hardly distinguishable from criminal fines), often without the due process protections which the courts provide. They usurp the function of the judiciary when this occurs.

It is argued that tribunals are necessary because certain areas of law are so specialized the courts can't handle them, and second, the separation of powers is not really violated because an individual can still appeal an adverse decision of an administrative tribunal to the courts (not true in the case of tax courts). These arguments contradict each other. If social security law is so specialized that the courts can't handle it properly, then how can the courts properly exercise appellate review over administrative decisions on such matters? Instead of administrative courts, the nation should establish special courts to deal with social security tax, and OSHA matters. Except for military courts, specialty courts should be under the judicial branch of government, not the executive. Military courts existed before the Constitution and were deemed essential to military discipline. The founding fathers indicated no intention of changing military courts.

A key concept of the Constitution is separation of powers. It is a principle by which the founding fathers sought to prevent any one person or group from becoming too powerful. It is essential to free government.

Growth of Big Government

The erosion of the separation of powers goes unnoticed today because of the rapid speed in which all branches and levels of government are expanding.

When George Washington became President in 1789, the federal government had 350 federal civilian employees to govern a population of three million—and they accomplished the task without automobiles, Lear jets, telephones, word processors, and other conveniences.

Today's federal government has over three million civil service employees, governing a population of 218 million. The total number of civil service employees has increased 8,571 times since 1789. The ratio of civil service employees to private citizens has grown from 1:8,500 in 1789 to 1:70 today. Each government employee is financed by taxes, and each regulates some aspect of citizens' lives. State and local governments have experienced similar growth.

The founding fathers believed Big Government was a threat to personal freedom. They tried to limit the size of government by carefully restricting its powers. Individuals wanting to expand the power of government have used ingenious means of getting around these restrictions. For many years the courts stood in the way, but in recent decades the courts have ignored some original restraints.

The general welfare clause was one such restriction. Article 1, Section 8, Paragraph (1) of the Constitution authorizes Congress to tax and spend for the "general Welfare of the United States." The founding fathers intended this phrase as a limit on federal power: the federal government can tax and spend only for that which benefits the nation *generally*, as a whole. It may not tax and spend for the *specific* welfare of individuals or groups.

In recent decades the courts have frequently ignored the word *general* as a limitation of power. They have reasoned that the nation is so interdependent, that expenditures which benefit specific groups in turn benefit the nation as a whole. For example, a subsidy to milk producers would enable them to produce better and spend more, and this would promote the general welfare of the nation. Such reasoning has made the general welfare restriction meaningless.

The "commerce clause" is another such limitation. Article I, Section 8, Paragraph (3) empowers Congress to regulate commerce "among the several states." By granting Congress the power to regulate *interstate* commerce, the founding fathers intended to withhold from Congress power to regulate *intrastate* commerce—

commerce within a state. That was to be left to the state governments.

But the courts have reasoned that if *intra*state commerce affects
*inter*state commerce it can be regulated—and the courts almost
always find that it does. For example, when the federal government
tried to regulate train passenger fares, a railroad objected. The
railroad conceded that Congress had the power to regulate rates
between Dallas and Shreveport; that was interstate commerce. But
the railroad argued that Congress has no power to regulate rates
between Dallas and Abilene; that's intrastate commerce and beyond
the power of Congress. But the Supreme Court ruled that if rates
between Dallas and Abilene were left unregulated, it could affect
whether people chose to travel to Abilene or to Shreveport; in other
words, it affected interstate commerce. And the regulation of
intrastate train fares was upheld.[7]

This rationale moved from ingenious to bizarre in *Wickard v.
Filburn.* The Court previously ruled that Congress could not only
regulate intrastate commerce if it affected interstate commerce; it
could also regulate production and manufacturing if it affected
interstate commerce—and again, it almost always does. So Congress sought to restrict the amount of grain a farmer could grow on
his farm. Farmer Filburn raised more grain than the regulations
allowed, but fed the excess grain to his pigs. How, he asked, could
the grain I raise on my own farm and feed to my own pigs, possibly
be considered interstate commerce? The Court answered: If you
hadn't raised that grain on your own farm and fed it to your pigs,
you might have bought some grain on the market and fet it to your
pigs; and that might have affected the price of grain in interstate
commerce! Thus the judge's gavel becomes a judicial magic wand,
and the distinction between interstate and intrastate, production
and commerce, is miraculously swept away. Another constitutional
barrier to Big Government fell by the wayside.[8]

A third barrier to Big Government was the doctrine of delegated
powers. The founding fathers understood that the federal government had been given only certain powers, and the federal government possessed only those powers and no others. The founding
fathers thought this was clear to everyone. But they wrote in the
Tenth Amendment: "The powers not delegated to the United States

7. Houston, *East and West Texas Railway Co. v. United States,* (The Shreveport Rate
Case), U.S . 342 (1914).
8. *Wickard v. Filburn,* 317 U. S. 111 (1942).

by the Constitution, nor prohibited by it to the States, are reserved to the States respectively, or to the people."

These men did their best, in Jefferson's words, to bind government down with the "chains of the Constitution."[9] But they failed to anticipate the evolutionary view of law.

Evolution, Legal Positivism, and Beyond

Most legal scholars of the twentieth century have a different outlook from those in the late eighteenth century. Woodrow Wilson capsulized the difference in his book *The New Freedom:*

> One of the chief benefits I derived from being President of the University was that I had the pleasure of entertaining thoughtful men from all over the world. I cannot tell you how much has dropped into my granary by their presence. I had been casting around in my mind for something by which to draw several parts of my political thoughts together but it was my good fortune to entertain a very interesting Scotsman who had been devoting himself to the philosophical thought of the 17th Century. His talk was so engaging that it was delightful to hear him speak of anything, and presently there came out of the unexpected region of his thought the thing I had been waiting for. He called my attention to the fact that in every generation all sorts of speculation and thinking tend to fall under the formula of the dominant thought of the age. For example, after the Newtonian Theory of the Universe had been developed, almost all thinking tended to express itself in the analogies of the Newtonian Theory and since the Darwinian Theory has reigned amongst us, everybody is likely to express whatever he wishes to expound in terms of development and accommodation to environment.
>
> Now, it came to me, as this interesting man talked, that the Constitution of the United States had been made under the dominion of the Newtonian Theory. You have only to read the papers of *The Federalist* to see that fact written on every page. They speak of the "checks and balances" of the Constitution, and use to express their idea the simile of the organization of the universe, and particularly of the solar system, how by the attraction of gravitation the various parts are held in their orbits; and then they proceed to represent Congress, the Judiciary, and the President as a sort of imitation of the solar system.
>
> They were only following the English Whigs, who gave Great Britain its modern Constitution. Not that those Englishmen analyzed the matter, or had any theory about it; Englishmen care little for

---

9. Thomas Jefferson; quoted by Edwin Meese, III, "Toward a Jurisprudence of Original Intention," *Benchmark*, Vol. II, No. 1, p. 10.

theories. It was a Frenchman, Montesquieu, who pointed out to them how faithfully they had copied Newton's description of the mechanism of the heavens.

The makers of our Federal Constitution read Montesquieu with true scientific enthusiasm. They were scientists in their way—the best way of their age—those fathers of the nation. Jefferson wrote "the laws of Nature"—and then by the way of after thought—"and of Nature's God." And they constructed a government as they would have constructed an orrery—to display the laws of Nature. Politics in their thought was a variety of mechanics. The Constitution was founded on the law of gravitation. The government was to exist and move by virtue of the efficacy of "checks and balances."

The trouble with the theory is that government is not a machine, but a living thing. It falls, not under the theory of the universe, but under the theory of organic life. It is accountable to Darwin, not to Newton. It is modified by its environment, necessitated by its tasks, shaped to its functions by the sheer pressure of life. No living thing can have its organs offset against each other, as checks, and live. On the contrary, its life is dependent upon their quick co-operation, their ready response to the commands of instinct or intelligence, their amicable community of purpose. Government is not a body of blind forces; it is a body of men, with highly differentiated functions, no doubt, in our modern day, of specialization, with a common task and purpose. Their co-operation is indispensable, their warfare fatal. There can be no successful government without the intimate, instinctive co-ordination of the organs of life and action. This is not theory, but fact, and displays its force as fact, whatever theories may be thrown across its track. Living political constitutions must be Darwinian in structure and in practice. Society is a living organism and must obey the laws of Life, not of mechanics; it must develop.

All that progressives ask or desire is permission—in an era when "development," "evolution," is the scientific word—to interpret the Constitution according to the Darwinian principle; all they ask is recognition of the fact that a nation is a living thing and not a machine.[10]

The founding fathers were Newtonians. They believed in a God who created the heavens and the earth, and established fixed physical laws by which the world operates and fixed laws of nature by which governments operate. Their world view was also Newtonian. They believed in fixed, unchanging absolutes: Scientific laws don't change (though man's perception of them might), and the laws that govern national and international relations don't change.

10. Woodrow Wilson, *The New Freedom* (New York: 1914), pp. 44-48.

So except for an occasional amendment to accommodate changing conditions, the Constitution is valid for all ages.

Twentieth-century jurisprudence is based on a Darwinian world view. Life evolves, men evolve, society evolves, and therefore laws and constitutions evolve. According to the Darwinian principle, the Constitution's meaning evolves and changes with time.[11] An example of this Darwinian view of law is found in the Supreme Court's use of the "cruel and unusual punishment" clause of the Eighth Amendment. *Trop v. Dulles*, 356 U. S. 86, involved the State Department's effort to strip a man of his citizenship because he deserted from the armed forces in World War II. Trop argued that to strip him of his citizenship constituted cruel and unusual punishment. The State Department argued that this could not be considered cruel and unusual punishment because the authors of the Eighth Amendment would have approved of such punishment, if not something more severe like execution. But Chief Justice Warren ruled in favor of Trop, writing "that the words of the Amendment are not precise, and that their scope is not static. The Amendment must draw its meaning from the *evolving standards of decency that mark the progress of a maturing society*" (emphasis added).

Justice Brennan picked up the same theme in his concurring opinion in *Furman v. Georgia*, 408 U. S. 238 (1972). Justice Brennan contended that capital punishment is per se cruel and unusual punishment and therefore unconstitutional. The fact that capital punishment was practiced in 1789 when the Eighth Amendment was adopted, and that the same Congress which passed the Eighth Amendment also passed the Fifth Amendment which expressly recognizes capital punishment, was deemed irrelevant. Brennan said, quoting Warren in *Trop v. Dulles*, that the Eighth Amendment must be interpreted according to an "evolving standard of decency"; and even though capital punishment was acceptable in 1787, it is cruel and unusual by the enlightened standards of today. Brennan's opinion did not speak for the majority, but it combined with others to strike down Georgia's capital punishment statute as applied in that case.

Four years later the Court again considered a capital punishment statute, in *Gregg v. Georgia*, 428 U. S. 153 (1976). A 5-4 majority ruled the statute was constitutional. Many states since 1972 have adopted new capital punishment statutes, and many polls showed

---

11. We speak today about the "evolution" of a legal doctrine; and as judges guide the evolution of the legal system, they "make law." Blackstone would not had spoken of "making law"; in his more humble view judges "discover" or "apply" the law of nature and of nature's God. But judges today think they "make" law.

that a majority of the public favored the death penalty. The majority said that society's standards of decency have not evolved to the point where capital punishment is cruel and unusual.

However, Justice Thurgood Marshall dissented and argued that public opinion polls and votes of legislators could not be relied on to ascertain society's standards of decency, because legislators and private citizens do not really comprehend how barbaric capital punishment is.

Marshall and the minority claim society has evolved to the point where capital punishment is cruel and unusual. Stewart and the majority say society has not evolved to that point—yet. But neither the majority nor minority deny the basic evolutionary interpretation. They merely question at which stage of the evolutionary scale we are!

This is not the way the founding fathers viewed constitutional interpretation. They saw the Constitution as the supreme law, and also as a covenant or contract. The Constitution like all legal documents was viewed as a fixed document, to be interpreted according to its plain meaning. And if its meaning was ambiguous as applied to a specific situation, it was to be interpreted according to the intent of those who wrote it, signed it, and ratified it.

James Madison expressed this view when he wrote, "(If) the sense in which the Constitution was accepted and ratified by the Nation . . . be not the guide in expounding it, there can be no security for a faithful exercise of its powers."[12] His views were echoed by Thomas Jefferson: "The Constitution on which our Union rests, shall be administered by me according to the safe and honest meaning contemplated by the plain understanding of the people of the United States, at the time of its adoption."[13] George Washington recognized that the Constitution is changed by the amendment process the Constitution provides, not by evolutionary interpretations:

> If, in the opinion of the people, the distribution or modification of the Constitutional powers be at any particular wrong, let it be corrected by an amendment in the way the Constitution designates. But let there be no change by usurpation; though this may in one

12. James Madison, *The Writings of James Madison*, ed. G. Hunt, (1899-1910), p. 191; quoted by Raoul Berger, *Government by Judiciary* (Harvard University Press, 1977), p. 364; quoted by William D. Graves, Brief of Defendants, *Bell and McCord v. The Little Axe Independent School District No. 70 of Cleveland County*, in the U. S. District Court for the Western District of Oklahoma, filed May 13, 1982, p. 17.

13. Thomas Jefferson; quoted in *Thomas Jefferson* (Salt Lake City, Utah: Freeman Institute, American Classic Series, 1981), p. 65.

instance be the instrument of good, it is the customary weapon by which free governments are destroyed.[14]

Joseph Story, Professor of Law at Harvard and Associate Justice of the U. S. Supreme Court, was the leading constitutional scholar of the nineteenth century. In *Commentaries on the Constitution* (1833) he called for interpreting the Constitution according to its plain meaning and the intent of its authors, "The first and fundamental rule in the interpretation of all instruments is, to construe them according to the sense of the terms, and the intention of the parties."[15] He declared that the Constitution was to be understood in terms of its plain, commonsense meaning:

> The reader must not expect to find in these pages any novel constructions of the Constitution. I have not the ambition to be the author of any new plan of interpreting the theory of the Constitution, or of enlarging or narrowing its powers, by ingenious subtleties and learned doubts. . . . Upon subjects of government, it has always appeared to me that metaphysical refinements are out of place. A constitution of government is addressed to the common sense of the people, and never was designed for trials of logical skill, or visionary speculation.[16]

Harvard law professors don't address themselves to the "common sense of the people" today. Consider this paragraph from Professor Unger's analysis of the Critical Legal Studies movement (a loosely-knit group of radical lawyers, law professors, and law students) which appeared in the *Harvard Law Review*:

> The modern lawyer may wish to keep his formalism while avoiding objectivist assumptions. He may feel happy to switch from talk about interest group politics in a legislative setting to invocations of impersonal purpose, policy, and principle in an adjudicative or professional one. He is plainly mistaken; formalism presupposes at least a qualified objectivism. For if the impersonal purposes, policies, and principles on which all but the most mechanical versions of the formalist thesis must rely do not come, as objectivism suggests, from a moral or practical order exhibited, however partially and ambiguously, by the legal materials themselves, where could they come from? They would have to be supplied by some normative theory

---

14. George Washington, *American Historical Documents* (New York: Barnes and Noble, Inc., 1960), p. 144.

15. Joseph Story, *Commentaries on the Constitution of the United States*, 3rd ed. (Boston, 1858), pp. 283, 400.

16. Ibid., p. viii.

extrinsic to the law. Even if such a theory could be convincingly established on its own ground, it would be a sheer miracle for its implications to coincide with a large portion of the received doctrinal understandings. At least it would be a miracle unless you had already assumed the truth of objectivism. But if the results of this alien theory failed to overlap with the greater part of received understandings of the law, you would need to reject broad areas of established law and legal doctrine as "mistaken." You would then have trouble maintaining the contrast of doctrine to ideology and political prophecy that represents an essential part of the formalist creed": you would have become a practitioner of the free-wheeling criticism of established arrangements and received ideas. No wonder theorists committed to formalism and the conventional view of doctrine have always fought to retain some remnant of the objectivist thesis. They have done so even at a heavy cost to their reputation among the orthodox, narrow-minded lawyers who otherwise provide their main constituency.[17]

After wading through 125 pages of this complex legal jargon, one comes to understand that backers of the Critical Legal Studies movement repudiate objective standards of law and the formal, apolitical, rational legal structure built upon those objective standards.

The Critical Legal Studies movement is not alone in rejecting objective standards of law. Legal positivism, the school of thought developed by Dean Christopher Columbus Langdell of Harvard in the 1870s and followed by Dean Roscoe Pound, Supreme Court Justice Oliver Wendell Holmes, Jr., and others, has been the predominant philosophy taught in law schools during the 1900s. Legal positivism can be summarized by the following points: (1) There are no objective, God-given standards of law, or if there are, they are irrelevant to the modern legal system. (2) Since God is not the author of law, the author of law must be man; in other words, law is law simply because the highest human authority, the state, has said it is law and is able to back it up by force. (3) Since man and society evolve, therefore law must evolve as well. (4) Judges, through their decisions, guide the evolution of law (Note again: Judges "make law"). (5) To study law, get at the original sources of law, the decisions of judges; hence most law schools today use the "case law" method of teaching law.[18]

17. Roberto Mangabeira Unger, "The Critical Legal Studies Movement," *Harvard Law Review*, 96:561 (1983), pp. 561-675, at 565-66.

18. For a more detailed discussion of legal positivism, see John Eidsmoe, *The Christian Legal Advisor* (Grand Rapids, Michigan: Baker Book House, 1984, 1986), pp. 63-93, and the sources cited therein. See John H. Hallowell, *Main Currents in Modern Political Thought*

Many judges have gone beyond the legal positivist position. "Legal realists" openly proclaim the desire to use the legal system to promote their own ends and use positivism as the basis for denying divine law and/or natural law. In this sense the Critical Legal Studies movement is one aspect of legal realism, though all legal realists are not necessarily leftist as is the Critical Legal Studies movement.

Others expand on the role of the judge as social policy maker. Professor Alexander Bickel suggested that:

> The function of Justices . . . is to immerse themselves in the tradition of our society and of kindred societies that have gone before, in history and in the sediment of history which is law, and . . . in the thought and the vision of the philosophers and the poets. The Justices will then be fit to extract "fundamental presuppositions" from their deepest selves, but in fact from the evolving morality of our tradition.[19]

Judges do this, rather than businessmen, dentists, legislators, or auto mechanics because, "Courts have certain capacities for dealing with matters of principle that legislatures and executives do not possess. Judges have, or should have, the leisure, the training, and the insulation to follow the ways of the scholar in pursuing the ends of government."[20] Justice Robert H. Bork of the U. S. Court of Appeals for the District of Columbia, citing Bickel's words, simply says, "Other than to heave a wistful sigh, I will pass by this vision of a judge's life without comment."[21]

These writers are saying that courts—and legal profession in general, particularly law professors—should make policy for the nation without having to rely on the will of the majority as

---

(New York: Holt, Rinehart & Winston, 1950, 1960), pp. 340-67. For a good exposition of the positivist position by one who at the time supported it, see Jerome Frank, *Law and the Modern Mind* (New York: Coward-McAnn, Inc., 1935). However, later Frank rejected positivism and embraced a form of natural law.

19. Alexander Bickel, *The Least Dangerous Branch*, p. 236.

20. Ibid., pp. 25-26.

21. Robert H. Bork, "Styles in Constitutional Theory," *South Texas Law Journal*, Vol. 26, No. 3 (Fall 1985), pp. 383-96, at 389. For further discussion of the non-interpretivist position, see John Hart Ely, "Constitutional Interpretivism: Its Allure and Impossibility," *Indiana Law Journal*, Vol. 53, pp. 399-448; Mark v. Tushnet of Georgetown University Law Center, "Following the Rules Laid Down: A Critique of Interpretivism and Neutral Principles," *Harvard Law Review*, Vol. 96, No. 4 (February, 1983), pp. 781-827; Tushnet, "Critical Legal Studies and Constitutional Law: An Essay in Deconstruction," *Stanford Law Review*, Vol. 36, pp. 623-47; Michael J. Perry, *The Constitution, the Courts, and Human Rights: An Inquiry into the Legitimacy of Constitutional Policymaking by the Judiciary* (New Haven, Conn.: Yale University Press, 1982).

expressed by the legislators, or on the letter of the Constitution as intended by its writers. Lino Graglia, professor of Constitutional law at the University of Texas School of Law, asks:

> Do the proponents of judicial review truly understand that under those judicial robes there are only lawyers, not persons selected for the job because of unusual depth or breadth of learning, or exceptional ethical, political, or historical insight? Do they realize that, far from necessarily possessing expertise in any substantive area of human knowledge, our judges typically rejected post-graduate education in favor of going to law school? The study and practice of law has many advantages, including the acquisition of great skill in the manipulation of words, but few would recommend it as a means of inculcating habits of ethical fastidiousness or devotion to candor. No person knowledgeable as to the making of lawyers or the practice of law can possibly believe that it is from among lawyers that we should select our ethical leaders or that to the lawyers selected we may safely grant governmental authority. . .[22]

Professor Graglia makes a most piercing indictment of judicial policy-making:

> . . . *judicial usurpation of legislative power has become so common and so complete that the Supreme Court has become our most powerful and important instrument of government in terms of determining the nature and quality of American life.* Questions literally of life and death (abortion and capital punishment), of public morality (control of pornography, prayer in the schools, and government aid to religious schools), and of public safety (criminal procedure and street demonstrations), are all, now, in the hands of judges under the guise of questions of constitutional law. The fact that the Constitution says nothing of, say, abortion, and indeed, explicitly and repeatedly recognizes the capital punishment the Court has come close to prohibiting, has made no difference.
>
> The result is that *the central truth of constitutional law today is that it has nothing to do with the Constitution* except that the words "due process" or "equal protection" are almost always used by the judges in stating their conclusions. Not to put too fine a point on it, constitutional law has become a fraud, a cover for a system of government by the majority vote of a nine-person committee of lawyers, unelected and holding office for life. The desirability of this form of government should be the central question in any realistic

22. Lino A. Graglia, "Judicial Review on the Basis of 'Regime Principles': A Prescription for Government by Judges," *South Texas Law Journal*, Vol. 26, No. 3 (Fall 1985), pp. 435-52, at 446.

discussion of judicial review today. It is a question, however, that defenders of judicial review are ordinarily more concerned to obscure than to discuss.[23]

The two philosophies of jurisprudence can be summarized in the statements of two Supreme Court justices. Justice Felix Frankfurter, a political liberal but advocate of judicial restraint, declared, "What governs is the Constitution, and not what we have written about it."[24] In constrast was a statement by New York Governor Charles Evans Hughes, later named Chief Justice: "We are under a Constitution, but the Constitution is what the judges say it is."[25]

Note his wording: The Constitution *is* what the judges say it *is*. He didn't say the Constitution *means* what the judges say it *means*. Some say the Constitution is a "living document" that embodies all subsequent court decisions incorporating it. One constitutional law professor declared, with the approval of most of his colleagues, that the Constitution is more than the written document signed in 1787; rather, the various decisions of the Supreme Court are part of the Constitution, and these along with the original written document, are the true "Constitution" of the land. It has even been said that the Supreme Court sitting in session is a "continuous constitutional convention."

In contrast, those who believe in original intent would say the Convention ended in 1787, and from that point on the letter of the Constitution was fixed (except for the ratification and amendment processes), just as the canon of Scripture was complete when the last book of the New Testament was written. According to this view courts interpret and apply the Constitution, but they do not expand it or guide its evolution.

The debate continues. The immediate influence of these professors and their disciples may be less than they think. They mostly talk to each other, and write in law reviews which they along with their disciples read. But their long-term influence is staggering. They

23. Ibid., p. 441. Let me add that while I hold the highest respect for Professor Graglia, I share his objections to judicial policy-making but not necessarily his objections to judicial review. Professor Graglia develops his position more fully in "How the Constitution Disappeared," *Commentary*, Vol. 81, No. 2 (February 1986), pp. 19-27. Professor Graglia is justifiably concerned about the "tyranny of the minority," the nine unelected justices of the Supreme Court. But his remedy is the "tyranny of the majority," virtually unchecked majority rule without due regard for the unalienable rights of minorities. My remedy for both is the rule of law under the Constitution interpreted according to the framers' intent.

24. Justice Felix Frankfurter; quoted by Judge Brevard Hand, *Wallace v. Jaffree*, reversed, affirmed in part, 105 S. Ct. 2479 (1985).

25. Charles Evans Hughes; quoted by Craig R. Ducat and Harold W. Chase, *Constitutional Interpretation* (St. Paul: West Publishing Co., 1974, 1983), p. 3.

train the future lawyers of the nation, who become the nation's judges, law professors, and, to a large extent, politicians. The American public, and Christians in particular, need to pay attention to this debate.

A courageous Christian, Attorney General Edwin Meese, has done the nation a great service by bringing public attention to the debate. In a 1985 address to the American Bar Association which was later revised for publication, Meese declared:

> It was not long ago when constitutional interpretation was understood to move between the poles of "strict construction" and "loose construction." Today, it is argued that constitutional interpretation moves between "interpretive review" and "non-interpretive review." As one observer has pointed out, under the old system the question was *how* to read the Constitution; under the new approach, the question is *whether* to read the Constitution. . . .
>
> The result is that some judges and academics feel free (to borrow the language of the great New York jurist, Chancellor James Kent) to "roam at large in the trackless fields of their own imaginations."[26]

Meese called for a return to a "Jurisprudence of Original Intention" in which the words of Justice Story would be taken seriously:

> In construing the Constitution of the United States, we are in the first instance to consider, what are its nature and objects, its scope and design, as apparent from the structure of the instrument, viewed as a whole and also viewed in its component parts. Where its words are plain, clear and determinate, they require no interpretation. . . . Where the words admit of two senses, each of which is conformable to general usage, that sense is to be adopted, which without departing from the literal import of the words, best harmonizes with the nature and objects, the scope and design of the instrument.[27]

Reaction to Meese's views from the liberal community was swift and critical. Justice Brennan—who had spoken of "evolving standards of decency" in *Furman v. Georgia*—declared in an October 12, 1985, symposium at Georgetown University:

> It is arrogant to pretend that from our vantage we can gauge accurately the intent of the Framers on application of principle to

26. Edwin Meese, III, address to American Bar Association, 1985; adapted in "Toward a Jurisprudence of Original Intention," *Benchmark*, Vol. II, No. 1, January-February 1986, pp. 1-10, at 6.

27. Joseph Story; quoted by Meese, ibid., p. 10.

specific, contemporary questions. All too often, sources of potential enlightenment such as records of the ratification debates provide sparse or ambiguous evidence of the original intention. Typically, all that can be gleaned is that the Framers themselves did not agree about the application or meaning of particular constitutional provisions, and hid their differences in cloaks of generality. Indeed, it is far from clear whose intention is relevant—that of the drafters, the congressional disputants, or the ratifiers in the states? or even whether the idea of an original intention is a coherent way of thinking about a jointly drafted document drawing its authority from a general assent of the states. And apart from the problematic nature of the sources, our distance of two centuries cannot but work as a prism refracting all we perceive. One cannot help but speculate that the chorus of lamentations calling for interpretation faithful to "original intention"—and proposing nullifications of interpretations that fail this quick litmus test—must inevitably come from persons who have no familiarity with the historical record.[28]

Brennan continued:

. . . the genius of the Constitution rests not in any static meaning it might have had in a world that is dead and gone, but in the adaptability of its great principles to cope with current problems and current needs. What the constitutional fundamentals meant to the wisdom of other times cannot be their measure to the vision of our time. Similarly, what those fundamentals mean for us, our descendents will learn, cannot be the measure to the vision of their time.[29]

What are the "great principles" of the Constitution? According to Brennan, the greatest is human dignity—even though the Constitution never uses the term. He says, "There is no worse injustice than wrongly to strip a man of his dignity."[30] But Justice Brennan supports abortion on demand, so apparently an innocent unborn baby is not stripped of his or her dignity during an abortion. Except as applied to unborn babies, capital punishment should be avoided, even though the Constitution expressly approves capital punishment. He believes that the United States continues an upward progress to become as a "shining city upon a hill,"[31] unbounded by the fetters of original intent or the literal words of the Constitution,

28. William J. Brennan, Jr., "The Constitution of the United States: Contemporary Ratification," Teaching Symposium, Georgetown University, Washington, D. C., October 12, 1985, p. 39.

29. Ibid., p. 42.

30. Ibid., p. 47.

31. Ibid., p. 51.

through an *"evolutionary process (that) is inevitable and, indeed,
it is the true interpretive genius of the text.''*[32]

There are however, several arguments for a jurisprudence of
original intent:

1. To a large extent, the intent of the framers of the Constitution
can be determined. The founding fathers were united in their basic
world view and principles of law and government; their disagreements centered on the application of those principles to specific
structures of government. Even then, they generally talked over
their differences until an agreement was reached—except for
compromises on issues like representation and slavery. The view
that the Constitution is a "bundle of compromises" does not stand
up under careful examination.[33]

This does not mean the framers of the Constitution anticipated
every future problem. To determine their intent on current issues it
is necessary to assume their mindset, of adopting their world view
and basic values, and ask, "Given those basic values, how would the
framers of the Constitution have handled this problem if they had
been confronted by it?"

For example, consider the abortion issue. Legally the issue
concerns the Fourteenth Amendment which states in part, "nor
shall any State deprive any person of life, liberty, or property,
without due process of law . . . ." there are two fundamental issues:
(1) Does the term *liberty* include the right to an abortion? (2) does
the term *person* include an unborn child and thereby guarantee the
unborn child the right to life? These questions probably never
occurred to those who passed and ratified the Fourteenth Amendment in 1868; they certainly do not appear in any of the recorded
debates. In determining how to apply the Fourteenth Amendment
to the abortion issue, suppose that someone had asked "Does
'person' include unborn children?" or "Does 'liberty' include the
right to abortions?" during the floor debates on the Fourteenth
Amendment. What would have been the likely response, given the
basic morals and values and perceptions of those involved at the
time? In an effort to interpret the founding fathers' initial intent the
following question could be asked, "Given the founding fathers'
basic values, what would have been their view of abortion, had they

32. Ibid., p. 51.
33. Ralph A. Rossum, "A Means-Ends Approach to the Study of the Constitution and
Constitutional Law," *Politics in Perspective*, Vol. 13, No. 1, Fall 1985, pp. 36-48, at 44;
Skousen, *"Miracle of America" Study Guide*, p. 69; John P. Roche, "The Founding Fathers:
A Reform Caucus in Action," *The American Political Science Review*, LV (December, 1961),
pp. 799-816.

known the latest scientific and technical information about the unborn child? The fact that the Fourteenth Amendment was passed and ratified in 1868 when most states had either passed or were in the process of passing laws to prohibit abortion—a fact that Justice Blackmun overlooked in *Roe v. Wade*—may help interpret and apply the signers of the Constitution intent.

There may be areas in which the original intent is difficult to perceive. But that should not prevent efforts to ascertain and apply the founding fathers' intent—it is possible to do so more often than Justice Brennan believes.

2. A jurisprudence of original intent does not preclude flexibility as the previous discussion points out. The principles are fixed and unchanging, the application of those principles may vary in different circumstances.

3. The framers of the Constitution were not infallible. A jurisprudence of original intent does not mean citizens are bound to follow the letter of the Constitution for eternity. The Constitution provides a means for amendment. When circumstances require amendments (which is seldom since the Constitution is a broad statement of principle rather than a book of detailed specifics), or when citizens perceive that the framers of the Constitution were mistaken, the Constitution can be changed by amendments.

Amending the Constitution is a serious step which should not be undertaken lightly. But there is more danger of "tampering with the Constitution" through judicial reinterpretation (read: misinterpretation), than by the amendment process.

The amendment process is accused of being cumbersome. It is; and it should be. The Constitution, as the embodiment of the fundamental principles of the nation, should not be changed unless over a period of time, a substantial majority concurs in that change.

4. In every other field of law—statutory construction, interpretation of contracts, construction of testamentary documents such as wills and trusts—the plain meaning of the document is considered first. If that is not clear, we look to the makers' intent. Why should Constitutional interpretation be any different? The Constitution is actually entitled to more deferential respect than other legal documents.

5. The Constitution is a law—the supreme law—but it is also a contract or covenant. Americans pledged to uphold it by signing and ratifying it. Millions of Americans take oaths to uphold the Constitution of the United States: judges, public officials, and those in military service. In a larger sense, all members of society are part of this covenant.

6. An analogy can be drawn between constitutional law and theology. At the time of the Reformation, some church officials insisted that church tradition was equal to or nearly equal to Scripture, as divine revelation. Luther and Calvin rejected that view. They vowed that they would be governed *"sola scriptura"*— by Scripture alone. Most of the founding fathers held this Protestant view.

This is similar to the controversy in constitutional interpretation. Those rejecting jurisprudence of original intent insist that the decisions of the court are just as binding as the Constitution, if not more so. Some speak of a "living Constitution," or a "dynamic Constitution," exists which consists of the original document and the court decisions which are built on it. Charles Evans Hughes, later Chief Justice of the Supreme Court, expressed this view: "We are under a Constitution, but the Constitution is what the judges say it is."[34]

Against this view, the jurisprudence of original intent insists, with Justice Felix Frankfurter, that "What governs is the Constitution, and not what we have written about it."[35] Legal authorities and case precedents are entitled to great deference. But when they conflict with the plain wording of the Constitution or the intent of those who signed it, the original intent must govern.

7. Those who claim to reject original intent often quote the framers of the Constitution when it suits their purposes. Frequently the liberal wing of the Court cites (out of context and out of proportion to its importance) Jefferson's statements about church and state.

8. Justice Brennan's remarks assume an upward progress of history and only make sense if one accepts that optimistic view. In his opinion, history is "inevitably" evolving upward toward greater appreciation of liberty, democracy, and human dignity. So any departures from original intent must be in the direction of bigger and better things for all mankind.

History does not indicate an upward progress toward freedom and human dignity. Rather, history reveals that periods of freedom are rare and short-lived; that free and humane civilizations rise and flourish briefly, then fall back into the darkness of despotism and barbarism. A survey of the world of today—supposedly the most enlightened age of all history—shows that much of the world is

34. Charles Evans Hughes; quoted by Ducat and Chase, *Constitutional Interpretation*, p. 3.
35. Justice Felix Frankfurter; quoted by Judge Brevard Hand, *Wallace v. Jaffree*, reversed, affirmed in part, 105 S. Ct. 2479 (1985).

enslaved under one form or another of tyranny and/or communism.

It is tempting to depart from the absolute principles of the Constitution when there is assurance that the exchange or change will be for something better. But history indicates the greater likelihood of exchanging them for something worse.

Consider again the Eighth Amendment prohibition of cruel and unusual punishment. Justice Brennan opposes capital punishment, believing the death penalty violates the principle of human dignity. So he would rule that capital punishment constitutes cruel and unusual punishment and therefore violates the Eighth Amendment, even though it is clear the founding fathers didn't think so.

He believes in the "inevitable evolutionary process" upward toward an even greater realization of his lofty ideals. So he leaves the founding fathers' intent behind with cheerful confidence that society is moving on to something better.

What if that confidence is misplaced and society isn't getting better? What if society is getting worse—more cruel, inhumane, barbaric, and totalitarian? What about the "evolving standards of decency"? Suppose that a state legislature were to pass a law that anyone convicted of manslaughter as a result of drunk driving shall be skinned alive—a punishment employed by the Assyrians and other ancient peoples. The founders would have thought such a punishment cruel and unusual; and if the courts were to follow a jurisprudence of original intent, they would strike it down as violating the Eighth Amendment.

But what would a court do under an evolving standard? Picture a court saying, in paraphrase of *Trop v. Dulles*:

> The defendant claims that his sentence—being slowly skinned alive—is cruel and unusual under the Eighth Amendment. We recognize that the authors of that hallowed amendment would have thought so. But our inquiry must not stop there. For the words of the Amendment are not precise, and their scope is not static. The Amendment must draw its meaning from the evolving standards of decency that mark the progress of a maturing society. It is now 200 years later, and our society has clearly matured. Through rising crime rates, and through violence graphically portrayed in movies and television, we have become inured to practices that would have shocked the delicate consciences of that earlier era. While being skinned alive may have been cruel and unusual in 1789, we cannot say it is cruel and unusual under today's standards. We therefore uphold the sentence and direct that the defendant be delivered to the local taxidermist for execution.

Granted, this paraphrase is far-fetched. But where will an evolving standard end? What limits can be placed on evolutionary jurisprudence? Its boundaries are as wide as the judges' imaginations, aided by massive doses of mind-expanding injections from the nation's law reviews. Departures from the fixed standard of original intent puts interpretations on a "slippery slope" that can lead anywhere.[36]

The framers of the Constitution held no utopian dreams. They recognized with John Adams that human nature had not changed "since the Garden of Eden," and that there had been "no improvements in morals since the days of Jesus."[37] The idea of an upward evolutionary progress was foreign to them. They labored to produce a "Constitution for the ages" that would stand the test of time.

One of the main values of a Constitution is that *it buys time for a nation.* A constitution is never a match for an immoral or ignorant people determined to trample on its provisions. But when properly enforced it can buy time for the nation. During periods of national degeneracy or irrationality, it can form a temporary barrier against majority or minority tyranny and keep liberty and order alive until morality revives and sobriety returns.

The fixed principles of the Constitution are based on the "Laws of Nature and of Nature's God" set forth in the Declaration of Independence. The jurisprudence of original intent, based on the fixed principles of the Constitution as understood by its signers, stands solid in an era of uncertainty. For human rights, freedoms, and dignity to survive, they must be based on the intended original principles.

The Secularization of America

Law is not the only secularized field. There appears to be a comprehensive effort to remove religious influence from the American scene or relegate it to second-class status.

---

36. Readers may recognize that the phrase "slippery slope" is borrowed from the late Dr. Francis Schaeffer and was used in regard to the debate over the inerrancy of Scripture. Schaeffer argued that if we depart from the fixed standard of inerrancy, we are on a "slippery slope" that can lead anywhere. While the two issues are not necessarily dependent on each other, there is a clear relationship between the debate over the inerrancy of Scripture and the debate over jurisprudence of original intent. However, this does not mean the Constitution is considered to be equal with Scripture. God guided and gave his assistance to the writers of the Constitution, but he did not inspire them in the sense that he inspired the authors of Scripture. The fallibility of the Constitution is recognized in the fact that it contains provisions for its own amendment. There is and should be no provision for amending Scripture.

37. John Adams; quoted by Zoltan Harasett, *John Adams and the Prophets of Progress* (Cambridge: Harvard University Press, 1952), p. 187.

In many schools throughout the nation, children are free to meet in voluntary groups to study and promote literature, philosophy, politics, even gay rights, but are *not* free to meet for prayer, worship, or Bible study. In *Widmar v. Vincent*, 454 U.S. 263 (1981), the U.S. Supreme Court ruled that if a public university allows other student groups to meet on campus, it must grant the same privilege to religious groups. The court has not determined whether the same right extends to students in secondary or elementary schools.

In many schools, baccalaureate or commencement speakers are free to expound on an endless variety of ideas, but are sometimes barred from speaking about religious subjects. In other schools teachers are free to use occult symbols such as witches and goblins at Halloween, but are prohibited from using Christian symbols at Christmas. Students are taught evolution but are not allowed to hear the evidence for special creation. In the name of academic freedom, teachers are free to force unwilling students to read semi-pornographic books but are sometimes prevented from sharing books about Jesus Christ. Taxpayer-funded student newspapers publish all sorts of materials, even if they contain foul language or anti-religious messages, but have been stopped from printing pro-religious material.

These policies are *not* mandated by the Supreme Court (at least, not yet), but the practical effect of such policies is to relegate Christians and other religious-minded people to the status of second-class citizens. The religious person has *less* freedom than the secular-minded person to publicly discuss and promulgate ideas that are important to him.

This downgrading of religion is especially prevalent in American history courses. The material in this book may seem new, strange, almost foreign because it is not what the textbooks are teaching about America's founding.

The religious factor in American history is not *denied*; it is simply *ignored*. The biggest problem with most textbooks about America's founding, is not what they *say*, but what they *leave out*. And since the textbooks omit mention of the nation's religious heritage, many public school teachers are also inclined to omit it in classroom discussions.

Dr. Paul Vitz, Professor of Psychology at New York University and principal author of a federally-funded study titled "Religion and Traditional Values in Public School Textbooks," concluded that textbook authors "have a deep-seated fear of any form of active contemporary Christianity, especially serious, committed Protestantism, and the result is an "obvious censorship of religion" much like sex was censored during the Victorian period.

Recently public schools were barred from showing a film about the settlement of Jamestown, because the film depicted the erection of a cross at the settlement.

But according to historical facts, a cross *was* erected at the Jamestown settlement; the Pilgrims at Plymouth *did* give thanks to God for their blessings; Thomas Jefferson *did* make plain references to God in the Declaration of Independence; early congresses *did* call on the President to proclaim days of prayer and thanksgiving; religion *did* play an important role in the lives of the early American settlers and in the founding of the American republic (these facts have not been censored out yet). But if and when these facts are censored from curricula, students receive a distorted picture of American history.

The religious writings of the founding fathers are available to those who will look for them—even though textbooks and encyclopedias ignore the religious beliefs of the founding fathers and treat these men as secular humanists. That is what makes this cultural censorship all the more ominous—because the information is so readily available, its omission cannot be due to ignorance; it must be by design.

A great deal is being said by saying nothing about God and religion. The basic message that comes across is that God is either nonexistent or irrelevant, and that religion was not very important in American history and American life. This needs to be corrected.

Christians: Get Involved

America's legal and political system needs a massive transfusion of Christian blood.

A society which has been conditioned to think in terms of moral and ethical relativism needs the input of those who recognize absolute principles. A nation which has been convinced that human reason and human experience are the only means of attaining truth, needs to hear from those who read God's special revelation, the Bible. A thought system based on faith in an upward evolutionary process, human goodness, and unlimited human potential, needs to be challenged by those holding a biblical view of God, man, and human sin.

In *The Stealing of America* John Whitehead notes the takeover of American institutions by secular humanists. But as Dr. Gary North pointed out, they didn't steal America. It was given to them!

American Christians created a vacuum by retreating from public life during the late 1800s and early 1900s. Part of this was due to legitimate concern over the "social gospel" which came close to being salvation by works through left wing social reform. Part of it was due to the influence of pietism which commendably stressed Bible study, prayer, conversion, and personal morality, but neglected the Christian responsibility to be salt and light to the world. As a result, Christians developed a "ghetto mentality." They associated mostly with each other, read their own literature, listened to their own music, and stayed out of politics, and let the rest of the world go by. As a result, secular-minded people took over the influential posts in academia, government, media, and scientific research. They used these positions to promulgate their own humanistic goals. This simply confirmed the ghetto mentality that said the "world" was an evil place to be shunned whenever possible.

But the Bible's command is to be "salt of the earth" (Matt. 5:13). Salt does three things. It gives flavoring; Christians are to give a Christian flavor to the nation's culture, arts, music, movies, laws, and politics. It preserves; Christian morality helps preserve the nation from the disastrous consequences of immorality. And third, when salt is rubbed into wounds, it hurts!

When Christians start applying biblical solutions to national problems, furious reactions result. Sometimes this opposition is the result of Christians' insensitivity; sometimes it is a measure of effectiveness. The opposition doesn't complain unless it's been hurt. Harry Truman used to say, "If you can't stand the heat, get out of the kitchen"; to which the late Iowa Attorney General Richard Turner added, "If there's no heat in your kitchen, you probably aren't doing much cooking!"[38]

Today, Christians are reentering the political arena—and as Christians become more knowledgeable about politics, their effectiveness will increase.

Christians need to be involved in every field. Our culture should be permeated with a distinctively Christian flavoring.

Scholars often come to non-Christian conclusions because they start with non-Christian presuppositions and use non-Christian sources.

Christians need to enter the legal system. The number of Christian lawyers is increasing, but more are needed to serve as judges,

---

38. Richard Turner, Speech, Sioux City, Iowa, 1966.

law professors, and in other influential positions. Imagine the impact of another Supreme Court Chief Justice like John Jay!

The phrase *separation of church and state* appears nowhere in the Constitution. It comes from Thomas Jefferson's comment made many years later. The First Amendment says, "Congress shall make no law respecting an establishment of religion, or prohibiting the free exercise thereof. . . ."

The church and state have separate functions, so the phrase *separation of church and state* is a legitimate interpretation of the First Amendment.

Those who object to Christian expression in public life frequently use the phrase as a code-word to mean, *separation of church from reality.* They say, "Christians can stay in church and pray and sing, but leave the *real* problems of the world to *us.*"

God's people in the Bible didn't shrink from the "real" world. David served as king of Israel. Daniel was prime minister of Babylon and later Persia. Joseph became prime minister of Egypt. Esther was queen of Persia. Erastus served as the city treasurer (Rom. 16:23). The prophets did not hesitate to speak out on the political issues of their day.[39]

It is not the American tradition for Christians to stay out of politics. Reverend Witherspoon was teacher of Presidents, member of the Continental Congress, and signer of the Declaration of Independence. A majority of the delegates to the Constitutional Convention were professing Christians, many had theological training, and at least one had been a licensed preacher. At least forty-four of the delegates to the various state ratifying conventions were ordained ministers. In 1789 when James Madison introduced the First Amendment on the floor of Congress, the Speaker of the House was Rev. Frederick Conrad Augustus Mühlenberg, an ordained Lutheran clergyman.

Alexis de Tocqueville made an interesting observation about religion in America:

> Religion in America takes no direct part in the government of society, but it must be regarded as the first of their political institutions; for if it does not impart a taste for freedom, it facilitates the use of it. Indeed, it is in this same point of view that the inhabitants of the United States themselves look upon religious belief. I do not know whether all Americans have a sincere faith in their

---

39. For a more detailed discussion of biblical reasons and precedents for Christian involvement in politics, see John Eidsmoe, *God and Caesar: Christian Faith and Political Action* (Westchester, Illinois: Crossway, 1984), pp. 54-69.

religion—for who can search the human heart?—but I am certain that they hold it to be indispensable to the maintenance of their political institutions.[40]

Church and state do have separate functions, but religion and politics cannot be totally separated. For every aspect of politics and law involves moral principles. By denoting such acts as murder and theft as crimes, moral decisions are being made. When deciding whether or not abortion is a crime, moral decisions are again being made. When overhauling tax laws, moral decisions are made as to who shall bear what portion of the nation's expenses.

Morality cannot be separated from religion. Washington noted in his farewell address that "reason and experience both forbid us to expect, that national morality can prevail in exclusion of religious principle."

Morality always deals with ultimate values which find expression in some type of religion. The question is, which religion and what values—those of the Judeo-Christian tradition on which the nation was founded, or those of Secular Humanism, the New Age, or others? R. J. Rushdoony said it well:

Behind every system of law there is a god. To find the god in any system, look for the source of law in that system. If the source of law is the individual, then the individual is the god of that system. If the source of law is the people, or the dictatorship of the proletariat, then these things are the gods of those systems. If our source of law is court, then the court is our god. If there is no higher law beyond man, then man is his own god, or else his creatures, the institutions he has made, have become his gods. When you choose your authority, you choose your god, and where you look for your law, there is your god.[41]

Can the United States of America be classified a Christian nation? Was it ever a Christian nation; could it become so again?

In the first sense of the word—that of a nation composed of people who are regenerate through the power of Jesus Christ—the answer is no. Luther emphasized a truly Christian nation must be thoroughly won for Christ. However:

This you will never accomplish; for the world and the masses are and always will be unchristian, although they are all baptised and are nominally Christian. Christians, however, are few and far between,

40. de Tocqueville, *Democracy in America*, I:316.
41. R. J. Rushdoony, *Law and Liberty* (Fairfax, Virginia: Thoburn Press, 1971), p. 33.

as the saying is. Therefore it is out of the question that there should be a common Christian government over the whole world, nay even over one land or company of people, since the wicked always outnumber the good. Hence a man who would venture to govern an entire country or the world with the Gospel would be alike a shepherd who should place in one fold wolves, lions, eagles, and sheep together and let them freely mingle with one another and say, Help yourselves, and be good and peaceful among yourselves; the fold is open, there is plenty of food; have no fear of dogs and clubs. The sheep, forsooth, would keep the peace and would allow themselves to be fed and governed in peace, but they would not live long; nor would any beast keep from molesting another.

For this reason these two kingdoms must be sharply distinguished, and both be permitted to remain; the one to produce piety, the other to bring about external peace and prevent evil deeds; neither is sufficient in the world without the other. For no one can become pious before God by means of the secular government, without Christ's spiritual rule.[42]

But Luther also stressed that the state officials must seek wisdom from God: "A prince must act also in a Christian way toward his God, that is, he must subject himself to Him in entire confidence and pray for wisdom to rule well, as Solomon did."[43]

In this latter sense—people whose basic views and values are consistent with those of the Christian religion, or a nation whose basic foundational principles are consistent with the Bible—America was and to a large extent still is a Christian nation. For the principles on which this nation was founded are based on the Bible.

Christians have a vital contribution to make to the health and well-being of America. They are needed to articulate biblical principles of government in every courtroom, legislative hall, and precinct meeting in the nation. They must also articulate these principles with human reason consistent with God's revealed Word. God has revealed his truth not only by special revelation (the Bible) but also by general revelation (nature, reason and conscience: Rom. 2:14-15), sometimes called natural grace, or common grace. Christians must appeal to general revelation when dealing with people who do not accept special revelation.

Christians are needed to reestablish the moral tone of society. The founding fathers recognized that freedom cannot exist in an immoral society—the nation will crumble from within or be con-

---

42. Martin Luther, "Secular Authority: To What Extent It Should Be Obeyed," 1523; reprinted in *Works of Martin Luther* (Grand Rapids: Baker Book House, 1982), III:237.
    43. Ibid., III:270-71.

quered from without. Christians must supply the moral fiber that comes from obedience to God and his natural and revealed laws if America is to survive as a free society. Christians must be salt of the earth and light of the world. "Righteousness exalteth a nation: but sin is a reproach to any people" (Prov. 14:34).

Suggested Reading List

The National Center for Constitutional Studies, P.O. Box 33722, Washington, D.C. 20033, (202) 371-0008 has developed a series titled *I Love America* which is suitable for public and private schools and recommended for ages five to fourteen. The Center has a lecture series for adults and older children which can be used in churches and public meetings, titled *"Miracle of America" Study Guide*; and has recently published a book titled *The Making of America*.

The founder of the National Center for Constitutional Studies is Dr. W. Cleon Skousen, a constitutional scholar and dedicated conservative. Dr. Skousen is a leader in the Mormon Church, and in a few respects his materials reflect a Mormon perspective. For example, pp. 19-21 of the *"Miracle of America" Study Guide* imply that the Anglo-Saxon peoples are descendents of the Israelites. Pages 33-34 imply that the "religion of all mankind" is one of works-righteousness which could be inconsistent with the Christian view of salvation by grace through faith. These isolated references are easily spotted and distinguished.

The Foundation for American Christian Education (P.O. Box 27035, San Francisco, California 94127) publishes materials on America's constitutional history. Their publication, *The Christian History of the Constitution of the United States of America: Christian Self-Government* contains reproductions of the Magna Charta, the English Bill of Rights, excerpts from Locke's "Of Civil Government," Montesquieu's "The Spirit of Laws," Blackstone's "Commentaries," Bradford's "History of Plimoth Plantation," and other materials. The Foundation has produced a second volume, titled *The Christian History of the Constitution of the United States of America: Christian Self-Government with Union* which contains additional material such as excerpts from Grotius, Pufendorf, and Vattel. Other works produced by the Foundation include *The Christian History of the American Revolution, The Bible and the Constitution of the United States of America*, and *Teaching and Learning America's Christian History*.

American Vision (P.O. Box 720515, Atlanta, Georgia 30328) publishes a study guide titled *God and Government: A Biblical and Historical Study*, by Gary DeMar, written from a Calvinist perspective.

The Foundation for Christian Self-Government, (P.O. Box 1087, Thousand Oaks, California 91360, 213-340-1294) publishes another study guide for use in churches and homes, titled *The American Covenant: The Untold Story*. David Marshall and David Manuel have published two books on America's Christian history, *The Light and the Glory* and *From Sea to Shining Sea* (Old Tappan, New Jersey: Revell, 1977, 1986). The original sources are also available, *The Federalist Papers* by Hamilton, Madison, and Jay (New York: Mentor Books, 1961) and Madison's *Notes of Debates in the Federal Convention* (Athens, Ohio: Ohio University Press, 1985). A good compilation of sources from the Constitutional Convention is Catherine Drinker Bowen's *Miracle at Philadelphia* (Boston: Little, Brown & Co., 1966).

Appendix 1:
Treaty of Tripoli

T he Treaty of Tripoli of 1797 should be explained when discussing the role of religion in Washington's career. It is alleged that Washington signed this Treaty, Article 11 of which declares that

> ... the government of the United States of America is not in any sense founded on the Christian Religion,—as it has in itself no character of enmity against the law, religion or tranquility of Musselmen.[1]

The Treaty was negotiated in 1796 between U.S. officials and the Dey of Tripoli and the Dey of Algiers to secure safe passage for American ships through waters near the Barbary Coast of North Africa.

Incomplete historical information and translation problems have left many unanswered questions about the Treaty of Tripoli. The following has been verified:

(1) The copy of the treaty recently circulated which bears Washington's signature is a fraud. Washington never signed the Treaty of Tripoli. The treaty never reached the President's desk until after March 1797 when John Adams was President. The treaty was first signed by Jussuf Bashaw Mahomet, the Dey of Tripoli, on

---

1. Treaty of Tripoli; cited by Loren P. Beth, *The American Theory of Church and State* (Gainesville, Florida: University of Florida Press, 1958), p. 74.

November 4, 1796. Then it was sent to Algiers, where Hassan Bashaw, the Dey of Algiers, signed it January 3, 1797. It was then sent to Lisbon, Portugal, where U.S. Minister to Portugal David Humphreys signed it February 10, 1797. Then it was sent to the United States, where the Senate approved it on June 7, 1797. President Adams signed it June 10.[2]

(2) The Treaty was translated into English sometime in January or February 1797, probably by an Algerian court official. The U.S. official in charge of the signing in Algiers, Joel Barlow, did not know Arabic, but signed his name to a statement, "The foregoing is a literal translation of the writing in Arabic on the following page."[3] Barlow's "translation" removed many cultural and religious references and in some instances changed the meaning to give the Dey of Algiers more authority and enforcement powers than was intended. For example, Barlow's translation of Article 12 reads:

> In case of any dispute arising from a violation of any of the articles of this treaty no appeal shall be made to arms, nor shall war be declared on any pretext whatever. But if the Consul residing at the place where the dispute shall happen shall not be able to settle the same, an amicable reference shall be made to the mutual friend of the parties, the Dey of Algiers, the parties hereby engaging to abide by his decision. And he by virtue of his signature to this treaty engages for himself and successors to declare the justice of the case according to the true interpretation of the treaty, and to use all the means in his power to enforce the observance of the same.[4]

Barlow's translation differs greatly from a more literal translation of Article 12 made in 1930 by Dr. C. Snouck Hurgronje of Leiden.

> Praise be to God! Declaration of the twelfth article. If there arises a disturbance between us both sides, and it becomes a serious dispute, and the American Consul is not able to make clear (settle) his affair, and (then) the affair shall remain suspended between them both, between the Pashna of Tripoli, may God strengthen him, in the well-protected Algiers, has taken cognizance of the matter. We shall

2. Ray W. Irwin, *The Diplomatic Relations of the United States with the Barbary Powers, 1776–1816* (Chapel Hill: University of North Carolina Press, 1931), p. 84; cited by John W. Whitehead, "The Treaty of Tripoli," *The Rutherford Institute*, Vol. 2, No. 1 (January/February 1985, 1986), pp. 10–11.

3. Charles I. Bevans, *Treaties and Other International Agreements of the United States of America, 1776–1949* (Department of State, 1974), XI: 1073–1074; cited by Whitehead, ibid.

4. Barlow's translation, Treaty of Tripoli, Article 12; reprinted in Bevans, *Treaties*, XI:1072; cited by Whitehead, ibid.

accept whatever decision he enjoins on us, and we shall agree with this condition and his seal (i.e., the decision sealed by him); may God make it all permanent love and a good conclusion between us in the beginning and the end, by His grace and favor, amen![5]

These inconsistent translations reveal the confusion which existed concerning the treaty.

(3) Translation interpretation is possibly the source of confusion on Article 11. There is evidence that Article 11 was actually not part of the Treaty of Tripoli. Consider the following entry from *Treaties and Other International Agreements of the United States of America, 1776-1949:*

> Most extraordinary (and wholey unexplained) is the fact that Article 11 of the Barlow translation with its famous phrase, "the government of the United States of America is not in any sense founded on the Christian religion," does not exist at all. *There is no Article 11.* The Arabic text which is between Articles 10 and 12 is in form a letter crude and flamboyant and withal quite unimportant, from the Dey of Algiers to the Pasha of Tripoli. How that script came to be written and to be regarded, as in the Barlow translation, as Article 11 of the treaty as there written, is a mystery and seemingly must remain so. Nothing in the diplomatic correspondence of the time throws any light whatever on the point."[6] (emphasis added)

One explanation is that the Dey of Algiers wrote this note on the Treaty to mollify certain concerns of the Pasha of Tripoli about entering into a Treaty with an "infidel" (non-Islamic) nation. The Algerian court official translating the document translated everything on the page without regard to its nature or source. It is also possible that American foreign service officials, eager to conclude a treaty, allowed the Barbary officials to continue under that impression.

(4) Piracy continued despite the Treaty; the United States went to war with Tripoli in 1801. A new treaty with Tripoli, which does not contain the phrase in question, was accepted on April 17, 1806.[7]

While this information does not completely resolve the mystery of the Treaty of Tripoli, it certainly establishes that the Treaty cannot be used as evidence that Washington—or Adams, for that matter—did not believe this nation was founded on Christian principles.

---

5. Hurgronje's translation, Treaty of Tripoli, Article 12; reprinted in Bevans, *Treaties,* XI:1078; cited by Whitehead, ibid.

6. Cited in Bevans, *Treaties,* XI:1070; cited by Whitehead, ibid.

7. Leo Pfeffer, *Church, State and Freedom* (Boston: Beacon Press, 1953), p. 211.